A HANDBOOK AND READER OF OTTOMAN ARABIC

A Handbook and Reader of Ottoman Arabic

Edited by Esther-Miriam Wagner

UNIVERSITY OF CAMBRIDGE
Faculty of Asian and Middle Eastern Studies

OpenBook Publishers

https://www.openbookpublishers.com

Updated digital material and resources associated with this volume are available at https://doi.org/10.11647/OBP.0208#resources

Semitic Languages and Cultures 9.

ISSN (print): 2632-6906
ISSN (digital): 2632-6914

ISBN Paperback: 9781783749416
ISBN Hardback: 9781783749423
ISBN Digital (PDF): 9781783749430
DOI: 10.11647/OBP.0208

Cover images: Upper left, T-S 10J16.26 (Hebrew script); upper right, CUL Or.1081.2.75.2 (Syriac script), both reproduced with kind permission of the Syndics of Cambridge University Library. Image below, from box HCA 32/212 from the The National Archives.

Cover design: Anna Gatti

CONTENTS

INTRODUCTION.. xi

I. HANDBOOK

Michiel Leezenberg

1. Vernacularisation in the Ottoman Empire: Is Arabic the Exception that Proves the Rule?..................... 1

Necmettin Kızılkaya

2. From Means to Goal: Auxiliary Disciplines in the Ottoman *Madrasa* Curriculum 23

Guy Burak

3. On the Order of the Sciences for He Who Wants to Learn Them.. 39

Guy Burak

4. Rumi Authors, the Arabic Historiographical Tradition, and the Ottoman *Dawla/Devlet* 43

Christopher D. Bahl

5. Arabic Grammar Books in Ottoman Istanbul: The South Asian Connection 65

E. Khayyat

6. Bastards and Arabs.. 87

II. READER

Dotan Arad and Esther-Miriam Wagner

1. Bodl. Ms. Heb. C. 72/18: A Letter by Isaac Bayt ʿAṭṭān to Moses B. Judah (1480s)................................ 143

Benjamin Hary

2. The Purim Scroll of the Cairene Jewish Community 149

Dotan Arad

3. Appointment Deed of a Cantor in the Karaite Community, Cairo (1575) 155

Naḥem Ilan

4. Aharon Garish, *Metsaḥ Aharon* 161

Humphrey Taman Davies

5. *Kitāb Hazz al-Quḥūf* (1600s) 173

Boris Liebrenz and Kristina Richardson

6. A Weaver's Notebook from Aleppo (10th/16th century) 193

Michael Erdman

7. Selections from Arabic Garshūnī Manuscripts in the British Library 197

Liesbeth Zack

8. Excerpt from Yūsuf al-Maġribī's *Dafʿ al-iṣr ʿan kalām ahl Miṣr* (1606) 209

Jérôme Lentin

9. Lebanon: Chronicle of al-Ṣafadī (early 17th century [?]) 227

Werner Diem

10. A Jew's Testimony Regarding a Statement Made in His Presence by a Muslim, Testified on Monday 20th Kislev 5418 (1657) 233

Werner Diem

11. A Jew's Testimony Regarding a Statement Made in His Presence by a Muslim (1681) ... 237

Omer Shafran

12. A Basra Passover *Haggadah* with Judaeo-Arabic Translation (ca. 1700) ... 239

Ghayde Ghraowi

13. *Qahwa* 'Coffee' (16th–17th centuries) ... 243

Jérôme Lentin

14. Egypt: Damurdāšī's *Chronicle of Egypt* (first half of 18th century) ... 251

Ani Avetisyan

15. Matenadaran Collection MS No.1751: A Medical Work (1726) ... 255

Esther-Miriam Wagner and Mohamed Ahmed

16. A Clerical Letter by Rafael al-Ṭūḵī from the Prize Papers Collections (1758) ... 261

Esther-Miriam Wagner and Mohamed Ahmed

17. A Christian Mercantile Letter from the Prize Papers Collections (1759) ... 267

Feras Krimsti

18. Ḥannā al-Ṭabīb, *Riḥlat al-Shammās Ḥannā al-Ṭabīb ilā baldat Istanbūl* (1764/65) ... 275

Jérôme Lentin

19. Syria 1: Chronicle of Ibn al-Ṣiddīq (1768) ... 283

Ahmed Ech-Charfi

20. A Letter Transmitted by Ambassador Hajj Mahdī Bargash from Sultan Muḥammad Bin ʿAbdallah to Sultan Abdul Ḥamīd (1789 CE)....................................289

Boris Liebrenz

21. Arab Merchant Letters from the Gotha Collection of Arabic Manuscripts..293

Matthew Dudley

22. A Judaeo-Arabic Letter from the Prize Papers Collection, HCA 32/1208/126.2 (1796) 307

Olav Ørum

23. The Cairo-Ramla Manuscripts, or the Ramle KAR, 13 (1800s) 315

Magdalen M. Connolly

24. A 19th-Century Judaeo-Arabic Folk Narrative.......333

Jérôme Lentin

25. Libya 1: Ḥasan al-Faqīh Ḥasan's *Chronicle Al-Yawmiyyāt al-Lībiyya* (early 19th century)...............349

Jérôme Lentin

26. Libya 2: Letter from Ġūma al-Maḥmūdī (1795–1858) to ʿAzmī Bēk, *Daftardār* of the *ʾIyāla* (Province) of Tripoli (undated)...................................353

Geoffrey Khan and Esther-Miriam Wagner

27. T-S NS 99.38 (1809) 359

Esther-Miriam Wagner and Mohamed Ahmed

28. Rylands Genizah Collection A 803 (1825) 365

Jérôme Lentin

29. Syria 2: Chronicle of Muḥammad Saʿīd al-ʾUsṭuwānī (1840–1861) 371

Jérôme Lentin

30. Arabia: A Letter from Abdallah Ḥiṣānī to ʿAbdallah Bāšā (1855) 375

Liesbeth Zack

31. Excerpts from Yaʿqūb Ṣanūʿʾs *Abū Naḍḍāra Zarʾa* and ʿAbd Allāh al-Nadīm's *al-Ustāḏ* 381

George Kiraz

32. A Disgruntled Bishop: A Garshūnī Letter from Bishop Dinḥā of Midyat to Patriarch Peter III 399

Alex Bellem and G. Rex Smith

33. Aḥmad b. Muḥammad al-Jarādī: *Sīrat al-Ḵawāja al-ʾAkram al-Marḥūm Harmān al-ʾAlmānī* 415

Esther-Miriam Wagner

34. Ora ve-Simḥa (1917) 427

Charles Häberl

35. A 'Mandæo-Arabic' Letter from Lady Drower's Correspondence 431

Tania María García-Arévalo

36. An Anecdote about Juḥā (1920s) 441

REFERENCES 445

INTRODUCTION

The idea for this *Handbook and Reader of Ottoman Arabic* grew from a small seed. Originally, I had planned on an informal gathering with Geoffrey Khan, Rex Smith, and some fellow postdocs and students to talk about our respective Ottoman Arabic projects. To my great astonishment, a number of eminent Arabic linguists agreed to join us when I presented the idea, and from there we started drawing in Ottoman historians working on literacy and experts working on other languages in the Ottoman Empire. Our intended small workshop thus grew into the first conference on the topic, which took place in the Faculty of Asian and Middle Eastern Studies in Cambridge in 2016.

I had begun pondering the need for a volume focused on Ottoman Arabic after working on Early Modern sources in the Cairo Genizah, where the lack of reference works available to consult when working on these materials made for tedious checking of fringe dictionaries and dialectal grammar books. In my own experiences of being an Arabic student in Germany in the 1990s, in a very traditional German philology department, the Arabic texts taught had a chronological cut-off in the late medieval period. Students were provided with introductions to pre-Islamic poetry, Classical literature, and excursions into Muslim Iberian authors, but a contemptuous attitude prevailed towards anything written from the 15th century onwards.

Khaled Rouayheb (2015, 1) has summarised this attitude towards Ottoman Arabic in his description of the Ottoman period in the context of Arabic history as the perception of a "bleak

 https://doi.org/10.11647/OBP.0208.43

chapter of cultural, intellectual, and societal 'decadence' (*inḥiṭāṭ*) that began with the sacking of Baghdad by the Mongols in 1258 and came to an end only with the 'Arab awakening' of the nineteenth and twentieth centuries." When it comes to Arabic sources, this frame of mind is still quite wide-spread: more purely minded Arabic philologists might still recoil at the mention of philological work on these late Arabic sources characterised by vernacular influence and Middle Arabic orthography. This is why the gathering of like-minded people brought about much joy and an enthusiastic network of people who appreciate and work on Ottoman Arabic, who investigate literacies of Arabic in the Ottoman Empire, and who want to discuss the political, historical, and sociolinguistic circumstances behind Ottoman Arabic phenomena.

1.0. Koineisation of Arabic in Ottoman Arabic

Under Ottoman rule, we see a shift in Arabic literacy, and marked changes in the use of Arabic can be observed in various registers in contrast to earlier time periods. To a degree, this transformation follows on from changes in the Ayyubid and Mamluk period, but occurs on a much larger scale and extends to a much larger number of vernacular features.

The frequency with which these features occur depends on the literary genre of the texts concerned. Poetic, medical, and theological texts may show very few deviations from the norms of early medieval texts, whereas utilitarian prose in particular is marked by large scale introduction of vernacular and koine forms.

Some of the more frequent changes are tied in with the religious affiliations of the writers.[1] Although particular changes can be found in the case of Muslim writers, too, Christian and Jewish communities appear to have been less guided than their Muslim counterparts by the literary ideal of *al-ʿarabiyya*. As a result, where appropriate, the writings of Jews and Christians include a larger number of colloquial forms than those composed by their Muslim compatriots. Especially when writers attempted to connect to one another on an emotional level, we see colloquial forms occur in correspondence, or vernacular forms may be used to render speech in court documents.

Although Christian and Jewish texts may show a greater number of non-Classical forms than Muslim texts, due to religiously-anchored attitudes towards Classical Arabic among writers of the latter, this does not mean there are no shared trends observable in all Ottoman Arabic texts. A methodological flaw haunting grammatical description of Judaeo-Arabic and Christian Arabic texts is the method by which materials are compared to one another. Rather than comparing those forms which diverge from the Classical inventory to comparable contemporary texts, i.e., other letters, documents, philosophical texts, etc., analyses often concentrated on divergences from Classical Arabic only, thus incorrectly marking shared confessional forms as particularly Jewish or Christian.

The reality of Jewish or Christian Arabic forms was thus compared to the ideal of Muslim Arabic. Yet, Muslim texts are

---

[1] For a discussion on confessional varieties and their validity as a category, see Holes (2019), den Heijer (2012), and Wagner (2018).

often slightly more prescriptive, and many progressive language features do indeed appear to emerge first in Jewish and Christian texts.

Language deviation is additionally facilitated by the use of a different alphabet—such as Hebrew, in the case of Judaeo-Arabic, or Syriac, in the case of Garshuni texts. The use of a different script appears to open avenues of orthography influenced by spelling conventions in the relevant contact language that are closed to writers only employing Arabic script.

2.0. Shared Trends and Divergences of Koineisation across Confessional Boundaries

Trying to answer the question of how the choice of alphabet influences the writing of Ottoman Arabic, the texts in this *Reader* reveal a heterogeneous picture. Obvious differences become apparent in terms of orthography. Double spelling of consonants in cases of gemination occurs increasingly in Judaeo-Arabic sources from the later medieval period, but is largely confined to *w* and *y*. In the 19th and 20th centuries this appears to spread to all consonants, as in texts II.34 and II.36. Judaeo-Arabic texts of the later Ottoman period, in particular utilitarian prose texts, also reveal certain patterns of the realisation of short vowels that are hidden in Arabic script. The same can be found in texts written in Mandaic script, which, in addition to a large number of *plene*-spelled vowels, also reveals the dialectal pronunciation of suffixes, such as Classical Arabic -*k* as vernacular -*č*. Yet, other texts, in particular those written in Garshūnī, show an astonishing affinity to Classical Arabic orthographical norms.

A divergent feature can be found in the spelling of otiose *ʾalif*. In Judaeo-Arabic, this appears in medieval works, such as the Bible translation by Saadya Gaon, but has been lost in documentary sources. Christian utilitarian prose composed in Arabic, however, keeps this norm inherited from Arabic scribal traditions. Another divergent phenomenon is the vocalism patterns frequently found in Ottoman Judaeo-Arabic sources. Whether these patterns are specific to spoken Jewish Arabic or whether the use of the Hebrew alphabet allows shared colloquial speech patterns which were later abandoned by the other communities to emerge still needs to be investigated further.

The definite article preceding the 'sun letters' is most often not spelled in Judaeo-Arabic sources, but may also, albeit rarely, be missing in Christian and Muslim texts.

The very frequent *plene*-spelled short vowels, defective spelling of Classical Arabic long vowels, ה for Classical Arabic short /a/, and *tafḵīm* and *tarqīq* in Judaeo-Arabic correspondence and in Mandaic sources is aided by the use of different alphabets and Hebrew and Mandaic orthographical conventions. *Tāʾ marbūṭa* for *tāʾ*, however, occurs only in Christian letters, where it appears to be associated with the use of Arabic script.

The replacement of interdental fricatives by stops and the omission of final *nūn* of the nunation is shared in texts written by all confessions.

When we focus on the morphological, syntactic, and lexical levels, the differences become somewhat less pronounced. For example, while the vernacular *bi*-imperfect and the written koine form of *lam* as a general negation seem to emerge somewhat earlier in non-Muslim sources, they are common features found in texts written by members of all confessions. Pronouns and pronominal suffixes appear to be spelled colloquially mostly in non-Arabic alphabets, but the phenomenon occurs in Arabic script as well.

The lexicon of non-Muslim writers often includes vocabulary from the liturgical languages of those communities, but these should be classed as register-specific loanwords. Utilitarian texts in all confessional groups, in particular, display a rich assortment of colloquial phenomena.

Overall, most Ottoman Arabic texts show increased influence of vernacular forms compared with medieval texts, and allow greater access to the spoken language. At the same time, written koine forms become customary in the texts.

In terms of shared and divergent features, the biggest faultline seems to be utilitarian prose versus literary texts, rather than along confessional boundaries, although non-Arabic scripts additionally facilitate the emergence of non-Classical forms.

3.0. Notes

Having met Efe Khayyat from Rutgers University at another conference and discovered our shared passion for Ottoman Arabic, the two of us set about organising another conference at Rutgers in 2017. With his support, more contributors to the volume were recruited. The meetings culminated in a third and final workshop at the Woolf Institute in Cambridge in 2019.

When we discussed what form the written output of the conference could take, the idea of a *Handbook and Reader of Ottoman Arabic* emerged. The aim of such a volume would be to make a large number of short 15th–20th-century Arabic texts available and easily accessible to students and scholars of Arabic. Commentaries would elucidate shared linguistic phenomena and language change reflected in the written sources.

The Handbook section thus gathers articles intended to educate about a wide range of topics pertaining to literacy and education in the Ottoman Empire. The Reader section contains samples of texts provided by over twenty-five different scholars. Some of the texts were reproduced from other publications, with the obligation to leave them unchanged in this edition. Classical Arabic transcriptions and conventions were used alongside colloquial modern counterparts. It was therefore not possible to employ a homogenous transliteration system. This was somewhat difficult for me, conditioned by my Germanic schooling, but I have embraced the spirit of variationism.

The articles in the Handbook section have the references added at the end of each article, while the references for the Reader section are gathered at the end of the volume.

All texts in the Reader part that were originally composed in scripts other than Arabic have been rendered in Arabic transcription in order to allow access for scholars unfamiliar with the Hebrew, Syriac, and Mandaic alphabets. The transcription follows the system developed by Werner Diem (2014), and serves to open up the original text to the uninitiated, especially to native readers of Arabic. In the transcriptions, no statements are made about place of articulation or vowel quality or quantity, and no attempt has been made to provide a normalised Arabic version of the original text.

The table below shows the transliterations for the Classical texts:

ا	ʾ	ض	ḍ
ب	b	ط	ṭ
ت	t	ظ	ẓ, ḏ̣
ث	ṯ, th	ع	ʿ
ج	j	غ	ġ, gh
ح	ḥ	ف	F
خ	ḫ, ḵ, kh	ق	Q
د	d	ك	K
ذ	ḏ, dh	ل	L
ر	r	م	M
ز	z	ن	N
س	s	ه	H
ش	š, sh	و	W
ص	ṣ	ى	Y

4.0. Acknowledgments

This volume would not have been possible without the support of many institutions and individuals. First and foremost, my heartfelt thanks go to all the scholars who have contributed to this volume: Dotan Arad, Ani Avetisyan, Christopher Bahl, Alex Bellem, Guy Burak, Magdalen Connolly, Humphrey Davies, Werner Diem, Ahmed Ech-Charfi, Matthew Dudley, Michal Erdman, Tania García-Arévalo, Ghayde Ghraowi, Charles Häberl, Benjamin Hary, Nahem Ilam, Geoffrey Khan, George Kiraz, Feras Krimsti, Efe Khayyat, Necmettin Kizilkaya, Michiel Leezenberg, Jérôme Lentin, Boris Liebrenz, Olav Orum, G. Rex Smith, Kristina Richardson, Omer Shafran, Liesbeth Zack.

The Woolf Institute supported me first through a Research Fellowship, then appointed me as Director of Research and finally as Executive Director, always allowing me to continue my research passions, with funding provided for all three workshops.

The Faculty of Asian and Middle Eastern Studies of the University of Cambridge provided funding towards the first and third workshops. Rutgers University and Efe Khayyat funded the second workshop, while the T-S Genizah Research Unit of the Cambridge University Library contributed to the first workshop.

My profound gratitude goes to Gottfried Hagen, whose advice was crucial for the organisation and conduct of all three workshops. Geoffrey Khan and Clive Holes were ever supportive, and we had great intellectual input from Enam al-Wer, Helen Pfeifer, and Hakan Karateke. Thanks also go to John-Paul Ghobrial, Didem Havioglu, Tuna Artun, Peter Hill, and Khaled el-

Rouayheb, a well as all Woolf Institute staff who facilitated the conferences.

Last but not least, I owe a great debt to Aaron Hornkohl, Alissa Symon and Flora Moffie, who with great enthusiasm and passion helped me in bringing this volume together.

I. HANDBOOK

1. VERNACULARISATION IN THE OTTOMAN EMPIRE: IS ARABIC THE EXCEPTION THAT PROVES THE RULE?

Michiel Leezenberg

1.0. Introduction to the Ottoman Cosmopolitan

Arabic, Charles Ferguson has famously told us, is—like modern Greek—a *diglossic* language, 'high' and 'low' varieties of which are used in different and complementary settings. Diglossia differs from bilingualism in that it involves two varieties of the same language; moreover, the high variety lacks native speakers, and is acquired only in formal educational settings, and used only in official and/or written forms of communication. This diglossia, he adds, has proved remarkably resilient and enduring. Since their original publication in 1959, however, Ferguson's ideas have been modified and refined: varieties of modern Arabic other than the two reified high and low registers have rightly been distinguished; and the diglossic situation in Arabic, and even more in modern Greek, has been shown to be rather less stable and

https://doi.org/10.11647/OBP.0208.01

more contested than Ferguson's irenic picture would have us believe.[1]

Here, I would like to suggest that we can fruitfully explore the topic of Arabic diglossia—and of the development of modern Arabic more generally—laterally, and in a comparative and diachronic manner. More concretely, when studied in their broader Ottoman and post-Ottoman settings, the diglossic constellations of Arabic and Greek turn out to be but two very distinct outcomes of a rather broader process of *vernacularisation*, that is, a shift from written classical to locally spoken language varieties, in which hitherto spoken languages started being used for new literate uses, such as, most importantly, official courtly communication, high literature, and learning. This broader process in fact occurred across virtually the entire the Ottoman Empire; its consequences are still visible in the Empire's various successor states. Here, however, I will not discuss the case of Arabic in detail; rather, I will briefly sketch the wider pattern of development, and leave discussion of the implications for the study of Arabic to another occasion.

I take my cue from Sheldon Pollock, who has, famously, identified a number of *cosmopolitan orders* in the world of Latinity and the Sanskrit-based civilization in and around the Indian subcontinent during the first millennium CE; both of these orders, he

[1] Ferguson has also identified a number of what he calls 'myths' about Arabic (or what we would nowadays call 'language ideologies' or 'folk-theoretical beliefs') among its native speakers; among the most important of these, he argues, is the widespread, and ardently defended, belief that, despite all the dialectal and other varieties one encounters, there is but one single Arabic language.

further argues, went through broadly similar processes of vernacularisation around the year 1000 CE.[2] In Western and Southern Europe, this process yielded written Romance languages like Italian, Catalan, and French; in South Asia, vernaculars like Tamil, Telugu, and Kannada were similarly promoted to written status. Thus, vernacularisation is not specifically or uniquely modern or European; it may occur at different times and in different places.

The Ottoman Empire, as I hope to show below, knew a cosmopolitan order similar to those of Sanskrit and Latinity; and it, too, went through a massive wave of vernacularisations, in the 17th and 18th centuries CE. These vernacularisations, moreover, paved the way for the new, vernacular language-based ethnic identities and national movements that emerged in the course of the 19th century. In their earlier stages at least, these identities and movements developed largely, if not completely, independently of any cultural, ideological, or political influence or interference from Western or Central Europe. Thus, the widely held but rarely investigated assumption that national identities outside Europe were crucially influenced by European (and, more specifically, German) romantic nationalism and shaped by the categories of philological orientalism would seem to deserve reconsideration.

Although many discussions of nationalism contrast the multilingualism of premodern empires with the monolingual ideals and the linguistic standardisation of modern nation states, few empires can match the diversity and complexity of the early mod-

---

[2] For a brief statement, see Pollock (2000).

ern Ottoman linguistic constellation. In the Ottoman Empire, Arabic enjoyed a high status as the language of the revelation of Islam and of Islamic religious learning; but it was not the only written language of prestige even among Muslims, let alone other population groups. Famously, the Ottoman elites recognised 'the three languages' (*elsine-i selâse*) that dominated literate communication: Arabic for religious learning, Persian for poetry, and Ottoman Turkish for administration and official correspondence. The latter, as is well known, was a form of Turkish with a large, if highly variable, proportion of vocabulary items and grammatical constructions borrowed from Arabic and Persian; being virtually incomprehensible to the uneducated masses, and deliberately so, it also served as a marker of social distinction for the Ottoman bureaucratic elites.[3]

Christians living in the Empire had a number of classical, or sacred, languages of their own: in theory, Koinè Greek served as the language of liturgy and learning for all Orthodox Christians in the Empire, although some Orthodox communities used other ancient tongues, like Old Church Slavonic in the Balkans or Arabic in the Levant. Armenians, who had had their own church for centuries, used Grabar, or classical Armenian, as a liturgical and learned language; and Eastern Christians of different denominations generally used Syriac, which had been the regional *lingua franca* in the Fertile Crescent prior to the arrival of Arabic, but by the early modern period had become a dead language, and was used exclusively in formal and/or written communication.

---

[3] Cf. Mardin (1961).

The spoken varieties of these languages had a rather lower status—so low, in fact, that, among Greeks and Armenians in particular, one observes substantial language loss and a shift towards locally dominant languages or spoken *linguae francae* like Turkish, colloquial Arabic, or Kurdish. There is no evidence that this language shift was due to repressive Ottoman policies, as some nationalist historians have claimed; in fact, there is little evidence of *any* substantial Ottoman language policies prior to the last decades of the 19th century CE.

Among Ottoman Jews, the 'Sacred Language' (*leshon haqodesh*), a blend of Hebrew and Syriac, was the main written language prior to the arrival of large numbers of Sephardic Jews from the Iberian Peninsula in the late 15th and early 16th centuries. The main written language of this group was 'Judaeo-Hispanic,' grammatically a calque of the sacred language with a large number of Hispanic lexical items; this was distinct from 'Ladino' in the strict sense, the commonly spoken variety of Judaeo-Hispanic, which was much closer to colloquial 15th-century Spanish.[4]

Apart from these, there were also languages that had little or no written tradition like, most significantly, the Romance varieties spoken by several Orthodox Balkan Christian groups, Al-

[4] Remarkably, Evliya Çelebi describes what he calls *lisân-ı Yahûdî*, or 'the Jewish language,' as spoken in Safed in Ottoman Palestine (Dankoff et al. 2011, 3/74); but this language turns out to be neither classical Hebrew nor Aramaic, nor any offshoot from the Sacred Language, but a spoken dialect of Judaeo-Hispanic.

banian, and Kurdish, not to mention a number of mixed languages like the famous 'Asia Minor Greek,' which was almost exactly half Greek and half Turkish in its vocabulary and grammar, and the language varieties spoken by the Dom, or 'Gypsy', groups in different parts of the Empire. Although we have rather less information about these spoken vernaculars on the verge of the vernacularisation wave, we are fortunate in having a rich and relatively reliable source of information in Evliya Çelebi's famous *Seyâhatnâme*, or 'Book of Travels', which was written in the mid-17th century CE but not published until three centuries later.[5] Spoken language is always foremost in Evliya's mind, with sex a close second. Accordingly, the *Seyâhatnâme* offers a plethora, not only of basic vocabulary and stock phrases in various Ottoman vernaculars, but also obscene expressions. The care and precision of its transcriptions make this work a precious source for linguists even today.

2.0. Early Modern Ottoman Vernacularisation

Evliya observes that in the medreses of the Empire's outlying regions, Arabic and Persian were the main languages of instruction; but he also describes how Muslims in Ottoman Bosnia used a small Turkish-Bosnian lexicon—a vocabulary that has become known, and in fact appears to have gained a rather wide circulation, under the title of *Potur shahidiyya* (Dankoff et al. 2011, 5/229–30). That is, he points to the vernacularisation of 'Bosnian', i.e., the locally spoken South Slavic dialect, which was very

[5] The best modern edition of the *Seyâhatnâme* is Dankoff et al. 2011); for a generous selection in English, see Dankoff and Kim (2010).

close to the varieties that have subsequently become known as Serbian and Croat. This is one of the earliest examples of a much broader pattern of vernacularisation in the early modern Ottoman Empire: between the 17th and the early 19th centuries CE, various Ottoman population groups in different parts of the Empire shifted to new written uses of local vernacular languages.[6] The best known, and best documented, examples of this process are probably those among the Empire's various Christian groups. First and foremost, among Ottoman Greeks, a movement arose in the mid-18th century, pioneered by authors and actors like Iosipos Moisiodax and Adamantios Korais, which propagated the use of language varieties closer to locally spoken dialects than the millennia-old Koinè Greek, with the aim of making Greek-language education easier and less time-consuming. Amidst fierce polemics, Korais—ultimately successfully—argued that a modern, civilised Greek nation should speak and write neither a vulgar dialect nor the old-fashioned Koinè Greek, but a purified form of language (subsequently called *Katharevousa*), which was free of Turkish loans and enriched with neologisms to express modern concepts. Likewise, among Ottoman Armenians, in early modern times a new, supraregional variety emerged, called *K'aghak'akan* or 'the civil language', which was much closer to—though not identical with—regionally spoken dialects, and hence

[6] For a more detailed overview, see Leezenberg (2016). A book-length account, provisionally entitled *From Coffee House to Nation State: The Rise of National Languages in the Ottoman Empire*, is currently in preparation.

much easier to learn, read, and write than classical Armenian.[7] In the Ottoman Balkans, authors like Dositej Obradovic and Vuk Karadzic encouraged the written use of South Slavic (subsequently labelled 'Serbian'), against the dominance of both Koinè Greek and Old Church Slavonic; among Ottoman Serbs that had sought refuge in the Austro-Hungarian Empire in the 1690 exodus headed by patriarch Arsenije III, a supraregional language for learned and literate communication emerged that was called 'Slaveno-Serbian;' its use was actively encouraged by the Habsburg authorities, as a way of countering Russian linguistic, religious, and political influences. Further Eastward, in the Danube provinces, mid-18th-century authors like Paisii Hilendarski and Sofronij Vracanski simultaneously preached and practiced the literate use of the Bulgarian, or as they called it, 'Slaveno-Bulgarian', vernacular; and already earlier in the century, the famous Dimitrie Cantemir had pioneered the written and printed use of Romance vernacular locally called 'Wallachian', but subsequently labelled 'Romanian.' Initially, Cantemir appears to have intended this Romance vernacularisation as a way of countering the influence of Old Church Slavonic; but its later proponents emphasised the venerable pedigree of this vernacular in the Latin of antiquity, in an obvious effort to counter the dominance and prestige of Koinè Greek.

But these developments were not restricted either to the Empire's European provinces or to its Christian population groups. The Sephardic Jewish communities witnessed (or rather,

---

[7] For Modern Greek, see, e.g., Horrocks (1997) chapters 13–17; Ridgway (2009); for Armenian, see Nichanian (1989).

caused) the emancipation of spoken Ladino as a medium of religious learning in the early 18th century. During the same period, Muslim Albanians started to produce Arabic–Albanian and other vocabularies for educational purposes, and started composing learned divan poetry in an Albanian enriched with Arabic, Persian, and/or Ottoman Turkish expressions, locally called *bejtexhi* or '*Bayt* poetry'. In the Empire's Easternmost provinces, Kurdish authors like Ehmedê Xanî started using Kurmanji or Northern Kurdish both for didactic works and learned *mathnawî* poetry. In Mesopotamia, different denominations of Eastern Christians started using different forms of modern Aramaic, as distinct from classical Syriac, for literate, literary, or liturgical purposes. Even Ottoman Turkish witnessed significant attempts at simplifying the written language of bureaucracy in the 18th century in the direction of the Turkish dialect spoken in Istanbul, to the dismay of some officials, who feared they could no longer show off their social and linguistic distinction.[8] This period also witnessed significant linguistic shifts among different Ottoman population groups: in the 18th century, substantial numbers of so-called Romaniotes, or Greek-speaking Jews of the Ottoman Balkans, started speaking Ladino; and many Copts in Egypt and some Eastern Christians in the Mashriq and in Mesopotamia, appear to have become Arabised, largely abandoning their traditional vernaculars in favour of colloquial Arabic.

[8] Cf. Mardin (1961).

3.0. Attempts at Explanation: The Role of Vernacular Philologies

The fact that similar processes of vernacularisation occurred across, and perhaps even beyond, the early modern Ottoman Empire calls for explanation. At present, however, we are at a loss for any such explanatory account. For linguists, it would seem reasonable to suspect some kind of areal convergence or other form of language contact; this would raise the further question of whether such common or converging innovations simultaneously occurred in several languages, or rather started in one language, which then triggered similar changes in others. Such areal explanations, however, may be only part of the story: given that vernacularisation involves written rather than spoken language forms, and literate elites rather than the uneducated masses, such questions of cultural contact may also involve factors that are not strictly or structurally linguistic. To mention but one example: although the spoken varieties of Southern Slavic known today as Serbian, Croat, and Bosnian were mutually intelligible, and were in contact in urban centres like Sarajevo, the written traditions developed by authors writing in each of these three vernaculars were, for all practical purposes, completely independent from one another, if only because they involved, respectively, the Cyrillic, Latin, and Arabic alphabet.

One obvious level to look for explanations is the Ottoman political economy, in particular the well-known phase of some form of economic 'liberalisation,' coupled with a relative political decentralisation, in the 17th and 18th centuries CE.[9] Perhaps, then, we may fruitfully relate early modern cultural and linguistic phenomena to the rise of mercantilism; and indeed, among the Greek and Armenian communities in the major cities of the Western Ottoman Empire, like Istanbul, Izmir, and Salonica, something like a mercantile bourgeoisie had emerged, which had become affluent through trade with Christian powers, especially in the Western Mediterranean and Central Europe. The rise of such new secularised elites may tempt us to see linguistic developments among them as triggered and inspired by the cultural epiphenomena of such commercial contacts, and in particular by imported ideas associated with the Enlightenment and early Romantic nationalism. But quite apart from the question of whether there were any concrete and coherent vernacularising doctrines or tendencies specific to the European Enlightenment, such an explanation overstates Western European influence and downplays local Ottoman dynamics. These vernacularising processes, after all, took place not only among the European-oriented mercantile bourgeoisie in the Empire's urban centres, but also among different population groups in its more remote and isolated rural peripheries.

Given these difficulties, we should perhaps first try to isolate and explicate all potentially relevant linguistic, sociolinguistic, and other factors before attempting any explanation. There are several such factors that may help in guiding our explanations; but here, I will discuss only the role of printing and of vernacular philologies. First, it should be noted that some, but by no

[9] See, e.g., Inalcik and Quataert (1994, parts II and III).

means all, of these vernacularising movements were accompanied and facilitated by the use of printing. Thus, texts in different varieties of Greek and Armenian were printed in centres like Venice and Vienna, primarily targeting publics living in Ottoman territory and often sponsored by wealthy Ottoman citizens. Even more intriguingly, these foreign presses also produced materials written in Turkish, but printed in Greek or Armenian characters (subsequently called, respectively, 'Karamanlidiki' and 'Armeno-Turkish literature'), indicating that by this time, a substantial part of the affluent reading publics could read these scripts, but had long since shifted to spoken Turkish. The Empire's Sephardic Jews had known-printing in Judaeo-Hispanic since the 16th century CE; but from the early 18th century on, printed works of religious learning (and, later, increasing numbers of secular texts) in colloquial Ladino started being published as well. Famously, Ibrahim Müteferrika's government-sponsored press printed a number of works in Ottoman Turkish in the first half of the 18th century; but in the face of protests from scribes and copyists, and more importantly of disappointing sales, it discontinued activity. Other vernacularising movements, however, like those among Albanians, Bulgarians, and Kurds, would not involve printed texts until well into the 19th century. In short, the mere availability of printing technology was in itself neither a causal factor nor a necessary feature of the various Ottoman vernacularisations.[10]

---

[10] This is one serious problem for Benedict Anderson's influential (1991) argument that it was 'print capitalism', or the mere availability of the

A second important if variable aspect of Ottoman vernacularisation is the appearance of vernacular grammars. The writing, let alone printing, of such grammars points to a later stage in the process of Ottoman vernacularisation, which stretches from the mid-18th to the mid-19th century. Until then, grammatical instruction was generally restricted to classical or sacred languages among Muslims, Christians, and Jews alike. In Muslim educational institutions, only Arabic grammar was studied systematically; Persian was acquired not by studying grammatical textbooks, but by reading works like Saʿdî's *Golestan*; and Ottoman Turkish, which had no fixed grammatical or stylistic rules or norms to begin with, appears to have been acquired informally, or simply to have been presumed as known. Even less current was any belief that locally spoken dialects were worthy of having their grammars written down and studied—or indeed that they had a system of grammatical rules to begin with. Generally, vernaculars appear to have been seen as deviations from classical norms or rules, rather than as full-fledged languages having rules of correctness of their own.[11]

This was to change in the 18th century: during this period, one witnesses the development of what one may call 'vernacular philologies', in particular through the writing of grammars and

technology of printing within a capitalist mode of production, which made possible the rise of superstructural or ideological 'imagined community' of the nation.

[11] An intriguing exception may be Evliya Çelebi, who in his *Seyâthatnâme*, conceives of all (spoken and written) languages as analogous to religions, each of them revealed by a specific prophet and having a sacred scripture of its own (*Seyâhatnâme* II:256a; Dankoff et al. 2/57).

lexica for various vernaculars. To mention but a few: in 1757, Dimitri Eustatievici wrote a Romanian grammar, *Gramatica Rumaneasca*; but this text would not be printed until well into the 20th century. Likewise, probably around the mid-18th century CE, Elî Teremaxî composed a *Tesrîfa Kurmancî* or 'Kurdish morphology' in Kurmanjî or Northern Kurdish. Written for young Kurdish-speaking medrese pupils taking their first steps in Arabic grammar, this work gained a wide circulation in the rural medreses of Northern Kurdistan, and, in fact, continued to be used clandestinely even after the rulers in the new republic of Turkey ordered the closing down of all medreses in the 1920s. In 1815 Vuk Karadzic wrote a grammar of his native dialect of Serbian, the *Pismenica serbskoga jezika*, at the request of his friend Jernej Kopitar; this work was to gain rather wider circulation in Northern European historical-comparative linguistic circles thanks to Jakob Grimm's 1824 translation, the *Kleine serbische Grammatik*. In 1835, Neofit Rilski had a *Bolgarska gramatika* printed for use in schools trying to rid themselves of Greek linguistic and cultural dominance. And as late as 1851, Ahmed Cevdet Pasha published a *Kavâ'id-i Osmaniyye* 'Principles of Ottoman [Turkish]', which was to go through numerous printed editions in the following decades.

It should be emphasised that these new vernacular philologies owe less to modern Western philological orientalism than to local classical traditions. Even in a relatively late work like Cevdet and Fuad Pasha's textbook, the categories employed are those of traditional Arabic grammar, rather than of modern Western philology. Thus, in its treatment of the locative and ablative case, evidentials, and vowel harmony, the *Kavâ'id-i Osmaniyye* differs radically from A. L. Davids's 1832 *Grammar of the Turkish Language*, which some modern scholars, mistakenly, have seen as a source of inspiration for Cevdet's work.[12] In short, a strong argument can be made that these vernacularising processes, and the emergence of new local vernacular philologies, *preceded* any influence or hegemony of modern Western orientalist philology.

The historical and theoretical significance of these vernacular grammars has not yet been assessed. Here, however, I wish to suggest that they not only mark an important dimension of the vernacularisation of various Ottoman languages; they also embody a step in what one may call the *governmentalisation* of language, that is, in a process that simultaneously turned vernacular languages into objects of knowledge and objects of governmental concern. One of the main aspects of modern nationalism, after all, is that all subjects are to be turned into full-blooded citizens, and into loyal members of the nation, by universal education in a standardised, unified and codified version of what is called 'the mother tongue'; and that the spread and implementation of this mother tongue through educational systems and institutions is one of the primary responsibilities of the new institution of the nation state. The history of modern nationalism, that is, is also a history of how vernacular languages—or new forms of language much closer to spoken dialects—simultaneously became instruments of mass communication, symbols of identification, and objects of government.

[12] For a more detailed argument, see Leezenberg (2021).

4.0. A *Sonderweg* for Arabic?

At first blush, Arabic seems to form the most important, if not virtually the sole, significant exception to this empire-wide process of vernacularisation. Although dialectal or colloquial traces appear in various Arabic-languages of different ages, no authors openly proclaim or propagate either the written use of vernacular forms of Arabic, or the modernisation or purification of the Arabic language prior to the *nahda*, or literary Renaissance movement, that emerged in the mid-19th century. But perhaps we simply have not looked closely enough, or have been misled to some extent by the pervasive linguistic ideologies concerning the unity and uniqueness of Arabic.

Considerations of space, and lack of relevant expertise, prevent me from pursuing these questions in greater detail; but here, I would merely like to suggest that the study of Ottoman Arabic may be enriched by a more systematic contextualisation: we can, and perhaps should, ask whether and how the structure, use, and ideologies of Arabic were affected by developing institutions and practices of government, and compare and contrast the development of Arabic with that of other languages in the Ottoman Empire. To take but one example, one may think of so-called 'Middle Arabic' typologically as a specific style or register of Arabic between the normative ideal of Classical Arabic and the colloquial realities of local dialects, rather than historically, as a developmental stage or period as was done by earlier scholars.[13] In doing so, however, we may come to see the similarities and divergences

[13] I owe this suggestion to Clive Holes (personal communication).

between Arabic and other Ottoman languages in a rather different light. As discussed above, speakers of several other Ottoman languages also developed supraregional forms that consciously differed from, and acted as intermediaries between, on the one hand, the classical norm and, on the other hand, the regional, 'vulgar' dialects. The modern Greeks developed *Katharevousa*; among Ottoman Armenians, a supraregional 'civil language' (*K'aghak'akan*) emerged; and Serbian exiles produced an educated Slaveno-Serbian. Only Greek and Arabic, however, retained an enduring diglossia, whereas both Civil Armenian and Slaveno-Serbian disappeared in the 19th century.

There was nothing inevitable about these outcomes. Prior to the 1815 publication of Karadzic's *Pismenica serbskogo jezika*, several grammars of Slaveno-Serbian had been written and printed; in fact, Karadzic's own grammar has been shown to be a calque of one of these grammars, which simply replaced Slaveno-Serbian items and paradigms with dialectal ones.[14] And Nichanian (1989) describes how a substantial literature (both translated and original) in Civil Armenian had circulated before being replaced by a variety closer to the dialects spoken in the Empire, called 'Western Armenian'. Thus, even if the process of vernacularisation occurred throughout the Ottoman Empire, its outcomes varied widely across different languages.

The brings up the substantial question why *only* Greek and Arabic retained a relatively stable diglossic constellation, whereas languages that emerged from broadly similar backgrounds, like Armenian and the Slavic languages, did not.

---

[14] This was argued in detail by Thomas (1970, 14–21).

One crucial factor appears to have been the role of language ideologies: among Greeks and Arabs alike, the belief that, despite all dialectal differences and diachronic developments, their language—like their nation—was and should remain a unitary and unified entity appears to have predominated, and to have created the preconditions for relatively stable and enduring—if by no means uncontested—diglossia. Among Armenians, by contrast, the language-ideological belief that a modern language should be closer to the dialects of 'the people' appears to have carried the day. Finally, Slavic languages, and apparently also the various forms of Neo-Aramaic, appear to have been shaped by what has been called 'fractal logic' (cf. Gal 2005), which leads to ever-greater linguistic differentiation alongside the proliferation of new ethnic or sectarian antagonisms. In the mid-19th century, attempts at creating a unified 'Serbo-Croat' language seemed to be successful, but the two main varieties continued to be written in different scripts; and since the wars of the 1990s, efforts to emphasise the linguistic differences—not only between Serbian and Croat, but also with Bosnian and Montenegran—have been further stepped up. Another South Slavic vernacular, Bulgarian, appears to have followed a similar fractal logic: it came to be seen, and used, as a distinct Slavic language only in the later 18th century, and by the turn of the 20th, a movement had emerged that claimed 'Macedonian,' which hitherto had been classified as 'Western Bulgarian,' as a language in its own right; and the fractalising process may not have ended there. Similarly, in Northern Iraq, among Eastern Christians of different denominations, a bewildering variety of modern and not-so-modern standards of written Modern Aramaic has emerged, without any one variety gaining a wider currency.[15]

In short, common processes of vernacularisation have had very different results in different languages, depending in part on linguistic ideologies, on ethnic and sectarian relations, and on vernacular philologies. Most, if not all, of these outcomes, it should be noted, had already been more or less decided (though by no means completed) by the end of World War I, that is, prior to the formation of the Ottoman successor states and the imposition and permeation of national languages through educational institutions and mass media. Thus, they were not dependent on, or decided by, sovereign state power; hence, it may be useful to study Ottoman processes and patterns of vernacularisation neither in purely linguistic terms nor in terms of sovereign state power, but with an eye to the development of vernacular philological traditions as a crucial factor in linguistic governmentalisation.

References

Anderson, Benedict. 1991. *Imagined Communities*. 2nd edition. London: Verso Books.

[15] One might also argue that, in early modern times, speakers of Turkish knew an Ottoman-colloquial Turkish diglossia; but there was little if any sense that these were two levels or registers of the *same* language. The labels used for both may be significant: generally, Ottoman Turkish was called *Osmanlıca* or *Osmanî*, and colloquial Turkish *Türkçe* or *Kaba Türkçe* 'coarse Turkish'; Evliya refers to the former as *Lisan-ı Rum*, and to the latter as *Lisan-ı etrâk*.

Burke, Peter. 2004. *Languages and Communities in Early Modern Europe*. Cambridge: Cambridge University Press.

Butler, Thomas. 1970. 'The Origins of the War for a Serbian Language and Orthography'. *Harvard Slavic Review* 5: 1–80.

Dankoff, Robert, et al. (eds). 2011. *Evliya Çelebi seyahatnamesi*. Istanbul: Yapı Kredi Yayınları.

Dankoff, Robert, and Sooyong Kim (trans.). 2010. *An Ottoman Traveller: Selections from the Book of Travels of Evliya Çelebi*. London: Eland.

Ferguson, Charles. 1959. 'Diglossia.' *Word* 15 (2): 325–40.

———. 1968 (1959). 'Myths about Arabic'. In *Readings in the Sociology of Language*, edited by J. Fishman, 375–81. The Hague: Mouton.

Foucault, Michel. 1978. 'La gouvernementalité'. *Dits et écrits* III: 635–57. Paris: Gallimard.

Gal, Susan. 2005. 'Language Ideologies Compared: Metaphors of Public/Private.' *Journal of Linguistic Anthropology* 15 (1), 23–37.

Horrocks, Geoffrey. 1997. *Greek: A history of the Language and Its Speakers*. London: Longman.

Inalcik, Halil, and Donald Quataert (eds). 1994. *An Economic and Social History of the Ottoman Empire*. Cambridge: Cambridge University Press.

Leezenberg, Michiel. 2016. 'The Vernacular Revolution: Reclaiming Early Modern Grammatical Traditions in the Ottoman Empire'. *History of Humanities* 1 (2): 251–75.

———. 2014. 'Elî Teremaxî and the Vernacularization of Medrese Learning in Kurdistan'. *Iranian Studies* 47: 713–33.

———. 2021. 'Internalized Orientalism or World Philology? The Case of Modern Turkish Studies'. *History of Humanities* 6 (1): 109–19.

Mackridge, Peter. 2009. *Language and National Identity in Greece, 1766–1976*. Oxford: Oxford University Press.

Mardin, Serif. 1961. 'Some Notes on an Early Phase in the Modernization of Communications in Turkey'. *Comparative Studies in Society and History* 3 (3): 250–71.

Nichanian, Marc. 1989. *Ages et usages de la langue arménienne*. Paris: Éditions Entente.

Pollock, Sheldon. 2000. 'Cosmopolitan and Vernacular in History'. *Public Culture* 12: 591–625.

2. FROM MEANS TO GOAL: AUXILIARY DISCIPLINES IN THE OTTOMAN MADRASA CURRICULUM

Necmettin Kızılkaya

1.0. Introduction

The Ottoman Empire established madrasas since its formation. It met the needs of these madrasas, first, by inviting teachers from adjacent regions and, soon after, by employing their students. Thus, students who successfully graduated from the madrasa then became the teachers, who would in turn become the pioneers in systemising the Ottoman madrasa (Āşıkpaşazāde 1332). The curriculum became methodised in a short time. To ensure the continuation of this system, it was continually revised and developed by the Ottoman scholars.

There were many factors that facilitated this constant revision of the Ottoman madrasa system. The most important of these was that the madrasa was an institution in which qualified individuals were produced in every area needed by the Empire. The madrasa curriculum, which had been structured to respond to a wide range of expectations and issues, from bureaucracy to *ilmiye* institutions, had to be continually developed. That being said, the effort to develop the curriculum does not mean that there were

 https://doi.org/10.11647/OBP.0208.02

no fixed disciplines within the madrasa system. On the contrary, in some fields there were books that were taught for centuries throughout the Empire. Therefore, there were constants and variables in the madrasa curriculum; and the variables were shaped according to the needs of each period.

Despite this, we still do not have much knowledge about the books taught in the Ottoman madrasa system, as there has not yet been much scholarly attention by researchers in the field of history and education on the subject. Studies regarding the madrasa mainly focus on its structures, its architecture, its relations with politics, teacher-student relationships, and *ilmiye* hierarchy. Many issues, such as the curriculum, the range of the courses taught, the differences encountered within different regions, and the reasons for changes to the curriculum have not been elucidated as of yet. The absence of specific scholarship regarding this subject in Western languages, with the exception of a few general studies, has led to a lack of understanding regarding the nature of the Empire's educational system among modern researchers. Although some Turkish studies partially fill the gap on this subject,[1] a significant number of them provide only general information about the curriculum, and more detailed studies are needed.

The Ottoman madrasa curriculum was structured in different stages, with different disciplines taught at each step. The main aim of the curriculum was to understand the Islamic disciplines and to meet the needs of society. Therefore, the madrasa

[1] For details see Hüseyin 1983; İsmail 1984; Cevat 1997; Murat 2019.

curriculum focused on understanding three disciplines. These disciplines are *fiqh* 'deep understanding', *kalām* 'theology', and *taṣawwuf* 'mysticism', which are called *al-ʿulūm al-ʿāliyya* 'the high disciplines'. However, the discipline of *fiqh* stands in a central place among them. It is not an exaggeration to posit that the madrasa education was designed for the discipline of *fiqh*. There was a preparatory process that trained students for these three disciplines, in general, and *fiqh*, in particular. In this process, the auxiliary disciplines, which are *ʿulūm āliyya*, were taught and the students were provided with the necessary knowledge and sophistication to understand the Islamic disciplines. The preparatory/auxiliary disciplines are mostly Arabic disciplines. The auxiliary disciplines, which serve as the key for students to comprehend texts written in various branches of the Islamic disciplines that emerged in Muslim societies, especially the texts of the Qurʾān and the Sunna, are *ṣarf* 'morphology', *naḥw* 'grammar/syntax', *manṭiq* 'logic', *ādāb al-baḥth wa-l-munāẓara* 'dialectic', *waḍʿ* 'philosophy of language', and *balāgha* 'rhetoric'.

There are many classical sources about the disciplines taught in Ottoman madrasas. Both the divergent sources and the teaching of various works in different centuries in the Empire, which lasted for six centuries, make it difficult to draw a unified picture of the curriculum. However, the fact that the disciplines taught did not undergo much change in these periods, together with the continuity of some of the utilised texts, allows us to make general comments on some points. Three types of sources are available to investigate the taught courses. The first of these are books dealing with the *tartīb* 'organisation' and *tasnīf* 'classification' of disciplines. I will examine the curriculum based on these sources. The second of these are biographies and autobiographies of scholars. In these sources, the books that a scholar read and taught give a particular idea to the reader about which books were in circulation, accepted, and included in to the curriculum. The third type are *ijāza* 'diplomas'. These diplomas reveal to us the lessons and from whom those lessons were taken. Yet, in general, they do not mention the names of the books studied. In this article, I will briefly examine the works taught in the field of auxiliary disciplines in the Ottoman madrasa curriculum. Although different works were taught in different periods and regions, I will focus on the most widely read books.

2.0. Auxiliary Disciplines in the Madrasa Curriculum

Kawākib-i Sabʿa Risālesi is an anonymous work authored in 1155/1741 as a response to an inquiry by the French ambassador to Bāb-i Ali (High Porte) about the character of the Ottoman madrasa curriculum. It consists of important material regarding the pre-madrasa education. I will briefly summarise the information about the pre-madrasa process in the *risāla*. According to this *risāla*, upon starting his education, a student first learned the Arabic alphabet and then began reading the Qurʾān from *ʿamma juzʾ*.[2] Then, under the supervision of a teacher, the student would

[2] A *juzʾ* is one of the thirty parts of the Qurʾān.

read the whole Qurʾān along with a book of *tajwīd.*[3] Later, the process continued with memorising the Qurʾān and Birgili Mehmed Efendi's (d. 981/1573) *ʿAqāʾid Risālesi*, which was written in Turkish. After the ceremony of completing the memorisation of the Qurʾān, a dictionary—such as the poetic dictionary of Ibn al-Farishta (d. after 821/1418)—was taught to impart familiarity with Arabic words. Additionally, in order to get used to Persian, brāhīm Shāhidī's (d. 957/1550) Persian verse dictionary *Tuḥfa-i Shāhidī*) was taught. Having completed this process, the student was able to begin the auxiliary disciplines (Cevat 1997). The disciplines taught in the madrasa were divided into three main parts: the auxiliary disciplines, Islamic disciplines, and *juzʾiyyāt* 'particular cases, details', such as mathematics, geometry, and astronomy). The main purpose was to learn the Islamic disciplines; the auxiliary disciplines were taught in support of understanding them. Of course, this never demoted the auxiliary disciplines to a secondary position. On the contrary, in some periods and madrasas, they were given equal importance to the Islamic disciplines.

2.1. Morphology (*Ṣarf*)

The first discipline taught in auxiliary disciplines was the discipline of morphology (*ṣarf*). The *Amthila* (*Amthila-i Mukhtalifa wa-Muttarida*) was the first book read in this discipline. This text examines words and their forms. The students first memorised the text. An interesting feature of this text is that it is an anonymous

[3] *Tajwīd* is a set of rules for the correct pronunciation of the letters with all their qualities.

text/or that its author is unknown. After this, *Bināʾ al-afʿāl*, also anonymous, was studied. This book was written to afford basic knowledge of morphology based on the sound, structure, and semantic variation of the past and present tenses of Arabic verbs. In this respect, the basic education given in *Amthila* is deepened in the *Bināʾ* by taking Arabic verbs as the core of the discussion. The *Maqṣūd*, which is read at the next stage, is, like *Amthila* and *Bināʾ*, also anonymous. In this book, after emphasising the importance of the discipline of morphology, the patterns of verbs, conjugations of verbs and the declension of nouns, the rules to be applied in these conjugations and declensions and their explanations are all expounded upon and the kinds and descriptions of the verbs are elucidated (Khalīfa 2007, 1:255; 2:1078, 1806–7).

Al-ʿIzzī fī l-taṣrīf is one of the five classical works known as the *sarf cümlesi* and taught in the Ottoman madrasas. It is an important book written by ʿIzz al-Dīn al-Zanjānī (d. 660/1262) on the discipline of Arabic morphology. Because of its importance, scholars like Saʿd al-Dīn al-Taftāzānī (d. 792/1390), Sayyid Sharīf al-Jurjānī (d. 816/1413), ʿImād al-Dīn Ibn Jamāʿa (d. 819/1416), Niksārī Ḥasan Pasha (d. 827/1424), Khoja Zāda Musliḥ al-Dīn (d. 893/1488), Khatīb al-Shirbīnī (d. 977/1570), and ʿAli al-Qārī (d. 1014/1605) have written commentaries on it. Among them, the commentary by Taftāzānī became famous and dozens of sub-commentaries were written on it (Khalīfa 2007, 2:1139–40). Like other books of morphology, Aḥmad b. ʿAlī b. Masʿūd's (d. 8th/14th century) comprehensive work *Marāḥ al-arwāḥ* was widely taught in Ottoman madrasas. This book consists of seven chapters and provides detailed information first on infinitives and then on the different forms and types of verbs (Khalīfa 2007, 2:1651).

Ibn al-Ḥājib's (d. 646/1249) *al-Shāfiya fī l-Taṣrīf*, was written on Zamakhsharī's (d. 538/1144) *al-Mufaṣṣal fī ṣanʿat al-iʿrāb*, which is a summary (*khulāṣa*) of Abū Bishr Sībawayhi's (d. 180/796) *al-Kitāb*. This was a key text in morphology within the madrasa curriculum. Ibn al-Ḥājib combined the subjects related to morphology in Zamakhsharī's *al-Mufaṣṣal* by making the necessary additions as well as sorting, correcting, and summarising them in his *al-Shāfiya*. This book is considered the first concise work on morphology, covering almost all subjects of the discipline. Another significant feature of this text was that the author, Ibn al-Ḥājib, though based in an Ottoman and Ḥanafi tradition madrasa, was a Mālikī scholar. *Al-Shāfiya* explains the rules of morphology in a concise yet systematic way. It has been taught as a textbook for centuries in madrasas throughout the Ottoman and Islamic world. Many studies from commentaries, sub-commentaries, poeticisation, and translation have been added to it. Moreover, not only the text itself, but also its commentaries were taught in the Ottoman madrasas (Khalīfa 2007, 2:1021).

2.2. Grammar/Syntax (*Naḥw*)

The second discipline taught was Arabic grammar/syntax (*naḥw*). The first book that was used as a textbook in Arabic grammar was the *ʿAwāmil*. Although there were several books that bore this title, two of them were widely used for teaching in the Ottoman madrasas over the centuries. The first one was ʿAbd al-Qāhir bin ʿAbd al-Raḥmān al-Jurjānī's (d. 471/1078) *al-ʿAwāmil*, which was called *al-ʿAwāmil al-ʿatīq*; the second one was Muḥammad Birgiwī's (d. 981/1573) *al-ʿAwāmil*, which was referred to as *al-ʿAwāmil al-jadīd*. However, there are significant differences between these two books in terms of a number of factors (*ʿāmils*) and the way they were treated. Al-Jurjānī's *al-ʿAwāmil* was taught in some parts of Anatolia, though mainly in Arab regions, Iran, and the Indian Subcontinent. As for Birgiwī's text, it was taught in the madrasas of Istanbul and the Balkans for a long period (Durmuş 1991). After memorisation of Birgiwī's *al-ʿAwāmil*, students moved to another book, *Iẓhār al-asrār*, which was written based on the principles of the Basran language school of grammar, i.e., to teach the main subjects of Arabic grammar in a concise way and in a short time. The grammatical rules that were mentioned only by name and with a single example in the *ʿAwāmil* were extended in *Iẓhār al-asrār* by giving their definitions, conditions, and detailed examples (Khalīfa 2007, 1:117).

Ibn al-Ḥājib's *al-Kāfiya* is one of the main texts that was used in the Ottoman madrasas. It is, along with Sībawayhi's *al-Kitāb* and Zamakhsharī's *al-Mufaṣṣal*, one of the three most recognised books written on Arabic grammar. Although Sībawayhi's *al-Kitāb* contains rich material and examples, its contents are unclassified. Zamakhsharī classified its subjects and summarised it in his *al-Mufaṣṣal*. Ibn al-Ḥājib's *al-Kāfiya* relied on *al-Mufaṣṣal*. All of the subjects of *naḥw* were studied to allow students to understand complex topics. Thanks to the accomplishment of *al-Kāfiya*, it was used as a text book in Ottoman madrasas for centuries (al-Zamakhsharī 2004; Khalīfa 2007, 2:1370–76). Ibn al-Ḥājib's *al-Kāfiya* was used not only as an independent textbook in the madrasa curriculum, but also as the main text and subject of commentary by Nūr al-Dīn ʿAbd al-Raḥmān Jāmī's (d. 898/1492) *al-Fawāʾid al-Dhiyāʾiyya*. *Al-Fawāʾid*, which is also known as *Jāmī* or *Molla Jāmī*. It was one of the main grammar books that was taught at the advanced level. *Molla Jāmī* was not the only advanced textbook that students studied in madrasa; other books were also taught, such as Ibn Hishām's (d. 761/1360) *Mughnī al-labīb* and *Alfiyyat Ibn Mālik* (Ibn Khaldūn 2005, 5:297–98).

Besides some other features, *Mughnī al-labīb* is original in terms of its classification of subjects. By that time, grammar books had come to classify subjects based on *ʿāmil-maʿmūl-iʿrāb*, *marfūʿāt-mansūbāt-majrūrāt-majzūmāt*, but Ibn Hishām followed a different method, which made his book renowned and one of the most circulated since his time. He divided its eight sub-chapters into two main chapters, which are *mufradāt* 'propositions' and *jumal* 'sentences' (Ibn Hishām 1964; Khalīfa 2007, 2:1751–54). As for the *Alfiyyat Ibn Mālik fī l-naḥw wa-l-taṣrīf*, it was composed of thousands of grammatical rules explained using examples from Qurʾānic verses, Prophetic traditions, and Arabic poems. It was memorised by students at the advanced level (Khalīfa 2007, 1:151–55).

2.3. Logic (*Manṭiq*)

After completing grammar, students would study logic (*manṭiq*). Most of the *manṭiq* books taught in Ottoman madrasas belonged to the last period of the pre-Ottoman era, which is denominated the *mutaʾakhkhirūn* period. The first textbook taught in the madrasa on logic is Asīr al-Dīn al-Abharī's (d. 663/1265), *al-Risāla al-Aṯīriyya fī l-manṭiq*, with a condensed version known as *Īsāgūcī*, along with its commentaries and the glosses written on it. *Īsāgūcī* is an abridgement that contains all the subjects of classical logic. Because of this feature, it became the first textbook taught in the discipline of logic in the madrasa curriculum and many commentaries and sub-commentaries written on it have received the attention of scholars. The first of these commentaries is Ḥusam al-Dīn Ḥasan al-Kātī's (d. 760/1359) *Ḥusam-i Kātī* and Muḥy al-Dīn al-Tālishī's (d. 887/1482) sub-commentary on it are famous. Mullā Fanārī's (d. 834/1431) *al-Fawāʾid al-Fanāriyya*, which is the second well-known commentary, and its sub-commentary, Aḥmad Ibn Khizir's (d. 950/1543) *Qūl (Qawl) Aḥmad*, were also central textbooks in the madrasas (İzgi 1997). These two books differ from the other logic books taught in the madrasa in the way that both, especially the latter, employ tight and comprehensive language. By reading these texts, the student not only learned logic, but also had to grapple with difficult phrases of the Arabic language.

At a higher level, students were taught ʿAlī Ibn Omar al-Kātibī al-Qazwīnī's (d. 675/1277) *al-Risāla al-Shamsiyya fī l-qawāʿid al-manṭiqiyya* and Saʿd al-Dīn al-Taftāzānī's *Tahdhīb al-manṭiq wa-l-kalām*, with its commentaries and super commentaries. In the following period, Qutb al-Dīn al-Rāzī's (d. 766/1365) *Taḥrīr al-qawāʿid al-manṭiqiyya fī sharḥ al-Risāla al-Shamsiyya*, a famous commentary on al-Qazwīnī's *al-Risālat al-*

Shamsiyya, was taught. Along with *Taḥrīr al-qawāʿid al-manṭiqiyya*, its sub-commentaries in Sayyid Sharīf al-Jurjānī's (d. 816/1413) *Taḥrīr al-qawāʿid* and in Kara Dāwūd Izmitī's (d. 948/1541) *Ḥāshiya ʿalā Ḥāshiya Küçük (Kuçek) ʿalā Taḥrīr al-qawāʿid al-manṭiqiyya* were studied. The student who read and completed these books proved his scientific talent and desire. Finally, in the discipline of logic Qutb al-Dīn al-Rāzī's commentary, *Lawāmiʿ al-asrār Sharh Maṭāliʿ al-anwār fī l-manṭiq* on Sirāj al-Dīn al-ʿUrmawī's (d. 682/1283) *Maṭāliʿ al-anwār*, was taught (al-Rāzī 1384; Sāçaklīzāde 1988).

2.4. Dialectic (*Ādāb al-baḥth wa-l-munāẓara*)

After logic, dialectic (*ādāb al-baḥth wa-l-munāẓara*) was studied to help students avoid inconsistency and contradiction in debate. At the elementary level, Taşkuprizāde Aḥmed Efendi's (d. 968/1561) *Sharḥ ʿalā Risāla fī ʿilm ādāb al-baḥth wa-l-munāẓara*, which is his commentary on his own *al-Risāla*, was taught. After that, students studied Kamāl al-Dīn Masʿūd al-Rūmī's (d. 905/1499) commentary on Shams al-Dīn Muḥammad Ibn Ashraf al-Samarqandī's (d. 722/1322) *al-Risāla al-Samarqandiyya fī ādāb al-baḥth*, which has around twenty-one super commentaries. At the same time, they were studying Shah Ḥusayin Efendi's (d. 1130/1718) *al-Risāla al-Ḥusayniyya fī fanni ādāb al-baḥth* with its commentaries and sub-commentaries . Following this stage, students studied Qādī ʿAḍud al-Dīn al-Ījī's (d. 756/1355) *Ādāb al-baḥth* and its commentary *Sharḥ Ādāb al-baḥth*, written by Muḥammad al-Ḥanafī l-Tabrīzī (d. around 900/1494) and its sub-commentary, Mīr Abū al-Fatḥ Muḥammad Ibn Amīn's (d. around 875/1470) *Ḥāshiyat al-Mīr* (İzgi 1997).

2.5. Philosophy of Language (*Waḍ*ʿ)

One of the important disciplines taught in madrasas was *ʿilm al-waḍʿ*. *Waḍʿ*, which deals with the origins and nature of language, focuses on the relationship between utterance and meaning and the circumstance/state of indication of utterance to meaning. The subjects of *waḍʿ*, whose history did not go as far back as that of other disciplines, were examined in the context of the relationship of utterance and meaning in the works of philology, logic, and legal theory before becoming an independent discipline. ʿAḍud al-Dīn al-Ījī's *al-Risāla al-waḍʿiyya* is the first independent work written on the relationship of words and meaning by focusing on the *waḍʿ*. *Al-Risāla al-Waḍʿiyya* became famous soon after it was written, and many commentaries and sub-commentaries were written on it. The discipline of *al-waḍʿ* reached a certain depth due to discussions between Saʿd al-Dīn al-Taftāzānī and Sayyid Sharīf al-Jurjānī, in particular on the relationship between utterance and meaning. Alī Kuşçī's (b. 879/1474) *ʿUnqūd al-zawāhir fī l-ṣarf* systematised *waḍʿ* and changed its subjects, shifting the focus from utterance meaning to *waḍʿ*. The subjects were newly systematised under the chapters *waḍʿ*, *wāḍiʿ*, *mawḍūʿ*, *mawḍūʿ lahu*, and *hikma al-waḍʿ* and were made more advanced. In this way, the process which deals with language from a philosophical perspective was followed at various stages in numerous texts throughout the Ottoman Empire (Kuşçī 2001; Fazlıoğlu 2012).

In the discipline of *al-waḍʿ*, whilst commentaries and glosses were being written within Ottoman lands, so too were independent works being written and taught within the madrasa. The first commentary on al-Ījī's *al-Risāla al-Waḍʿiyya* was Abū al-Qāsim al-Laythī al-Samarqandī's (d. 888/1483) *Sharḥ Risāla al-Waḍʿiyya.* It was one of the main texts taught in the Ottoman madrasa. Another commentary written on *al-Risāla al-Waḍʿiyya* and taught in the Ottoman madrasa was 'Iṣām al-Dīn al-Isferāyīnī's (d. 951/1544) *Sharḥ Risāla al-Waḍʿiyya,* which was known in madrasa circles as *ʿIṣām al-waḍʿ* or *ʿIṣām al-waḍʿiyya.* This commentary by al-Isferāyīnī was usually taught with the commentary of al-Samarqandī, but found comparatively more space in the curriculum relative to that book. Another work that was studied in this field was *Risāla fī l-waḍʿ*, which was penned by Ibrāhīm Ibn Khalīl al-Agīnī (d. 1311/1894), who lived in the last period of the Ottoman Empire (Özdemir 2006, 203, 206, 212; Khalifa 2007, 1: 898).

2.6. Rhetoric (*Balāgha*)

Rhetoric (*balāgha*) examines the rules and methods of *mot juste* and proper speech. It examines the pronunciation of the word in a clear, understandable, and beautiful manner in accordance with the situation required by the interlocutor. It is divided into three sub-sections: *ʿilm al-maʿānī* 'semantics', *ʿilm al-bayān* 'figures of speech', and *ʿilm al-badīʿ* 'embellishments'. Rhetoric as a discipline is as old as morphology and syntax. This discipline emerged and was developed in order to cultivate appreciation of the style and subtle meanings of the Qur᾿ān (al-Qazwīnī 1932, 36–37; al-Sakkākī 1987, 161–62).

In the Ottoman madrasa, Muḥammad Ibn ʿAlī al-Sakkākī's (d. 626/1228) *Miftāḥ al-ulūm* was the main text taught. The third part of this work—which examines various disciplines, such as morphology, syntax, poetry—bears the title *ʿilmā al-maʿānī wa-l-bayān*. In this chapter, Sakkākī expands on the discipline of rhetoric as a discipline, using rational methods of knowledge that were employed in the fields of theology, philosophy, and logic. With this approach, he transformed rhetoric from being an individual experience and pleasure to a discipline with its own rules and principles. In this respect, Sakkākī introduced an innovation no one else initiated before him, and seriously influenced those who came after. Therefore, *Miftāḥ al-ʿulūm* was the basis for almost all of the books written on *balāgha* (Ibn Khaldūn 2005).

Khaṭīb al-Qazwīnī's (d. 739/1338) *al-Talkhīs fī ʿulūm al-balāgha* comes first among the books taught in the discipline of rhetoric, which has an important place in the madrasa curriculum. This book, which is the summary of Sakkākī's *Miftāḥ al-ʿulūm*, is still read in the discipline of rhetoric in today's madrasas. Because of its importance, numerous studies have been made on Khaṭīb al-Qazwīnī's *al-Talkhīs*. Among these studies, two commentaries written by Saʿd al-Dīn al-Taftāzānī are especially important. Of these, *al-Sharḥ al-Mukhtaṣar* was short and taught after *al-Talkhīs* in Ottoman madrasas. He wrote the second commentary, *al-Sharḥ al-Muṭawwal*, after examining the books written in the discipline of rhetoric, especially Abd al-Qāhir al-Jurjānī's (d. 471/1079) *Dalā᾿il al-iʿjāz* and *Asrār al-balāgha* (al-

Taftāzānī 2013). In some madrasas, instead of *al-Muṭawwal*, Khaṭīb al-Qazwīnī's *Īḍāḥ al-maʿānī* which is the author's own commentary on the *al-Talkhīs fī ʿulūm al-balāgha* was studied. In some madrasas, as a final book, Burhān al-Dīn Ibrāhīm Ibn Muḥammad al-Halabī al-Qabāqibī's (d. 850/1446) *al-Alfiyya li l-maʿānī wa-l-bayān* was memorised (İzgi 1997).

References

Āşıkpaşazāde. 1332. *Tevārih-i Āl-i Osman'dan Āşıkpaşazāde Tarihi.* Istanbul: Matbaayı Āmire.

Atay, Hüseyin. 1983. Osmanlılarda Yüksek Din Eğitimi: Medrese Programları, İcazetnāmeler, Islahat Hareketleri. Istanbul: Dergah Yayınları.

Çelik, Murat. 2019. Osmanlı Medreseleri ve Avrupa Üniversiteleri (1450–1600). Istanbul: Küre Yayınları.

Durmuş, Ismail. 1991. 'El-ʿAvāmilü'l-mie'. In *Turkiye Diyanet Vakfi Islam Ansiklopedisi.* Istanbul: Turkiye Diyanet Vakfi Yayinlari.

Fazlıoğlu, Şükran. 2012. 'Vaz'. In *Turkiye Diyanet Vakfi Islam Ansiklopedisi.* Istanbul: Turkiye Diyanet Vakfi Yayinlari.

Ḥajī Khalīfa, Kātib Çelebi. 1972. *Kashf al-ẓunūn ʿan asāmī al-kutub wa-al-funūn.* Baghdād, Maktabat al-Muthannā.

Ibn Hishām, ʿAbd Allāh ibn Yūsuf. 1964. *Mughnī al-labīb ʿan kutub al-aʿārīb.* Cairo: al-Maktabah al-Tijārīyzh al-Kubrā.

Ibn Khaldūn, ʿAbd al-Raḥmān. 20005. *Al-Muqaddimah.* Casablanca: al-Dār al-Bayḍāʾ.

İzgi, Cevat. 1997. *Osmanlı Medreselerinde İlim* I–II. Istanbul: İz Yayıncılık.

Kuşçī, ʿAlī. 2001. *ʿUnqūd al-zawāhir fī l-ṣarf*. Cairo: Dār al-Kutub al-Miṣriyya.

al-Qazwīnī, Jalāl al-Dīn Muḥammad ibn ʿAbd al-Raḥmān. 1932. *al-Talkhīṣ fī ʿulūm al-balāghah.* Miṣr: al-Maṭbaʿah al-Raḥmānīyah.

al-Rāzī, Qutb al-Dīn. 1384. Taḥrīr al-qawāʿid al-manṭiqiyya fī sharḥ al-Risālat al-Shamsiyya. Qum: Manshūrāt Baydar.

Sāçaklīzāde, Muhammad b. Abī Bakr. 1988. *Tartīb al-ʿulūm.* Beirut: Dār al-Bashāʾir al-Islāmiyya.

al-Sakkākī, Yūsuf ibn Abī Bakr. 1987. *Miftāḥ al-ʿulūm.* Beirut: Dār al-Kutub al-ʿIlmiyya.

al-Taftāzānī, Saʿd al-Dīn. 2013. al-Muṭawwal harḥ Talkhīs Miftāḥ al-ʿulūm. Beirut: Dār al-Kutub al-ʿIlmiyya.

Uzunçarşılı, İsmail Hakkı. 1984. *Osmanlı Devletinin İlmiye Tekilātı.* Ankara: Türk Tarih Kurumu Basımevi.

3. ON THE ORDER OF THE SCIENCES FOR HE WHO WANTS TO LEARN THEM

Guy Burak

Muḥammad ibn Abī Bakr Sājaqlīzādah (Saçaklızade, d. 1732/3) was an influential scholar who devoted a work to the organisation of the Islamic sciences (titled accordingly *Tartīb al-ʿulūm,* completed ca. 1715).[1] The following passage is the section from this work in which he discusses the training of a scholar. Interestingly, Sājaqlīzādah is aware of the different linguistic backgrounds of the students across the Empire and structures the curriculum, which consisted primarily of texts in Arabic, accordingly. It is for this reason that he insists on the memorisation of the Arabic–Turkish dictionary by Ibn Malak (or Ibn Firishta).

> Confidence that he is capable of understanding [the material] should be instilled in the novice. If he is young (*ṣabiyan*), he should be ordered to study the Qurʾān with a teacher whose transmission [of the Qurʾān] is sound, until he completes [the study of the entire Qurʾān]. Then he should be ordered to study the minutiae of faith, the principles of the creed of the People of the Sunna, the prescribed ability [to comprehend] the science of ethics and the science of prayer.

[1] On Saçaklızade see Özcan (2005); El-Rouayheb (2015, 116–20).

 https://doi.org/10.11647/OBP.0208.03

He who masters (*mutakaffil*) all those [sciences should study] Muhammad Birgivi's *Turkish Epistle*,[2] which is easy for novices who are not speakers of Arabic (*ʿajamī*).[3] Then he should be ordered, if he is a non-speaker of Arabic, to study *Lughat Ibn Firishta*[4] and memorise it. If he is mature (*bāligh*), after [gaining] confidence in his ability to comprehend [the materials], he should be ordered to study [*Surat*] *al-Fātiḥa* and short *suras*. Then he should be ordered to study that [i.e., Birgivi's] Epistle or any [other epistle] that will be of use. Then he should be ordered to study the entire Qurʾān. Then he should be ordered to study *Lughat Ibn Firishta* and memorise it. After having studied *Lughat Ibn Firishta*, be he young or mature, he should be ordered to study the science of morphology (*ṣarf*), then grammar (*naḥw*), then [jurisprudential] practical rulings (*ʿilm al-aḥkām*), then logic, then disputation (*munāẓara*), then theology (*kalām*), then rhetoric (*maʿānī*), then the fundamentals of jurisprudence and then jurisprudence. By 'jurisprudence' I do not mean only the science of practical rulings (*al-aḥkām al-ʿamaliyya*) without evidence [for this judicial opinion], as in *Mukhtaṣar al-Qudūrī*,[5] but the understanding of [jurisprudence] with [jurisprudential] evidence, as in *al-Hidāya*.[6] As for *Mukhtaṣar al-Qudūrī*, or whatever replaces it in the science of practical rulings, he should study it after

---

[2] Birgivi (1898), and Birgivi (1876).

[3] *ʿAjamī* can mean 'Persian' or 'speaker of Persian', though in this context it seems to be a generic term referring to non-Arabic speakers.

[4] ʿIzz al-Din ʿAbd al-Laṭīf ibn Malak's (also known as Ibn Farishta or Firişteoğlu, d. After 1418) was one of the first Arabic–Turkish dictionaries; see Baktır (1999).

[5] Al-Qudūrī (2005).

[6] Al-Marghīnānī (2000).

having studied the science of phonetic forms and grammar. Otherwise, his understanding will remain [at the level of] the principles (*qawāʿid*) of Fundamental of Jurisprudence, unlike the understanding [required for texts] like *al-Hidāya*. By 'theology' I do not mean only the theological issues (*al-masāʾil al-iʿtiqādiyya*), but what appears [in works] like *al-Maqāṣid*[7] on essences (*jawāhir*) and attributes (*aʿrāḍ*) and theological issues with proofs and responses to opponents. Then, after [having studied that] he should study the principles of *hadith*, then *hadith riwāya*, and *hadīth dirāya*, and then Qurʾānic exegesis. As for the study of Qurʾānic recitation (*tajwīd*) and the Qurʾānic readings (*qirāʾāt*) and Qurʾānic orthography (*marsūm al-maṣāḥif*), the student should learn [these sciences] whenever he can, before studying Qurʾānic exegesis. As to arithmetic, geometry, astronomy, and the science of metres and rhymes, he should study them whenever he can, but it is recommended to study arithmetic before the study of practical rulings and especially [before the study] of inheritance rules (*farāʾiḍ*).[8]

References

Baktır, Mustafa. 1999. 'İbn Melek'. *Türkiye Diyanet Vakfı İslâm Ansiklopedisi* 20: 175–76.

Birgivi, Mehmet. 1876. *Risale-i Birgivi*. Istanbul (?).

———. 1898 [1314]. *Vasiyetname*. Istanbul (?).

El-Rouayheb, Khaled. 2015. *Islamic Intellectual History in the Seventeenth Century: Scholarly Currents in the Ottoman Empire and the Maghreb*. New York: Cambridge University Press.

[7] *Al-Maqāṣid* (1989); see also Özen (2011).

[8] Sajaqlizādah (Saçaklızade) (1988, 209–10).

al-Marghīnānī, ʿAlī ibn Abī Bakr. 2000. *Al-Hidāya: Sharḥ Bidāyat al-Mubtadiī*. Cairo: Dār al-Salām li-l-Ṭibāʿa wa-l-Nashr.

Özen, Şükrü. 2011. 'Tetazani'. *Türkiye Diyanet Vakfı İslâm Ansiklopedisi* 40: 299–308.

Özcan, Tahism. 2008. 'Saçaklızade Mehmed Efendi'. *Türkiye Diyanet Vakfı İslâm Ansiklopedisi* 35: 368–70.

al-Qudūrī, Aḥmad ibn Muḥammad al-Qudūrī. 2005. *Mukhtaṣar*. Beirut: Muʾassasat al-Rayyān li-l-Ṭibāʿa wa-l-Nashr wa-l-Tawzīʿ.

Sajaqlizādah (Saçaklızade), Muḥammad ibn Abī Bakr al-Marʿashī. 1988. *Tartīb al-ʿUlūm.* Beirut: Dār al-Bashāʾir al-Islāmiyya.

Taftāzānī, Masʿūd ibn ʿUmar.' 1989. *Kitāb Sharḥ al-Maqāṣid.* Beirut: ʿĀlam al-Kutub.

4. RUMI AUTHORS, THE ARABIC HISTORIOGRAPHICAL TRADITION, AND THE OTTOMAN DAWLA/DEVLET

Guy Burak

In Jumādā II 965/April 1558, the envoy of the *sharīf* of Mecca, the Hanafi jurist, scholar, and chronicler Quṭb al-Dīn Muḥammad b. Aḥmad b. Muḥammad al-Nahrawālī (d. 1582) visited Istanbul and met with Semiz Ali Paşa, then second vizier and future grand vizier of the Empire (served as grand vizier from 1561 to 1565).[1] The Meccan envoy was impressed by the vizier's scholarly interests and, particularly, by the latter's interest in history (*taʾrīkh*). When the vizier informed the envoy of his successful military campaigns against the infidels, al-Nahrawālī warned the vizier:

> if what you have mentioned is not recorded, it will perish from memory and its virtues will not be known after a few years, and when whoever was present in that campaign perishes, his narration [of events, *khabar*] will perish as well. No one will remember [the campaign] and its

[1] On al-Nahrawālī see Blackburn (2012). See also the Introduction in Blackburn (2005). On Semiz Ali Paşa, see Mantran (2012). Al-Nahrawālī left two reports of this encounter: in his travelogue (Blackburn 2005, 168–69) and in his chronicle; for the latter see al-Nahrawālī (2004, 310–11).

 https://doi.org/10.11647/OBP.0208.04

> knowledge will vanish from the pages of existence (*ṣafaḥāt al-wujūd*) after a short while.

The Meccan envoy immediately mentioned the interest of Arab scholars (*ʿulamāʾ*) in the science of history and even provided the vizier with a relevant example: the 13th-century chronicler Abū Shāma's (d. 1267) *al-Rawḍatayn fī akhbār al-dawlatayn* (Abū Shāma 1997). Abū Shāma's chronicle, al-Nahrawālī explained, records the military campaigns against the crusaders undertaken during the reigns (*dawla*) of Nūr al-Dīn (d. 1174) and Ṣalāḥ al-Dīn al-Ayyūbī (d. 1193). "This most exquisite and beautiful book," the Meccan pointed out, "remained in the pages of time." Al-Nahrawālī then concluded with a question: "Why aren't your histories (*akhbārakum*) and deeds (*āthārakum*) recorded in the books [of history], eternalised in the pages of the eras and time periods?" Upon hearing the envoy's question, Semiz Ali Paşa asked the scholar and jurist Kınalızade Ali Çelebi (d. 1572), whom al-Nahrawālī described as "the time's most virtuous composer in Arabic" (*faḍīl dhalika al-waqt fī al-inshāʾ al-ʿArabī*), to compile a work like Abū Shāmah's. According to al-Nahrawālī, Kınalızade started working on the Arabic chronicle, which he never completed (Al-Nahrawālī 2004, 310–11).[2]

---

[2] On Kinalizade see Tezcan (1996) and Köker (1999). Kinalizade's familiarity with the Arabic scholarly traditions may have been one of the reasons for his eventual appointment, in 1562, to the chief judgeship of Damascus. On his encounters with the Damascene scholars see Pfeifer (2015).

The vignette is revealing for several reasons. First, the exchange between the three protagonists reveals intriguing dynamics between the different parts of the Empire and their respective intellectual/historiographical/literary traditions. Al-Nahrawālī, a Meccan jurist and scholar, was well-versed in the Arabic historiographical tradition. The vizier, who was of Bosnian descent and had entered the imperial administration as a young boy, on the other hand, was known for his patronage of at least two works in 'simple Turkish' over the course of his career: a short treatise on the Ottoman construction projects in Mecca, which he commissioned during his tenure as governor of Egypt, and the Book of Prayer (*duʿā-nāme*), which he commissioned during his grand vizierate.[3] And Kınalızade, "the most virtuous writer in Arabic [among the Rumis]," emerges as one of the relatively few scholars from the core, predominantly Turkish-speaking lands of the Empire sufficiently familiar with the Arabic historiographical tradition to compile a chronicle like Abū Shāma's.

Secondly, al-Nahrawālī's comment on the state of Ottoman historiography merits attention. By the mid-16th century, when al-Nahrawālī visited the Ottoman capital, numerous chronicles devoted to the history of the Ottoman dynasty had already been written.[4] Al-Nahrawālī clearly misrepresented the state of histor-

[3] For the treatise on the Ottoman construction projects see Burak (2017, 315 n. 2). On the *Duʿa-name*, which was authored by the famous chief mufti Ebuʾs-Suʿud Efendi (d. 1574), see Kaleli (2014).

[4] The literature on 15th-century historiography in the Ottoman lands is quite vast. See, for instance, Mengüç (2013) and the bibliography

ical writing in the core lands of the Empire. His implicit observation, however, that few historical works were written in Arabic in the core lands of the Empire, was quite accurate, as most historical works were compiled in Ottoman Turkish and Persian. But assuming that both the Meccan envoy and the vizier knew about the historiographical corpus in Turkish (and Persian), the former's statement about the lack of historical writing, presumably in Arabic, in the core lands of the Empire implied a hierarchy between the Arabic and Turkish historiographical traditions: it was only historical writing in Arabic, according to al-Nahrawālī, that was truly eternal. This was obviously a view of a scholar versed in the Arabic historiographical tradition. But in the second half of the 16th century, several scholars and chroniclers from the core lands of the Empire (known as *Rumis*, 'from the Land of Rum')[5] followed in Kınalızade's footsteps and were receptive to this view of historical writing.

The differences between the historiographical traditions that coexisted throughout the empire were more than simply a matter of language. Each historiographical tradition employed conceptual and stylistic conventions that were not easily translatable. The emergence of a Rumi Arabic historical writing in the second half of the 16th century was also intended to provide the Ottoman ruling and administrative elite with a vocabulary to le-

---

therein. See also the section on historical writings in the palace library of Bayezid II: Fleischer and Şahin (2019, 569–96).

[5] On 'Ruminess' see Kafadar (2007).

gitimise their rule over the newly conquered Arabic-speaking territories of Greater Syria, Egypt, the Hijaz, and, slightly later, Arab Iraq.

This essay seeks to focus on one of these conventions: the Arabic expression *al-Dawla al-ʿUthmāniyya.* This expression, I would like to suggest, was embedded in the Arabic historiographical tradition, but was quite alien to the Turkish (and Persian) ones. It is for this reason that this expression opens a window into broader dynamics that await further study. I will return to this point in the concluding section of this essay.

1.0. Rumi Authors, Arabic Chronicles

In the chapter on History/Historiography (*ʿIlm-i Taʾrīh*) in his work on the classification of the sciences, Nevʿi Efendi (d. 1599) provides his readers with "the books associated with this [science" (*el-Kütübüʾl-musannefetü fīh*): The History of Ibn Kathīr, the History of al-Ṭabarī, the History of Ibn Athīr al-Jazarī, the History of Ibn al-Jawzī and his *Mirʾāt al-Zamān*, the History of Ibn Khallikān, the History of Ibn Ḥajar [al-ʿAsqalānī], the History of al-Ṣafadī, the History of Jalāl al-Dīn al-Suyuṭī, *Siyar al-ṣaḥāba wa-l-zuhhād*, *Ḥilyat al-abrār*, the History of Ḥakīm al-Nīsābūriī, the History of al-Baghdādī, *Taʾrīkh al-ḥukamāʾ*, *Kashf al-ghamm*, and *Taʾrīkh al-umam.* It is worth pointing out that all the titles in this list were compiled in Arabic (Prochazka-Eisl and Çelik 2015, 53). This fact is particularly striking, as Nevʿi Efendi chose to write his work in Turkish and included works written in Persian. In addition, it is quite evident that he relied on chronicles written in Turkish for his survey of the history of the Ottoman dynasty

(Prochazka-Eisl and Çelik 2015, 72–77). Nevʿi Efendi was probably inspired by the work of his earlier colleague, Ahmed Taşköprüzade (d. 1560). In the section devoted to History in his comprehensive work on the classification of the sciences, Taşköprüzade offers a remarkably similar, though much longer, list of works. Among the works Taşköprüzade's lists are The History of Ibn Kathīr, the History of al-Ṭabarī, the History of Ibn al-Athīr al-Jazarī, the History of Ibn al-Jawzī, Ibn al-Jawzī's *Mirʾāt al-zamān*, the History of Ibn Khallikān, the History of Ibn Ḥajar and his *Anbāʾ al-ghamr fī abnāʾ al-ʿamr* and *al-Durar al-kāmina fī aʿyān al-miʾa al-thāmina*, the History of al-Ṣafadī, the History of Jalāl al-Dīn al-Suyutī and his *Ṭabaqāt al-nuḥāh* (his *Bughyat al-wuʿāh fī ṭabaqāt al-lughawiyyīn wa-l-nuḥāh*), the History of al-Baghdādī, the supplement to al-Baghdādī's History by Ibn al-Najjār, the History and works of Abū Saʿd al-Samʿānī, the supplement to al-Samʿānī's History by al-Dabīthī, the History of al-Dhahabī, *Kitāb al-bāriʿ* by Ibn Abī Manṣūr, and *Yatīmat al-dahr* by al-Nīsābūrī. At the conclusion of the list, Taşköprüzade briefly states that "the chronicles in Persian are too numerous to be counted," but does not include a similar list of noteworthy Persian and Turkish chronicles (Tāshkubrīzāda [Taşköprüzade] 1968, 1:251–70).[6] It appears that for Taşköprüzade, much like for Nevʿi Efendi, the point of reference was the historiographical tradition in Arabic.

Nothing attests more to Taşköprüzade's historiographical preferences to writing history in Arabic than his own introduction to his biographical dictionaries of the jurists and scholars

[6] For an English translation of this section, see Rosenthal (1968, 530–35).

who were affiliated with the Ottoman dynasty. In the introduction to this work, he explains why he decided to compile this work:

> Since I [learned to] distinguish between right and left, between the straight [path] and trickery, I sought passionately the merits of the *ʿulamāʾ* and their histories (*akhbār*), and I was obsessed with memorising their important deeds and their works, until I would accumulate a large [body of knowledge] in my weak memory [so] it would fill the books and notebooks. Historians have recorded the merits of the *ʿulamāʾ* and the notables according to what has been established through transmission or was confirmed by eyewitnesses, [but] no one has paid attention to the *ʿulamāʾ* of these lands, and [consequently] their names and practices have almost vanished from the tongues of every present [i.e., living person] and [their memory] perished. When the people of excellence and perfection noticed this situation, they asked me to gather all the merits of the *ʿulamāʾ* in Rum. (Tāshkubrīzāda [Taşköprüzade] 1975, 5)

Note the similarities between the passage from Taşköprüzade's introduction and the comment al-Nahrawālī made to the Grand Vizier. Writing in Arabic, Taşköprüzade claims that only the recording of the histories of the Rumi scholars as part of the Arabic historiographical corpus—a corpus that was compiled elsewhere, beyond the Ottoman lands—can perpetuate their memory.

It appears that the perception of and anxiety about the Arabic historiographical tradition as more eternal than historical writings in Turkish and Persian subsided over the course of the 17th century. For instance, in the universal history he wrote in Arabic, Müneccimbaşı (or Munajjim Bāshī, d. 1702) includes a bibliography of historical works on which he drew. Although he organised the list according to the languages in which the works were written, his bibliography represented the historiographical traditions in the three languages: Arabic, Persian, and Turkish. Yet, it seems significant that Müneccimbaşı (*Jāmiʿ al-duwal,* 2a) retained the distinction between the traditions. Clearly, he knew that each of these traditions followed different conventions and employed distinctive vocabularies.

Most studies of historical writing in the Ottoman lands have tended to focus on the historiographical production in a specific language. The insightful collection of essays on Ottoman courtly historiography focuses almost exclusively on works written in Ottoman Turkish (Çıpa and Fetvaci 2013). On the other hand, Michael Winter, in his survey of Arabic historiography in the Ottoman Empire, ignores the writings in Persian and Turkish (Winter 2006, 171–90). To be sure, most scholars acknowledge that writings in Turkish include many expressions from Arabic and Persian and that expressions in Arabic frequently feature in Persian texts. But little scholarly attention has been paid to the manner in which the historiographical traditions relate to one another: are there particular expressions or conventions that can be associated (or, at least, more commonly associated) with a certain tradition? Which expressions and conventions were borrowed and, equally important, which were not? And when and why did authors choose to write in a specific historiographical tradition?

These questions draw attention to differences among the various historiographical traditions that coexisted and interacted throughout the Ottoman realms. In a recent study of 15th-century debates among five thinkers writing in Arabic and Persian about the nature of historical inquiry, Christopher Markiewicz (2017, 221) argues that

> monolingual approaches to Islamic historiography further obscure the full extent of the fifteenth-century discourse on history. The tendency to divide Islamic historiography between its Arabic, Persian, and Ottoman Turkish expressions reinforces an understanding of the historical traditions as separate, linguistically delineated dialectics. Moreover, while considerations of Ottoman historical writing generally acknowledge its relationship to Arabic and especially Persian historiography, the interrelationship between the three remains only superficially acknowledged.

Markiewicz thus concludes that

> the wide-ranging interaction between Arabic *and* Persian historical thought since the tenth century—and Turkish historiography, as well, beginning in the fifteenth century—constituted a fundamental aspect of the development of Islamic historiography as a vibrant cultural tradition until the rise of national historiographies in the late nineteenth and twentieth centuries.

I do not disagree with Markiewicz's general observation, but, in this short essay, I would like to highlight the special semiotic baggage that writing in Arabic carried in the context of a multilingual empire and the dynamics between multiple historiographical traditions. It seems to me that the study of historical writing in the Ottoman lands—and, in fact, across the Islamic(ate) world more broadly—ought to acknowledge the fairly wide range of interactions between these traditions, from the retention of differences to translations and borrowings. In this sense, what follows seeks to nuance the idea of a single historiographical project as a singular "vibrant cultural tradition."

Paying attention to these differences can also reveal how members of various learned circles across the Empire employed historiographical traditions and conventions to legitimise Ottoman rule and to enrich the Ottoman repertoire of power. At the same time, studying the manners in which certain expressions were employed may reveal tensions between competing claims and political projects. To illustrate this point, I now turn to examining in some detail the use of the expression "the Ottoman *Dawla*" (or *al-Dawla al-ʿUthmāniyya*) in the 16th and 17th centuries.

2.0. Ottoman *Devlet*/Ottoman *Dawla*

In what is perhaps the most systematic study of the meaning of the term *dawla* during the Mamluk period (1250–1517), Jo Van Steenbergen (2016, 55) observes that

> [i]n the course of many centuries of Arabic and Islamic history the Arabic noun *dawla* has appeared as a generic qualifier in many different contexts of rule, with complex meanings that are not always easily rendered in other languages. However, in its semantic essence, as suggested by Arabic lexicographers, *dawla* is always meant to refer in these contexts of rule to a particular political formation's temporary local monopoly of violence and of access to resources [. . .] But historically the Arabic noun *dawla* has always also been imbued with the transcendent, religious meaning of a God-given "turn"—the literal translation of the Arabic noun *dawla*—or term of rule in the monotheist trajectory of human history. In the hearts, minds and ears

> of those who used it, *dawla* therefore appealed to the idea of a universal empire as much as to that of a territorial state.

The multi-layered nature of the term *dawla*—a political and authoritative order and a divinely ordained mandate to rule—poses considerable questions when one encounters the use of the possessive adjective attached to it (or the compound noun), as in the case of *Dawlat al-Atrāk* 'the *dawla* of the Turks' or *al-dawla al-ʿUthmāniyya* in Mamluk Arabic sources. Evidently, Mamluk authors imagined a

> trans-regional hierarchy of (West-Asian or even wider) legitimate political leadership, which included Syrian viceroys as well as all kinds of Mongol, post-Mongol and other leaders, and which was topped by the royal *persona* of the sultan in Cairo. (Steenbergen 2016, 55)

Moreover, this perception of multiple *dawlas*, each with its own political and institutional orders, was also based on a sense of temporality, hence the succession of several *dawlas* in Mamluk historiography (Steenbergen 2016, 65).

One could argue that Ottoman authors were not oblivious to the perception of *dawla* from the Mamluk sources. But Ottoman sources, mostly written in Turkish, tended to focus on the more universal dimensions of *dawla* or *devlet.*[7] For 15th- and 16th-century Ottoman writers, following Dimitris Kastritsis'

---

[7] The Ottoman authors were drawing on a well-established use of the term *dawlat* in Persian sources from the Ilkhanid period onward (Allsen 2009, 1–7). I am grateful to Yoni Brack for bringing this piece to my attention and for an illuminating discussion on the use of the term *dawlat* in the Ilkhanid context.

(2007, 98, 200–3) translation of the term, *devlet* conveyed a sense of charismatic rule, or, in Hüseyin Yılmaz's (2018, 139, 157) translation, fortune or "auspicious turn to rule." Importantly, while many contenders to the throne may have some degree of *devlet*, once enthroned, *devlet* temporarily resided with the ruling sultan. As an early 15th-century source quips with regard to the competition among Ottoman princes during the interregnum, "Although *devlet* existed in Musa,/The *devlet* of Mehmed [the future Mehmed I] was truly greater!" (Kastritsis 2007, 219, 226). This is not to say that Ottoman dynasts did not recognise the legitimacy of other Muslim rulers or did not assume that the House of Osman as a whole had a right to rule, but it is important to note that, for the most part, authors writing in Turkish over the course of the 15th through the 17th centuries were quite reluctant to attach a possessive adjective 'Ottoman' to the noun *devlet*. Instead, in the 16th century, as Yılmaz (2018, 275) has observed, they stressed its eternity.

3.0. Rumi Authors and Their Use of *al-Dawla al-ʿUthmaniyya*

In the second half of the 16th century, several Rumi authors, that is, authors from the core, predominantly Turkish-speaking regions of the Empire, engaged in writing works in Arabic. Being Rumi, it should be emphasised, was not simply a matter of geography. In the context of an expanding empire, it was also a matter of political affiliation with the Ottoman dynasty. These Rumi authors who were writing in Arabic were astutely aware of the conventions of the Arabic historiographical tradition. In fact, the encounter of what was now the core lands of the Ottoman empire, and of Anatolia more generally, with historical writings in Arabic long predated the Ottoman conquest. Indeed, the inventory of the library of Bayezid II includes historiographical essays and chronicles in Arabic, some of which were even sent directly to members of his close retinue from the Mamluk capital (Markiewicz 2017, 236–40). What is intriguing about the second half of the 16th century is the Rumi authors' experiment with, participation in, and response to the Arabic historiographical tradition.

Perhaps the most extreme example of this engagement is the probably early 17th-century compilation of a text that was falsely attributed to the renowned 13th-century mystic Muḥyī al-Dīn Ibn ʿArabī (d. 1241), titled *al-Shajara al-nuʿmāniyya fī al-dawla al-ʿUthmāniyya* ('the Tree of Nuʿmān on the Ottoman Rule/Good Fortune'). In this short and popular text, Ibn ʿArabī allegedly foresaw the Ottoman conquest of the Arab lands. As Ahmed Zildzic, who studied in great detail the *Shajara* and its commentaries, has noted (Zildzic 2012, 85)

> [t]he oldest existent copy of *al-Shajara* comes from the first half of the XVII century, and if we accept that the date is not a later interpolation, we can conclude the text of *al-Shajara* as it reached us originated more than a century later than the events it discusses. What is evident, however, is the universal acceptance of the work in the Ottoman cultural and intellectual context.

For our purpose here, the important point is that the late anonymous author used the term *al-Dawla al-ʿUthmāniyya* in the title of the treatise to indicate that it originated in the early 13th century in the Arabic-speaking lands. Indeed, one could argue that the invocation of the term was quite antiquarian.

As I have already suggested above, Taşköprüzade was interested in writing an Arabic biographical dictionary that would commemorate the names and deeds of jurists and Sufi masters who were affiliated with the Ottoman dynasty. Clearly, he sought to be part of the Arabic historiographical tradition. Fittingly, the work is replete with references to that tradition and the conventions of the genre of the biographical dictionary. He even decides to call the Ottoman political project *al-Dawla al-ʿUthmāniyya*.

Several decades later, during the reign of Murad III (r. 1574–1595), a third author, Mustafa Cenabi (d. 1590/1591), chose to pen a work in Arabic, a universal history from the creation of the world to the Ottoman dynasty. Cenabi devoted chapters to the various dynasties who ruled the world, from the ancient Persian kings to his patrons, the Ottomans. Throughout, Cenabi (*Cenabi Tarihi*) selectively employs the term *dawla*: the Ḥasanī *dawla* of Mecca, the Hāshimīi *dawla* of Medina, the Circassian *dawla* (the Mamluks), the ʿAlawī/Ḥasanī *dawla* of Tabaristan and Jurjan, the Samanid *dawla*, the *dawla* of Chinggis Khan, the Uzbek *dawla*, the *dawla* of the Ak Koyunlu and the Ottoman *dawla*. Indeed, this list of *dawlas* seems to reflect the "trans-regional hierarchy of (West-Asian or even wider) legitimate political leadership" (Steenbergen 2016, 55) that one finds in Mamluk sources and the sense that *dawla* can be divided among rulers and dynasties.

4.0. Conclusion

The macaronic nature of the language that is commonly referred to as 'Ottoman Turkish' is quite well known and frequently mentioned in handbooks for students of the language. Students of 'Ottoman Turkish' are encouraged to study Arabic, Persian, and Modern Turkish/Turkic language and, based on this knowledge, to understand the logic of 'Ottoman Turkish'. This is, of course, an anachronistic perception of languages in general and of 'Ottoman Turkish' in particular, as it assumes fairly well-defined linguistic traditions or languages which are macaronically intertwined. But both Persian and Turkic languages have accumulated over the centuries numerous words that are morphologically Arabic. In many cases, the words retained their 'original' Arabic lexicographical meaning. But this has not always been the case. This linguistic entanglement raises an intriguing question: Where does 'Arabic' end and 'Ottoman Turkish' begin?

This short essay is an attempt to explore these complex dynamics between 'Arabic' and 'Turkish' in the Ottoman lands. My goal is not, to paraphrase Nile Green's (2019, 2) comment on Persian in the introduction to the recent volume on the Persianate world, "to promote Arabic [...], but rather to analyze Arabic as a field of sociolinguistic contact, and in doing so recognise the roles of hegemony and competition [...]." Indeed, as Murat Umut Inan (2019, 88) argues in his essay on Persian in the Ottoman world in the same volume, the history of Persian—and, one may add, of Arabic—in the Ottoman context is "intertwined with multiple histories of the empire." Much like Persian, Arabic afforded

Rumi writers a range of possibilities to promote political and intellectual claims, but also engendered anxiety and envy. The manner in which Rumi writers employed the terms *al-Dawla al-ʿUthmāniyya* and the anecdote with which I opened this essay capture these possibilities and anxieties.

Furthermore, the tension between *devlet* and *dawla*, which draws on the distinction between different linguistic/historiographical traditions, poses a translation challenge: how should one translate *al-Dawla al-ʿUthmāniyya* into, say, English? This translation challenge is what got me interested in exploring the relationship between *devlet* and *dawla* in the first place. Moreover, as I have argued elsewhere (Burak 2015, 94–98), in his *al-Shaqāʾiq al-nuʿmāniyya*, Taşköprüzade employed Mamluk (and Arabic) historiographical conventions to legitimise and record the history of the Ottoman learned hierarchy and the Sufi masters that were associated with the Ottoman domains. Accordingly, the narrative arc of the *Shaqāʾiq* diverges in terms of its historiographical and, indeed, political assumptions from those of Mamluk biographical dictionaries. Most notably, the Ottoman dynasty is the organising principle of Taşköprüzade's work. Further, when Taşkörüzade's *Shaqāʾiq* was translated by Mehmed Mecdi Efendi (d. 1591) into 'Ottoman Turkish', *al-Dawla al-ʿUthmāniyya* entered 'Ottoman Turkish' historiography. This Turkified expression raises yet another, though related, translation question: how should one translate the 16th-century expression *Devlet-i ʿOsmaniyye* into English?

References

Abū Shāma. 1997. *ʿAbd al-Raḥmān ibn Ismāʿīl al-Rawḍatayn fī akhbār al-dawlatayn*. Beirut: Muʾassasat al-Risāla.

Allsen, Thomas T. 2009. 'A Note on the Mongol Imperial Ideology'. In *The Early Mongol Language, Culture and History: Studies in Honour of Igor de Rachewiltz on the Occasion of his 80th Birthday*, edited by Volker Rybatzki et al., 1–8. Bloomington: Indiana University Press.

Blackburn, J. R. 2005. *Journey to the Sublime Porte: The Arabic Memoir of a Sharifian Agent's Diplomatic Mission to the Ottoman Imperial Court in the Era of Suleyman the Magnificent*. Beirut: Ergon Verlag Würzburg in Kommission.

———. 2012. 'al-Nahrawālī'. In *Encyclopaedia of Islam, Second Edition*, edited by P. Bearman et al. http://dx.doi.org/10.1163/1573-3912_islam_SIM_5759, consulted online 6 February 2021.

Burak, Guy. 2015. The Second Formation of Islamic Law: The Hanafi School in the Early Modern Ottoman Empire. New York: Cambridge University Press.

———. 2017. 'Between Istanbul and Gujarat: Descriptions of Mecca in the Sixteenth-Century Indian Ocean'. *Muqarnas* 34: 287–320.

Cenabi, Mustafa. *Cenabi Tarihi*, Süleymanıye Library, MS Ayasofya 3099.

Cenatar, Mehmet. 2005. 'Mustafa Cenabi'. In *Historians of the Ottoman Empire, The University of Chicago*: https://ottoman-historians.uchicago.edu/tr/historian/mustafa-cenabi, consulted online 28 January 2018.

Çıpa, H. Erdem, and Emine Fetvaci (eds.). 2013. *Writing History at the Ottoman Court: Editing the Past, Fashioning the Future.* Bloomington: Indiana University Press.

Fleischer, Cornell H. and Kaya Şahin. 2019. 'On the Works of a Historical Nature in the Bayezid II Library Inventory'. In *Treasures of Knowledge: An Inventory of the Ottoman Palace Library (1502/3–1503/4)*, edited by Gülru Necipoğlu, Cemal Kafadar, and Cornell H. Fleischer, 569–96. Leiden: Brill.

Green, Nile. 2019. 'Introduction'. In *The Persianate World: The Frontiers of a Eurasian Lingua France*, edited by Nile Green, 1–71. Oakland: University of California Press.

Inan, Murat Umut. 2019. 'Imperial Ambitions, Mystical Aspirations: Persian Learning in the Ottoman World.' In *The Persianate World: The Frontiers of a Eurasian Lingua France*, edited by Nile Green, 75–92. Oakland: University of California Press.

Kafadar, Cemal. 2007. 'A Rome of One's Own: Reflections on Cultural Geography and Identity in the Lands of Rum'. *Muqarnas* 24: 7–25.

Kaleli, Abdullah. 2014. 'Du'a-name (İnceleme-Çeviri Yazılı Metin-Özel Adlar Dizini-Tıpkıbasım'. MA thesis, Adiyaman Üniversitesi Sosyal Bilimler Enstitüsü.

Kastritsis, Dimitris J. 2007. The Sons of Bayezid: Empire Building and Representation in the Ottoman Civil War of 1402–1413. Leiden: Brill.

Köker, Ahmet Hulusi (ed.). 1999. *Kinalizade Ali Efendi (1510–1572*). Kayseri: Erciyes Üniversitesi Matbaası.

Mantran, R. 2012. "ʿAlī Pas̲h̲a Semiz'. In *Encyclopaedia of Islam, Second Edition*, edited by P. Bearman et al. http://dx.doi.org/10.1163/1573-3912_islam_SIM_0537, consulted online on 06 February 2021.

Markiewicz, Christopher. 2017. 'History as Science: The Fifteenth-Century Debate in Arabic and Persian'. *Journal of Early Modern History* 21: 216–40.

Mengüç, Murat Cem. 2013. 'Histories of Bayezid I, Historians of Bayezid II: Rethinking Late Fifteenth-century Ottoman Historiography'. *Bulletin of SOAS* 76: 373–89.

Müneccimbaşı. *Jāmiʿ al-duwal*. Süleymaniye Library MS Esad Efendi 1201, 2a.

al-Nahrawālī, Muḥammad b. Aḥmad b. Muḥammad. 2004. *Kitāb al-Iʿlām bi-aʿlām Bayt Allāh al-ḥarām*. Cairo: Maktabat al-Thaqāfa al-Dīniyya.

Pfeifer, Helen. 2015. 'Encounters After the Conquest: Scholarly Gatherings in 16th-Century Ottoman Damascus'. *International Journal of Middle East Studies* 47: 219–39.

Prochazka-Eisl, Gisela, et al., 2015. Texts on Popular Learning in Early Modern Ottoman Times, volume II: 'The Yield of the Disciplines and the Merits of the Texts': Nevʿi Efendi's Encyclopedia Netayic el-Fünun. Cambridge, MA: The Department of Near Eastern Languages and Civilizations, Harvard University.

Rosenthal, Franz. 1968. *A History of Muslim Historiography*. Leiden: Brill.

Steenbergen, Jo Van. 2016. 'Appearances of *Dawla* and Political Order in Late Medieval Syro-Egypt: The State, Social Theory, and the Political History of the Cairo Sultanate (Thirteenth–Sixteenth Centuries)'. In *History and Society During the Mamluk Period (1250–1517): Studies of the Annemarie Schimmel Institute for Advanced Study II*, edited by Stephen Conermann, 51–85. Bonn: Bonn University Press.

Tāshkubrīzāda (Taşköprüzade), Aḥmad ibn Muṣṭafá. 1968. *Miftāḥ al-saʿāda wa-miṣbāḥ al-siyāda fī mawḍūʿāt al-ʿulūm.* Cairo: Dār al-Kutub al-Ḥadītha.

———. 1975. ibn Muṣṭafá *al-Shaqāʾiq al-nuʿmāniyya fī ʿulamāʾ al-dawla al-ʿUthmāniyya.* Beirut: Dār al-Kitāb al-ʿArabī.

Tezcan, Baki. 1996. 'The Definition of Sultanic Legitimacy in the Sixteenth-Century Ottoman Empire: The Ahlak-i Ala'i of Kinalizade Ali Çelebi (1510–1572)'. MA thesis, Princeton University.

Winter, Michael. 2016. 'Historiography in Arabic during the Ottoman Period'. In *Arabic Literature in the Post-Classical Period*, edited by Roger Allen and D. S. Richards, 171–88. Cambridge: Cambridge University Press.

Yıldız, Sara Nur. 2012. 'Ottoman Historical Writing in Persian, 1400–1600'. In *Persian Historiography*, edited by Charles Melville, 436–502. New York: I. B. Tauris.

Yılmaz, Hüseyin. 2018. Caliphate Redefined: The Mystical Turn in Ottoman Political Thought. Princeton, NJ: Princeton University Press.

Zildzic, Ahmed. 2012. 'Friend and Foe: The Early Ottoman Reception of Ibn 'Arabi'. PhD dissertation, University of California, Berkeley.

5. ARABIC GRAMMAR BOOKS IN OTTOMAN ISTANBUL: THE SOUTH ASIAN CONNECTION[1]

Christopher D. Bahl

The transregional transmission of Arabic grammar books from South Asia to the Ottoman Empire contributed significantly to the scholarly curriculum of Ottoman Istanbul and beyond over the 16th and 17th centuries. Based on a study of several manuscripts of al-Muḥammad al-Damāmīnī's (d. 827/1424) and Shihāb al-Dīn al-Dawlatābādī's (d. 848/1445) commentaries (*shurūḥ*, sg. *sharḥ*), this article will argue that commentaries from South Asia on Arabic grammar treatises from earlier periods circulated widely among learned groups of Ottoman Istanbul. Thereby, they formed a crucial part of the scholarly engagement with the Arabic philological tradition and its broader cultural idiom in the Ottoman Empire. A focus on the variety of manuscripts, their marginalia and paratexts can shed light on cultural

[1] I am grateful to Prof. Konrad Hirschler for valuable comments and to several audiences at conferences in Ghent, Berlin, and Oxford for their feedback on earlier drafts of this paper. I thank Alice Williams for her suggestions.

 https://doi.org/10.11647/OBP.0208.05

practices in the circulation and reading of philological texts that emerged over the course of the 16th and 17th centuries.

A burgeoning field of scholarship on the early modern Middle East and South Asia has diversified its sources and approaches to the study of elite formation, scribal cultures and text circulation over the last years. Francis Robinson and Maria Szuppe expounded various scholarly connections and a shared canon of Islamicate works across the Ottoman, Safavid and Mughal dispensations (Robinson 1997; Szuppe 2004). Sanjay Subrahmanyam's 'connected histories' across Eurasia interrelated synchronous historical processes on commensurable levels of inquiry to study the workings of cultural encounters (Subrahmanyam 1997 and 2012). In particular, a focus on scribal cultures and traditions of *adab* and *akhlāq* informed the study of Indo-Persian forms of governance and bureaucracies, mainly across the Mughal world, but with implicitly strong connections across Western Asia (Alam 2004; Kinra 2015). Yet, while there is a general consensus that early modern entanglements facilitated forms of exchange among imperial elites and other sociabilities such as Sufi networks (Choudhury 2016), there is still room for further explorations regarding the empirical and material foundations of such cultural exchanges.

While Persian was central to these trans-imperial connections, Arabic has been considered as a major complementary idiom among mobile imperial and scholarly elites, but for different reasons. On the one hand, Arabic was a significant communicative medium among mobile learned groups between the regions of Gujarat and the Deccan with Yemen and the Hijaz (Robinson

1997; Ho 2006) but also across the wider Indian Ocean region (Ricci 2011). On the other hand, Arabic served in inquiries relating to a wider Islamicate canon across the disciplines of Quranic exegesis (*tafsīr*) and Islamic law (*fiqh*) (Ho 2006). Still, it could serve a variety of further social and cultural purposes. Recent studies by Rajeev Kinra on the Mughal bureaucratic elite have pointed out Arabic's integral part in the educational curriculum of a Mughal civil servant responsible for running the day-to-day imperial administrative business (Kinra 2010, 552). Similarly, Khaled El-Rouayheb's recent work on Islamic intellectual currents in the Ottoman Empire made implicit the central place of Arabic philology in the linguistic schooling of scholarly elites (El-Rouayheb 2015, 97–105).

Thus, Arabic philology was a requisite for the cultural refinement of the learned elites across early modern Islamicate cultures. Yet, while scholarship has explored the multifaceted terrain of Arabic philology over earlier periods, especially the disciplines of grammar (*ʿilm al-naḥw*), rhetoric (*ʿilm al-balāgha*) and lexicography (*ʿilm al-lugha*), research into later commentarial traditions is only in its infancy (Simon 1993; Gully 1995; Bauer 2005). At the same time, these studies mainly focus on the Arabic scholarship from the medieval central Arab lands and Persia, but often do not acknowledge contributions from learned centres across other regions.

As I will argue in the following, scholarly contributions from South Asia became more important from the 15th century onwards, when intellectual conversations and debates in Arabic philology extended further to the East. Scholars across the South

Asian subcontinent composed treatises and commentaries on Arabic syntax, morphology and rhetoric which circulated widely across learned groups of the Ottoman worlds further west by the 16th and 17th centuries (Ahmad 1946). A survey of the manuscript collections of the Süleymaniye Library in Istanbul discloses a large number of copied commentaries in the field of rhetoric by well-known figures such as al-Siyalkūtī, a courtier of the Mughal Emperor Shāh Jahān (Ed. 2018). However, there are also commentaries in the field of grammar from less-prominent figures, such as Muḥammad al-Damāmīnī (d. 827/1424) and Shihāb al-Dīn al-Dawlatābādī (d. 848/1445). And these are spread across a wide range of the individual collections of the Süleymaniye (Hitzel 1999).

1.0. Writing *Naḥw* in 15th-century South Asia

Al-Damāmīnī's and al-Dawlatābādī's contributions to Arabic grammar have to be situated within the wider processes of decentralisation that shaped the political landscape of 15th century South Asia. The declining Delhi sultanate was superseded by a regionalised configuration of courts from Gujarat, Malwa in the West to Jawnpur and Bengal in the East, and the Bahmanī kingdom in the Deccan (Schimmel 1980, 36–74; Asher and Talbot 2006, 85). These new political dispensations began to compete for service elites and scholars and could offer lavish patronage to those seeking to live their lives as migrant scholars. Muḥammad al-Damāmīnī (763–827/1362–1424) was born in Alexandria in Egypt and had passed through various educational stages in Mamlūk Egypt and Syria, teaching at the al-Azhar mosque among other learned sociabilities (al-Sakhāwī 1934–1937, VII:184–87). His change of career into the weaving business was unsuccessful and after the pilgrimage to Mecca he embarked on a career as a mobile scholar which first brought him to Zabīd in Yemen, but then even further across the Western Indian Ocean to Cambay and Nahrwāla (Patan) in Gujarat (see prefaces in MS Ragip Pasa 1326 and MS Carullah 1941). He received patronage from the court of Aḥmad Muẓaffar Shāh and composed, amongst other works, three grammar commentaries. The first work, written after his arrival in the western port city of Kanbāyat (Cambay) in Gujarat during the years 820–821/1417–1418, is the *Taʿlīq al-farāʾid ʿalā tashīl al-fawāʾid* 'Explanation of the precious pearls on the facilitation of benefits', a commentary on Ibn Mālik's (672/1274) *Tashīl al-fawāʾid wa-takmīl al-maqāṣid* 'The facilitation of benefits and the completion of objectives' (see prefaces in MS Ragip Pasa 1326 and MS Carullah 1941; Fleisch 2017a; 2017b). The second work, composed while he resided in the famous scholarly centre of Nahrwāla in Gujarat in 824/1421, is entitled *Tuḥfat al-gharīb ʿalā l-kalām mughnī al-labīb ʿan kutub al-aʿārīb* 'Gift of the extraordinary concerning the speech of sufficient understanding on the books of declinations', a commentary on Ibn Hishām's (d. 760/1360) treatise on syntax, *al-Mughnī al-labīb* (see preface and colophon of MS Bijapur 7; Fleisch 2017b). He then continued his vagrant life and travelled on to the Deccan. A third work, written while on his way from Gujarat to the city of Aḥsānābād (Gulbarga) in the Bahmanī realm of the Deccan during the years 825–826/1422–1423, is entitled *al-Manhal al-ṣafī fī sharḥ al-wāfī* 'The pure watering place in the explanation of the perfect', again a commentary, in this case on al-Balkhī's (d. 8th/14th c.) grammatical work al-*Wāfī* (see preface in MS Nahw 108). This was presented to the sultan Aḥmad Shāh Bahmanī and seems to have been his last scholarly composition before he died in 1424.

Al-Damāmīnī's contemporary Shihāb al-Dīn Aḥmad b. Shams al-Dīn al-Hindī al-Dawlatābādī (d. 848/1445) had a different professional trajectory, but he similarly benefitted from the increasing availability of courtly patronage during the 15th century. Al-Dawlatābādī was born in Dawlatābād in the Deccan, studied in Delhi and after Timur Tamerlane's invasion in 1398 he left and became attached to the court of Sulṭān Ibrāhīm Sharqī (804–844/1400–1440) in Jawnpūr as prime judge (*qāḍī al-qudāt*) and scholar (Nizami 2018). And there he joined a larger group of learned men who turned the court of Jawnpur into a flourishing centre of learning during the 15th century (Würsch 2018). He soon received the title Malik al-ʿUlamāʾ (Nizami 2018). Among the works he composed during his courtly tenure are the commentary *Sharḥ al-Hindī* on the famous treatise *al-Kafiya* by Ibn al-Ḥājib (d. 646/1249) as well as the work *al-Irshād*, a treatment of Arabic syntax (Nizami 2018).

With their texts in the field of *naḥw* both scholars primarily provided crucial commentaries for the refinement of Arabic. The *shurūḥ* were written with a South Asian audience in mind that engaged with the Arabic cultural idiom on a different canonical textual background in comparison to what for example al-

Damāmīnī had been accustomed to in Mamlūk Egypt[2]. Ultimately, such works served to develop skills in the exegesis of Islamic canonical works. And this intellectual purpose had also shaped the textual fabric of these commentaries. Grammar works were thick intertextual re-fabrications of Islamicate canonical texts. Excerpts of Islamic canonical works, specimen of poetry and by the early modern period a diverse commentarial layer had turned Arabic grammar books not only into foundational readings in the acquisition of Arabic language skills, but also substantiated them as digests of Islamicate cultural traditions (Gully 1995).

While these commentaries thereby contributed to the larger discourse and perpetuation of Islamicate textual traditions, the extent of the contribution of al-Damāmīnī's and al-Dawlatābādī's commentaries to different regional and local learned sociabilities can only be gauged by tracing the transmission of their texts as manuscript copies. Marginalia and paratextual elements on manuscripts offer a window into the world of reading practices, the conditions of the perception of texts among audiences and the

---

[2] This becomes especially clear when comparing two of al-Damāmīnī's commentaries on the same treatise, one written in Egypt and the other composed in Gujarat. The intertextual variety and reference to scholarly authorities differs considerably, a venue of research that I elaborated on in Bahl (2018).

forms of circulation among scholarly networks (Görke/Hirschler 2011).[3]

2.0. Manuscript Circulation in Ottoman Istanbul

In comparison to al-Damāmīnī, who was an established scholar before he had left Egypt for India, knowledge about al-Dawlatābādī's scholarly background and oeuvre must have slowly spread across scholarly networks from South Asia to Ottoman Istanbul. A survey of his commentaries on *naḥw* in the Süleymaniye Library in Istanbul reveals 30 manuscripts of his *Sharḥ Hindī* on the treatise *al-Kāfiya* for the 9th–11th (roughly 15th–17th) centuries, and only one version of the *Irshād*, his summary on Arabic syntax. The majority of these versions can be dated to the 16th and 17th centuries. Even if other works circulated in larger quantities, the numbers for the *Sharḥ Hindī* point to a considerable circulation of al-Dawlatābādī's texts in Istanbul and beyond. And the general reference to his commentary in various short-hands such as *Sharḥ Hindī, Kitāb Hindī,* and simply *Hindī* suggest that his work had become common parlance in the early modern Ottoman Empire.

Due to fragmentary spatial data, it is often difficult to clearly trace a direct transfer of manuscripts from South Asia to Ottoman Istanbul. The inscription of a specific paratext can serve as a very tentative indicator for an initial circulation of a text in South Asia. Across South Asia the phrase *yā kabīkaj* (the term

[3] The terms and concepts paratexts, hypertexts, intertextualities and other forms of transtextualities throughout this article are taken from Genette (1993; 2001).

kabīkaj refers to wild parsley and 'king of the cockroaches') was often written on the fly-leaf of a book in the belief that this formula would save the manuscript from cockroaches (Steingass 1977)[4]. Adam Gacek (1986) further referred to the regional varieties in the use of such talismanic paratexts locating the use of *yā kabīkaj* in the subcontinent. Among the collections in Istanbul, four manuscripts of al-Dawlatābādī's commentary come with this inscription on the fly-leaves and one of them even contains a separate inscription on the folios with the table of contents (see the fly-leaves of MSs Aya Sofya 4501, Darulmesnevi 1504, Laleli 3416, Yusuf Aga 347). However, even if the phrase *yā kabīkaj* developed in this form in South Asia, the practice of its inscription on manuscripts could have (and probably did) circulated as far as the Ottoman Empire among mobile learned groups. Thus, the use of the phrase *yā kabīkaj* can only situate the respective manuscript within a wider circulation of cultural practices and scribal traditions that extended as far as the subcontinent. A more precise assessment of the geographical spread of the use of *yā kabīkaj* awaits the study of larger surveys of manuscripts.

Additionally, since references to places were not always provided in the colophons, the exact origin of most of the manuscripts cannot be traced in detail. Yet, some versions demonstrate copying efforts across the Ottoman Empire making manifest a proliferation of the *Sharḥ Hindī* among its learned audiences. In two versions the respective scribes located their transcriptions in the city of Constantinople (*qusṭanṭīnīyya*) (see the colophons in

[4] I am grateful to Olly Akkerman for pointing this out to me.

MS Esad Efendi 3082 and MS Sehid Ali Pasa 2453). Still, manuscripts also hailed from other regions of the Empire. MS Carullah 1931 of the *Sharḥ Hindī* was copied by a certain Muḥammad b. Aḥmad b. Yūsuf in 966/1559 in Kefe (also Kaffa), a city on the south-eastern coast of Crimea, and since the reign of Bayezid II (886–918/1481–1512) a *sanjak* (administrative subdivision of a province) of the Ottoman Empire (Orhunlu 2018). These examples indicate multiple local demands and interests for al-Dawlatābādī's commentary.

Al-Dawlatābādī's text circulated across different scholarly sociabilities in the early modern period and thereby had a crucial share in the learned encounters across the field of Arabic philology. Paratextual profiles on several of his manuscripts demonstrate the minutiae of multiple interpersonal transmissions of the commentary and thereby a high velocity of the text. MS Lala Ismail 635 is a transcription of the *Sharḥ Hindī* with the appended *ḥawāshī* 'marginalia' of a certain Ibn al-Qalʿī on al-Dawlatābādī's commentary (MS Lala Ismail 635, fol. 171r). After the transcription of both texts by different scribes, the manuscript was first in the possession of a certain Aḥmad b. Abī [...] al-Maḥāsīnī in 1060/1650 and then came into the possession of a certain ʿAbd al-Karīm b. Muḥammad b. [...] al-Ḥusaynī in 1073/1662 (see MS Lala Ismail 635, fol. 1r). Similarly, another version of the *Kitāb Hindī*, which was finished in 1028/1619 with a *yā kabīkaj* note, was transmitted (*naqala*) and owned (*ṣāḥabahu*) by at least three different people and annotated extensively in this process (MS Laleli 3416, fol. 1r). Al-Dawlatābādī had arrived in the scholarly circles of the Ottoman world.

Similar paratextual profiles of extensive circulation mark al-Damāmīnī's commentaries, in principle his *Tashīl al-fawāʾid* and the *Sharḥ al-Mughnī* or *Tuḥfat al-gharīb* on Ibn Hishām's work of grammar, which, given the numbers of 19 and 35 manuscript versions respectively, circulated more prominently than the *Manhal al-ṣāfī*, with only four copies. Most importantly, the circulation of his commentaries was subject to larger changes in the paratextual anatomy of Arabic manuscripts. These can highlight the high degree of incorporation of these commentaries into learned sociabilities of Ottoman Istanbul and beyond.

3.0. The Emergence of the *Fihrist*

Manuscripts in Istanbul of both al-Damāmīnī's and al-Dawlatābādī's commentaries show that by the late 16th and 17th centuries the *fihrist* (table of contents) emerged as a new paratextual element. The term *fihrist* comes with a variety of forms and meanings stretched out over a considerable period. Here, I want to distinguish between two types of *fihrists*, the internal and the external. The internal *fihrist* refers to the authorial table of contents and constitutes an intertextual feature that often appears at the end of the *muqaddima* 'introduction' or 'preface' to a work. Internal *fihrists* form crucial textual elements of transition in an introduction after outlining authorial intention, reason, method and purpose of a work, framed in religious formulae and a localisation in a scholarly genealogy. They offer a 'road map' for the reader, locking the successive evolution of ideas of the work into a set of succinct terms or phrases. Thereby they precondition the reading experience by previewing how the larger argument is going to unfold successively. In general, the internal *fihrist* sprang from the pen of the authors, although the layout in manuscripts could be changed later on by the respective scribes.

In contrast to the internal *fihrist*, I want to focus on the use of the external *fihrist* in manuscripts of al-Dawlatābādī's and al-Damāmīnī's grammar commentaries, meaning a table of contents that was added subsequently by a reader or scribe. While the different forms of authorial internal *fihrists* indicate potential perusals of a text, manuscript notes in the form of paratexts, marginalia and other reading statements partially document the actual textual engagement of a reader with a text.[5] They register time and place, when and where a reader intervened or engaged with the text. Needless to say, this does not provide a full account of a reader's intellectual encounters with an oeuvre. Nevertheless, these manuscript notes can indicate changing cultural engagements through their own emergence or alteration over time. Most importantly, the focus on the intertextuality of *matn* and paratexts provides a perspective that goes beyond the interpretative exercise of a text. It encompasses its appropriation by a reader and thereby the historical significances it had in its perusal at a particular point in time. This means that texts could be appropriated in various ways, which highlights changing cultural practices among communities.[6]

---

[5] A strong argument for tracing such textual engagements in a different context was made in Krimsti (2019, 202–44).

[6] For a more detailed discussion of the *fihrist*, see Bahl (2018, chapter 4).

For the current purpose, I argue that the emergence of external *fihrists* during the late 16th and early 17th centuries on manuscripts of al-Damāmīnī's and al-Dawlatābādī's texts underscore their incorporation into scholarly curricula in Ottoman Istanbul. Readers introduced this device to render the texts more accessible. Here, I refer to the external *fihrist* that does not spring from the pen of the author but was added by a reader at a later stage. I base this argument on an extensive survey of al-Damāmīnī's texts and their 58 manuscripts, as well as on 30 manuscripts of al-Dawlatābādī 's text. Such a survey reveals a period of relative absence, relative because there might have been individual cases where such a *fihrist* was added to the manuscript but did not survive because it would have been located among the more vulnerable fly-leaves, which could have easily been torn away. Still, with the absence of 'tables of contents' for the 15th century, and their appearance during the late 16th and throughout the 17th century, there is a diachronic argument to be made. And although 16th and 17th century copies are empirically based on earlier 15th century transcriptions, they do not feature *fihrists* from the 15th century. As far as my research has shown, only late 16th and 17th century copies come with *fihrists*. Their appearance throughout the 17th century indicates a change over time in these Arabic manuscript cultures.

The more common appearance of external *fihrists* suggests a historical trend that took off during the early modern period in the wider field of Arabic philology. Four of the 30 manuscripts of al-Dawlatābādī's *Sharḥ Hindī* survive with a *fihrist*. Similarly, al-Damāmīnī's texts, as they survive on manuscripts in the Süleymaniye in Istanbul, show that the process of *fihrist*isation was not an all-encompassing phenomenon. Altogether 35 transcriptions of either al-Damāmīnī's *hindī* or *yamanī* commentary on Ibn Hishām's *Mughnī al-labīb* survive among the Süleymaniye collections. Only one transcription of the *hindī* commentary, the *Tuḥfat al-gharīb*, comes with a *fihrist*, and this version was copied in 1092/1681 (MS Carullah 1941). Of the four transcriptions of the *al-Manhal al-ṣāfī* in Istanbul again only one version has a *fihrist*, however not dated (MS Haci Selim Aga 1170-001, fol. 1v–2r). Yet, of the 19 copies of the *Taʿlīq al-farāʾid* in Istanbul, eight versions entail a *fihrist* and these versions date to the second half of the 16th and the 17th century (see MS Hekimoglu 888, MS Murad Molla 1675, MS Murad Molla 1676, MS Murad Molla 1677, MS Sehid Ali Pasha 2413, MS Sehid Ali Pasha 2414, MS Laleli 3176, MS Fatih 4909). Two of these versions can be pinned down to a circulation within Istanbul and from Mecca to Istanbul, and thus the wider Ottoman world of the mid-16th century (MS Muradmolla 1675, fol. 248r; MS Hekimoglu 888, fol. 445r).

Scribes and readers added external *fihrists* to the fly-leaves of a manuscript version. Three manuscripts of al-Dawlatābādī's *Sharḥ Hindī* come with a *fihrist* (MS Darulmesnevi 504, MS Servili 306, MS Yazmabagislar 342). All three are decorated in different ways. MS Darulmesnevi 504 was copied in 1027/1618. It simply consists of an enumeration of terms and sections of the treatise and its commentary, not in the form of a list, but spread out across the two pages together with corresponding folio numbers. MS Servili 306 is not dateable. Here, the *fihrist* contains a similar set of terms, but their arrangement is ordered and framed through a grid pattern, each field containing one term and the respective folio number across three pages. MS Yazmabagislar 342, copied in 978/1571, contains a *fihrist* that only stretches across one half-folio (probably incomplete).

Style and execution suggest several characteristics and functions of these *fihrists*. Firstly, their location on the fly-leaves before the title-page marks the process of creating the *fihrist* as separate from the transcription of the *matn* (main text). Readers or scribes most probably added it later after the completion of the manuscript copy. Secondly, this is further corroborated with the addition of folio numbers. Folio numbers locate the respective grammatical phenomena in the manuscript. Thus, the foliation broke up the text and made it more accessible. Significantly, this also enhanced the readability of the text, since readers could now browse through the *fihrist* to look up a specific grammatical term or phenomenon which they wanted to study. Thirdly, these terms or phenomena were formalised or standardised in all three manuscript copies. The *fihrist* functioned like an index that helped a reader navigate the text.

Thus, individual readers began to engage with these texts by creating a *fihrist* for individual manuscript versions. I argue that readers introduced this device to render the texts more accessible, which would serve them in their study pursuits. The overall location among the fly-leaves defined the paratextual characteristics of the external *fihrist* as a meaningful written elaboration of a hypertextual appropriation of a text. In general, they functioned as practical guides and provided a condensed overview of a work's contents. *Fihrists* in manuscripts of al-Damāmīnī's texts worked in a similar way. They were added to the manuscript at a later stage and appear before the title-page and the introduction to the text. Chapters, sections, important terms and phenomena were often referred to with a particular folio number. In one of the Istanbul versions of the *Tuḥfat al-gharīb* the *fihrist mā fī l-kitāb* 'index of what is in the book' goes over one and a half folios before the start of the *matn*'s foliation and was marked as completed with the symbol *tamma* at the end (MS Carullah 1941, fly-leaves). Chapter names were written in red and section titles in black. They were specified with a folio number and corresponded with their counterparts in the *matn* in red ink. In other cases, *fihrist*, *matn* and marginalia seem to be written in the same hand, yet the *fihrist* still was a final addition, because the foliation of the work conformed with the numbers given in the table of contents (MS Carullah 1941, fly-leaves). In contrast to this, a version of the *Manhal al-ṣāfī* entitled *fihrist hādhā al-kitāb* 'index of this book' is produced without foliation (MS Haci Selim Aga 1170-001, fol. 1v–2r). The *fihrist* offers only a bullet-point summary of grammatical terms and phenomena covered in this commentary.

Changing paratextual profiles in manuscripts of al-Damāmīnī's and al-Dawlatābādī's texts document changing textual practices of scribes and readers in this period. They emphasise the high degree to which al-Damāmīnī's and al-Dawlatābādī's texts had become a part of scholarly engagements with Arabic grammar in Ottoman Istanbul and beyond. Thus, both examples showcase empirically substantiated transregional connections between early modern South Asia and the Ottoman Empire and how such forms of text transmission were shaped by readers and their needs in the field of Islamicate learned pursuits.

References

Arabic Manuscripts

Al-Damāmīnī, M. *Taʿlīq al-farāʾid ʿalā tashīl al-fawāʾid*. MS Ragip Pasa 1326. Süleymaniye Library, Istanbul.

———. *Taʿlīq al-farāʾid ʿalā tashīl al-fawāʾid*. MS Hekimoglu 888. Süleymaniye Library, Istanbul.

———. *Taʿlīq al-farāʾid ʿalā tashīl al-fawāʾid*. MS Murad Molla 1675. Süleymaniye Library, Istanbul.

———. *Taʿlīq al-farāʾid ʿalā tashīl al-fawāʾid*. MS Murad Molla 1676. Süleymaniye Library, Istanbul.

———. *Taʿlīq al-farāʾid ʿalā tashīl al-fawāʾid*. MS Murad Molla 1677. Süleymaniye Library, Istanbul.

———. *Taʿlīq al-farāʾid ʿalā tashīl al-fawāʾid*. MS Sehid Ali Pasha 2413. Süleymaniye Library, Istanbul.

———. *Taʿlīq al-farāʾid ʿalā tashīl al-fawāʾid*. MS Sehid Ali Pasha 2414. Süleymaniye Library, Istanbul.

———. *Taʿlīq al-farāʾid ʿalā tashīl al-fawāʾid*. MS Laleli 3176. Süleymaniye Library, Istanbul.

———. *Taʿlīq al-farāʾid ʿalā tashīl al-fawāʾid*. MS Fatih 4909. Süleymaniye Library, Istanbul.

———. *Tuḥfat al-gharīb ʿalā l-kalām mughnī al-labīb ʿan kutub al-aʿārīb*. MS Carullah 1941, Süleymaniye, Istanbul.

———. *Tuḥfat al-gharīb fī l-kalām ʿalā mughnī al-labīb*. MS IO Bijapur 7, British Library, London.

———. *al-Manhal al-ṣafīy fī sharḥ al-wāfīy*. MS Haci Selim Aga 1170-001. Süleymaniye Library, Istanbul.

———. *al-Manhal al-ṣafīy fī sharḥ al-wāfīy*. MS Sehid Ali Pasa 2535. Süleymaniye Library, Istanbul.

———. *al-Manhal al-ṣafīy fī sharḥ al-wāfīy*. MS Nahw 108. Salar Jung Museum Library, Hyderabad.

Al-Dawlatābādī, Shihāb al-Dīn. *Al-Irshād*. MS Husrev Pasa 663. Süleymaniye Library, Istanbul.

———. *Sharḥ al-Hindī ʿalā l-Kāfiya*. MS Aya Sofya 4501. Süleymaniye Library, Istanbul.

———. *Sharḥ al-Hindī ʿalā l-Kāfiya*. MS Darulmesnevi 504. Süleymaniye Library, Istanbul.

———. *Sharḥ al-Hindī ʿalā l-Kāfiya*. MS Esad Efendi 3082. Süleymaniye Library, Istanbul.

———. *Sharḥ al-Hindī ʿalā l-Kāfiya*. MS Hamidiye 612. Süleymaniye Library, Istanbul.

———. *Sharḥ al-Hindī ʿalā l-Kāfiya*. MS Lala Ismail 635. Süleymaniye Library, Istanbul.

———. *Sharḥ al-Hindī ʿalā l-Kāfiya*. MS Laleli 3416. Süleymaniye Library, Istanbul.

———. *Sharḥ al-Hindī ʿalā l-Kāfiya*. MS Sehid Ali Pasa 2453. Süleymaniye Library, Istanbul.

———. *Sharḥ al-Hindī ʿalā l-Kāfiya*. MS MS Servili 306. Süleymaniye Library, Istanbul.

———. *Sharḥ al-Hindī ʿalā l-Kāfiya*. MS Yazmabagislar 342. Süleymaniye Library, Istanbul.

———. *Sharḥ al-Hindī ʿalā l-Kāfiya*. Yusuf Aga 347. Süleymaniye Library, Istanbul.

Secondary Literature

Ahmad, M. G. Z. 1946. *The Contribution of Indo-Pakistan to Arabic Literature. From Ancient Times to 1857*. Lahore: Sh. Muhammad Ashraf.

Alam, Muzaffar. 2004. *The languages of political Islam. India, 1200–1800*. Chicago: University of Chicago Press.

Asher, Catherine B., and Cynthia Talbot. 2006. *India before Europe*. New York: Cambridge University Press.

Bahl, Christopher. 2018. 'Histories of Circulation: Sharing Arabic manuscripts across the Western Indian Ocean, 1400–1700'. PhD dissertation, SOAS, University of London.

Bauer, Thomas. 2005. 'Rhetorik: Arabische Kultur'. In *Rhetorik: Begriff – Geschichte – Internationalität*, edited by Gert Ueding, 283–300. Tübingen: Niemeyer (= Gert Ueding [ed.]. 2007. *Historisches Wörterbuch der Rhetorik* 8:111–37. Tübingen: Niemeyer).

Choudhury, Rishad. 2016. 'The Hajj and the Hindi: The Ascent of the Indian Sufi Lodge in the Ottoman Empire". *Modern Asian Studies* 50/6, 1888–931.

Eds. 2018. 'al-Siyālkūtī'. In *Encyclopaedia of Islam, Second Edition*, edited by P. Bearman, Th. Bianquis, C. E. Bosworth, E. van Donzel, W. P. Heinrichs. http://dx.doi.org/10.1163/1573-3912_islam_SIM_7082, consulted online on 30 January 2018.

El-Rouayheb, Khaled. 2015. *Islamic Intellectual History in the Seventeenth Century: Scholarly Currents in the Ottoman Empire and the Maghreb*. New York: Cambridge University Press.

Fleisch, H. 2017a. 'Ibn Mālik'. In *Encyclopaedia of Islam, Second Edition*, edited by P. Bearman, Th. Bianquis, C. E. Bosworth, E. van Donzel, W. P. Heinrichs. http://dx.doi.org/10.1163/1573-3912_islam_COM_0336, consulted online on 21 February 2017.

———. 2017b. 'Ibn Hishām'. In *Encyclopaedia of Islam, Second Edition*, edited by P. Bearman, Th. Bianquis, C. E. Bosworth, E. van Donzel, W. P. Heinrichs. http://dx.doi.org/10.1163/1573-3912_islam_COM_0326, consulted online on 21 February 2017.

Gacek, Adam. 1986. 'The Use of *kabīkaj* in Arabic Manuscripts'. *Manuscripts of the Middle East* 1: 49–53.

Genette, Gerard. 1993. *Palimpseste: Die Literatur auf zweiter Stufe*. Translated by W. Bayer and D. Honig. Frankfurt: Suhrkamp.

———. 2001. *Paratexte: Das Buch vom Beiwerk des Buches*. Frankfurt: Suhrkamp.

Görke, Andreas, and Konrad Hirschler. 2011. 'Introduction: Manuscript Notes as Documentary Sources'. In *Manuscript Notes as Documentary Sources*, edited by Andreas Görke and Konrad Hirschler, 9–20. Beiruter Texte und Studien 129. Würzburg: Ergon-Verlag.

Gully, Adrian. 1995. *Grammar and semantics in Medieval Arabic: A study of Ibn-Hisham's 'Mughni l'labib'*. Richmond (Surrey): Curzon Press.

Hitzel, Frédéric 1999. 'Manuscrits, livres et culture livresque à Istanbul'. In *Livres et lecture dans le monde ottoman, thème sous la responsabilité de Frédéric Hitzel*, 19–38. *Revue des mondes musulmans et de la Méditerranée* 87–88.

Ho, Engseng. 2006. *The Graves of Tarim: Genealogy and mobility across the Indian Ocean*. Berkeley: University of California Press.

Kinra, Rajeev. 2015. *Writing self, Writing Empire: Chandar Bhan Brahman and the Cultural World of the Indo-Persian State Secretary*. Oakland: University of California Press.

———. 2010. 'Master and Munshi: A Brahman Secretary's Guide to Mughal Governance'. *Indian Economic and Social History Review* 47/4: 527–61.

Krimsti, Feras. 2019 'Arsāniyūs Shukrī al-Ḥakīm's Account of His Journey to France, the Iberian Peninsula, and Italy (1748–1757) from Travel Journal to Edition'. *Philological Encounters* 4: 202–44.

Nizami, K. A. 2018. 'al-Dawlatābādī'. In *Encyclopaedia of Islam, Second Edition*, edited by P. Bearman, Th. Bianquis, C. E. Bosworth, E. van Donzel, W. P. Heinrichs. http://dx.doi.org/10.1163/1573-3912_islam_SIM_1751, consulted online on 31 January 2018.

Orhonlu, Cengiz. 2018. 'Kefe'. In *Encyclopaedia of Islam, Second Edition*, edited by P. Bearman, Th. Bianquis, C. E. Bosworth, E. van Donzel, W. P. Heinrichs. http://dx.doi.org/10.1163/1573-3912_islam_SIM_4096, consulted online on 26 January 2018.

Ricci, Ronit. 2011. *Islam Translated: Literature, Conversion, and the Arabic Cosmopolis of South and Southeast Asia.* Chicago and London: University of Chicago Press.

Robinson, Francis. 1997. 'Ottomans-Safavids-Mughals: Shared Knowledge and Connective Systems'. *Journal of Islamic Studies* 8/2: 151–84.

Schimmel, Annemarie. 1980. *Islam in the Indian Subcontinent.* Leiden: Brill.

Simon, Udo Gerald. 1993. *Mittelalterliche arabische Sprachbetrachtung zwischen Grammatik und Rhetorik: 'ilm al-ma'ānī bei as-Sakkākī.* Heidelberg: Heidelberger Orientverlag.

Steingass, Francis. 1977. *Persian-English Dictionary.* London.

Subrahmanyam, Sanjay. 1997. 'Connected Histories: Notes towards a Reconfiguration of Early Modern Eurasia'. *Modern Asian Studies* 31/3: 735–62.

———. 2012. *Courtly Encounters. Translating Courtliness and Violence in Early Modern Eurasia.* Cambridge, MA and London: Harvard University Press.

Szuppe, Maria. 2004. 'Circulation des lettrés et cercles littéraires: Entre Asie centrale, Iran et Inde du nord (XVe–XVIIIe siècle)'. *Annales: Histoire, Sciences sociales* 59/5–6: 997–1018.

Würsch, Renate 2018. 'Abū l-Fatḥ b. ʿAbd al-Ḥayy b. ʿAbd al-Muqtadir'. In *Encyclopaedia of Islam, THREE,* edited by Kate Fleet, Gudrun Krämer, Denis Matringe, John Nawas, Everett Rowson. http://dx.doi.org/10.1163/1573-3912_ei3_COM_22611, consulted online on 31 January 2018.

6. BASTARDS AND ARABS

E. Khayyat

> Herr, du sollst den Streit beenden, der die Welt entzweit.
> So wie du bist haben unsere Alten den beschrieben, der es
> tun wird. Frieden müssen wir haben von den Arabern...
> Reinheit, nichts als Reinheit wollen wir...
>
> Jackals, from Kafka, "Schakale und Araber"

Commenting on Ziya Pasha's (1825–1880) anthology *Harabat*, the great poet Tevfik Fikret (1867–1915)—one of the pioneers of modern Turkish poetry—suggests that "even the *sahib-i fazlı*," which is to say 'the author of [this] gift or treasure', but also, as Fikret underlines, "the father of [this] illegitimate child [...]," confessed to the shortcomings of his final product (Fikret, 1898).[1] Ziya Pasha started off his anthology with disclaimers, explains Fikret, and announced his regrets already in the Introduction to *Harabat* "with a thousand *pîç-tâb-ı derûn*."

[1] *Sahib-i fazlı*: *sahib* is literally 'master' or 'owner'. The expression could alternatively be read 'the recipient of this blessing or grace', *fazlı* referring to Ziya Pasha's God-given talent, describing Ziya Pasha as blessed. In addition to 'that which is given as a gift or favour', *fazlı*, referring to *Harabat*, could be interpreted as 'the great service' Ziya Pasha provided. I use Ziya Pasha (1291–1292).

 https://doi.org/10.11647/OBP.0208.06

Fikret thus comes unglued already in the second paragraph of his critical essay on *Harabat*, showing off his twisted command of Ottoman Turkish. He demonstrates what a poet could make with the words of *elsine-i selase* 'the three languages, i.e., Arabic, Farsi, and Ottoman Turkish', the tri-lingual combination of the Ottoman Empire. *Derûn* is 'deep' and *pîç* is 'bastard'; *pîçtâb* 'distress or trouble' and *tâb* 'strength, light, or sparkle', also the act of 'annealing or tempering', and much more. Pushing things a little, one could easily hear تاب as طبع or 'print', since corrupting (bastardising?) Arabic, in writing as in speech, is quite the Turkish habit. Ziya Pasha's three-volume anthology (*mecmua-i müntehabât*, in Fikret's vocabulary) of Ottoman Turkish poetry, which was one of a kind when it was published between 1874–1875, contains poems in *elsine-i selase*. Its multilingualism (*avant la lettre*, as it were) was considered its main shortcoming by Ziya Pasha's fellow reformists and revolutionaries, who were calling for the elevation of the oral tradition in vernacular Turkish over and against *elsine-i selase* around the time when *Harabat* was published. Vernacular Turkish was the cornerstone of the Ottoman Turkish future that these revolutionaries sought to build through their literary-political activism (Levend 1972; Lewis 1999).[2] Instead *Harabat* covers and builds on Arabic and Farsi literary canons and focuses on Ottoman poetry under the influence of these traditions to develop a canon of modern Ottoman letters.

---

[2] The canonical history of the Turkish vernacular from the perspective of Turkish modernity is Levend (1972), which is somewhat teleologically minded. Also see Geoffrey Lewis (1999).

How does Ziya Pasha express his regrets, then, according to Fikret? Through a thousand painful sighs from the depths of his heart? Through a thousand adopted bastards in his orphanage of an anthology? Through the displaced, bastardised poems of the old? Through Arabic and Farsi poems of time immemorial that Ziya Pasha adopted as his very own, perhaps? Through the poems that do not belong to *us* but that *we* have made our own—Arabic and Farsi poems that, so deeply ingrained in our hearts and souls, are now part of our way of expressing ourselves, for better or for worse? Then again, what does *Harabat* show us when it sheds light on, prints, tempers the traits and movements in the depths of our souls? If the origins of Ottoman Turkish language, culture, literature, and self-expression—according to the logic of *Harabat*—might also be Persian and/or Arab, and thus perhaps even doubtful, what does that make of Ottoman Turks? Could the latter be the source of the anguish Fikret reads into Ziya Pasha's words?

Many before and after Fikret, including the giants of Turkish criticism, such as Namık Kemal (1840–1888) and Mehmet Fuat Köprülü (1890–1966), Rıza Tevfik (1869–1949), and Ahmet Hamdi Tanpınar (1901–1962), scrutinised Ziya Pasha's Ottoman Turkish canon as it took shape in this unique anthology.[3] They asked questions similar to the ones I summed up above, at times refuting the premises that guide Ziya Pasha's choices while acknowledging his ambition and great service, or sympathising with his politics while raising objections to some of his specific

---

[3] See *Tahrib-i Harabat*, 1303. Rıza Tevfik's 'Harabat ve Harabati' was published in *Yeni Sabah* (1944). See also Fuad Köprülü (1917).

choices. Yet almost every critic since Kemal has made a point of addressing our reformist Pasha's revolutionary agenda and his reactionary attitude in *Harabat* as paradoxical. It is high time we scrutinise the theologico-political premises underlying Ziya Pasha's sense of literary history to make better sense of this most productive paradox. Ottoman Arabic was central to the theologico-political horizon that shaped Ziya Pasha's branch of what I shall refer to as Islamicate humanism, just as *Harabat* had an absolutely crucial role to play in the history of this Islamicate humanism at large. *Harabat* both fulfils and destroys that humanism—it announces the end of Islamicate humanism right at the peak of its centuries-long, cross-cultural trajectory, hailing the beginning of a new era. Gerschom Scholem's pioneering vision on the paradoxical moments of Jewish history will guide us to account for this productive paradox.

Unfortunately, by focusing almost exclusively on the limited role that *Harabat* played in the history of modern Turkish and Turkish literary modernity, critics, scholars, and students of Ziya Pasha have obscured the immense potentials *Harabat* still carries. The pure 'Turkish vernacular' that Ziya Pasha's fellow reformists and revolutionaries, and Ziya Pasha himself at one point, sought to elevate for the future of the Ottoman people, was not a reality at that point in time, but more of an idea or an ideal to pursue. *Harabat*'s emphasis on Arabic, Farsi, and Ottoman Turkish, or the tri-language of the Ottoman Empire over and against the ideal of a Turkish vernacular, articulates another, a much older idealism, while carrying that idealism to its radical conclusions. A review of *Harabat*'s languages and literatures, and, finally, its Arabic canon, in the following pages will provide an opportunity to acknowledge these unaccounted-for aspects of *Harabat*, while raising an uncanny question: that of the relevance of Ottoman Arabic today.

1.0. The Bastards

Fikret's 1898 '*Harabat*'tan Bir Sahîfe', or 'A Page from *Harabat*', was a response to the reformist and/or nationalist critics of Ziya Pasha's anthology, who found the anthology's selection and multilingualism a little too reactionary. As mentioned, *Harabat* was published tri-lingually and covered the millennium-long history of Islamicate verbal arts in many of its genres and forms, from the *qasaid* to *khamriyyat*. The first volume, from which I have chosen a page to analyse closely in the concluding section of this essay, contains 37 Arabic, 38 Farsi, and 22 Ottoman Turkish *qasaid*. The curious thing is that, like Fikret and his other critics, Ziya Pasha was a reformist—a proto-nationalist of sorts, no less, and a member of the revolutionary Young Ottoman movement, who himself had a particular interest and investment in the vernacular, everyday, 'simple' Turkish, or Turkish as the tongue of the simple Ottoman folk.

About a decade before *Harabat*, when he and other like-minded reformists published a newspaper named *Hürriyet* in London exile, Ziya Pasha wrote a ground-breaking essay on reading

Figure 1: *Harabat* title page

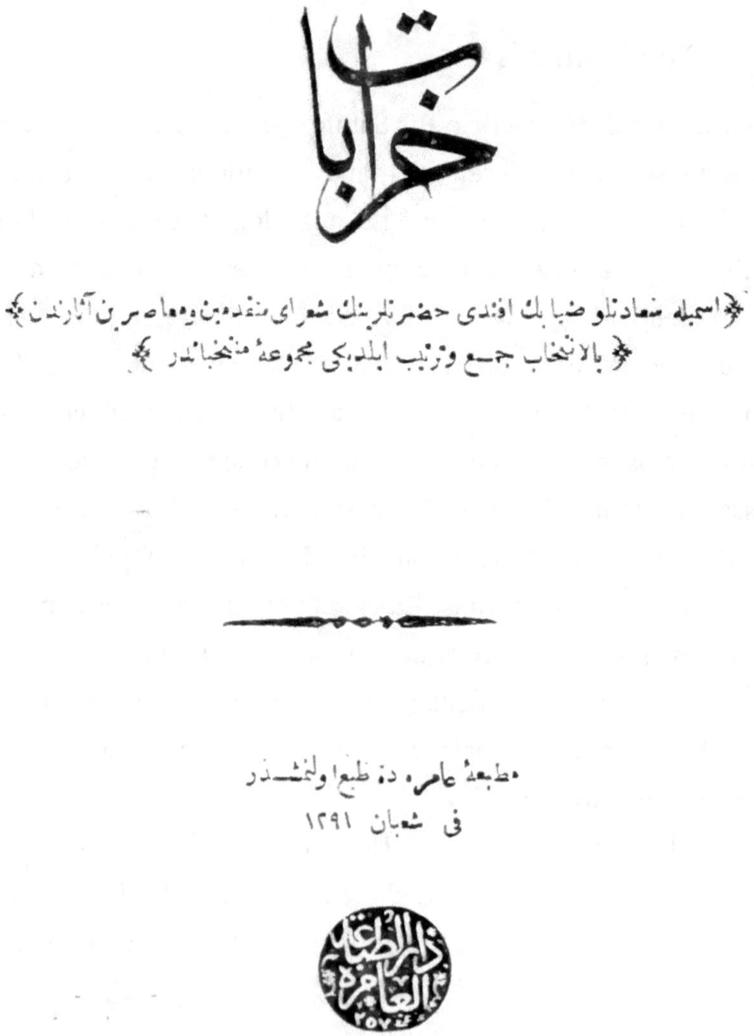

خرابات

اسمیله سعادتلو ضیا بك افندی حضرتلرینك شعرای متقدمین و معاصرین آثارندن
بالانتخاب جمع و ترتیب ایلدیکی مجموعهٔ منتخباتدر

مطبعهٔ عامره‌ده طبع اولنمشدر
فی شعبان ١٢٩١

دار الطباعة العامرة

and writing in the Ottoman language.[4] 'Poetry and Prose', which was meant to translate 'literature' in the modern, Western sense, is an essay about the insurmountable impossibility of drafting ground-breaking essays in Turkish. Not that our Pasha lacked the gift. But the language in which he wrote did not allow such a thing, the essay suggests.

Ziya Pasha and his comrades had fled the Empire because of their oppositional views, which were not perceived favourably by the Sublime Porte. They had become outcasts, living far away from their fellow Ottoman subjects. These concerned intellectuals, also known as the Young Ottomans, felt an urgency to reach out to those whom they took to be the true 'subjects' of Ottoman imperial history, which is to say the Ottoman multitude, to warn them of the difficulties ahead. The problem was *not* just that they had no option but to publish their oppositional views in the London-based *Hürriyet*, which was smuggled to Istanbul through the British embassy. Ziya Pasha and other luminaries, from our Pasha's perspective, had difficulty reaching out to the people even when they lived right in the heart of the Ottoman capital. The distance between the vernacular and their written, literary, Ara-

---

[4] Ziya Pasha's essay, '*Şiir ve İnşa* ['Poetry and Prose']' was published in the London-based *Hürriyet* in 1868. For the story of the newspaper, see Mardin (2000). Among some sources about Young Ottomans and Ziya Pasha in this context are Ebüzziya (1973); Akçura (1981); Kaplan (1948) and Yetiş (2000), which has a comparative discussion of the pasha's essay and its significance. Additionally, Tanpınar (2006) addressed the significance of the essay on multiple occasions.

bic- and Farsi-infused high Ottoman Turkish made literary address (in the modern sense), which is to say communicative action, or, more generally, mobilisation, practically impossible:

İşte bu sebebledir ki elân
Türkîde yok irticâle imkân

For this reason, in our day and age
Authenticity is not possible in Turkish (*Harabat* 1: v)[5]

In search of that vernacular, that pure medium, 'Poetry and Prose' challenged its readers to ask if Ottomans have, or ever had, a language of their own in which to produce poetry and prose free of Arabic and Farsi, and whether there existed a literature in that language, an archive of wordy material, per concrete evidence. The pasha responded in the affirmative, but with reservation, since he also seemed to admit that one cannot take this kind of thing as given, just as one cannot take the identity of one's biological father or mother as given.

Why else would he call for the standardisation of orthography for Ottoman Turkish, the language of the ruling Ottoman Turks, if not in search for a birth certificate of sorts? Our pasha also recommended the promotion of mass literacy, to turn to the streets of the Empire, to the oral tradition in the vernacular, where the living language of the ruling Ottoman Turks could perhaps be found. His thinking, therefore, was that the true Ottoman

[5] I translate ارتجال as 'authentic self-expression', relying on context here. In other contexts it can be translated 'speaking wittily extempore, successful improvisation, or clear extempore expression of what is in one's mind'.

language, the live language of the living multitude, and its literature, were potentially out there, but in an immaterial, non-tangible way in the people's mouths. So were the Ottomans as a unique nation: out there, yet nowhere to be found in the flesh, as if their unique identity, language, and culture (as distinct from—yet similarly to—the French, the British, Arabs, or Persians) amounted to hearsay. For as of Ziya Pasha's day, Ottomans (unlike the French, the British, Arabs, or Persians) existed in an ephemeral way, or, rather, more like a promise or potential, or, better still, silenced and invisible. That potential had to be objectified and the promise fulfilled, and the literary-humanistic archive—the birth certificate—organised and printed in actual, material books so that Ottomans might rightfully acknowledge their father- or mother-tongue and raise their voice.

Once the living language was elevated in this manner, and all these other measures were taken, then the sort of address such as the one Ziya Pasha sought to draft would easily reach the addressee—the people—and the interpellation would be felicitous. The Turk then would stop being Turk in name only and turn to, come to the name Turk. When Ziya Pasha drafted the essay in London, however, none of these conditions, and not even the condition of a uniform orthography, had been met yet. What sort of other changes the measures he listed would incite, or whether or not the creation of the conditions Ziya Pasha desired—or the interpellation itself, for that matter—would amount to fabricating an Ottoman Turkish language, literature, and identity, did not seem to concern him at this point. In other words, he was not concerned with the validity of the premises justifying the engineering of a new media technology. The Ottoman masses had to be mobilised if the Empire was to survive, and mobilisation required a new media technology—of that much he was certain.

From the point of view of the future of the Empire, then, that "Türkîde yok irticâle imkân" at that point in time, or the present silence and invisibility of the vernacular Ottoman Turkish identity and tongue, appeared as an urgent problem to be addressed. What turns out to be problematic in this moderately optimistic, future-oriented point of view, which is emblematic of the haste that marks the late Ottoman intellectual universe, would appear in a completely different light when Ziya Pasha moved on to develop an alternative, strictly historical perspective on the very same issues. Ziya Pasha's call in 'Poetry and Prose' voiced the concerns of his generation, which feared the unforeseeable future unfolding before them with the hasty reforms, oppressive rulers, and silent masses of the Sublime State. *Harabat*, in turn, takes a pause, and views the same state of affairs from the perspective of the Islamicate past, offering a sort of intellectual history on the silence or invisibility in question.

Perhaps Ziya Pasha himself took a first step in pursuit of the prescriptions of 'Poetry and Prose' when he put together *Harabat*. One could consider this anthology, then, the birth certificate that he called for—one that he himself drafted after a decade of research.

He set to work with his own archive, which had enabled and motivated him to consider his cultural identity unique and distinct from any other. He apologises in his Introduction, drafted in verse, for his limited sampling bias, which Fikret does not fail to underline, but, at the same time, does not consider significant.[6] Ziya Pasha organised the poems he grew up with, systematising, to the best of his ability, the one and only literary cultural archive of his era, collecting traditional verses in *elsine-i selase*. *Harabat* provides us with insight into the making of the traditional Ottoman intellectual and his/her lifeworld and, therefore, also outlines the fundamentals of the sort of humanism underlying such *Bildung*. The oral tradition in vernacular Turkish also figures in *Harabat*, but in a rather more critical manner, while Ziya Pasha of *Harabat*, looking back at his own intellectual journey, does not, of course, even consider offering translations of the Arabic and Farsi poems of his selection into Turkish.

Nor can he disentangle the centuries-old knots or cut off 'Turkish' poetry and prose from the Arabic and Farsi of his very own *Bildung*. In Fikret's terms, when Ziya Pasha, and, through him, the proto-nationalist Young Ottoman movement, look into their father's or mother's face from up close, they end up finding themselves in sorrowful doubt, at a paralyzing moment of decision, and yet before a future ripe for poetry as well.[7]

In the section of his "Introduction" to *Harabat* that addresses the motives behind his compilation of the poems, Ziya Pasha praises vernacular Turkish poetry for its educational value, describing his exposure to folk literature as an early station in his

[6] Ziya Pasha's 'Introduction' (*Mukaddime*) was soon after published separately as *Mukaddime-i Harabat* (1311).

[7] The poetry of the sort I have in mind here is that of the poet in the Vicoean key, i.e., ποιητής 'maker, inventor, lawgiver'.

intellectual journey and an inspiration for his own early verse. What marks this moment in his intellectual journey, though, is some half-learned, childish pride, and inability to handle criticism:

Kim şiirime atsa tane taşı
Uğrardı benimle derde başı
Hicv idi muârıza cevâbım
Şemşir-i zeban idi kitabım

Whoever threw stones at my poems
Would get in trouble with me
Sarcasm was my response to opposition
Scimitar of the tongue my constitution (*Harabat* 1, iv)

One can surmise that folk literature in any language of the Ottoman universe could potentially serve the same purpose, which is initiation into culture. Mastery over cultural matter would require more than mere initiation. For soon after his exposure to folk literature, Ziya Pasha laid his hands on two *diwans* in Ottoman Turkish, the study of which proved to be a humbling experience for him. Then again even that was just another step in his intellectual trajectory. Only after reading Farsi poetry did he find true enlightenment, he admits, beginning to figure out what a poem is and what it takes to be a poet proper, or to claim mastery over words, speech, and culture:

Amma okudukda Gülistan'ı
Derk etmeğe başladım lisânı[8]

Yet only after reading Golistan

[8] The *lisân* at issue here is the 'poetic' or Farsi language.

I began to understand the tongue (*Harabat* 1, v)

To be a poet one must leave behind the childish pride that comes with the gift, then—the gift of a mother tongue and talent. One must learn to look beyond and even overcome the self (*Harabat* 1, xi). Talent is a must to be a poet, but it is only one of the conditions for being a poet proper. Talent needs to be cultivated through learning and morals, through something like a humanities education:

Şâni-i şurüt-ı şâiriyyet
Tahşil-i maârif ü fazilet
İlim olmasa şâir olmaz insan
Dilsiz söze kadir olmaz insan

The second condition for becoming a poet
Is the study of culture and manners
There is no poetry without wisdom
One cannot command words without tongues (*Harabat* 1, x)

The humanities training of this sort requires moving beyond Turkish for the Turkish pupil, beyond the oral tradition and more, as we shall see shortly. This is not to say that *Harabat* disregards issues concerning the state of Turkish that Ziya Pasha voiced in 'Poetry and Prose'. Again, *Harabat* simply reframes Ziya Pasha's earlier questions in 'Poetry and Prose'. Ziya Pasha leaves behind his terror at the unforeseeable future of the Sublime State, along with his youthful haste, resentment, and pride. He develops a new perspective on the circumstances he observes in Turkish, which reflects a peculiar historicism and even realism, in so far as *Harabat* was based on his own actual, material library and lived experience.

According to the Ziya Pasha of *Harabat*, the very nature of the Turkish tongue is corrupt, or bastardised, as Fikret would say, due to the immense influence of the Persianate cultural universe on Turkish and the insistence of some Ottoman poets on imitating the great Iranian masters in Turkish:

Taklid ile çün lisân bozulmuş
Evzân-ı arazi ğâib olmuş
Çıktıkça lisân tabiatinden
Elbette düşer fesahatinden

For imitation corrupted the tongue
Verses of the land vanished
The more the tongue betrays its nature
The weaker its ability for expression (*Harabat* 1, v)

The source of all the difficulties Ziya Pasha observes in Turkish and the weakness of the Ottoman Turkish tongue is the confusion that results from such influence corrupting the nature of Turkish. Instead of elaborating more on what the true nature of Turkish might be, Ziya Pasha of *Harabat* welcomes what he finds in his archive and interprets his contemporary moment of 'weakness' and corruption in the history of Turkish as a station on a centuries-long cultural trajectory. First, he suggests that the Turkish condition is not unique; that Iranians once imitated Arabs in the exact same way that some Ottoman gentlemen of his day imitated the Iranians:

Türki'de değil bu hâl evvel
Olmuş idi Fâriside muhtel
Anlar da edip lisânı tecdîd

Etmiş Arab'a sühanda taklid

It is not in Turkish that this happened first
Farsi too once got corrupt
They too refreshed their tongue
And imitated the Arabs in discourse (*Harabat* 1, v)

Imitation leads to interesting outcomes in the case of Farsi. Its bond with Arabic only strengthens and eventually 'perfects' Farsi, enabling the Persianate cultural universe to dominate the Muslim world before the Ottoman Turks took the stage:

Zira Arabi lisânla evvel
Olmuş idi Fârisi mükemmel

For it was with the Arabic tongue
That Farsi reached perfection (*Harabat* 1, x)

Addressing what appears to be weakness in Ottoman Turkish requires not a search for the true nature of Turkish from this perspective, then, but to go beyond imitating Iranians, just as to get to the Persianate peak of Islamicate humanism, Iranians had to stop imitating Arabs, appropriated the Arabic archive, and produced in Arabic as well. The evident weakness of Turkish, similarly, required *appropriating* Farsi and reaching out all the way back to the source of learning to dig out wisdom.

The source of wisdom, the origin of learning, the ultimate reservoir of humanism in this mental theatre is Arabic. Arabic also serves as the measure of all things in this regard. It is not entirely clear whether Ottoman Turkish would be 'weaker' or stronger after appropriating Farsi and Arabic, or whether the goal here is to praise or condemn what Ziya Pasha regards as Turkish weakness or corruption. Then again, using his recurrent metaphors of the seas, rivers, and oceans, Ziya Pasha suggests that Turkish and Farsi are but two rivers when it comes to wisdom, while Arabic is the ocean:

Var ise de bazı fazla noksan
Evzân-ı Arab'dır anda evzân
Biz anlara nisbeten cedidiz
Güya ki Arablar'a hafidiz
Âşâr-ı Arab'dır ümm-i irfan
Bunlar iki nehrdir o umman

If we are deficient or excessive at times
Arabic metre is its metre [measure]
We are novices by comparison
Being supposedly Arabs' heirs
Arabic poetry is the mother of wisdom
It is the ocean: the other two, rivers (*Harabat* 1, v)

The continuity Ziya Pasha relies on here—from Arabic to Farsi and Ottoman Turkish—is based on the theologico-political horizon of Islamicate humanism and its sense of history, which I will address at length in the next section with Tanpınar's guidance. Suffice it to say that the obligation to study Arabic is the obligation to have a particular mindset, if not historical consciousness, for Ziya Pasha:

Şiir-i Arab'a tevessül eyle
Nahv ü lügata tevaggul eyle
Nazm-ı kudemâ vü fenn-i târih
Gül-nahl-i fesahate bün ü bih

Embrace Arabic poetry
Study its syntax and vocabulary

> The poems of the old and the science of history
> Are the root of this rose sapling of self-expression (*Harabat* 1, x)

Harabat, therefore, is a literary historical quest that, with its peculiar realism, forced our pasha to contradict the revolutionary politics he articulated in his earlier, proto-nationalist call to zoom in on and elevate the Turkish of the simple folk. *Harabat* shares the observations about the state of Turkish that Ziya Pasha first voiced in 'Poetry and Prose', but, elaborating on a historical continuity leading to that state of affairs, it offers an alternative, more complex path to literary-political action for the future. It still calls for action, like 'Poetry and Prose', but to 'perfect', or democratise the Ottoman tongue in a different way—through a more rigorous investment in Islamicate humanism by way of completely appropriating the Arabic and Farsi languages, literatures, and libraries into the Ottoman Turkish lifeworld.

From *Harabat* on there are two paths before the Ottoman Turkish intellectual history. Either dive deeper into that ocean of *harabat*, devour that ocean of wine—more to follow on *harabat* and wine poetry—and have Turkish, Arabic, and Farsi get further ruined and bastardised; or set Ziya Pasha's archive, library, and that orphanage of an anthology on fire, claim poetic license for a new era, and start from scratch. Ziya Pasha comes to opt for the former, for, additionally, there is still a huge potential in Ottoman Turkish, according to him, when one considers it a fruit of Islamicate humanism.

If Arabic is the true ocean of our ancient wisdom where the Farsi and Turkish rivers must meet—flowing backwards if need be—it is potentially Ottoman Turkish, or rather *elsine-i selase* as the native-Ottoman tri-language, that is the ocean of an infinite future where Arabic might finally become one with Farsi and Turkish. The three of them then would dissolve into one another to create something completely unprecedented: an ocean of oceans (*bahr-ı â'zam* as opposed to *umman*; *Harabat* 1, ix–x).[9] That would truly 'perfect' Ottoman Turkish—by dissolving it.

Then again, for some, *Harabat*'s realism was so destructive, so ruinous, that none of this was feasible after its publication. For this realism had made both the Islamicate past and the Turkish future mere phantasy. I shall clarify how and why I read 'realism' into *Harabat*'s mental theatre, and how this realism differs from realism in the Western sense, at the end of the next section. Suffice it to remember for now that *Harabat*'s literary-political vision was based on Ziya Pasha's actual library and archive, his real and material books, as opposed to the ideal, the pure phantasy of a distinctly Turkish identity, vernacular, or literature. Let me first explain how and why Ziya Pasha's critics found his work 'ruinous'.

Ziya Pasha himself wrote traditional poetry—his verse Introduction to *Harabat* is of the same genre. He was truly a *harabati*. *Harabat* is both 'the tavern' and 'ruins', and it is the proverbial and real gathering place of poets (who are called the *harabati* literally 'the wasted') to sing poems, literally being ruined and laid waste with the divine ecstasy of the words of poetry or with

[9] Alternatively, for a recent discussion of Ziya Pasha's anthology within the context of world literature, see Arslan (2017).

wine.[10] The poems of the *harabati* directed one to the drunkenness of the wine, where one gave up on worldly concerns and differences to give in to whatever one was, and guided other perplexed, inquisitive souls to do so as well. This amounts to turning and turning in circles, like the whirling dervishes, to avoid reading too much into this world, and to go about one's business in divine ecstasy. Once, the word *harabat* in Farsi and Ottoman Turkish had a more general, mystical connotation within these parameters, but as the Ottoman Turkish literary modernity evolved, and especially after the immense impact of Ziya Pasha's *Harabat*, in Turkish the word came to mean more specifically the canon of pre-modern Islamicate poetry, as opposed to Turkish literature in the modern sense, while *harabati* came to refer specifically to the author of traditional poetry. Ziya Pasha's work and the stir it created would over time suppress the immensely rich connotations of the word *harabat* in Turkish, then. This is to

---

[10] On Islam and wine, see Wensinck and Sadan (2018), and also Ahmed (2016). *Harabat* once referred to both the proverbial gathering place of mystics, poets, and lovers of poetry, and the actual space of worship and meditation of the Sufis (*tekke* or *hankah*); see Uludağ (2017). Dabashi (2013) explains:

> Persian literary historians have concurred that the word [*kharabat*] originally meant a 'house or tavern of ill repute' but was eventually appropriated by the mystics to mean a place that they frequent by way of suspending all hypocritical pretense to piety.... The idea is that there are places that you can frequent that will dismantle your beliefs, and yet, in doing so, will also restore your faith. The proverbial tavern in Persian poetry is that *kharabat*.

say that if Ziya Pasha, with *Harabat*, contradicts his own revolutionary politics, and comes out as rather reactionary than progressive according to his own proto-nationalist vision, this is not to say that his *Harabat* is necessarily *of* the *harabat* of old either.

Some of his critics suggested that Ziya Pasha's scandalous work served as a bookend to the tradition, that Ziya Pasha's work at large did not open up new horizons and venues of action, but merely created an impasse. *Harabat*'s path to *harabat*, accordingly, was a dead end. From this point of view, *Harabat* articulates the absence of a distinctly Turkish culture and identity (as distinct from Arabic and Farsi, to say the least) in Ottoman Turkish history not merely to terrorise Ziya Pasha's comrades. Its perspective on *harabat* also makes something new out of the material in Ziya Pasha's library, of his literary cultural archive. It makes out of a lively, mystical, proverbial gathering place, which was at once a place of worship and celebration, performance and deliberation, something that comes close to a canon in the European sense, or something like a proverbial cemetery. The Ottoman-Turkish literary cultural history Ziya Pasha framed, so that Ottoman Turks might know about their ancestry, turned the mystical *harabat* and its vibrant tradition into history, thereby ruining it, while it also ruined the reformist project to elevate vernacular Turkish and the nationalist vision of a future-oriented, Turkish cultural history. This latter judgment belongs to Namık Kemal, the poet-prophet of modern Turkey and one of Ziya Pasha's closest friends, whose *Tahrib-i Harabat*, meaning the destruction of the *harabat* or the damage *Harabat* brought about, was only the beginning of the torrent of criticism Ziya Pasha would receive in the coming decades. According to this school of thought, Ziya Pasha's work was ultimately 'ruinous', his Arabic and Farsi threatening to make out of the Turks mere bastards, helpless drunkards with no wisdom whatsoever.[11]

Yet "there is only *Harabat*," writes Fikret defending Ziya Pasha, "and non-other [*sic*] than *Harabat*"—that *Harabat* ruined nothing but remained, even almost three decades after its publication, the only edifice, the only anthology worthy of the name (Fikret 1898, 67). Whether one takes *Harabat* to be ruinous or regards it as an edifice that survived the test of time, it should now be clear that by all accounts *Harabat* marks a crucial moment of an extremely difficult, painstaking decision—a moment that lasted over half a century, no less. This is because, from the point of view of Ahmet Hamdi Tanpınar, *Harabat* both fulfils and destroys Islamicate humanism. That is how *Harabat* makes space for the articulation of modern Turkishness. I shall explain what this slightly more complex critique of *Harabat*'s Arabic entails in the next section, titled 'The Rings'.

In the section after 'The Rings', titled 'The Arabs', we will see what the Ottoman Arabic of the sort we find in *Harabat* does to Arabic language and literature. For *Harabat* bastardises not only 'Turkish', but Arabic as well. With its peculiar canon of Arabic poetry, it takes us beyond any idea of Arabic language and literature as the language and literature of Arabs. *Harabat*'s reactionary vision of Arabic could also be interpreted as a progressive model for the study of Arabic today. As if to embarrass our

[11] Thus concurs Köprülü (1917), for instance. Also see Bilgegil (1972).

Figure 2: Tahrib-I Harabat title page

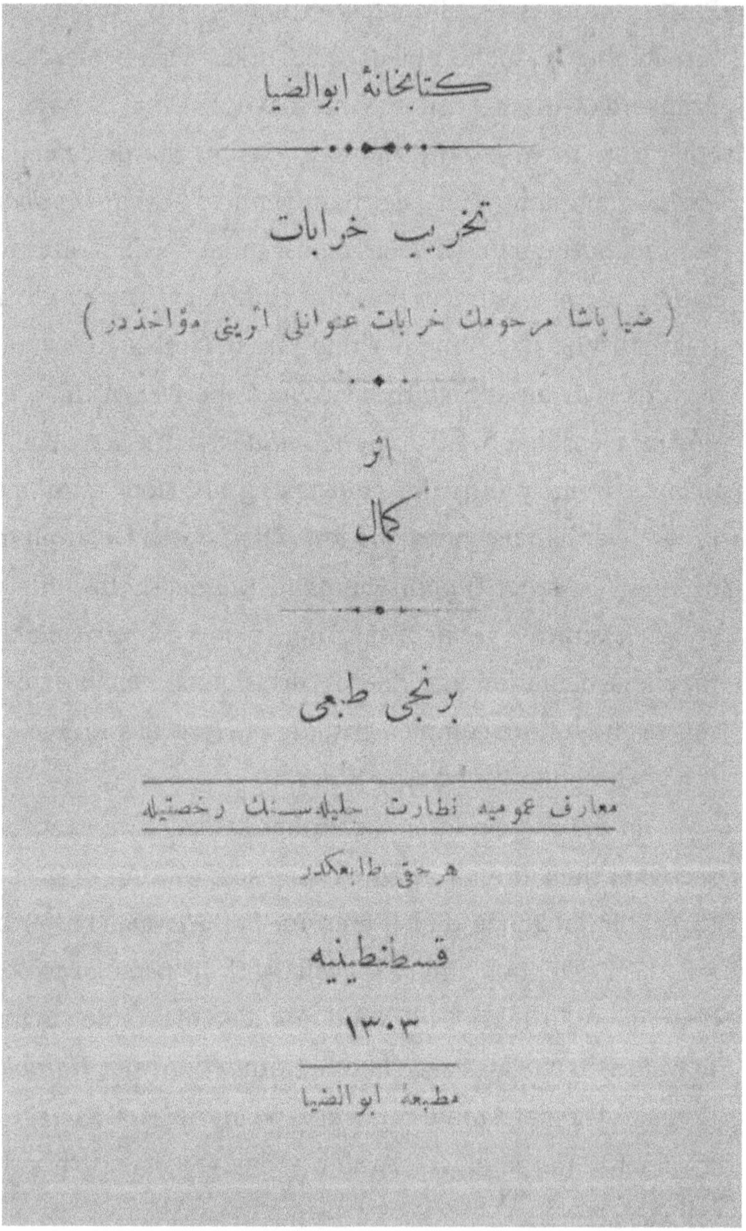

كتابخانهٔ ابوالضيا

تخريب خرابات

(ضيا پاشا مرحومڭ خرابات عنوانلى اثرينى مؤاخذه‌در)

اثر

كمال

برنجى طبع

معارف عموميه نظارت جليله‌سنڭ رخصتيله

هر حقى طابعكدر

قسطنطنيه

١٣٠٣

مطبعهٔ ابوالضيا

contemporary departments of Arabic in the US and elsewhere, Ziya Pasha's Arabic language and literature are Ottoman and Turkish, African, South Asian, and European all at once: it is 'global Arabic'.

2.0. The Rings

Young Ottomans Namık Kemal and Ziya Pasha, despite their revolutionary thirst, managed to cling to tradition, thus also to appear reactionary at times, thanks to their belief that the modern Western values and ideals they so admired had already been announced by Islam in its golden age. Modern democracy, for instance, was essentially the fulfilment of Islamic principles of faith for them.[12] The Qurʾān was the source of the law before which all persons were already equal, which conviction they could not stop explaining over and over again by turning to the Book and the *hadith*. To this end they developed a new critical vocabulary and political concepts as based on the sources of *sharia*. Through *biat* (the 'election' of the caliph by the community of Muslims) they argued for the parliamentarianism of Islam, or through *meshveret* for the Islamic sources of a politics of consensus and so on and so forth (Mardin 1962; Çiçek 2010).

[12] Ottoman Turkish intellectuals—from the drafters of the Tanzimat declaration (1839), which announced the first major reforms towards modernity and secularisation, to Young Ottomans and revolutionary Young Turks—often emphasised the continuities between modernity and Turkish or Islamicate pre-modernity. Historians of the late Ottoman era often find such rhetoric disingenuous, and the piety involved in it as rather opportunistic or pretentious.

Tanpınar's response to his predecessors' simultaneously revolutionary and reactionary, somewhat Eurocentric, yet equally Islamist mindset suggests that to have access to that mental theatre, one must be ready to rethink the fundamental concepts of the critique, beginning with history, historiography, tradition, and progress, and all these as they relate to the future and the past. Tanpınar does not agree with Ziya Pasha or Namık Kemal, yet he affords them the benefit of the doubt, and knows how to learn from them, too. This article is an attempt to learn from Tanpınar and Ziya Pasha in the same spirit.

Like Ziya Pasha, whom he regards as the "prototypical intellectual of the Tanzimat era," Tanpınar (2006, 19) thought that Ottoman Turkish letters followed "Arabic and Persian letters as the last great creative ring circling our common civilisation." This observation reads like a prose translation of the lines from Ziya Pasha's Introduction to *Harabat* that I have addressed above in a different context: Arabic, Persian, and Turkish are but three seas joining together in the Ottoman tongue to make up the ocean of oceans, or the ocean of Islamicate humanism (*Harabat* 1, ix–x). There is something distinct about the Ottoman language after all, yet this distinctiveness does not sit well with the thought of a history of a distinctly Turkish identity in the modern, European sense.

This distinctiveness has to do with a potential for (or the threat of, according to Tanpınar's double-dealing) radical fluidity or 'diffuseness', in Tanpınar's vocabulary, as opposed to homogeneity and groundedness. As mentioned earlier, one must trace the theologico-political premises underlying Ziya Pasha's thought of an ocean of oceans to get a better sense of the singularity of his Ottoman mindset. This is exactly what Tanpınar did, interpreting the cultural history of the 'Muslim Orient' (*Müslüman Şark*) against the background of the millennia-long development of identity and self-expression in the West, while ascribing a crucial role to Ziya Pasha in this history.

Tanpınar did not think that Islam was born as democracy *avant la lettre*. Yet he underlines that it is almost impossible to be guilty of blasphemy in Islam so long as one practices worship and verbally attests to the One—the practice or the performative, or the performance generally, being the core of this religion of the deed as opposed to faith (Tanpınar 1969, 41). This is why Islam could effortlessly accommodate countless contrary theological views and all sorts of mysticisms, Sufisms and orthodoxies alike, for Tanpınar.

There is indeed something radically democratic about Islam in its very essence, then, according to Tanpınar: already at its birth, Islam comes with a set of "democratic principles" (Tanpınar 1969, 43). Nevertheless, this democracy arrives "before its time," says Tanpınar, as if prematurely, and involves no sanctions or enforcement mechanisms to be politically relevant in modern times. In Tanpınar's view, these principles articulate an idea of justice without legal mechanisms; moreover, they do not allow historical, or rather historiographic space in the Islamicate intellectual universe for this idea to evolve.

Since Allah, unlike God in Christianity, is absolutely devoid of any human quality, and since Islam does not accommodate original sin and unequivocally denies the Incarnation as mere idolatry, it does not offer a human tragedy of salvation or allow for a human "notion of historical intentionality" to develop (Tanpınar 2006, 43). "Tragic realism" is not a possibility in the Islamicate lifeworld, nor is a tragic (as opposed to comic) view of mundane, human reality: "in a world that is no more than the variety of transient manifestations of the same absolute being that would always return to itself," there could not be anything of tragic import (Tanpınar 2006, 39). The Muslim Oriental does not "own up to the real," earthly life, but instead denies and ignores as immaterial its pomp, glory, poverty, wealth, or inequality (Tanpınar 2006, 44). Accordingly, "in our former civilization," ideally, "human beings would never even imagine standing before their own fate… the human found its true dimensions not in relation to this mundane world, which is nothing more than shadow play… but in his grand destiny in infinity" (Tanpınar 2006, 40). Now, paradoxically, this also means that Muslims once sought to be at constant peace with their earthly destinies in indifference—such indifference is the ideal to strive for in Islam.

Islam ends up preventing the emergence of class consciousness, moreover, and thus the class structure in the Muslim Orient according to Tanpınar, which in turn disables the "struggles that have been the heart and soul of progress in the West." This overly accommodating, a little too democratic attitude disables intellectual disagreement and trivialises opposition (Tanpınar 2006, 43). It renders all oppositional politics equally relevant or irrelevant—as a result, even the alterity of the pre-Islamic world is easily subsumed into the Islamicate lifeworld.

All the knowledge of "humanity's past was ascribed to Islam" and yes, "anachronistically" if need be. Greek antiquity was embraced as part of a struggle between Islam and blasphemy, explains Tanpınar, which was resolved for good with the arrival of the Muslim peak of human history and civilisation (Tanpınar 2006, 38–39). Plato, for instance, was admired for "having defended Islam" long before Islam's arrival. The true alterity of ancient, pagan cultures and civilisations was never recognised in Islamicate cultures. Needless to say, this indifference toward *alterity*, which is at once an ideal of diffuse or fuzzy *self*, could also be interpreted as an expression of a boundless humanism.[13]

Diffuseness and disintegration mark the Islamicate idiom in a variety of ways for Tanpınar. Above all, it is what structures Muslim Oriental self-expression. For instance, the pre-modern Muslim Oriental mind, *ideally*, had hardly any investment in prosaic composition, argues Tanpınar, although there are many exceptions, of course, and many historical movements that contradict the ideal. Regardless, this horizon has implications for temporal culture generally, but also for historiography and, eventually, for the development of a historical consciousness. Islamicate civilisational trajectory resembles "running backwards in time," which is to say that, while world history evolves, and identity and self-expression mature in other parts of the world, the Islamicate lifeworld progresses in the exact opposite direction for Tanpınar (2006, 35). While Tanpınar appears to regard this Islam

[13] The 'fuzziness' of premodern, non-Western identities has been an important issue for subaltern studies. The studies of Chatterjee (1993; 1996) are among the most often quoted in this context.

as an obstacle on Muslim Oriental peoples' path to self-expression, his comparativism enables him to elaborate on the distance between two alternative horizons—generally speaking, one Western and the other Muslim Oriental—shaping different ways of being and saying, and leads him to surprising conclusions as well.

The essence of 'Muslim Oriental art' as a form of self-expression is the *beyit* (couplet), Tanpınar argues, slightly overstressing the Muslim Oriental difference: the fragmented couplet as opposed to the solid 'stanza' of European poetry. The plot-driven 'narrative' that binds statements into stories or novels, or the 'frame', visible or invisible, of the Western plastic arts, contradicts the basic premises of this aesthetics. Tanpınar argues that the second line of most couplets appears redundant, unnecessary or superficial. The saying in the first line gives a motif. The second line says almost nothing, interrupts the discourse by way of expressing a forceful submission to form. It follows the first line strictly formulaically, thereby making the overall couplet—the form—appear empty of content, transforming the words of the couplet into an embellishment of the motif introduced in the first line. One half of the couplet annuls the content promised in the other, thereby rendering the couplet primarily, or even purely style. Individual couplets resemble precious stones bearing motifs. Couplets, *ideally*, should not join together in a singular and meaningful, plot-driven work or composition, regardless of the length of the poem. This is where style meets political theology in Tanpınar's literary history.

Now, on the one hand, this ideal, Islamicate-poetic way of making things with words could not have enabled the writing of novels or histories proper because it was stuck to the intransitivity of the Muslim tongue. Tanpınar translates all this into the language of the society. After Louis Massignon, he argues that "there is no time in the Muslim Orient, but only moments" (Tanpınar 2006, 32). The sort of teleology that could enable plot-driven story-telling and narratives—history or fiction—does not sit well with this logic. Again, there are numerous exceptions to the rule, of course, and Tanpınar addresses them as well, *but critically*. "Islamicate civilization was forever bound to its golden age around which it was formed," writes Tanpınar, which is to say that its progression could not be easily reconciled with a future-oriented teleology (Tanpınar 2006, 38). There is progress here—backward as it may be, according to Tanpınar's reasoning—toward the golden age of Islam, and there are stages to this trajectory.

Let us get to the 'exceptions' to the rule or the deviations from the ideal I have been mentioning in passing, to make better sense of the stages in the development of the *idea*. Based on what we have seen, and given that the Islamicate mindset as Tanpınar has it is an obstacle on Muslim Oriental peoples' path to self-expression, one would think that every deviation from this Islamicate path would be a welcome development from Tanpınar's perspective. Obviously, it is also a simple fact that histories, historical fictions, and plot-driven narratives abound in every era of Arabic, Farsi, and Ottoman Turkish as well. Then again, in Tanpınar's mind, it is as though the Islamicate ideal affects Arabic, Farsi, and Ottoman Turkish in different ways and to different degrees, and it is in Ottoman Turkish that we come closest to the ideal, for better or for worse. It is here that Tanpınar's conclusions become slightly ambivalent.

As expressed earlier, Ottoman Turkish letters follow "Arabic and Persian letters as the last great creative ring circling our common civilization" (Tanpınar 2006, 19). Despite the peculiarities of Islamicate-poetic writing described above, "[Arabs] had embraced some sort of narrative vision," writes Tanpınar—one that enables a sort of historical consciousness in the modern, European sense (Tanpınar 2006, 19). After all, pre-Islamic Arabic poetry, the Qurʾān, and later poetry and prose in Arabic at least involve linguistic continuity that easily lends itself to the building of a library in Arabic; not in the form of an actual, national library of sorts, but as an accumulation of books that reference and build on each other, i.e., an archive of writing. Persia—the second ring circling "our common civilization"—preserves its language and the library that it had built before Islam, and thus also the ability for self-expression, because Islam finds "Iranians in a particular geography and at the end of a war that concludes decisively." Yet the ability of Persians to Islamise themselves, to heed the Quranic call and merge with the Islamicate ocean is greater than the Arabs', accordingly, in so far as Islamised Persia embraces the Arabic archive as theirs alongside their own.

Then again, it is as though in Tanpınar's mind, these previous 'rings' fail to completely Islamise those whom they encircle. It is in Ottoman Turkish that we reach the peak—or the rock bottom—of this overall civilisational track. It is as though, in the final ring—the Oriental Turkish ring—Islam becomes more of what it was meant to be from the outset, fulfilling itself, again for better or for worse in Tanpınar's double-dealing. It is with the Turk—who did *not* come to the name Turk—that the Islamicate idiom sets on its most adventurous journey. Let us see what makes this all-engulfing, final creative ring so different.

There is a radical diffuseness, fuzziness to the Muslim Turk from the outset—some sort of separation from the origin, language, self, and earthly reality as well. It is this diffuseness that seems to have always already been the ultimate Islamicate-humanist horizon in Tanpınar's mind, as we have seen, i.e., the closest proximity to the 'golden age' of Islam, which remains in the past while shaping "our *common* civilization" traversing the future (Tanpınar 2006, 19).

Unlike Persians, Turks turn Muslim as small groups of people here and there, slowly and only gradually and as they move from one region to another. Until the 15th century, Turkic peoples only "struggled to control the changing conditions of life," moreover, which is why they could not even imagine building a library—a library in the sense that I have mentioned above, as an accumulation of books referencing and building on each other to enable, over time, a language of self-expression (Tanpınar 2006, 46). Only after the 15th century does the last great creative ring circling "our common [Islamicate] civilisation" emerge.

From the 15th century on, as Muslim Turks built their library and Islamicate idiom, they had already become a little too Muslim, a little too integrated into "our common civilization," expressing themselves, but only from within the boundaries of the common civilisation. Writers of "the last great creative ring circling our common civilization," thus, while writing in Turkish, also mastered, read, and wrote in the common languages of the Muslim world to build on its common civilisational archive. They read and wrote in *elsine-i selase* and even miraculously merged these tongues in their poems. As a result, 'alien' linguistic sensitivities—the prosodic laws of Arabic and Farsi—and vocabulary came to dominate Turkish self-expression.

Ottoman Turkish poets often borrowed words from the people's mouths, from the shared tongue of the common Turkish people, to mix them up with Arabic and Farsi and to subject them to the laws of these 'alien' tongues. Their art would thereby take those people, the humble Turks, beyond the cultural, linguistic, ethnic, etc. walls they were surrounded by and have them merge with humanity at large in the ocean of "our common civilization." Such was the *social* character of the *harabati*'s craft: "The ability to express one's self with such ready-made elements, to say what one had to say in this manner, which is what our old poetry mastered, constitutes both the weakness and the astonishing attraction of the Oriental imagination" (Tanpınar 2006, 33).

At the peak of the history of this Islamicate cultural trajectory, Ottoman Turkish poetry, over-determined as it was by the influences of multiple traditions, had become so "abstract" (*mücerret*) that it was hardly communicative. Its "world of imagination" was more of a toolbox containing the imagery, figures, syntax, and vocabulary that had already become frozen over the previous centuries of our common civilisation. It was in fact more craft than art at this point (Tanpınar 2006, 31). It was precisely these conditions, though—this "abstract" and overdetermined, frozen language and its frozen world of imagery, motifs, and figures—that reduced this poetry to pure *voice.* Voice, in turn, enabled the most concrete (*muayyen*) praise of a most concrete beauty and provided us with a most concrete way of loving, too (Tanpınar 2006, 22). No made-up story, narrative, or history could produce or match such purity of voice. This voice, Tanpınar explains, was the most essential element and greatest accomplishment of Ottoman poetry—a voice that, like the Arabic call-to-prayer that one still hears in Turkey, called for a particular way of being and living-in-common, constantly transforming the lives of people by way of finding its way to the people's mouths in recitations.

Having turned into pure style and voice over many a century, the language of Muslim Oriental poetry at its Turkish peak did not and could not depict mundane reality and its imperfections. Concrete reality was denied all imperfection in this tongue: "An entire inner world is visible in this literature, with gardens of roses and tulips painted in colors distilled through thousands of different kinds of alembics, with scents of spring and amber and all the refinements of a wisdom tired of pursuing life" (Tanpınar 1969, 55). Yet it continued to *express* and *represent*, as if in an endless recitation of a prayer in a partly familiar, foreign tongue, something far bigger, more real and equally this-worldly, with a clear voice: love for the Muslim way of life, for the real and everyday life of an entire Muslim humanity. It was the very "reflection on the individual of the order of a life-in-common whose entire history was built around the One and is nothing other than the violent and passionate struggle to defeat everything that is other than the One" (Tanpınar 1969, 25). Everything moves around the One in this mental theatre (Tanpınar 1969, 25). There is only One Source that anyone and everything came from and would return to.

As the entire world turns around the One, earthly fortunes and all other accidents being immaterial under His infinite power and beauty, the human selves become one, too. What is at stake here is the making of a "common life of mankind on earth" then, and in Tanpınar's Muslim Orient, poems and books were the building blocks for this edifice (Auerbach 1953, 552). Muslim Orient "constantly pushed its given limits" to reach out beyond the self, to undo the self dialectically to this end (Tanpınar 2006, 44). The cure that the poetry of the Muslim Orient prescribed to those who could not get over the self and come to terms with the infinite power and beauty of the One, for those who got distracted by the countless stories, wealth of events, and differences in this world, was wine. This is how Tanpınar accounts for the main figures and motifs of Islamicate letters: love, separation, desire, the passion and struggle to be one with the world and the One, and—perhaps most significantly—wine. Hence the significance of *Harabat*, of its multilingualism and its ocean-like coverage of the entirety of "our common civilization," and its ambition to merge Arabic, Farsi, and Turkish together with indifference toward earthly differences.

Ottoman Turkish poems, thus, lead to the fulfillment of what Tanpınar repeatedly describes as diffuseness and disintegration, of the speaking self, of language and discourse itself, analogous to the way the *beyit*, itself an image of diffuseness, was based on the disintegration of its dual nature, and the disintegration of the overall work (Tanpınar 2006, 21, 32, 46). By the 19th century, written, poetic Turkish had hardly anything distinctly Turkish about it—it was not even called Turkish; thus, it disabled 'Turkish' self-expression in the distance between the written and living languages. This poetry, the only means of self-expression, destroyed almost everything distinctly Turkish about the Turk. It dragged the Turk closer and closer to the singular, common humanity of "our common civilization," as if to have the Turk deserve the designations that the Western imagination reserved for the simultaneously fabulous and terrible Turk of Orientalism.[14] This 'Ottoman Turkish' discursive formation required "always to speak from without one's self, even to live outside one's own self.... This type of self-denial of the speaking self, a self-denial of such persistence" is "rare" indeed (Tanpınar 2006, 28).

Here we *also* have the two sides of a "latent conflict" Tanpınar traces in his history: the living Turkish of the humble and the language of Islamicate humanism (Tanpınar 2006, 20). The former lives secretly in people's mouths and can hardly make it to the archive; the latter carries in itself the traces of its struggle against the *self* and the living tongue, thus archiving that conflict as well. Until the 19th century, Islamicate humanism is always one step ahead of the living Turkish tongue, mind, and self within the parameters of the dialectic outlined above. In the meantime,

---

[14] See Khayyat (2018) for some commentary on this Turk and references.

the gap between the living tongue and the written word, between the humble and the poet-historian, grows bigger and bigger. According to Tanpınar, in the late Ottoman era the distance between *harabat*'s poetry and the language of the humble, illiterate, simple-Turkish-speaking Anatolian multitudes had become insurmountable. It is as if Ziya Pasha's traditional poems had gradually lost their *social* character and their *voice*. Toward the middle of the century there comes a moment when, no longer able to reach out to the life-in-common or to find nourishment there, this poetry turns into a mere affront to the self and nothing more. This is the moment when *harabati* turn into wasted souls producing bastards at best, just "insulting Turkishness," as it were.

By the time *Harabat* was compiled, right at the peak of a centuries-long crescendo, Ziya Pasha and his expression of pure joy at the persistent "self-denial of the speaking self" that, paradoxically, was also the very means of self-expression of the human of his Islamicate humanism, had become inaudible. The three volumes and languages of *Harabat* were simply inaccessible precisely to the simple-Turkish-speaking multitude. His humanism had left behind the very people whom it was meant to unite and bring into the fold of "our common civilization," of Muslim humanity. Despite having reached a peak, Islamicate humanism could no longer even come close to fulfilling its task at this point. In its flight "backward in time," it had left behind an entire future, the living tongue of the living people, and consequently, the people themselves. This is to say that the figure of the 'fabulous' Turk, finding perfection in ultimate diffuseness in Ziya Pasha's

Harabat, also announces the end of the Islamicate humanism of "our common civilization," making space for the modern Turk.

3.0. The Arabs

This interpretation of *Harabat* from the point of view of Turkish modernity and as the 'fulfilment in destruction' of Islamicate humanism might remind some the readers the way in which the great Gerschom Scholem (1973) interpreted another moment in Ottoman history, but from the point of view of modern Jewish history. I have in mind Scholem's disgraced messiah, Sabbatai Sevi of Izmir. For Scholem, modern Jewish history begins with Sabbatai's conversion to Islam, which left this messiah's followers with one of the most difficult paradoxes in the history of religion. From Sabbatai on, salvation becomes a strictly this-worldly matter in Jewish thought for Scholem, Sabbatai's antinomianism being more of a tragic inevitability than mere disaster. Needless to say, Sabbatai's apostasy is not the end of Jewish history for Scholem, nor do I wish to suggest that *Harabat* is the end of the history of Islam or Turks. The point is that both Sabbatai Sevi and Ziya Pasha mark turning points in their respective cultural historical trajectories. There is no doubt that the theologico-political horizon of *Harabat* belongs to an earlier moment in Islamicate cultural histories, a moment that since the publication of *Harabat*, has become history, and in part thanks to *Harabat*.

This analogy should clarify the way in which I interpret *Harabat* here: just as Scholem had a keen eye on the ways in which Sabbatai *fulfilled* pre-modern Jewish history while destroying it, opening up a new horizon for a variety of Jewish futures, so *Harabat* is capable of guiding us today as the yardstick that it is, exposing us to a bygone horizon for a number of possible Islamicate futures. Only some of those 'futures' came to take hold of our present. This is to say that it is important to underline the potentially enabling aspects of *Harabat*'s mental theatre as we observe the way in which it serves as a bookend to a centuries-long history. This is how, in the footsteps of Tevfik Fikret, I open 'a page from *Harabat*' here.

Fikret opens a random page to prove the anthology's worth, hence the title of his essay. The page that I have reproduced here is not random like the one Fikret chose: it is a page from the table of contents of the first volume of *Harabat*. The page lists Ziya Pasha's choice of canonical Arabic *qasidahs* that are as indispensably Ottoman Turkish as the canonical *qasidahs* in Ottoman Turkish in his mind. Under the title 'el-Qasâidü'l-'Arabiyye', the page gives us a sense of the canon of Ottoman Arabic literature, which is quite different from the canon of Arabic literature we teach today in contemporary academia.

Let us start with some of Ziya Pasha's remarks, which put this page, his Ottoman Arabic canon, or his Ottoman Turkish bastardisation of the canon of Arabic poetry, into context. His verse Introduction to the anthology contains separate sections that describe the different statuses and statures of Turkish, Persian, and Arab poets within the Ottoman cultural universe. The section

Figure 3: Table of contents from *Harabat*

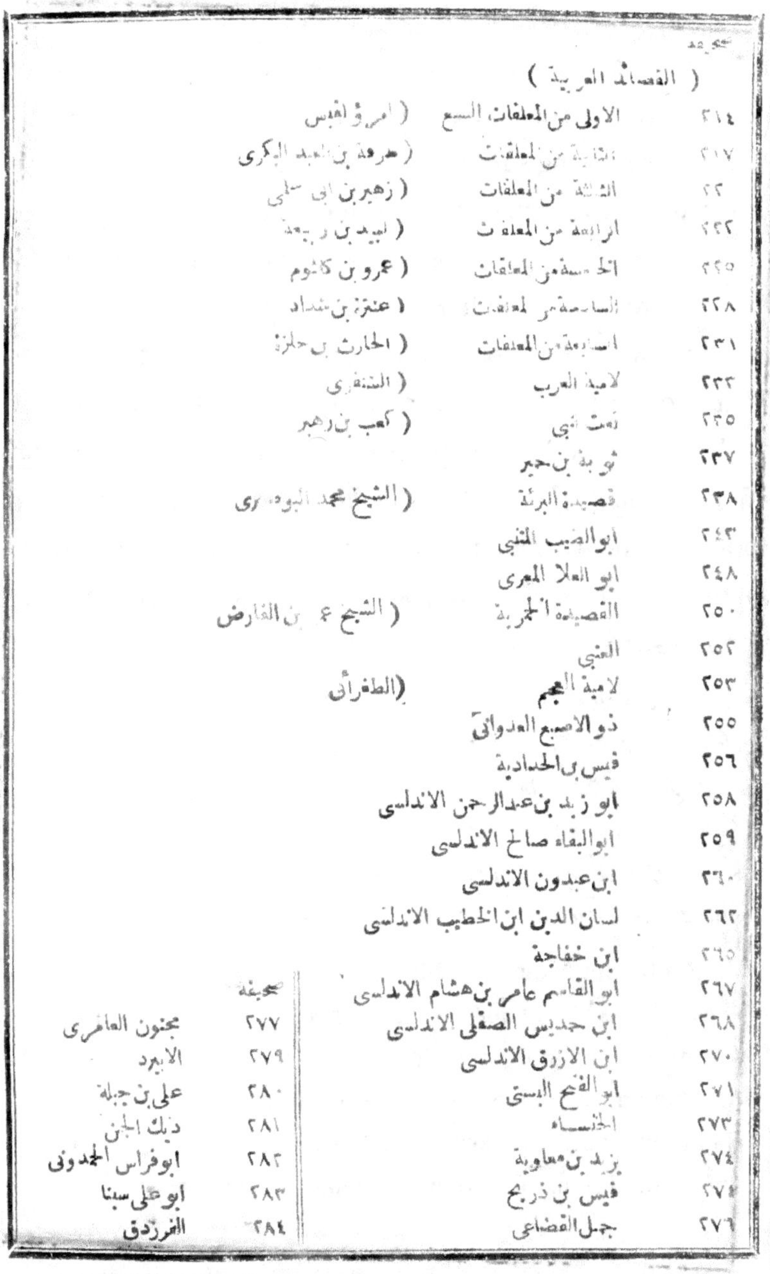

صحيفة

(القصائد العربية)

٢١٤ الاولى من المعلقات السبع (امرؤ القيس
٢١٧ الثانية من المعلقات (طرفة بن العبد البكرى
٢٢ الثالثة من المعلقات (زهير بن ابى سلمى
٢٢٢ الرابعة من المعلقات (لبيد بن ربيعة
٢٢٥ الخامسة من المعلقات (عمرو بن كلثوم
٢٢٨ السادسة من المعلقات (عنترة بن شداد
٢٣١ السابعة من المعلقات (الحارث بن حلزة
٢٣٣ لامية العرب (الشنفرى
٢٣٥ نعت النبي (كعب بن زهير
٢٣٧ ثوبة بن حمير
٢٣٨ قصيدة البردة (الشيخ محمد البوصيرى
٢٤٣ ابو الطيب المتنبي
٢٤٨ ابو العلا المعرى
٢٥٠ القصيدة الخمرية (الشيخ عمر بن الفارض
٢٥٢ العتبي
٢٥٣ لامية العجم (الطغرائي
٢٥٥ ذو الاصبع العدوانى
٢٥٦ قيس بن الحدادية
٢٥٨ ابو زيد بن عبد الرحمن الاندلسى
٢٥٩ ابو البقاء صالح الاندلسى
٢٦٠ ابن عبدون الاندلسى
٢٦٢ لسان الدين ابن الخطيب الاندلسى
٢٦٥ ابن خفاجة
٢٦٧ ابو القاسم عامر بن هشام الاندلسى
٢٦٨ ابن حمديس الصقلى الاندلسى
٢٧٠ ابن الازرق الاندلسى
٢٧١ ابو الفتح البستى
٢٧٣ الخنساء
٢٧٤ يزيد بن معاوية
٢٧٥ قيس بن ذريح
٢٧٦ جميل القضاعى

صحيفة
٢٧٧ مجنون العامرى
٢٧٩ الابيرد
٢٨٠ على بن جبلة
٢٨١ ديك الجن
٢٨٢ ابو فراس الحمدونى
٢٨٣ ابو على سينا
٢٨٤ الفرزدق

titled 'Ahval-ı Şuara-yı Arab' determines three eras for Arabic poetry: primal, middle (or mediocre), and recent. Alternatively: pre-Islamic, Islamic, and contemporary. Pre-Islamic Arabic poetry is that of al-Rāwiya's seven poets, the *Muʿallaqat*, or the suspended odes. There is nothing surprising here, of course. What is surprising is the way Ziya Pasha perceives these poets.

Given my description of the political theology that found its penultimate expression in *Harabat*, one might assume that our pasha's 'reactionary' outlook would lead him to look down on the *Muʿallaqat* or perhaps attempt to Islamise—or why not, even exclude the pagan Arab poets from his anthology altogether. Not only does *Harabat* embrace the *Muʿallaqat* wholeheartedly, it also appropriates them, making the quintessentially Arabic seven odes Ottoman Turks' very own, while Ziya Pasha just cannot sing enough praises for them:

Hakka ki Muallât-ı Seb'a
Hayret virir âşinâ-yı taba
Anlarda hakâyık-ı belagat
Anlarda menâbi-i fesahat
Kuran eğer etmeseydi iskât
Bunlar idi eblâğ-ı makâlât

Truthfully the seven suspended
Are a source of wonder for the learned
At times the truth of rhetoric
At others the source of eloquence in expression
Had the Qurʾān not taken them down
They would remain supreme articulation (*Harabat* 1, xxiii)

Then comes the Qurʾān. The miraculous Book, or the miracle of the Qurʾān, brings about nothing less than destruction to the poets of the old, to those great men who, along with their *Muʿallaqat,* lose their lustre vis-à-vis the penultimate Poem:

> *Mahv etdi anı Kitab-i Muciz*
> *Zâil oldı güneşle yıldız*
>
> The miraculous book destroyed their moment
> The sun and the stars then expired (*Harabat* 1, xxiii)

This is because the beauty and originality of the Book's poetry, according to the doctrine of *iʿjaz al-Qurʾān,* or 'the inimitability of the Qurʾān' are bound to remain unmatched forever.[15] After all creaturely talent is no match to the power of God:

> *Kur'an ne aceb olursa faik*
> *Mahlûka şebih olur mu Hâlık*
>
> The superiority of the Qurʾān can only be a wonder
> How could the mortal match up to the Creator (*Harabat* 1, xxiii)

It is not only the Almighty's power that is the issue here. Once the Qurʾān takes the stage, the Book elevates Arabic to its ultimate peak—and this peak, or the beauty of Quranic Arabic, does not belong exclusively to some crafty loquacious men and women of good fortune and stature. That language and that poetry belong to anyone and everyone.

On the one hand, from then on Arabic is 'level' or 'smooth', as opposed to oscillating between the great performances of one

[15] For a general introduction to the topic, see Martin (2019). For an elaborate introduction, see Larkin (1998), and Rahman (1996).

great orator or another and the Arabic of the simple, illiterate folk. On the other hand, from the Qurʾān on, anyone and everyone is a poet.

What Muslims celebrate every *laylat al qadr* is not only the power of God Almighty.[16] Every year Muslims remember and celebrate 'the night of empowerment', or the night when the revelation began in the depths of a cave, as the illiterate Prophet miraculously learned to read/recite the penultimate Poem to share it with humanity as a whole, including the illiterate majority or the simple folk. The ultimate 'message' of the Qurʾān, then, is that we can all be poets—that the Qurʾān gives us voice:

Ol rütbe Arab lisânı emles
Ez-tab ile şâir anda herkes

At this stage the Arab tongue goes smooth
With its lustre turns everyone a poet (*Harabat* 1, xxiii)

Thus, with the Quranic (and literary-humanistic) revolution, Arabic becomes radically democratised, as it were. Ziya Pasha's way of building a hierarchy between different stages of Arabic poetry proves his indebtedness to this very traditional, yet hardly ever discussed, aspect of the Muslim Mind and the literary politics of the Qurʾān.

For Ziya Pasha does not just appropriate the pre-Quranic Arabic *Muʿallaqat*, but goes so far as to take the logic of the Quranic revolution to its radical conclusions when he continues to draw a rigorous hierarchy in his interpretation of *Islamicate* Arabic poetry.

[16] For a general introduction see Marcotte (2018).

He does not feel obliged to hold in high regard Arabic poetry drafted by Muslims in his evaluation out of religious concerns, but rather prioritises the idea of poetry as it took shape with the Qurʾān, or the very politics of literature, as it were, of the inimitable Qurʾān. For instance, right after the miracle of the Quranic revolution, things go south in Arabic. The middle, or Islamicate Arabic poetry in Ziya Pasha's periodisation is also flat out mediocre in comparison to pre-Islamic Arabic poetry, and it starts with the coming to power of Umayyads:

Andan sonra gelen kabile
Başlar Emeviyye devletiyle
Ancak zâil olup bedâvet
Yokdur bu takımda eski lezzet

The tribes that come after
Start with the Umayyad State
Yet with the end of the *badawi* ways
This new folk no longer please (*Harabat* 1, xxiv)

Here the problem is that a dynasty gets established in Damascus, betraying the political-theological horizon and the literary politics of the Qurʾān. This ends up damaging Arabs morally, equates the Islamicate idea of freedom to bondage, and transforms Arabic poetry into mere worship or praise of power:

Çün Şam'da saltanat kuruldu
Ahlak-ı Arab da fasid oldu
Mecidd oldu redâ ete muhavvel
Hürriyet esarete mübeddel
Bünyân-ı duruğ olub müesses
Medh-i ümerâya düşdü herkes

For a dynasty was founded in Damascus

And left Arabs morally damaged
Evil replaced sublimity
Freedom became slavery
A wall of lies was erected
All began to merely praise the powers that be (*Harabat* 1, xxiv)

Moreover, Muslim conquests mix Arabs with non-Arabs, which renders 'secular' Arabic less poetic, a little too levelled perhaps, even if out of necessity. Arabs become one with the اعجام (un-idiomatic, vulgar-tongue-speaking) and the power of Arabic poems diminish:

Icem ile oldular muhâlit
Etdi bu da kadr-i şiiri sakıt

They mixed with the vulgar ones
And this diminished the power of poems (*Harabat* 1, xxiv)

Yet this state of affairs translates into the empowerment of Farsi poems, the two seas of Arabic and Farsi joining together to open a new chapter in the history of Islamicate humanism. Moreover, while Farsi becomes empowered thanks to its encounter with Arabic, this does not mean that Farsi becomes the exclusive literary language of the new era: Iranian poets drafting their verse in Arabic take the stage at this point, Iranians inheriting the glorious literary Arabic past and returning Arabic its poetic lustre.

As we have seen in the previous section, this second ring of Islamicate humanism would later meet its end when the Ottoman Turkish ring comes to encircle both Farsi and Arabic. Ziya Pasha's canon of Arabic poetry reflects a continuity that constantly underlines this dialectic. I would like highlight some of his choices to make this point clearer.

I will not dwell on all the great Arab poets whose works we still consider part of the Arabic canon today and who also take their rightful place in this anthology, but instead underline the choices that make *Harabat* unique in its strategy. Right after the *Muʿallaqat,* Ziya Pasha's anthology gives us *Lāmiyyāt 'al-Arab* by the quasi-legendary poet of the pre-Quranic universe, namely Al-Shanfarā. Not much later, though, we find *Lāmiyyāt 'al-Ajam* by Al-Togharayi of Isfahan in *Harabat*'s canon of Arabic poetry, which was Al-Togharayi's response to Al-Shanfarā. Ziya Pasha amplifies Al-Togharayi's voice with his choice to reflect the sort of continuity he had in mind as the history of a developing Islamicate humanism.

Then comes a rather more surprising and obvious set of choices that bring us to the moment of the Europeanisation of Arabic. Out of thirty-seven poets in Ziya Pasha's Arabic canon, eight of them, which is to say almost a quarter, are from Spain: Ebû Zeyd bin 'Abdu'r-rahman al-Andalusî, Ebu'l-Beqâ Sâlih al-Andalusî, Ibn 'Abdûn al-Andalusî, Lisânu'd-dîn Ibn al-Hatîb al-Andalusî, Ibn Hafâce, Ebu'l-Qâsım 'Amir bin Hishâm al-Andalusî, Ibn Hamdîs al-Sıqıllî al-Andalusî, and finally Ibn Al-Azraq al-Andalusî.

Other choices of Ziya Pasha, for instance, to include in the canon Abd al-Salam Ibn Raghbân al-Himsî's—known as Dik al-Jinn of Homs—suggest that our Pasha did his best to cover as

Figure 4: 'Ahval-ı Şuara-yı Arab' title page

مقدمه

واردر بر صنف اهل گفتار — مقصودلری دکلدر اشعار
مولانا مثنوی بی یازمش — هم گلشنی معنوی بی یازمش
یازمش نیجه برگزیده آثار — محمود شبستری وعطار
مقصدلری بونلرك عیاندر — نظم ایله حقیقتی بیاندر
شاعر دیمك او یله اهل حاله — استاد نقیصه در کماله
بیکدن صکره کلور اواخر — برشاعر تام ایچنده نادر
دیوانلرین آراسەك سراپا — آزدر اعلاسی چوقدر ادنا
وادئ جدید آچدی صائب — بولدی نیجه نکتهٔ مناسب
نظمنده ایدر زیاده کلفت — آندن گورینور براز بطائت
ارسال مثلده مثلی یوقدر — اما بیقدجق قدرده چوقدر
مجموعهٔ محتشمده یکسر — مرثیه‌سی وار برابکی خوشتر
مدح ایتدکه مکتبی محالدر — ایلا مجنونی پك گوزلدر
وحشی ووصال اکا یقیندر — طهرانلی سلیم پك متیندر
امیدی واوحدی انیسی — ایران شعراسنك نفیسی
صادق شرف ونصیر وآذر — نوعی وجلال ایله برابر
اکثر سوزی طالب وکلیمك — اشکنجه‌سی طبع مستقیمك
شوکت بیدل بتون خیالات — ادراککی مقولهٔ محالات
چون بوایکی شاعر اولدی موجود — ایرانه بلاغت ایتدی بدرود
قاآنی کلنجه صوك زمانده — رد العجز ایلدی بیانده
اشعارده اشرف خلفدر — حقاکه بقیة السلفدر
کلمه نجب سلفدن آخر — مجلسلره گیج گلور اکابر

احوال شعرای عرب

اشعار عربده اوچ زماندر — اول اوسط دخی اواخر
اسلامدن اول اولان آثار — هنگام شباب عمر اشعار
جهل ایله برابر اول زمانلر — مردانه یازاردی نکته دانلر
حقاکه معلقات سبعه — حیرت ویرر آشنای طبعه
آنلارده حقایق بلاغت — آنلارده منابع فصاحت
قرآن اگر ایتمسیدی اسکات — بونلار ایدی ابلغ مقالات
محوایتدی آنی کتاب معجز — زائل اولدی کونشله یلدز
قرآن نجب اولورسه فائق — مخلوقه شبیه اولورمی خالق
اول رتبه عرب لسانی املس — ازطبع ایله شاعر آنده هرکس
مشهورلری ذوات سبعه — اصحاب معلقات سبعه

much ground as possible and had an almost geographic and inclusive vision as he sought to provide a genealogy of the globalised Arabic of his times. Dik al-Jinn, a contemporary of Abu Nuwas and one of the masters of Abu Tammam, is hardly studied along with these illustrious figures, but was included in *Harabat* probably because of his famously ruinous ways, his drunkenness and debauchery.

Thus, in *Harabat* step by step the glorious tongue of the miraculous Book, or Quranic Arabic, becomes globalised, as it were—not simply through Arab conquests or 'colonialism' of one sort or another, but by appropriations of Arabic by the newly Islamised masses of the world, and/or through the bastardisation of Arabic, to go back to Fikret's terms. In other words, if modern Turkish is to be analysed within the context of a broader history of vernacularisation—vernacularisation of writing, of knowledge, and of power—then *elsine-i selase* must be interpreted within the context of the vernacularisation of Arabic itself. The latter, despite being the heart and soul of Islamicate intellectual histories more generally, is hardly ever addressed seriously by critics.

Arabic may not be the only language that went through vernacularisation of this order. Perhaps one might be so creative as to lay the grounds for comparing Ottoman Arabic to medieval Latin, or the 'Middle Latin' of 'Catholic cosmopolitanism'. I was more interested in elaborating the unique character of Arabic from the point of view of the late Ottoman intellectual universe, and the very specific theologico-political context that nourished this universe. Additionally, it may be the case that the vernacularisation of Arabic as a theologico-political matter (or of Latin, for that matter) does not sit well with, or cannot even have a place in, our modern historical narratives of vernacularisation and the democratisation of language. This is the reason why I welcome Fikret's vision and prefer the term 'bastardisation'.

Let me be clear that the bastardisation in question is no mere metaphor here: *Harabat*'s Arabic contains many errors and typos, some of which could be considered ruinous mistakes in a dissertation on Arabic poetry today. For instance, *Harabat* has the name of one of the greatest figures of classical Arabic poetry, namely Abu Firas al-Hamdani's name in this table of contents as ابو فراس الحمدوني or al-Hamdouni. Then again, with respect to the liberties and limitations that Ottoman Turkish appropriation of Arabic reflect within the overall context of Islamicate humanism, this is hardly surprising—suffice it to say that one of the most popular names in modern Turkish is Mehmet, and Turkish armies are known to consist of *mehmetçiks* or 'little Mehmets', from the prophet's name, محمد.

There is no doubt that *Harabat* was an imperialist, Ottomanist and also 'Islamist'—and 'Sunni'—although this is beyond the scope here. It reflects a certain degree of bias and bigotry, no doubt, especially when it is considered an anthology of Islamicate or even pan-Ottoman poetry and literature, and given what it lays claim to and appropriates and what it excludes. It merely reflects the ruling Muslim Ottoman Turks' self-perception at a crucial moment in the history of the Ottoman Empire. With its emphasis on the Islamicate pasts, and the insistence on the place of Ottoman

Turks in Islamicate history, *Harabat* is at the same time an Islamicate-humanist response to the burgeoning Turkish nationalism.

When *Harabat* was published, the ideal of a pure Turkish vernacular was still in the process of taking shape in the minds of revolutionaries and reformists, among whom we must count Ziya Pasha himself, as I have explained. The pure Turkish vernacular was not a reality yet, but at best a *literary*-political ideal. For no one wrote or spoke that pure vernacular. Arabic never became one with Farsi and Turkish in that ideal Ottoman Turkish tongue, or rather in *elsine-i selase* as the native-Ottoman tri-language. No one wrote or spoke that language either, and therefore, it, too, was a literary-political ideal. Both vernacular Turkish and *elsine-i selase* as the native-Ottoman tri-language were ideals, then—and they nourished two conflicting ideologies.

Clearly *Harabat* presents Ottoman culture and literature as the peak of Islamicate civilisation, and in that there is a degree of Ottoman Turkish pride and nationalism. This said, it is the paradoxical—most productively paradoxical—nature of this bias and pride that I find more interesting, and more instructive as well, with respect to the study of Islamicate pasts. Let me summarise this paradoxical condition once again.

In the mental theatre of *Harabat*, Ottoman-Turks stand right on top of the peak of the history of Islam. They are the perfect Muslims right at the end of that history, but *only in so far as* they are the most selfless, *only in so far as* their 'identity' and distinctiveness amount to the penultimate *self-denial* that fulfils the Islamicate-humanist ideals within the parameters I have outlined above with Tanpınar's help. In other words, what we have here is *also* a politics of 'anti-identitarianism' that necessitate religiously systematic acts of self-denial—acts of literature no less—in favour of a common Muslim humanity. "This type of self-denial of the speaking self, a self-denial of such persistence" *is* "rare" (Tanpınar 2006, 28).

This is also what *Harabat* reflects with its Arabic canon. Paradoxically, then, the degree to which the Ottoman Turks could distance themselves from everything that made them a unique and distinct collectivity, the readiness with which they embraced Arabic and Farsi as their own at the expense of a unique culture, language, and identity, and the fanaticism with which they embraced the Islamicate-humanist ideals to develop a language and literature that over time would become completely self-destructive, make them unique and distinct and place them right on the peak of this civilisational track.

How inclusive this 'self-denial' was or could have been is another question—suffice it remember, though, that in the context of Ottoman Arabic, the appropriation of pre-Quranic Arabic and the pagan *Muʿallaqat*, notwithstanding recognition of their alterity, displays at least an attempt to take the logic of self-denial in question to another level and move toward embracing non-Muslim antiquity in the name of an Islamist politics. This Islamism beyond Islam, which is in no way modern or unique to Ottoman Turkish outlook, was perhaps on the path toward an even more inclusive humanism within the history of Islamicate civilisation.

For the Islamist-humanist readiness to embrace the other's language and words as one's own did require Ziya Pasha to take other steps in that regard. The ambition to always look beyond and eventually overcome the self, having paved the way to what Tanpınar describes as Ottoman Turkish 'self-denial', additionally requires learning European languages *in the present* for our pasha:

İster isen anlamak cihanı
Öğrenmeli Avrupa lisânı
Etmiş orada fünün terakki
Tahsilden eyleme tevakki
Bilmek gerek andaki funünu
Terk eyle taassub-u cününu
Ansız kişi tâm şâir olmaz
Bir kimse lisânla kâfir olmaz

If you wish to comprehend the world
You must learn European tongues
Science has progressed there
Never fear its study
You must know the science of the present
You must avoid fanaticism and bigotry
Without the present there is no poetry proper
Learning a tongue is no apostasy (*Harabat* 1, xi)

But let us go back to *Harabat*'s Ottoman-Arabic canon. With the 'Ottoman Turkish' *Muʿallaqat,* we observe an exemplary moment in the history of Islamicate humanism. In conclusion, I contend that Ziya Pasha's canon of Arabic poetry as a whole is another extraordinary achievement that perfectly articulates the basic premises of what I am tempted to call 'literary-political Islam'. This literary-political Islam, with its 'reactionary' vision of Arabic, could also be a progressive model for the future of the study of Arabic today—as 'global' Arabic.

References

Ahmed, Shahab. 2016. *What Is Islam? The Importance of Being Islamic*. Princeton, NJ: Princeton University Press.

Akçura, Yusuf. 1981. *Tanzimat Edebiyatında Türkçülük İzleri: Şinasi ve Ziya Paşa*. Ankara: KB.

Arslan, Ceyhun. 2017. 'Canons as Reservoirs: The Ottoman Ocean in Ziya Pasha's *Harabat* and Reframing the History of Comparative Literature'. *Comparative Literature Studies* 54 (1): 731–48.

Auerbach, Erich. 1953. *Mimesis: The Representation of Reality in Western Literature*. Translated by Willard R. Trask. Princeton, NJ: Princeton University Press.

Bilgegil, Kaya. 1972. *Harabat Karşısında Namık Kemal*. Istanbul: Irfan.

Chatterjee, Partha. 1993. *The Nation and Its Fragments: Colonial and Postcolonial Histories*. Princeton, NJ: Princeton University Press.

———. 1996. 'The Manifold Uses of Jati'. In *Region, Religion, Caste, Gender and Culture in Contemporary India*, vol. 3, edited by T. V. Satyamurthy, 281–92. Delhi: Oxford University Press.

Çiçek, Nazan. 2010. *The Young Ottomans: Turkish Critics of the Eastern Question in the Late Nineteenth Century*. New York and London: Tauris.

Dabashi, Hamid. 2013. *Being a Muslim in the World*. London: Palgrave Macmillan.

Kaplan, Mehmet.1948. *Namık Kemal, Hayatı ve Eserleri*. Istanbul: İstanbul Üniversitesi Edebiyat Fakültesi Yayinlari.

Khayyat, Efe. 2018. *Istanbul 1940 and Global Modernity*. London: Rowman & Littlefield.

Köprülü, Fuad. 1917. 'Harabat'. *Yeni Mecmua* 10: 186–88.

Larkin, Margaret. 1998. 'The Inimitability of the Qur'ān: Two Perspectives'. *Religion and Literature* 20: 31–47.

Levend, Agah Sırrı. 1972. *Türk Dilinde Gelişme ve Sadeleşme Evreleri*. Ankara: TDK.

Lewis, Geoffrey. 1999. The *Turkish Language Reform: A Catastrophic Success*. Oxford: Oxford University Press.

Mardin, Serif. 2000. *The Genesis of Young Ottoman Thought*. Syracuse, NY: Syracuse University Press.

Marcotte, Roxanne D. 'Night of Power.' *Encyclopaedia of the Qur'ān*, edited by Jane Dammen McAuliffe. http://dx.doi.org/10.1163/1875-3922_q3_EQSIM_00299, consulted 19 July 2018.

Martin, Richard C. 'Inimitability'. *Encyclopaedia of the Qur'ān*, edited by Jane Dammen McAuliffe. http://dx.doi.org/10.1163/1875-3922_q3_EQCOM_00093, consulted 19 July 2018.

Pasha, Ziya. 1868. 'Şiir ve İnşa'. *Hürriyet* 11, September 7: 4–8.

———. 1291–1292 [1874–1875]. *Harabat*. 3 vols. Istanbul: Matbaa-i Âmire.

———. 1311 [1893]. *Mukaddime-i Harabat*. Istanbul: Matbaa-i Ebüzziya.

Rahman, Yusuf. 1996. 'The Miraculous Nature of Muslim Scripture: A Study of ʿAbd al-Jabbār's *Iʿjāz al-Qur'ān*'. *Islamic Studies* 35: 409–24.

Scholem, Gershom. 1973. *Sabbatai Sevi: The Mystical Messiah, 1626–1676*. London: Routledge Kegan Paul.

Tanpınar, Ahmet Hamdi. [1946] 2006. *Ondokuzuncu Asır Türk Edebiyatı*. Istanbul: YKY.

———. 1969. *Edebiyat Üzerine Makaleler*. Istanbul: MEB.

Tevfik, Ebüzziya. 1973. *Yeni Osmanlılar Tarihi*. Istanbul: Kervan.

Tevfik, Fikret. 1303 [1886]. *Tahrib-i Harabat*. Istanbul: Matbaa-i Ebüzziya.

———. 1898. 'Harabat'tan bir Sahife'. *Servet-i Fünûn* 395: 67–71.

Tevfik, Rıza. 1944. 'Harabat ve Harabati'. *Yeni Sabah* 2372, December 29: 6.

Uludağ, Süleyman. 'Hankah'. *Islam Ansiklopedisi*. http://www.islamansiklopedisi.info/?idno=160068&idno2=c160028#2, consulted 17 July 2017.

Wensinck, A. J., and Sadan, J. 'Khamr'. *Encyclopaedia of Islam, Second Edition*, ed. by P. Bearman, Th. Bianquis, C. E. Bosworth, E. van Donzel, W. P. Heinrichs. http://dx.doi.org/10.1163/1573-3912_islam_COM_0490, consulted 19 July 2018.

Yetiş, Kazım. 2007. *Dönemler ve Problemler Aynasında Türk Edebiyatı*. Istanbul: Kitabevi.

II. READER

1. BODL. MS. HEB. C. 72/18: A LETTER BY ISAAC BAYT ʿAṬṬĀN TO MOSES B. JUDAH (1480S)

Dotan Arad and Esther-Miriam Wagner

Transcription

Recto

1. בעד אל סלאם אל גליל אל חביב אל כרים אל עאלם אל שאמל ה"ר ~~יזד~~ משה בן יודה
2. נעלמך באן בעד אלדי אפתרקנה מנכום קאציינה כתיר פי אל טריק מן גהה אל
3. אל מרכב אלדי כאנת תעמל מא אכתיר ואל כאלק תעאלה פריג עלינה ווצלנה
4. פי רודוס וקעדנה פי רודוס דקס שהריין ואפתרקנה מאע ואחד אל בארכה
5. באש נמורו פי סרקוסה ומורנא למדון ונקצנה שוי כובז ונביד וגיירה נזל ר̇ צוריאל
6. ור̇ מצליח באש יאשתריו אל כובז ואל נביד נאס אל בלד ומר אל קארב ואל נאס ואל
7. יהוד אלדי כאנו מן פוק ועמרו זוג מראכב באש יאכדו אל מרכב מתענה
8. אוחניו ריינה דאלךּ אל שי קטענה אל חבל והרבנה ובקיו אל יהוד פי מדון
9. וכדאלךּ בקא ר̇ צוריאל פי מדון ואנא אל יום סרקוסה נעלמך באן יגי ענדך
10. ואחד אל נצראני קטלאני אסמו מיסר ברנארד לו אזינה נסראני גיד נרגבך באן תאקף
11. שוי מעה בפיידה מתעך ומתעה אלדי דאלך אל נצראני אסתקצה אש אנסאן פי
12. סכנדרייא אלדי הו יסוא יאקף פי מטגר וגיירה ואנא קולת לה פיהא ואחד אסמו
13. ר̇ משה והו אנסאן סמסאר ויסוא פי כל שי איצ̇ה הו יגיב מעה כמס מית
14. קטעה גבון טהור באל חותם מתענה ויגיב מעה ואחד אל כותאב מן אל דיין מתענה
15. כאן דאלךּ אל גבון הו כשר וטהור ודאלךּ אל גבון אשתראה בריאיי אנא
16. נעלמךּ באן אל ספרים אלדי ועתך באש נבעתך מא כאן לי זמן נכתובהם לך לאכן

 https://doi.org/10.11647/OBP.0208.07

17. מן דאלךּ אלדי ועת[ד] מוסרע יגיאוךּ וסלם מן גהתי כתיר לשלום ה"ר אברהם
18. תלמיד איצ̇ה לחסיד הנכבד ה"ר צדקה קונטייס איצ̇ה לנכבד ר̇ יושוע המכונה
19. נגיב וסלם מן גהתי לגמיע אל חבאב ושלום
20. מהיי לאמרך יצחק בית עטאן

Verso

1. ליד היקר הנעים הנכבד
2. הנ[ח]מד איש חמודות
3. כה"ר משה בן יודה
4. מן סרקוסה לסכנדרייא

Arabic Transcription

Recto

1. بعد السلام الجيل الحبيب الكريم العالم الشامل ה"ר יצ"ו משה בן יודה
2. نعلمك بان بعد الدي افترقنه منكوم قاصيينه كتير في الطريق من جهه ال
3. ال مركب الدي كانت تعمل ما اكتير وال خالق تعاله فريغ علينه ووصلنه
4. في رودوس وقعدنه في رودوس دقس شهرين وافترقنه ما ع واحد ال باركه
5. باش نمورو في سرقوسه ومورنا لمدون ونقصنه شوي خبز ونبيد وغييره ن̇ز̇ل ר̇ צוריאל
6. ור̇ מצליח باش ياشتريو الخبز والنبيد ناسا لبلد ومر القارب والناس وال
7. يهود الدي كانومن فوق وعمرو زوج مراكب باش ياخدو المركب متعنه
8. احنيو رييىنه دالك ال شي قطعنه ال حبل وهربنه وبقيو ال يهود في مدون
9. كددالك بقا ר̇ צוריאל في مدون وانا اليوم سرقوسه نعلمك بان يجي عندك
10. واحد النصراني اسمو ميسر برنارد لو ازينه نسراني جيد نرغبك بان تاقف
11. شوي معه بفييده متعك ومتعه الدي دالك النصراني استقصه اش انسان في
12. سكندرييا الدي هو يسوا ياقف في مطجر وغييره وانا قولت له فيها واحد اسمو
13. ר̇ משה وهو انسان سمسار ويسوا في كل شي ايضه هو يجيب معه خمس ميت
14. قطعه جبون טהור بال חותם متعنه ويجيب معه واحد ال كوتاب من ال דיין متعنه
15. كان دالك ال جبون هو כשר و טהור ودالك ال جبون اشتراه بريايي انا
16. نعلم بان السفريم الدي وعتك باش نبعتك ما كان لي زمن نكتوبهوم لك لاكن
17. من دالك الدي وعتك موسرع يجيا ك وسلم من جهتي كتير לשלום ה"ר אברהם
18. تلميد ايضه לחסיד הנכבד ה"ר צדקה קונטייס ايضه לנכבד ר̇ יושוע המכונה
19. نجيب وسلم من جهتي لجميع ال حباب ושלום

20. מهيي לאמرك יצחק בית עטאן

Verso

1. ليد היקר הנעים הנכבד
2. הנ[ח]מד איש חמודות
3. כה"ר משה בן יודה
4. من سرقوسه لسكندرييا

Translation

Recto

(1) After greetings to the dear, the beloved, the honourable, the one of comprehensive knowledge, the honourable rabbi Moses b. Judah (2) we inform you that after we separated from you, we travelled for a very long time because of the (3) ship which could not do much better, but the Creator, may he be exalted, showed us the way out and we arrived (4) in Rhodes and stayed in Rhodes *Daqas*[?] for two months. We departed with a *barca* (5) in order to go to Syracuse, and went to Modon. We were lacking bread and wine, and other (things). Rabbi Ṣuriel and (6) Rabbi Maṣliaḥ went down (from the ship) in order to buy bread and wine [from] the country people, and then the (small) boat went off (to the shore), with both the (non-Jewish) people and the (7) Jews on it. Then a pair of ships approached in order to seize our ship. (8) They revealed themselves, and (when) we saw this, we cut the hawser and fled, while the Jews remained in Modon. (9) So Ṣuriel remained in Modon and I am now in Syracuse. I inform you that (10) one of the Catalan Christians will come to you, his name is Messer Bernard Lo Azina. He is a nice Christian. I want you to

support (11) him somewhat, for your and his benefit: this Christian inquired about someone in (12) Alexandria who is (his) equal, to support (him) in the market place, and in other things. I told him: there is someone in (Alexandria), his name is (13) Rabbi Moses. He is an agent and equal (to you) in every regard. Also, he will bring with him 500 (14) pieces of kosher cheese with our seal, and he will bring with him a letter from the Dayyan (Jewish judge), (15) also (certifying) that this cheese is indeed kosher and pure. He bought this cheese under my advice. (16) I inform you that the books which I promised you to buy for you—I did not have time to write them for you, but (17) those which I promised to you—I am making haste so that they will arrive at yours (soon). Relay from me many greetings to Rabbi Abraham (18) Talmid, and also to the honourable ḥasid Ṣedaqah Contias (?), and also to the honourable Joshua known as (19) Najīb, and greet for me all the loved ones. And *shalom*. (20) Ready for your command, Isaac Bayt ʿAṭṭān.

Verso

(1) for the beloved, the pleasant, the honourable (2) the lovely, you man greatly beloved[1] (3) the honourable Rabbi Moses b. Judah (4) from Syracuse to Alexandria.

Commentary

In some Judaeo-Arabic letters from the 15th century we start to see features that later regularly occur in Judaeo-Arabic Ottoman letters, such as *plene* spelling of short vowels; the shortening of

[1] Dan. 10.11.

long final [a] and subsequent spelling with ה; reflections of the raising of [a] vowels and other dialectal vocalisms; *tafḵīm* (velarisation) and *tarqīq* (de-velarisation) of consonants; non-standard personal pronouns and suffixes; the common occurrence of *bi*-imperfect forms and inclusion of vernacular vocabulary.

Recto

Line 2

אפתרקנה 'we separated'. Classical Arabic long final *ā* is spelled with ה throughout the letter.

Line 4

'Daqas' (דקס). The meaning of this word is not clear, but it appears here to be the name of a locality.

'barca'. A kind of a small boat (in Spanish and Italian).

Line 5

באש. The word *baš* is used throughout this letter as the connective 'so that', which points to the Moroccan background of the writer; see Wagner (2014, 148–49).

Line 6

יאשתריו 'they buy' probably reflects dialectal North African morphology of III-*y* verbs, according to which the final radical is treated like a strong consonant. See also ובקיו 'they stayed' in line 8.

Line 10

Tarqīq of [ṣ] in נסראני 'Christian', although earlier in the line it is spelled in its CA form.

Line 11

אש אנסאן reflects the North African form *ash*, for CA *aysh*.

Line 12

Tafḵīm of [t] in מטגר 'market place'.

2. THE PURIM SCROLL OF THE CAIRENE JEWISH COMMUNITY

Benjamin Hary

The Purim Scroll of the Cairene Jewish Community (*megillat pūrīm il-miṣriyyīn*) was probably composed by the spiritual leader of the Jewish community in Cairo, Rabbi Samuel (or Solomon) Sidilio. The Scroll records events following the deliverance of the Jews from the tyrannical rule of Ahmad Pasha, self-appointed governor in Ottoman Egypt in 1524. The community established the 27th of Adar as a day of fasting and the 28th of Adar as a festive holiday to be celebrated after the manner of Purim. On that day the Scroll was read in the local synagogues. There are two versions of the Scroll among the Cairene Jewish community. One is more detailed, mentions names of people and places, and exists in both Hebrew and Egyptian Judaeo-Arabic. The other is shorter, more general, and has survived only in Hebrew. Both versions are critically edited using several manuscripts, translated, and linguistically analysed in Hary (1992).

Transcription

Adler, Folio 4b

11. ופ̇י ד̇לך̇ אל יום

12. וקת טלוע אחמד באשה לל קלעה

 https://doi.org/10.11647/OBP.0208.08

13. גׄעלוה סולטאן עליהום ונאדו פׄי
14. גׄמיע רחבאת מצר עמל אחמד
15. באשה סולטאן עלא מצר ועלא גׄמיע
16. קראהא. ולמא עמל סולטאן
17. גׄדד אל טׄולם עלא אל נאס אלדׄי

Adler, Folio 5a

1. פׄי מצר וטלב יסלב
2. ארואחהום. ופׄי כול מדינה
3. ומדינה וכול בלד ובלד
4. מחל אן סמעו אן אחמד באשה
5. עוצׄי עלא אל מלךׄ סולימאן
6. עוציו הום איצׄא אהל אל
7. אריאף מעהו. ולמא סמעו
8. אל יאוד אן אחמד באשה עוצׄי
9. עלא אל סולטאן סלימאן ואנהו
10. עמל סולטאן פׄי מצר
11. פׄחוזנו חוזנן שדידן ועטׄים
12. גׄדא. וכׄאפׄו כׄופׄן עטׄים
13. ושקו אל אתואב לל גׄאיה
14. ואיצׄא גׄמיע אהל אל מדינה כׄאפׄו
15. כׄופׄן עטׄים. ושקו תיאבהום
16. כבירהום וצגׄירהום. וחוזנו אהל
17. אל בלד ואכׄתזו גׄמיע סוכאנהא

Arabic Transcription

Adler, Folio 4b

11. وفي ذلك ال يوم
12. وقت طلوع احمد باشه لل قلعه
13. جعلوه سولطان عليهوم ونادو في
14. جميع رحبات مصر عمل احمد
15. باشه سولطان علا مصر وعلا جميع

16. قراها. ولما عمل سولطان
17. جدد ال ظولم علا ال ناس الذي

Adler, Folio 5a

1. في مصر وطلب يسلب
2. ارواحهوم. وفي كول مدينه
3. ومدينه وكول بلد وبلد
4. محل ان سمعو ان احمد باشه
5. عوصي علا ال ملك سوليمان
6. عوصيو هوم أيضا اهل ال
7. ارياف معهو. ولما سمعو
8. ال ياود ان احمد باشه عوصي
9. علا ال سولطان سليمان وانهو
10. عمل سولطان في مصر
11. فحوزنو حوزنا شديدن وعظيم
12. جدا. وخافو خوفن عظيم
13. وشقو ال اتوا ب لل غايه
14. وأيضا جميع اهل ال مدينه خافو
15. خوفن غظيم. وشقو تيابهوم
16. كبيرهوم وصغيرهوم وحوزنواهل
17. ال بلد واختزو جميع سوكانها

Translation

(4b) On that day when Ahmad Pasha went up to the Citadel, they appointed him Sultan and (subsequently) people proclaimed in all the squares of Cairo that Ahmad Pasha had become the Sultan of Egypt and all of its towns. When (Ahmad) became the Sultan, he renewed the oppression over the people in Cairo, (5a) seeking to rob them of their wealth. In every district and town, whenever it was heard that Ahmad Pasha had rebelled against King Suleiman, the people of the countryside also rebelled with him. When the Jews heard that the Pasha had rebelled against Sultan Suleiman and that he had become the Sultan in Egypt, they grieved tremendously, became very fearful, and tore their clothes into pieces.[1] Furthermore, all the residents of the city became anxious, too, and both the young as well as the old tore their clothes. The townspeople became sorrowful and all of its dwellers became humiliated.

Commentary

Folio 4b

Line 11

אל יום. The separation of the definite article from its following noun and its manifestation as a separate written morpheme is common in Late Judaeo-Arabic (Khan 1991, 225; Hary 2009, 110–11).

Line 12

טלוע /ṭuluʿ/ reflects the preference in Egyptian Judaeo-Arabic for the vowel /u/ (Rosenbuam 2002, 37; Hary 2017, 16–17, 20–21) and the pattern /fuʿul/, which is widespread in Egyptian Judaeo-Arabic (equivalent to standard Egyptian Arabic /fiʿil/; Hary 2009, 117–18). For the pattern /fuʿul/ see also עוצי (line 5); עוצין (line 6); חוזנו (lines 11, 16).

Line 13

[1] Literally: 'they tore their clothes very much'. As is well known, the tearing of clothes is a sign of mourning in the Jewish tradition.

סולטאן reflects the (almost) obligatory spelling of short /u/ with a *waw* in the Hebraised orthography in Late Egyptian Judaeo-Arabic (Hary 2017, 16–17).

Line 15

עלא reflects the Hebraised orthography (Hary 1996) where the *ʾalif maqṣūra bi-ṣūrati l-yāʾ* is not spelled with a *yod* (as is more common in the Arabicised orthography in Classical Judaeo-Arabic); rather it is spelled with an *ʾalef* here, perhaps due to Aramaic influence (Hary 1992, 252–53).

Line 17

אלדׄי reflects the frozen form of the relative pronoun in Late Judaeo-Arabic (Hary 1992, 308).

Folio 5a

Line 8

אל יאוד reflects scribes' avoidance of the combination יהו for its perceived sacred significance (Blanc 1985, 306; Hary 1992, 90, 270).

Line 11

חזנן שדידן and also כׄופׄן in lines 12 and 15 reflect the spelling of the *tanwīn* accusative in Late Judaeo-Arabic (when is appears in the texts) with a final *nun*, rather than final *ʾalef*, as is more common in the Arabicised orthography of Classical Judaeo-Arabic (Khan 1991; Hary 1992, 296–98).

3. APPOINTMENT DEED OF A CANTOR IN THE KARAITE COMMUNITY, CAIRO (1575)

Dotan Arad

Transcription

MS St. Petersburg, Evr. Ar. II 1378[1]

It seems that the document is torn and its end is missing. On the verso there is an appointment deed for the same cantor in Hebrew, but its wording is different.

1. למא כאן בתא'[2] נהאר אל אתנין כ"ח שהר אב יא"ל[3] סנה ה'ש'ל'ה' ליצירה חצל קאל וקיל
2. וצ'ראב וכנאק ובקי כל מן קאם יחב יתקדם אלי וטאיף אלמר' כ'ר'[4] יעקב החזן לאנה כאן חזן כביר
3. ומשרת פי כנסת בית שמחה ומלמד נו'ע'[5] והם לא אהלא' לדלך ולא ירצ'א אחד בהם ואלדי

[1] Published with Hebrew translation in Arad (2016).

[2] = בתאריך.

[3] = יהפכהו אלהים לטובה.

[4] = אלמרחום כבוד ר'.

[5] = נוחו עדן.

 https://doi.org/10.11647/OBP.0208.09

4. ביחב דלך ומתעצב ענאדה לקול אד' הנ' הג'[6] אהרן יצ"ו וכ'ר'[7] יוסף אלתוריזי יצ"ו אלדינים תם אן אלדיינים
5. אלמד' אע'[8] אשארו במא ראוה בעין אליראה ואכ'תארו ר' יהודה אלתוריזי הרופא יצ"ו יכון חזן כביר
6. לאנה נעים קול ומבין בכל ענין ואנה יכון משרת פי בית הכנסת לאנה אהלא' לדלך ואנה
7. יכדם תלת סנין בלא ג'אמכיה ואנה יסמע לקול אלדיינים אלמד' אע' ולא יכאלפהם פי אמר מן אלאמור אלדינייא
8. ואנה יקים בואג'באת כדמת בית הכנסת כמא כאנו אלמשרתים אלדי כאנו קבלה ואנה יקים
9. בואג'באת אלחזון שמחות חופות ומילות ואבילות ואנה לא יתכלף ען פעל שי מן דלך לא לכביר
10. ולא לצג'יר ואנה יתואצ'ע מע אלקהל ויתנהג עמם בטוב לב וידרוש שלום הקהל גדולם וקטנם
11. ואנה לא יתקלק[9] מן דלך ולא יקול אנא באעמל בלא ג'אמכיה מא לאחד עליא חכם ואלדי אכתאר
12. אפעלה ואלדי מא אכתארה מא אפעלה ואנה יכדם עדוה וצאחבה פי הנא ועזא וג'ירה תם אן ר'
13. יהודה אלתוריזי אחצ'רוה וסמע ג'מיע מא כתב עליה אע' תם אנה רצ'י בג'מיע מא דכר אע'
14. וקבלה עליה כמא דכר אע' טואל אלמדה אלמד' אע' תם בעד דלך חתמו אלדינים אלמשאר אליהם
15. באן לא סביל לאחד מן אלקהל בר' יה'[10] יתקדם עליה ולא יבתדלה [ל]אנה מא ביעמל דלך [אלא לשם]
16. שמים ואן לא סביל לאחד יעאנדה ול[...] [ג]מיע מא פעל וכל דל[ד] חצל ברצ'אהם

---

[6] = אדוננו הנשיא הגדול.

[7] = ישמרו צורו וגואלו. וכבוד רבי.

[8] = אלמדכורין אעלאה. See Wehr (1994, 749), مذكور اعلاه.

[9] Should probably be: יתקלקל.

[10] = ברוכים יהיו.

Arabic Transcription

1. لما كان بتا' نهار الاثنين כ"ח شهر اب יא"ל سنه ה'ש'ל'ה' ליצירה حصل قال وقيل
2. وضراب وخناق وبقى من قام يحب يتقدم الى وظايف ال المر' כ'ר' יעקוב החזן لانه كان חזן كبير
3. ומשרת פי כנסת בית שמחה ומלמד נו'ע' وهم لا اهلاً لذلك ولا يرضا احد بهم والدي
4. بيحب دلك ومتعصب عناده لقول אד' הנ' הג' אהרן יצ"ו וכ'ר' יוסף אלתוריזי יצ"ו אלדינים ثم ان الדיינים
5. المد' اع' اشارو بما راوه بعين اליראה واختارو ר' יהודה אלתוריזי הרופא יצ"ו يكون חזן كبير
6. لانه נעים קול ומבין בכל ענין وانه يكون משרת في בית הכנסת لانه اهلاً لدلك وانه
7. يخدم تلت سنين بلا جماكية وانه يسمع لقول الדיינים المد' اع' ولا يخالفهم في امر من الامور الدينينيا؟
8. وانه يقيم بواجبات خدمة בית הכנסת كما كانو الמשרתים الدي كانو قبله وانه يقيم
9. بواجبات الחזן שמחות חופות ומילות ואבילות وانه لا يتخلف عن فعل شي من دلك لا لكبير
10. ولا لصغير وانه يتواضع مع الקהל ויתנהג עמם בטוב לב וידרוש שלום הקהל גדולם וקטנם
11. وانه لا يتقلق من دلك ولا يقول انا باعمل بلا جماكية ما لاحد عليا حكم والدي اختار
12. افعله والدي ما اختاره ما افعله وانه يخدم عدوه وصاحبه في هنا وعزا وغيره ثم ان ר'
13. יהודה אלתוריזי احضروه وسمع جميع ما كتب عليه اع' ثم انه رضى بجميع ما دكر اع'
14. وقبله عليه كما دكر اع' طوال المده المد' اع' ثم بعد دلك חתמו الדינים المشار اليهم
15. بان لا سبيل لاحد من الקהל בר' יה' يتقدم عليه ولا يبتدله [ل]انه ما بيعمل دلك [אלא לשם]
16. שמים وان لا سبيل لاحد يعانده ول[...] [ج]ميع ما فعل وكل دل[ك] حصل برضاهم

Translation

With God's help (1) On the date of Monday, 28th of Av, may God turn it for the better, of the year 5335 of the creation [=1575

CE],[11] prattle[12] (2) and quarrel and dispute had happened. Everyone who wanted to be appointed to the duties of the late, the honourable R. Jacob the cantor, because he was the chief cantor (3) and a beadle in the Bet Simcha synagogue, and a [children's] teacher—may he rest in heaven—was found unsuitable for it. None of them was acceptable. He who (4) wants it stubbornly stood up against our master, our great Exilarch Aaron—may his Rock and Redeemer [= God] protect him—and against the honourable R. Joseph al-Tawrīzī—may his Rock and Redeemer protect him—the judges. Thus, the aforementioned (5) judges ordered, according to what they saw "with the eye of fear [of God]," and chose R. Judah al-Tawrīzī the physician—may his Rock and Redeemer protect him—to be a chief cantor, (6) because he has a pleasant voice and he is expert on every matter; and to be a beadle of the synagogue, because he is suitable for it. He will (7) serve 3 years without salary;[13] and should obey the aforementioned judges' orders; and he should not disobey them in any religious matter. (8) He should fulfil the duties of the synagogue's service, as the former beadles have done; and he should fulfil (9) the duties of the cantorship in weddings, circumcision

[11] According to the Rabbanite calendar, 28th of Av 5335 occurred on Thursday, 14 August 1575. The Karaite calendar was not predetermined in that period. The date of the deed could be, therefore, one of the close Mondays to the Rabbanite date (11.8.1575 or 18.7.1575) or even a month later, if the Karaites added one month to the Hebrew Calendar that year.

[12] See Wehr (1994, 933): قال وقيل / قيل وقال 'long palaver; idle talk, prattle, gossip'. See also Kazimirski (1860, 837) قيل وقال.

[13] See Kazimirski (1860, 329).

celebrations, and mourning ceremonies, and should not be negligent[14] in doing any of it, in neither large nor (10) small matters. He should behave humbly with the congregation and relate to them with good heart, and greet the congregation, their old and their young (11), and not do it lazily.[15] He should not say: "I am working without salary, nobody has a claim on me, and I will do (12) only what I choose"; and he should serve his friend as well as his enemy, in greetings and condolences and the like. Then R. (13) Judah al-Tawrīzī was brought,[16] and heard all of what is written about him above, and he agreed with all that was mentioned above (14) and accepted it for himself, according to what is mentioned above for the aforementioned period. After that, the aforementioned judges assigned (15) that it is not possible[17] for any of the congregation (members)—may they be blessed—to be appointed instead of him, nor to replace him,[18] because he is doing it only "in the name (16) of heaven" [=with pure intentions], and there is no option for any to object to him with obstinacy. And [...] everything that was done. All of that happened of their [free] will...

---

[14] See Blau (2004, 193), خلف.

[15] See Hinds and Badawi (1986, 715), اتقلق.

[16] Before the judges.

[17] See Wehr (1994, 461), سبيل; Friedman (2016, 558), כאן לה סביל.

[18] I have not found the eighth form of the root بدل in the dictionaries. This is perhaps a scribal error for what should read יתבדלה. Blau (2004, 36) attests to the existence of بدل in the eighth form, translating 'to profane', but this meaning is not appropriate here.

Commentary

Line 2

ובקי. Used as auxiliary verb; see Blau (2006, 47); Friedman (2016, 60).

Line 4

ביחב. *Bi*-imperfect 'he wants'.

4. AHARON GARISH, METSAḤ AHARON

Naḥem Ilan

A commentary on Deuteronomy, MS London Or. 10704 (Gaster Collection 930), fols. 97a–99b:

Transcription

וקולה פין (!) יש בכם איש או אשה או משפחה או שבט אשר לבבו פונה היום מעים (!) ייי ומא הו מאסך אל תורה ואל מצות, פיגַ'ב אללה עליה וימחי אסמה ויבדילו ייי לרעה ולא יואבה (!) ייי סלוח לו ומחה ייי את שמו מתחת השמים, כמא גרת הל

מעשה גרא פי ואחד ואסמה שמואל, וכאן חכם עצ'ים, וזאל פיה אלקצא ונשתמד, וצאר ערל, ועבר פי דת אל ערילים, וערף פי דת אלדי להום, וצאר אויב לישראל, וערף פי עלמהום באל זאייד, וסמו אסמו אל ערילים פולו עלא אסמהום. וחסב פי באלו אן יפני ג'מעיית ישראל בר מנן, וגזר עלא ישראל אן יפניהום ולא יכלי בר מנן להום (97ב) אתר. פראח לענד אל צולטאן אל ערילים וקאל לה: האדול אל יהוד עד[...] לנא, ופי צלאה אלדי להום, ביודעו עלינא, ובירידו לנא אל וחיש, והום אעדא אל כובאר לנא, אסמע מני ואפניהום מן אל דוניא. ואלדי ידכול לדיינא נסתבקי להום אתר, ואן ידכול לדיינא נבקיה. פג'אובו אל אל (!) צולטאן וקאל לה: באיי חוג'ה נג'י עליהום חתא נפניהום? קאל להום: אנא ענדי ארבעין סואל. אן כאן ביג'אבוני עליהום כאן כיר, ואן כאן מא ביג'אובוני עליהום, ואלא אפניהום ג'מיעהום ג'ומלת אן ואחדה.

פי דאלך אל סאעא אבעת אל צולטאן ורא אכאביר ישראל ואל חכמים, פוקפו קודאם אל צולטאן ואל דיואן ואל וזרא ואל אומרא. פוקף דאלך אל משומד אל רשע אל ערל וגזר וקאל אן יג'אוובוה (!) עלא האד אל ארבעין סואל. פמא קדרו יג'אבוה ולא עלא סואל אן ואחד.

 https://doi.org/10.11647/OBP.0208.10

פבכיו ג'מעית ישראל בכא אן שדיד, וקאלו: יא מולאנא אל סולטאן, בנטלוב מנך רחמה, ותרחמנא אנך תעטינא מוהלת ארבעין יום עלא קדר ארבעין סואל אלדי ביריד יסאלנא האדא אל רג'ול. פחט אללה סו פי קלבה אל רחמה, ואעטאהום מוהלת ארבעין יום.

פג'ו לבית (98א) הכנסת וצלו ואתחננו קודאם אללה סו וגזרו תענית פי אל צבור, ובעתו רוסלא לג'מיע אל מודן אלדי קריבין אליהום, אנהו יצומו ויתחננו קודאם אללה סו.

תם אנה ואחד מן אל רוסלא ראח וג'אב מודת עשרין יום. והו פי אל עשרין יום, ואלא צאדף רג'ול שיך וכביר ומחתרם. סאל לדאלך אל רגול וקאל לה: איש לך חאגה פי האד אל בלד? קאל לה: יא סידי, ענדך תעלם אן אל יהודים פי שודה עצ'ימה, ואכדו מוהלה מן אל סולטאן ארבעין יום, ומצ'ת מנהא עשרים יום, בקא עשרין יום אאכר, ובר מנן יקתלוהום ג'מיעוהון, אן מא ערפו דאלך אל סואלאת אלדי ביריד יסאל דאלך אל רשע לל יהוד. ג'אובו דאלך אל שיך וקאל לה: לא תכאף, אגלוס ענדי, ומא יציר לכום אלא אל כיר ואל סלאמה. פאגצבן וקעד ענדה מודת יח' יום, בקי עליה יומין מן אל עשרין. קאל דאלך אל רג'ול לל שיך: יא סידי, אטלקני חתא ארוח ואסוח פי אל דוניא, מא בקא לי צבר אני אקעוד הל יומין. קאל לה: יא ולדי, טוול רוחך וכון מסתעקד באללה סו, באנה מא ביתרוך בני ישראל ומא ביתג'לא ענהו, כ"ק לא אעזוב את ישראל, אלא הו מעהו פי כול שדה, כ"ק עמו אנכי בצרה.

אל שיך כאן ענדה (98ב) ברכה מלאנה מייה. קאל לה: קום אל יום חתא נצלי לאללה סו, ונדעיה לגמעיית ישראל אן ינצרהום עלא דאלך אל רשע. פקאמו אתניהום והום ידעו ויצלו לרב אל עאלמין בכלאץ ישראל. קאל דאלך אל שיך לדאלך אל יהודי: אשלח תיאבך חתא אנזל אנא ואיאך נעמל טבילה פי האד אל ברכה. שלח דאלך אל רג'ול תיאבו, וג'ו מלאכים אכדו אל דאלך אל תיאב ווצלוהום לחמאם מדינת אל יהוד אלדי פיהא דאלך אל גזרה. ונזלו חתא ינטבלו, וטלעו אתניהון פי דאלך אל חמאם. קאל דאלך אל רג'ול לל שיך: יא סידי, נחנא מן גאבנא להאד אל מכאן? קאל לה אל שיך: אסכות ואנצ'ור עגאייב אללה סו.

פלמא וצלו להארת (!) אל יהוד, נצ'רו אל צולאם מאסכין אל יהוד, ועמאלין ביחצ'רוהום לחצ'רת אל סולטאן. קאל להום דאלך אל שיך: אפרגו האדא אל יהוד ואנא אטלע לחצ'רת אל סולטאן ואעטיה ג'ואבאתה. פאכדו דאלך אל שיך וקדמוה לל סולטאן.

וקאל לל סולטאן ואל חאצ'רין: יג'י האד אל רגול ויסאלני. אין רדת סואלתה (!) כאן כיר, ואן כאן מא רדית סואלאתה יכון קתלי אנא פי אל אול. קאל אל סולטאן: כלאם אן (99א) מליח קולת. פאחצ'רו דאלך אל רשע, וקאל לל שיך: אנתי, יא שיך, יא נחס, אנת תקדר תרוד לי גואבאתי? קאל לה: יא רשע, אנא בקדרת אלהים אלהי ישראל סו, באקדר ארוד לך ג'ואבאתך. לאכן אנא באתכלם כלמה באגאזת אל סולטאן ואל חאצ'רין, ואנא כדאלך ענדי בעץ' סואלאת. אן מא רדתהון, יכון דמך חלאל, אני אקתלך. קאל דאלך אל רשע: נעם, והכדא יציר.

פקאם דאלך אל רשע עלא חילה וסאל אל ארבעין סואל, ורדהם דאלך אל שיך ג'מיעהום, וצאר ישראל יכלצו באל סלאמה. קאל דאלך אל שיך: יא מולאנא אל סולטאן, ואנא באריד אן ירוד סואלי. פסאלה אול סואל ותאני סואל ותאלת סואל ומא קדר יג'אווב (!) ולא ואחד. פאל חין אלתזם דאלך אל רשע אל קתל. קאם דאלך אל שיך וקאל: יא סידי, האד אל רשע, מן תורת משה רבינו ע"ה מדכור פי פרשת אתם נצבים אנה מצירה ינקלב אסמה, ותג'ו אנתו ותסמוה פולו. ונחנא כאן ענדנא אסמו שמואל. ואנצ'ור כיף אנתו אעטאכום אללה פהם, אנכון תסמוה פולו. אל פ – אם יש בכם שורש **פ**ורה ראש ולענה; ואל ואו – **ו**הבדילו ה' לרעה; ואל ל – לא יאבה ה' סלוח לו; ואל ואו אלאכראנייה – ומחה ה' את שמו מתחת השמים.

פי דאלך אל סאעא קאל אל שיך: יא סבע, אטלע וכוד נציבך. פאנשק אל חיט וטלע סבע אן כביר וקתלה, ומא כלא מנה אתר. ודאר אל סבע חתא יפתרס לל סולטאן. קאם אל סולטאן מן עלא כורסיה וקאל לל שיך: בחיאתך ובחיתאת (!) תוראתך אלדי הי אמת ויציב, כוד מני עהד, לם בקית אאדיה אל יהוד בשי אן וחיש אלא אכרמהום ואעזהום ואג'עלהום ריסא עלינא, וארפע ענהום ג'מיע אל כ'צאייר. כלצני מן האד אל סבע! פקאם קאל דאלך אל שיך לל סבע: יא סבע, מתא מא האד אל סולטאן אאדא לל יהוד, תטלע ותקתלה קתלת שניעה. וג'לס אל סולטאן עלא אל כורסי, וכלצו ישראל מן דאלך אל צרה.

ומתל מא כלצו ישראל מן יד אל רשע, כדאלך יכלצו ישראל מן כל צרה וצוקה, ויהי ייי אלהים עמנו כאשר היה עם אבותינו, אמן וכן יהי רצון.

Arabic Transcription

وقوله פין (!) יש בכם איש או אשה או משפחה או שבט אשר לבבו פונה היום מעים (!) ייי وما هو ماسك ال תורה وال מצות, فيغضب الله عليه ويمحي اسمه ויבדילו (!) ייי לרעה ולא יואבה (!) ייי סלוח לו ומחה ייי את שמו מתחת השמים, كما جرت הל

מעשה جرى في واحد واسمه שמואל, وكان حكم عظيم, وزال فيه القضاء ונשתמד, وصار ערל, وعبر في דת ال ערילים, وعرف في דת الذي لهوم, وصار אויב לישראל, وعرف في علمهوم بال زاييد, وسمو اسمو ال ערילים فولو على اسمهوم. وحسب في بالو ان يفني جمعييت ישראל בר מנן, וגזר على ישראל ان يفنيهوم ولا يخلي בר מנן لهوم (97ב) اتر. فراح لعند ال صولطان ال ערילים وقال له: هادول ال يهود عد[و؟...] لنا, وفي صلاه الدي لهوم, بيودعو علينا, وبيريدو لنا ال وحيش, وهوم اعدا ال كوبار لنا, اسمع مني وافنيهوم من ال دونيا. والدي يدخول لديينا نستبقي لهوم اتر, وان يدخول لديينا نبقيه. فجاوبو ال ال (!) صولطان وقال له: بايي حوجه نجي عليهوم حتى نفنيهوم؟ قال لهوم: انا عندي اربعين سوال. ان كان بيجابوني عليهوم كان خير, وان كان ما بيجاوبوني عليهوم, والا افنيهوم جميعهوم جوملت ان واحده.

في دالك ال ساعا ابعت ال صولطان ورا اكابير ישראל وال חכמים, فوقفو قودام ال صولطان وال ديوان وال وزرا وال اومرا. فوقف دالك ال משומד הרשע الل ערל וגזר وقال ان يجاوبوه على هاد ال اربعين سوال. فما قدرو يجابوه ولا علا سوال ان واحد.

فبكيو جمعيت ישראל بكا ان شديد, وقالو: يا مولانا ال سولطان, بنطلوب منك رحمه, وترحمنا انك تعطينا موهلت اربعين يوم على قدر اربعين سوال الدي بيريد يسالنا هادا ال رجول. فحط الله סו في قلبه ال رحمه, واعطاهوم موهلت اربعين يوم.

فجو לבית (98א) הכנסת وصلو واتحننوا قودام الله סו[1] וגזרו תענית في ال צבור, وبعتوا روسلا لجميع ال مودن الدي قريبين اليهوم, انهو يصوموا ويتحننو[2] قودام الله סו.

تم انه واحد من ال روسلا راح وجاب مودت عشرين يوم. وهو في العشرين يوم, والا صادف رجول شيخ وكبير ومحترم. سال لدالك ال رجول وقال له: ايش لك حاجه في هاد البلد؟ قال له: يا سيدي, عندك تعلم ان ال יהודים في شوده عظيمه, واخدو موهله من ال

[1] سبحانه وتعالى.

[2] This could be a case of borrowing from the Hebrew verb יתחנן.

سولطان اربعين يوم, ومضت منها עשרים يوم, بقا عشرين يوم اخر , ובר מנן يقتلوهوم جميعوهون, ان ما عرفو دالك ال سوالات الدي بيريد يسال دالك الרשע لل يهود. جاوبو دالك ال شيخ وقال له: لا تخاف, اجلوس عندي, وما يصير لكوم الا ال خير وال سلامه. فاغصبن وقعد عنده مودت יח يوم, بقى عليه يومين من العشرين. قال دالك ال رجول ل شيخ: يا سيدي, اطلقني حتى اروح واسوح في ال دونيا, ما بقا لي صبر اني اقعود هل يومين. قال له: يا ولدي, طوول روحك وكون مستعقد بالله סו, بانه ما بيتروك بني ישראל وما بيتجلا عنهو, כ"ק[3] לא אעזוב את ישראל, إلا هو معهو في كول شده, כ"ק עמו אנכי בצרה.

ال شيخ كان عنده (98ב) بِركه ملانه مييه. قال له: قوم اليوم حتى نصلي لله סו, وندعيه لجمعييت ישראל ان ينصرهوم على دالك ال רשע. فقامو اتنيهوم وهوم يدعو ويصلو لرب ال عالمين بخلاص ישראל.

قال دالك ال شيخ لدالك ال يهودي: اشلح تيابك حتى انزل انا واياك نعمل טבילה في هاد البركه. شلح دالك ال رجول تيابو, وجو מלאכים اخدو ال دالك ال تياب ووصلوهوم لحمام مدينت ال يهود الدي فيها دالك ال גזרה. ونزلو حتى ينطبلو,[4] وطلعو اتنيهون في دالك ال حمام. قال دالك ال رجول لل شيخ: يا سيدي, نحنا من جابنا لهاد ال مكان؟ قال له ال شيخ: اسكوت وانضور عجاييب الله סו.

فلما وصلو لهارت (!) ال يهود, نضرو ال صولام ماسكين ال يهود, وعمالين بيحضروهوم لحضرت ال سولطان. قال لهوم دالك ال شيخ: افرجو هادا ال يهود وانا اطلع لحضرت ال سولطان واعطيه جواباته. فاخدو دالك ال شيخ وقدموه لل سولطان.

وقال لل سولطان وال حاضرين: يجي هاد ال رجول ويسالني. اين (!) ردت سوالاته كان خير, وان كان ما رديت سوالاته يكون قتلي انا في ال اول. قال ال سولطان: كلام ان (99א) مليح قولت. فاحضرو دالك ال רשע, وقال لل شيخ: انتي, يا شيخ, يا نحس, انت تقدر ترود لي جواباتي؟ قال له: يا רשע, انا بقدرت אלהים אלהי ישראל סו, باقدر ارود لك جواباتك. لاكن انا باتكلم كلمه باجازت ال سولطان وال حاضرين, وانا كدالك عندي بعض سوالات. ان ما ردتهون, يكون دمك حلال, اني اقتلك. قال دالك الרשע: نعم, وهكدا يصير.

---

[3] كما قال.

[4] Borrowing from the Hebrew verb טבל, means dive in the water, or go under water.

فقام دالك הרשע على حيله وسال ال اربعين سوال, وردهم دالك ال شيخ جميعهوم, وصار ישראל يخلصو بال سلامه. قال دالك ال شيخ: يا مولانا ال سولطان, وانا باريد ان يرود سوالي. فساله اول سوال وتاني سوال وتالت سوال وما قدر يجاووب ولا واحد. فال حين التزم دالك הרשע ال قتل. قام دالك ال شيخ وقال: يا سيدي, هاد הרשע, من ال תורת משה רבינו ע"ה مدكور في פרשת אתם נצבים انه مصيره ينقلب اسمه, وتجو انتو وتسموه فولو. ونحنا كان عندنا اسمو שמואל. (99ב) وانضور كيف انتو اعطاكوم الله فهم, انكون تسموه فولو. ال ف (פ) — אם יש בכם שורש פורה ראש ולענה; وال واو — והבדילו ייי לרעה; وال ل (ל) — לא יאבה ייי סלוח לו; والواو ال اخرانييه — ומחה ייי את שמו מתחת השמים.

في دالك ال ساعا قال ال شيخ: يا سبع, اطلع وخود نصيبك. فانشق ال حيط وطلع سبع ان كبير وقتله, وما خلا منه اتر. ودار ال سبع حتى يفترس لل سولطان. قام ال سولطان من على كورسيه وقال لل شيخ: بحياتك وبحيتات (!) توراتك الدي هي אמת ויציב, خود مني عهد, لم بقيت اديه ال يهود بشي ان وحيش الا اكرمهوم واعزهوم واجعلهوم ريسا علينا, وارفع عنهوم جميع ال خصايير. خلصني من هاد ال سبع! فقام قال دالك ال شيخ لل سبع: يا سبع, متى ما هاد ال سولطان اادا لل يهود, تطلع وتقتله قتلت شنيعه. وجلس ال سولطان علا ال كورسي, وخلصو ישראל من دالك הצרה.

ومتل ما خلصو ישראל من يد הרשע, كدالك يخلصو ישראל من كل צרה וצוקה, ויהי ייי אלהים (!) עמנו כאשר היה עם אבותינו, אמן וכן יהי רצון.

Translation

And his saying “lest there should be among you man, or woman, or family, or tribe, whose heart turneth away this day from the Lord” (Deut. 29.17) and he does not take hold of the Torah and the commandments, then the Lord shall be angry at him and shall blot out his name, and the Lord shall separate him unto evil […] and will not be willing to pardon him […] and shall blot out his name from under heaven” (Deut. 29.19), just like:

The story of a person named Shmuel, who was a great scholar, and he converted and became a Christian, and learned their religion, and became an enemy of Israel, and he became an expert in their ideas. The Christians called him Paulo. He thought to diminish the community of Israel—May it not befall us! He decreed to destroy Israel and not leave—May it not befall us—any (97b) survivors. So he went to the gentile Sultan and told him: "These Jews are our enemies, and in their prayers they curse us, they only want evil for us, and they are our worst enemies. Listen to me and I shall destroy them from the world. Whoever choses to convert to our religion we shall keep alive." The Sultan answered him: "On what pretext are we going to destroy them?" He told him: "I have forty questions. If they answer them, so be it; and if they don't, I shall surely destroy them all at once."

At that moment the Sultan sent for the Jewish leaders and scholars, and they came before the Sultan, the Prime Minister, ministers, and princes. That evil convert stood there and decreed, and said they needed to answer those forty questions. They could not answer, not even a single question.

The community of Israel wept hard, and said: "Our master the Sultan, we ask you for mercy, please spare us and give us an extension of forty days for the forty questions this man wants to ask us." God almighty put mercy in his heart, and he gave them a forty-day extension.

They came to the (98a) synagogue, and prayed and beseeched God almighty, and decreed a communal fast, and sent messengers to all the nearby towns to fast and pray to God almighty.

One of these messengers went missing for twenty days. On the twentieth day he saw an honoured, distinguished old man. The old man asked that person: "Do you have any business in this town?" He said: "Sir, you should know that the Jews are in serious trouble, and have received a forty-day extension from the Sultan, twenty of which have already passed. Twenty days are left, and—May it not befall us—they will kill everyone, if they don't know the questions this evil man wants to ask the Jews." The old man answered him: "Don't be afraid. Sit with me, and you will have nothing but good and peace." Against his will he sat with the old man for eighteen days. With two days left out of the twenty, the man told the old man: "Sir, please let me go and I will go wander the world. I have no patience left in me to wait these two days." He told him: "My son, be patient, and believe in God almighty, who will not leave the sons of Israel and will not desert them, as it is said "I will not forsake my people Israel" (1 Kgs 6.13; altered version), but he is with them in all trouble, as it is said "I will be with him in trouble" (Ps. 91.15).

The old man had (98b) a pool full of water. He told him: "Get up today in order we will pray to God almighty, and ask him on behalf of the community of Israel, to help them with that evil man." The two of them rose, and they were calling and praying to the Lord of the World for the redemption of Israel. That old man said to that Jew: "Take off your clothes, so that you and I can get into this pool for ritual immersion." The man took his clothes off, and angels came and took the clothes, and brought the men to the bath in the town of the Jews in danger of the decree. They went down for ritual immersion, and the two immersed in that bath. The man said to the old man: "Sir, who brought us to this place?" The old man said to him: "Be quiet and see the greatness of the Lord almighty."

When they got to the Jewish neighbourhood, they saw the evil ones taking the Jews to bring them to the Sultan. The old man told them: "Let these Jews go, and I will come to the Sultan, and give him his answers." They took the old man and brought him to the Sultan.

He said to the Sultan and the others who were present: "Let this man come and ask me. If I answer his questions, good; and if I don't answer his questions, kill me first." The Sultan said: "Well (99a) spoken." They brought the evil man, who said to the old man: "You, worthless old man, you can give me my answers?!" He told him: "Ho, evil one, I—with the power of God almighty, God of Israel—can give you your answers. But I will say something, with the permission of the Sultan and those present. I also have a few questions. If you don't answer them, your blood shall be permitted, and I will kill you." The evil man said: "Yes, and so be it."

That evil rose and asked the forty questions. That old man answered him all of them, and Israel were saved in peace. The old man said: "Our master, the Sultan, I want him to answer my questions." So he asked him a first question, and second and third, and he couldn't answer a single one. He immediately was condemned to death. That old man rose and said: "Sir, that evil man is mentioned in the Torah of Moses—may he rest in peace—in the portion of *Atem Nitsavim* 'Ye stand', and that eventually his name will be changed, and you would call him Paulo, and with us his name was Shmuel. See how God has given you wisdom to call him Paulo (פולו):

פ – אם יש בכם שורש פורה ראש ולענה; **ו** – והבדילו ייי לרעה; **ל** – לא יאבה ייי סלוח לו; **ו** – ומחה ייי את שמו מתחת השמים!

P – 'lest there should be among you a root that beareth gall and wormwood' (Deut. 29.17); W – 'And the Lord shall separate him unto evil out' (v. 20); L – 'The Lord will not spare him' (v. 19); W – 'and the Lord shall blot out his name from under heaven' (v. 19).

At that moment the old man said: "Lion, go out and take your share!" The wall broke open and a big lion came out, who killed him and left no remains. The lion turned around to kill the Sultan. The Sultan rose off his throne and told the old man: "By your life and the life of your Torah, which is true, take a promise from me that I will do nothing evil to the Jews, only respect and glorify them, and make them chiefs over us, and remove all troubles from them. Save me from that lion!" The old man rose and told the lion: "Ho, Lion, when this Sultan is ill-favoured toward the Jews, come out and kill him in a shameful death." The Sultan sat on his throne and Israel were saved from that trouble.

And as Israel were saved from that evil, they shall be saved from any trouble and calamity, "and may God be with us, like he was with our fathers" (1 Kgs 8.57). Amen.

Commentary

The story brought here is unusual in two dimensions: it is the only folk story mentioned in *Metsaḥ Aharon*, and it reflects a cultural setting that was foreign to Aleppo Jewry in the early 16th century. However, it fits well with Rabbi Aharon Garish's cultural background. The commentary was based mostly on *Midrashim* and early *Agadot*, Torah commentaries (Rabbenu Ḥananel, Rabbi Avraham Ibn Ezra, Ḥizkuni, Nahmanides, Baḥya ben Asher, Rabbi Yaacov ben Asher [Baʿal Ha-Turim], the Tosafotists), Rabbi Yehoshua Ibn Shuʿayb's sermons, Maimonides (*Mishne Torah* and *The Guide for the Perplexed*), and *Arbaʿa Turim—Oraḥ Ḥayyim*. Therefore, his cultural world was a blend of the best of Europe's composition—Spain, Provence, France, and *Ashkenaz*.

The background for this story is the public polemics that took place between churchmen, particularly converts, and Jewish leaders in Spain and France, especially during the 13th–14th centuries, which was unknown to the Muslim Orient. While strange to the Aleppo lifestyle, it shows that the thrilling plot, the eventual miraculous resolution, and anchoring the story in Torah verses were enough to include it in the commentary. It is a reflection of the commentator's (or his ancestors') cultural world, a heritage passed on from generation to generation, dearly cherished.

Various considerations (literary, linguistic, stylistic, and educational) suggest that it started as an oral sermon given by

Rabbi Aharon on Shabbat Nitsavim, which later resulted in it being included in the written commentary.[5]

[5] This story is found in a shorter version in Havlin (1995, 176–177), and the arena there is Provence, probably the 12th Century. See also Ilan (1996, esp. 181–184, 207–210).

5. KITĀB HAZZ AL-QUḤŪF (1600S)[1]

Humphrey Taman Davies

Al-Shirbīnī's work, which he probably wrote in or soon after 1686, is perhaps unique in pre-20th-century Arabic literature, and unusual in any pre-20th-century scholarly literature, in focusing on the countryside as a cultural, social, economic, and religious site in its own right. The work, which is in two parts, surveys, in the first, the three estates of rural (effectively, north-eastern Egyptian Delta) society: the peasant (and above all the poor peasant) as cultivator or *fallāḥ*; the country pastor or *faqīh*; and the mendicant rural Sufi or *faqīr*. A further section analyses and mocks bad verse written by peasants and other marginal figures (e.g., a Mamluk emir of Ethiopian origin). The second part of the work analyses at length and with numerous digressions a forty-seven-line poem, supposedly written by a peasant called Abū Shādūf. The poem describes its supposed author's rise and fall, evolves into an extended lament for the delicious foods that, in his decline, the poet can only dream of eating, and ends with the poet's describing his project to restore his fortunes by going to the city and stealing slippers from outside a mosque. The book winds up with a miscellany of anecdotes, mostly about grammarians.

[1] Reprinted from Davies (ed.) (2016, I:65–78, 122–27, 129–31).

 https://doi.org/10.11647/OBP.0208.11

The thrust of the argument throughout the book is that country people are coarse (*kathīf*) and their natures cannot be changed; they contrast in all things with the city dweller, who is refined (*laṭīf*). Coarseness in this context includes physical grossness, moral turpitude, and ignorance. Of particular concern to the author are the false claims to knowledge made by 'people of the countryside'; in a number of scenes, Azhari scholars are challenged to a battle of wits by a village man of religion, the hollowness of whose learning is exposed and ridiculed by his opponents.

There is evidence that, against the conventional notion of cultural decline, literacy increased during the Ottoman period, in part because of the spread of the *kuttāb*, a school in which young children memorised the Qurʾān and achieved basic literacy and numeracy. As a result, as Nelly Hanna (1998, 102–3) writes, "many more people knew how to read and write beyond those who were attached to institutions of higher education" and literacy spread, especially among artisans and tradesmen. It is possible that the traditional gatekeepers of learning became alarmed by this process and that the author, of whose career little is known beyond his having been at some point a bookseller, was commissioned to write *Brains Confounded* to undermine claims to knowledge by the non-scholarly non-elite. According to this interpretation, then, the 'people of the countryside' are but stand-ins for the great unwashed in general, and for those who threatened the scholarly hegemony over knowledge in particular.

The comic impact of *Brains Confounded* depends on two conceits. The first is that the Ode and other verses ascribed by the author to peasants are indeed of rural origin and represent actual rural literary production. This is obviously untrue, and we assume that such verses were manufactured by al-Shirbīnī or others of his milieu to be the butt of their satire. The discovery of a short work dating to some forty years before *Brains Confounded* and containing some of the same poems satirised by al-Shirbīnī offers an intriguing hint that such writings may have been in fashion in the second half of the 17th century.

The second conceit is that such verse merits the deployment of the tools of etymological, grammatical, rhetorical, and historical analysis developed by Arab philologists for the elucidation of the fundamental texts of their culture, such as the Qurʾān and classical verse, even while the author is at pains to stress that the material that is the object of these critical attentions is innately ridiculous and unworthy of consideration as literature by virtue both of its 'rural' language and the low social status, and concomitant vices, of its creators.

Taken as a whole, al-Shirbīnī's work provides an example of Arabic comic writing at its best, its arguments at base serious, its techniques inventive, its energy never flagging. It also provides, in its multiple digressions into subjects as diverse as fleas and farting, an intriguing window into the mind, or perhaps the mental lumber room, of an educated man of the mid-Ottoman period in Egypt.

The first two excerpts are from a passage in the first part of the work entitled 'Accounts of What Happened to Peasants Who Went to the City'. They exemplify the presentation of the peasant as irredeemably gross, both physically and morally, and touch on a number of frequently recurring themes: the peasant's trip to the city (Cairo) to pay taxes to his 'master' (the local tax-farmer, usually a Mamluk), such trips inevitably leading to misadventure; Turkish as a shibboleth of the elite; and the peasants' terror of forced labor. The second set of excerpts focuses on the pretensions to knowledge of the rural *faqīh* 'country pastor', and his actual ludicrous ignorance, which render him easy prey for the 'well-instructed'.

Transcription

3.22

(وقيل طلع رجل فلّاح يورِد لأستاذه المال) فأنزله في محل فيه طاقة مفتوحة تشرف على حريم الأمير فلمّا جاء الليل قال الفلّاح في نفسه يا ترى يابو معيكه الاماره لمّا تختلي بنسوانهم كيف يفعلوا ولكن انضر كيف ما يفعل استادك مع امراته ولمّا تروح الكفر احكى لامّ معيكه تعمل لك ديك العمله متل ما تعمل الاماره وتحظك امّ معيكه بديك العمله ولا بدّ ما يرطنوا على بعضهم البعض بالتركي وانت تنضر طريقة ما يفعلوا لحريمهم وتبقى تقول للجدعان انا بقيت متل الاماره وبقت امّ معيكه متل امراة الامير استاد البلد ثمّ إنّه صبر حتى أقبل الليل ودخل الأمير إلى منزله فقام الفلّاح ونظر من الطاقة فرأى الأمير جالس على سرير من العاج وعليه أنواع الفرش وجلست زوجته على سرير متله ثمّ إنّ الأمير صار يلاطفها وينادمها برقيق الكلام تارة بالتركي وتارة بالعربي إلى أن اشتهى منها قضاء الحاجه فأخذ من جانبه وردة ورماها بها فأتت إليه وتملّى بحسنها وجمالها على أحسن حال وأتمّ سرور وحبور ومنوال ثمّ إنّه كلّ واحد منهما انضجع على سريره ونام

3.23

قال فلمّا أصبح الصباح أخذ الفلّاح خاطر أستاذه وتوجّه إلى بلده فلمّا طلع الكفر لاقته زوجته أمّ معيكه وسلّمت عليه وجلست هي وإياه في منادمة مثل منادمة القرود أو بربرة الهنود إلى أن سألته عن المدينة وعن أستاذ البلد فقال لها يا أمّ معيكه المدينة مليحه ولا صعب غير الشخاخ فيها ولا مليح كماني إلّا امراة أستادنا تشنّ وترنّ وعليها خُلْقان مليحه كيف نَوار ابو النوم اصفر واحمر وعلى راسها قحف متل قحفي إلّي البسه نهار العيد إلّي شريته أيام الفرح بنصّ فضّه وجديد وفي ايديها اساور صفر الله أعلم أنّهم من اسباط النخل ولابسه قميص احمر مخيط متل الزكيبه إلّي نعبّي فيها الفول الاخضر وفي سيقانها حجل متل حجل أمّ دعموم إلّي شريته

لها بخمسة انصاف فلوس جدد ولابسه شايه خضره الله أعلم أنّها صبغتها ببرسيم ويا مَحْسَنْها في وقت ديك العمله الّي يعملوها الناس مع النسوان وخاطري يا امّ معيكه تعملي لي متلها حتى يقولوا الناس ومشايخ الكفر ابو معيكه بقا متل الاماره فقالت يابو معيكه إحكي لي يا ابو معيكه على إلّي شفته من امراة استادك فقال لها لمّا رحت المدينه وطلعت للاستاد وحطّني في موضع فيه طاقه تطلّ على الحريم وعلى الموضع الّي ينام فيه الامير فصبرت لمّا دخل الليل وبقيت اتخنّس كيف الكلب الزوام فشفت الامير استادنا قعد على خشبه سوده مربوطه بشراميط بيض لها اربع رِجلَين كيف عريشة المَقات الّي نعملها أيام البطّيخ في الغيط وقعدت امراته على خشبه كيفها متل جرّافة الغيط وبقا يكلّمها بكلام الجنادي يقول لها شلضم بلضم تقول له شقلب مقلب حتى اشتهى منها ديك العمله فحدفها بنواره حمره متل نوارة ابو النوم فقامت تشنّ وترنّ حتى جت له وعمل فيها العمله فقالت له أمّ معيكه واحيات شاربك الّي كيف شارب التيس لا أعمل لك متل عمل الاماره وتنفش على مشايخ الكفر اصبر لمّا يجي الليل تبلغ مرادك

3.24

قال فصبر الفلّاح حتى دخل الليل فقال لها اقعدي في مَدْود الحماره وانا أقعد في مدود البقره قصادك ففعلت وقعدت في المدود وعليها الشلاتيت والشراميط وآثار الجلّة وفيها الشُخاخ أيضًا قال فلمّا خطر التعيس الناصية قضاء الحاجة بعد أن صار ينادمها بكلام مثل نبيح الكلاب شياط وعياط وضراط وسؤال عن البقرة والعجلة والتور والجلّة وغير ذلك أراد أن يرميها بشيء مثل ما فعل الأمير فحطّ يده في المدود فرأى قالب طوب محروق فأخذه وحدفها به فوقع في وسط رأسها ففلقها وسال الدم فصرخت بأعلى صوتها فأقبلوا الجيران ومشايخ البلد ووصل الخبر إلى حاكم البلد فأقبل هو وطائفته وسأل عن القضية فأخبروه بها فأخذه وضربه ضربًا موجعًا وأحضروا للمرأة جرائحي قطب رأسها ومكث يجري عليها شهرًا كاملًا حتى برئت فانظر لهذا النحس التعيس * وقلّة عقله الخسيس * كيف ظهر من ملاعبته لزوجته الهمّ والنكد * وقيام الغارات في البلد *

3.25

(واتفق أنّ ثلاثة أنفار من قحوف الريف أرادوا طلوع المدينة) فساروا حتى قربوا منها فقال كبيرهم وصاحب الرأي فيهم إنّ مدينة مصر كلّها جنادي وعسكر يقطعوا الروس واحنا فلّاحين وانْ لم نعمل متلهم ونرطن عليهم بالتركي وإلّا يقطعوا روسنا فقالوا له أصحابه يابو دعموم إحنا ما نعرف تركي ولا غيره فقال لهم أنا تعلّمت التركي زمان إن كنت أقعد حدا المشدّ والنصراني ركبه بركبه فقالوا له أصحابه علّمنا التركي فقال لهم إذا طلعنا المدينه نروح الحمّام الّي يقولوا عليه نعيم الدنيا نستحمّا فيه ونغسل جلودنا ويقولوا فيه نقره غويطه يشخّوا ويخروا فيها وبعد ما نخرج من نعيم الدنيا ونقف نلتف في بردنا ونتمّ امرنا اقول لكم قَرْداش محمّد قولوا لبّيك وهاه

نوار أقول لكم معاكم شي بيرْ مُنْقار يعني جديد قولوا يوق يوق يعني ما معنا شي فيخاف صاحب الحمّام ويقول لعقله دول جنادي غُرْب يقطعوا الروس ويخلينا نخرج بلا فلوس وتهيبنا الناس ونبقى في مصر متل الاماره ويشيع خبرنا في الكفر انّنا بقينا أماره نرطن بالتركي فيخافوا منّا مشايخ الكفر ولا يبقى لهم علينا كلام أبدًا فقالوا له أصحابه دي شوره صواب يابو دعموم

3.26

قال فساروا حتى طلعوا مصر وسألوا عن الحمّام فدلّوهم عليه فدخلوا وشلحوا الزعابيط وأرموا البرد والشلاتيت وصاروا عريانين مثل ما يفعلوا في البرك والأبيار فقال لهم صاحب الحمّام استروا أنفسكم فأرادوا أن يأخذوا البرد يستتروا بها فأرموا لهم صنّاع الحمّام فوط قُدْم من رجيع الحمّام فربطوها على عوراتهم غصب عنهم وصارت عوراتهم في الغالب مكشوفة وأيورهم مدلية ودخلوا الحمّام مثل فحول الجاموس * أو المعيز أو التيوس *

3.27

حتى بقوا داخل الحمّام * وغسلوا ما عليهم من الوسخ والسخام * وغطسوا في الحيضان * مثل الثيران أو الجديان * وخرجوا مع بعضهم البعض * وقد تزلزلت منهم الأرض * وهم في حالة الأثوار * وصور الأبقار * حتى لبسوا الزعابيط * وتلفعوا بتلك الشلاتيت * وسحبوا النبابيت * على الأكتاف * وأرادوا الخروج بلا خلاف * قال فصاح عليهم صاحب الحمّام * هاتوا الأجره يا عرصات يا ليام * فالتفت كبيرهم وقال لأصحابه قرداش محمّد فقالوا له لبّيك وهاه نوار فقال لهم معاكم شي بير منقار يعني جديد فقالوا يوق يوق يعني ما معنا شي فقال لهم صاحب الحمّام في أي وقت يا تيوس اتعلّمتم التركي المعكوس وبقيتم أكابر وأمارة وما هذا التركي الذي يشبه الخرا أقسم بالله لا يخرج منكم عرص حتى يحطّ الأجره بزياده وإلّا حطّوا البرد رهن على الأجره قال ثمّ إنّه أمر أصحابه بصكّهم وضربهم وأخذوا البرد منهم وخرجوا من عنده وتداركوا في الأجرة واقترضوها من أهالي الكفر وخلّصوا بردهم وتوجّهوا إلى حال سبيلهم

3.28

(وطلع رجل منهم المدينة فصادف الجلاد) ينادي في الأسواق على رجل استحقّ القتل يقول يا معاشر الناس فظنّ أنه ينادي العونه يا فلّاحين ففرّ هاربًا حتى وصل إلى الكفر فرأى جماعة من بلده يريدوا الذهاب إلى المدينة فقال لهم لا تطلعوا المدينة فإنّهم ينادوا فيها للعونه والسخره قال فمكثوا أهل بلده ثلاث سنين ما يطلعوا مصر خوفا من السخرة والعونة فانظر إلى قلّة عقولهم وخساسة رأيهم

4.14

(وسأل فقيه ريف بعض العلماء) وقال له مرادي أقرأ الجُرّومية على مذهب الإمام الشافعي فضحك عليه من جهله وطرده

4.15

(ودخل على العلّامة الحُمَيدي رحمه الله تعالى رجل من فقهاء الريف) وقال له عندك مختصر القرآن وكان الحميدي شيخ الصحّافين بمصر فقال الشيخ رحمه الله نعم اجلس حتى أنظره لك فجلس عنده وإذا برجل أقبل على الشيخ وقال له عندك يا سيدي مختصر مسلم فقال له نعم خذ تعريص هذا فإنّه مختصر مسلم لا كلام وطرده من عنده فتعجّب الحاضرون منه غاية العجب ثمّ إنّهم سألوا فقيه الريف عن حاله فقال لهم أنا رجل اقرّي الأولاد في بلدي القرآن وقد ثقل عليهم لطوله فقلت لعل أحدًا اختصره فيكون سهل على الأولاد ويحفظوه بالسرعه فضحك عليه الحاضرون ومضى إلى حال سبيله

4.16

(وسعى رجل من الأكابر عند قاضي القضاة بمصر المحروسة ليأخذ لرجل فقيه نيابة في بعض المحاكم) ومدحه عنده فقال ائتني به فلمّا حضر بين يديه قال له القاضي هل تحفظ القرآن قال نعم أيد الله مولانا القاضي وعندي مصحف مليح بخط المؤلّف قال فتحقّق القاضي جهله وضحك عليه وطرده فمضى إلى حال سبيله

4.17

(ودخل بعض الفقهاء الجهّال على أبي حنيفة النعمان رضي الله عنه) ورجل الإمام ممدودة لوجع أصابها فلمّا رآه الإمام في هيئة حسنة وثياب فاخرة لمّ رجله وكان الإمام يقرّر في مسألة صلاة الصبح ما حكمها إذا طلعت الشمس ونحو ذلك فقال له هذا الجاهل إذا طلعت الشمس قبل الفجر ما حكم الصلاة فقال الإمام آن لأبي حنيفة أن يمدّ رجله ثمّ مدّها في وجهه ومضى على درسه ولم يلتفت إليه

4.18

(واتفق أنّ اثنين اختصما في آية من كتاب الله تعالى) فقال أحدهما لعلّهم يتفكّرون وقال الآخر لعلّهم يشكرون فبينما هم في المشاجرة إذ طلع عليهم فقيه من فقهاء الريف فسألوه لاعتقادهم أنّه يحفظ القرآن هل يتفكّرون أو يشكرون فقال الأولى أنّنا نأخذ من كلّ كلمة جانبًا ونجعلها لكما لعلّهم يتفشكرون ونبطّل المشاجرة بينكما فقالا قاتل الله الأبعد كفر وغير كلام الله

4.22

(ودخل بعض العلماء قرية من قرى البحر بنواحي الجبل) فرأى محلًّا يشبه المسجد وفيه البقر والغنم وقد اشتدّ به الجوع فجلس يقرأ في سورة الكهف فاجتمع عليه جماعة من تلك القرية يسمعوا قراءته إلى أن وصل إلى قوله تعالى {سَيقُولُونَ ثَلاَثَةٌ رَابِعُهُمْ كَلْبُهُمْ} فقالوا له يا شيخ نجست القرآن كلام الله ما فيه كلاب وأنت تجعل فيه كلاب اخرج من بلدنا وإلّا قتلناك قال فقام رجل منهم وقال لا تضربوه ولا تقتلوه حتى نرسل لفقي بلدنا الحاج مخالف الله ونسأله فإن قال لنا إنّ القرآن فيه كلاب تركناه وإلّا قتلناه قال فأرسلوا خلف هذا الرجل فحضر شخص كأنّه سارية الجبل من طوله أو عمود الصواري من غلظه وثقل ذاته ورؤيته تقشعرّ منها الجلود وهو ملفع بحِرام أبيض دنس لا غير فلمّا حضر وجلس أخبروه بالقضية فنظر يمينًا وشمالًا وقال لهم اصبروا حتى أبين لكم الأمر وأكشف لكم الحال ثمّ إنّه انضجع على قفاه وقال لهم اطرحوا علي الحرام فطرحوه عليه فسكت ساعة على هذه الحالة لا يتحرّك ثمّ إنّه قام بسرعة عريان مكشوف الرأس والعورة ووقف ساعة بهذه الحالة ينظر نحو السماء وهو في وجد وكرب ثمّ ادّعى بحرامه فالتف فيه وجلس وقال لهم طلعت العشر سماوات إلّي خلقها الله فرأيت أول سما فيها بقر وتاني سما فيها جاموس وتالت سما فيها عجول ورابع سما فيها تيران وخامس سما كذا وسادس سما كذا وصار يعدّ أصناف حيوانات إلى أن قال وشفت عاشر سما مليانه غنم وأنتم تعرفوا أنّ الغنم تعوز الكلاب ولا تفارقها وراعى الغنم لا بدّ له من كلب يحرس غنمه خلّوا الراجل يروح ولا تقتلوه واعطوه رغيفين دره يأكلهم قال فأخذ الرغيفين ومضى وهو يحمد الله الذي خلّصه من هؤلاء الجهلة

Translation

Accounts of What Happened to Peasants Who Went to the City

3.22

And it is said that a peasant came and brought his master his taxes and the latter put him up in a room that had an aperture that overlooked the private quarters of the emir. When night came the peasant said to himself, “I wonder, Abū Muʿaykah, what the emirs do with their women when they’re by themselves. Just watch what your master does with his wife and when you go back to the hamlet you can tell Umm Muʿaykah to do it like the emirs and she'll pleasure you the very same way. I bet they spout gibberish to one another in Turkish.[2] Just you watch the way they do it with their women and you'll be able to tell the brave lads, 'Now I'm just like the emirs and Umm Muʿaykah's like the wife of the emir, the master of the village!'" So he waited patiently until night came and the emir entered his house. Then the peasant got up and, looking through the aperture, saw the emir sitting on a bed of ivory furnished with all kinds of coverings, and his wife came and sat on another just like it. The emir engaged with her in gentle talk and conversation of a refined sort, now in Turkish and now in Arabic, till, desiring to consummate the act with her, he took a rose from his side and tossed it at her, and she came to him and he luxuriated in her comeliness and beauty to his heart's content, and with the most perfect pleasure, satisfaction, and abandonment, after which each one lay down on his own bed and went to sleep.

3.23

Come morning, the peasant took leave of his master and set off for his village. When he reached the hamlet, he was met by his wife, Umm Muʿaykah, and she greeted him and they sat down together for a conversation like the converse of apes or the jabbering of Indians, and so it went until she asked him about the city and about the master of the village, and he told her, "Umm Muʿaykah, the city's a fine place and there's nothing that's hard

---

[2] As the language of the Ottoman élite, Turkish was the shibboleth of the military caste.

there except for pissing![3] And there's nothing so fair either as our master's wife—she jingles and jangles and wears clothes pretty as poppy flowers, red and yellow, and on her head she wears a cap just like the one that I wear at the Feast that I bought when we got married for a silver piece and a copper piece, and on her wrists she has yellow bracelets made of God only knows what—date stalks or something. She was wearing a red shift sewn like the sacks we pack fresh-picked beans in and on her legs were anklets like Umm Duʿmūm's[4] that I bought her for five silver-pieces-worth of coppers and she was wearing a green jacket, God only knows what she'd dyed it with—clover or something. How fine she looked when they did the thing that people do with women, and I want you, Umm Muʿaykah, to do it for me just like she did, so that the people and the shaykhs of the hamlet say, 'Now Abū Muʿaykah's just like the emirs!'" Said she, "Tell me, Abū Muʿaykah, what you saw your master's wife do, Abū Muʿaykah." He told her, "When I went to the city and went to the master's and he put me in a room with an aperture looking down into the private quarters and the room where the emir sleeps, I waited till night came, crouched like a snarling dog. Then I saw our master the emir sit down on a black wooden thing tied together with white rags. It had four legs, just like the squash trellis

---

[3] The reference seems out of place because it has no equivalent in the earlier part of the story. However, jokes about peasants not being able to find a place to relieve themselves in the city are central to other stories that occur later (1.12.1, 2) and were apparently a stock element in the mockery of peasants.

[4] Umm Duʿmūm: presumably a second wife.

that we put up in the fields at the watermelon harvest. His wife sat down on a wooden thing of the same sort, like the shovel-sledge they use to flatten the fields. He started talking trooper talk to her, saying, 'Humpety-tumpety!' and she answered, 'Upsy-downsy!' and so it went on till he wanted to do it with her. Then he heaved a red flower like a poppy at her and she got up jingling and jangling and went to him and he did it to her." Said Umm Muʿaykah, "I swear by your billy-goat whiskers, I'll do it for you like the emirs do and then you can preen yourself in front of the shaykhs of the hamlet. Be patient until nightfall and you will attain your desire!"

3.24

So the peasant waited till night and then said to her, "You sit in the donkey's trough and I'll sit in the cow's in front of you!" So, she did as he said and sat down in the trough in her rags and tatters and traces of dung, not to mention the piss that was on her. When the miserable wretch decided to consummate the act—after he'd engaged with her in converse sweet as the barking of dogs, with hubbub and hullabaloo and farting and questions about the cow and the calf and the ox and the dung cakes and so forth—he wanted to toss something at her as the emir had done, so he put his hand into the trough and saw a piece of burnt brick, which he took and heaved at her. The brick hit her in the middle of her head and cracked it open and the blood ran and she screamed at the top of her lungs, and the neighbors and the shaykhs of the village came and the news reached the chief of police of the village, who proceeded to the place with his entourage and enquired into the matter. They told him what had happened and he took the man and beat him severely; and they got the woman a surgeon, who sewed up her head and spent a whole month treating her before she recovered. Observe this wretch with luck ungraced and the stupidity of his mind debased, and how, from his clowning with his wife, sorrow, woe, and mayhem in the village grew!

3.25

And it happened once that three clods from the countryside decided to go to the city. When they were almost there, their leader and counselor said, “The city of Cairo is all troopers and foot-soldiers that cut off people’s heads, and we are peasants, and if we don’t do as they do and gabble at them in Turkish, they’ll chop off our heads.” “Abū Duʿmūm,” said his companions, “we know nothing about Turkish or anything else!” “I learnt Turkish long ago,” he answered them, “when I used to sit next to the bailiff and the Christian, knee to knee.” So his companions said to him, “Teach us Turkish!” “When we get to the city,” he said, “we’ll go to the bathhouse, which people call Heaven on Earth, and take a bath and wash our hides—they say it has a deep hole that they shit and piss in! As we’re leaving Heaven on Earth and are wrapping ourselves in our cloaks and about to be on our way, I’ll say to you, ‘Kardeş Mehmet!’ (‘Brother Mehmet!’) and you say, ‘At your command!’ and ‘Hah! Ne var?’ (‘Huh! What’s up?’).

Then I'll ask you, 'Do you have bir munqār?'[5] meaning a copper piece, and you say, 'Yok yok!' meaning 'No, we don't.' Then the bathhouse keeper will get scared and say to himself, 'These are foreign troopers who chop off people's heads!' and he'll let us leave without paying and everyone will stand in awe of us and we'll be treated in Cairo like emirs. Word will spread in the hamlet that we've become emirs and speak Turkish, and the shaykhs of the hamlet will be afraid of us and they'll have no more authority over us at all!" "Sound thinking, Abū Duʿmūm!" said his companions.

3.26

So, they proceeded until they reached Cairo and asked for the bathhouse, and the people directed them to it and they entered, shedding their woolen wraps and throwing their cloaks and the rest of their rags on the ground and leaving themselves naked, just as they do at the ponds and wells. "Make yourselves decent!" the bathhouse keeper told them, and they were about to take their cloaks and cover themselves with those when the bathhouse workers threw them some old, used towels. Like it or not, they had to tie these over their privates, though these remained for the most part exposed, and, penises wagging, they went into the bathhouse, looking like buffalo bulls or billies and bucks.

---

[5] *Munqār*, i.e., *mangır*, an Anatolian Ottoman copper coin, the equivalent of the Egyptian copper piece *jadīd*; see further Pamuk (2000, 38).

3.27

Once inside, they washed off the muck and the mire, plunging into the tanks like young oxen or kids, and emerged again all together, the ground shaking beneath them as in a tremor, like oxen in condition and cattle in apparition. Then they donned their cloaks, wrapped themselves in their rags, shouldered their cudgels, and were about to leave without more ado, when the bathhouse keeper shouted after them, "Hand over the money, you pimps, you cheats!" At this the leader turned and said to his companions, "Kardeş Mehmet!" to which the others replied, "At your command!" and "Hah! Ne var?" and he said, "Do you have *bir munqār*?" meaning, "a copper piece" and they answered, "Yok yok," meaning "No, we don't." The bathhouse keeper said to them, "When did you bucks learn this Turkish that sucks and become big men and emirs, and what is this Turkish that sounds like shit? I swear to God, not one of you pimps leaves till he hands over the entrance fee and then some, or you leave your cloaks as pledges for it!" Then he ordered his friends to kick them and beat them and they took their cloaks from them and the peasants left and came up with the fee, which they borrowed from the people of the hamlet, and they redeemed their cloaks and went on their way.

3.28

And one of these people went to the city and arrived just as the public executioner was crying out "Oyez!" in the marketplaces apropos of a man who had been sentenced to die. The peasant thought that he must be calling, "All peasants to the corvée!" and fled back to the hamlet. There he found a party from his village about to set off for the city, so he said to them, "Don't go up to the city, for they're summoning people to the corvée!" and the people of his village then went for three years without going to Cairo, for fear of the corvée. Observe their stupidity and the baseness of their thinking!

Further Anecdotes Showing the Ignorance of Country Pastors

4.14

And a country pastor asked a question of a scholar, saying to him, "It is my wish to read the Jurrūmiyyah[6] according to the school of the Imam al-Shāfiʿī." The man mocked him for his ignorance and threw him out.

4.15

And a country pastor visited the learned scholar al-Ḥumaydī, may the Almighty have mercy on him, and asked him, "Do you have an abridged Qurʾān?" Shaykh al-Ḥumaydī being Shaykh of the Book Traders in Cairo. The shaykh, God have mercy on him, told him, "Certainly. Sit down while I find it for you." So, he sat down. Then another man came to the shaykh and said to him,

---

[6] I.e., the *al-Ājurrūmiyyah* of Abū ʿAbd Allāh Muḥammad ibn Dāʾūd al-Sanhājī, known as Ibn Ājurrūm (672/1273 or 1274 to 723/1323), "the most widely known and used Arabic grammatical textbook of all time [in which] the whole of Arabic grammar is reduced to about a dozen printed pages of easily memorised rules and stereotypical examples" (Carter 1998, 308). The point of the story is that the country pastor does not know the difference between grammar and jurisprudence.

"Sir, do you have an abridged Muslim."[7] "Indeed I do," said the shaykh: "Take this wretch, for he's an abridged Muslim, no two ways about it!" and he threw the pastor out. Those present were utterly amazed and asked the pastor about himself and he told them, "I am one who teaches the children in my village to read the Qurʾān, but they find it boring because it's so long, so I thought maybe someone had abridged it, which would be easier for the children and allow them to memorize it quickly." Those present mocked him and he went his way.

4.16

And a certain grandee exerted his influence with the chief judge in Divinely Protected Cairo to get a post for a pastor as a deputy judge in one of the courts, singing the man's praises. The judge said, "Send him to me." When the man was before him, the judge asked, "Have you memorized the Qurʾān?" and the man replied, "Yes indeed, God aid Your Worship, and I've got a lovely copy in the author's own handwriting!" The judge saw how ignorant he was and mocked him and threw him out, and he went his way.

4.17

And an ignorant country pastor paid a visit to Abū Ḥanīfah al-Nuʿmān—may God be pleased with him—at a moment when the imam had his leg stretched out in front of him because of some pain he was suffering from. When the imam saw that the man

---

[7] I.e., an abridged version of the famous collection of Prophetic traditions entitled *The Reliable Collection (al-Jāmiʿ al-Ṣaḥīḥ)*, compiled by Muslim ibn al-Ḥajjāj (d. 261/875).

was of dignified appearance and dressed in fine clothes, he drew in his leg. At the time, the imam happened to be giving instruction on the question of the morning prayer and what rule applied should the sun rise during the prayer and so on.[8] The ignoramus asked him, "What's the rule for the prayer, if the sun rises before dawn?" Said the imam, "It seems it's time for Abū Ḥanīfah to stretch out his leg again!" and he did so in the man's face and went on with his teaching and paid him no further attention.

4.18

And it happened that two men differed over a verse of God's Word, one saying *laʿallahum yatafakkarūn* ("perhaps they will bethink themselves"), the other *laʿallahum yashkurūn* ("perhaps they will be grateful").[9] While they were arguing, a country pastor appeared, and, believing him to have memorized the Qurʾān, they asked him, "Is it *yatafakkarūn* or *yashkurūn*?" That ignoramus told them, "The best thing to do is for us to take a little from each word and make it *yatafashkarūn*,[10] and put an end to your quarreling." "God strike you dead!" they said to him. "He has blasphemed, and changed the word of God!"

---

[8] Prayer must not be performed at the precise moment of sunrise, noon, or sunset. Traditions deal with the validity of the dawn prayer if initiated before but completed after sunrise.

[9] The occurrence of nearly identical passages in the Qurʾān increases the difficulty of memorising it. The phrase *la-ʿallahum yatafakkarūn* occurs in three places (Q Aʿrāf 7.176; Naḥl 16.44; Ḥashr 59.21), while *la-ʿallahum yashkurūn* occurs once (Q Ibrāhīm 14.37).

[10] *Yatafashkarūn* has no meaning, but is reminiscent of *yatafashkalūn* 'they are confused or disordered'.

4.22

And a scholar entered one of the villages on the banks of the river close to the desert and saw what looked like a mosque, with cattle and sheep and goats in it. He was extremely hungry, so sat down and recited from Sūrat al-Kahf,[11] and a group of people from the village gathered around to listen. However, when he came to the words of the Almighty "Some will say, 'They were three, their dog the fourth',"[12] they said to him, "Shaykh, you have defiled the Qurʾān! God's Word has no dogs in it, and you have put dogs in it! Get out of our village before we kill you!" One of them, however, stood up and said, "Don't beat him or kill him till we've sent for the pastor of our village, al-Ḥājj Mukhālif Allāh[13] and asked him. If he tells us that the Qurʾān has dogs in it, we'll leave him be. If not, we'll kill him!" So they sent for this man and an individual appeared, tall as a flagpole on a mountain and bulky and heavy in physique as the Pillar of the Columns, so that just looking at him was enough to make the skin crawl. He was enveloped in a filthy white blanket and nothing else. When he came and had sat down, they informed him of the situation. He looked to the right and to the left and then said to them, "Be patient till I reveal you the truth and discover you the essence of the matter!" Then he lay down on his back and told them, "Throw the blanket over me!" which they did. He remained thus for a while without speaking or moving, then suddenly leapt up, naked, head

---

[11] Q 18, Sūrat al-Kahf.

[12] Q Kahf 18.22.

[13] *Mukhālif Allāh* literally 'He who disagrees with God'.

and privates exposed, and stood thus for a while gazing into the sky in a state of ecstatic agony. Eventually, he called for his blanket and wrapped it about him and sat down. "I have visited the Ten Heavens that the Almighty created," he said, "and I saw that in the First Heaven are cows and in the Second Heaven buffalos and in the Third Heaven calves and in the Fourth Heaven oxen and in the Fifth Heaven such-and-such and in the Sixth Heaven such-and-such" and he went on enumerating the various types of animals until he said, "and I saw that the Tenth Heaven was full of flocks of sheep and goats, and as you know flocks need dogs, which they are never without, and the shepherd has to have a dog to guard his flocks. Let the man go and do not kill him, and give him two loaves of corn bread to eat!" So the scholar took the two loaves and went away, praising the Almighty for saving him from those ignoramuses.

6. A WEAVER'S NOTEBOOK FROM ALEPPO (10TH/16TH CENTURY)

Boris Liebrenz and Kristina Richardson

At the end of the 10th/16th century and the beginning of the 11th/17th century, the Aleppine Kamāl al-Dīn, a weaver by profession, kept a notebook.[1] Only a small fragment of it seems to have survived, held since the early 19th century in the Forschungsbibliothek Gotha in Germany. The remaining folios, from the years 997 and 998, contain descriptions of political and economic events, of meetings with friends and events in the market, or the weather; obituaries; riddles and sayings; stories and excerpts from books on history, religion, and law; a multitude of poems, many of his own making; in short, anything that this weaver deemed interesting to record at any point.

Kamāl al-Dīn had a keen interest in reading, literature, and scholarship, but was not a career scholar himself. While he had studied several sciences to some degree in his youth (fol. 55v: *al-maʿqūlāt wa-l-fiqh wa-ʿiddat ʿulūm*), his only teacher held a minor post and remains unknown outside of Kamāl al-Dīn's notebook.

[1] The notebook, its place in Arabic literature, as well as the biography of its author are the object of an extended study that will accompany our edition of the text, to appear within the series Bibliotheca Islamica at the Orient-Institut Beirut.

 https://doi.org/10.11647/OBP.0208.12

Colloquial language is a feature of the poetic genre called *zajal*, in which the author works several times. He does not willingly employ it in his prose. Kamāl al-Dīn certainly makes several smaller mistakes in these passages. Yet his idiosyncrasies rarely exceed contemporary manuscript practices. These practices include the replacement of an *ʾalif maqṣūra* with a *yāʾ*, of a *hamza* with a *yāʾ* , or the omission of the points on the *tāʾ marbūṭa*. Thus, the sole instance of the word اعطيطك in our sample probably serves as an attempt to introduce an element of spoken language into the story and to mark the speaker as an uneducated worker.

For the edition, we have adopted a set of orthographic standardisations to make the text more accessible: *tāʾ marbūṭa* with points; *ʾalif maqṣūra* without dots; *ḥamza* where necessary. We have also added some modern punctuation.

Transcription

Story of a hashish addict

MS Gotha orient. A 114, fol. 7r

يحكى

أن بليعاً زيهاويني اشترى حمصاً من الحمصاني في زبدية منه برهن كي لا يتهاون في ردها. فلما وصل إلى بيته قال لأهل الدار: "إذا أنا قمت صباحاً قولوا لي: خذ الزبدية!" فلما أصبح لبس ثيابه وهَمّ بالطلوع وإذا بقائلة: "خذ الزبدية!" وكان الوقت وقت لم تتعارف فيه الوجوه فمد يده ليأخذ الزبدية (سعي) ان (لصعاره) مستعملة جاء ليأخذ الزبدية أخذ المستعملة تحت أبطه. وكان الحمصاني بقدرة الله غفل عن عادته فلم يزل ينتظره حتى جاء. فناوله ما تحت أبطه فاخذها الحمصاني وطلّ رأيها مستعملة جرى وراءه لحقه فقال له: "عافاك! والله أين زبديتي؟" فقال: "اعطيطكها[2]!" فلم يزالا يتشاجرا حتى أن بن الزهاوي استيقظ رأى أن أباه غلط حمل الزبدية وهو لاحق لأبيه وإذا بهم في نزاعها فعلم أنها سهوة الزيهاوية.

---

2 كذا، والصواب: أعطيتك إياها.

Translation

It is told

that a *ḥashīsh* swallower bought hummus from the hummus vendor in a *zabdiyya* bowl that he borrowed from him against collateral, so that he wouldn't neglect to return it. When he came home, he said to the people of the house: "When I get up in the morning, say to me: Take the *zabdiyya*!" And when he awoke, he dressed and wanted to get out, there was a woman saying: "Take the *zabdiyya*!" This was at a time when one could not tell faces apart. So, he stretched out his hand to take the *zabdiyya*, (…) there was a chamber pot. He wanted to take the *zabdiyya*, but took the chamber pot under his armpit. And the hummus vendor, through God's power, against his usual habit, waited until he came. He handed over what he had under his armpit and the hummus vendor took it. When he saw that it was a chamber pot he came after him, reached him, and said: "Please! By God, where is my *zabdiyya*?" He said: "I gave it to you!" They wouldn't stop arguing until the son of the *ḥashīsh* addict woke up and saw that his father had erred in picking up (what he thought was) the *zabdiyya*. When he reached his father, there they were, fighting over it. Then he realised that the cause was the absent-mindedness of *ḥashīsh* addicts.

Commentary

زيهاويني. Cf. the form الزهاوي later in the same story. It is clear already from Kamāl al-Dīn's own use of the term in several locations (see the stories on fol. 22v and the judge on *ḥašīš* on 58r) that it must have something to do with drug abuse. Furthermore, a connection is apparent with زيه, which Ṣafī al-Dīn al-Ḥillī (d. 749/1350) used to mean 'hashish'. In his commentary on al-Ḥillī's verse, Bosworth (1976, II: 309) noted the following: "*Zīh* 'hashish' is a common term in the literature of hashish consumption from Ayyūbid and Mamlūk times onwards, with *zayyāh* occurring for 'hashish addict' (…)."

زبدية. A large bowl or deep dish.

لم تتعارف فيه الوجوه. Meaning it was too dark to discern shapes.

اعطيطكها. Instead of أعطيتك إياها.

7. SELECTIONS FROM ARABIC GARSHŪNĪ MANUSCRIPTS IN THE BRITISH LIBRARY

Michael Erdman

In the history of writing and literacy in the Middle East, Arabic written in Syriac characters, known as Arabic Garshūnī, presents us with an interesting, yet often forgotten, example of cultural adoption and adaptation. Arabic Garshūnī, similar to other allographic traditions, did not have a standardised orthography on which authors and scribes might base their writings. Nonetheless, the general need for language to function as a means of communication and wide dissemination of information implied that certain patterns were adhered to across the Christian Arab world. Previously, the corpus of Arabic Garshūnī manuscripts was limited to Levantine and southern Turkish sources, but an increase in our access to digitised manuscripts from Iraq and other regions has helped to broaden our understanding of this particular means of recording and reproducing cultural heritage (McCollum 2014, 16–19).

Within the patterns referred to above, the use of Syriac graphemes to represent Arabic sounds can be broken down into three separate categories: those for which there is a one-to-one correspondence between Arabic and Syriac graphemes; those

 https://doi.org/10.11647/OBP.0208.13

cases in which Syriac lacks a unique means of representing an Arabic phoneme or grapheme; and a third subset in which the Syriac script represents Arabic phonemes through the use of diacritics. It should be noted that the distinction between phoneme (a unique sound in a phonetic system) and grapheme (a unique letter in a writing system) is important here. The decision to match a grapheme to a grapheme, a phoneme to a phoneme, or a phoneme to a grapheme (and vice versa) tells us as much about the copyist's grasp of Classical Syriac and Classic Arabic as it does about their particular dialect of spoken Arabic (McCollum 2014, 227).

The first category of mappings presents the least difficulties. Here, a one-to-one correspondence is established and is easily recognizable. Thus, the Arabic letter *bāʾ*, for example, is represented by the Syriac letter *bēt*. Within this category, however, we also find that the core Arabic graphemes function as representatives of the Arabic graphemes based on them, regardless of pronunciation. In this respect, the Syriac *yōd* is used for both the Arabic *yāʾ* and the Arabic *ʾalif maqṣūra*, despite the latter's pronunciation as an *ʾalif*.

The second group of graphemes are slightly more problematic, but they do reveal the pre-modern scribe or writer's understanding of phonetics. Take, for example, the velarised consonants, for which there are two graphemes in Syriac and four in Arabic. In general, those who wrote in Garshūnī sought to replicate sounds by both the *ṣādē* with a dot over it and the *ṭēt* with a dot under it. This raises the question of vernacular pronunciations of these letters among the Arabic-speaking Christian communities of the Middle East. In particular, it focuses our attention on the merging of the velarised phonemes in some dialects, such as Lebanese, which are still present in others, such as Najdī and Khalījī Arabic.

Finally, the third collection of graphemes is the most unstable: those that can be represented fully in Syriac with the help of diacritics, the most common of which is the *rukākā*, a dot below the letter. Here, the Arabic *ghayn* is rendered with the Syriac *gāmal* and a dot below, the traditional Syriac means of rendering the voiced pharyngeal fricative. Occasionally, a conscientious scribe would also use a *qūshāyā*, or a dot above the letter, to indicate that it was to be read as the corresponding non-spirantized letter in Arabic. The problem with this group of graphemes is that the usage of the dot is far from routine. The reader is thus left asking herself if this phenomenon—which rarely impedes comprehension—is a reflection of vernacular phonology or simple laziness on the part of the scribe.

A final remark must be made on additional markers used in Arabic texts. The *hamza*, although a separate letter according linguists, never features in Garshūnī texts. When it would sit on an *ʾalif*, *waw* or *yāʾ* in Arabic, the basic grapheme is used. *Ḥarakāt* may or may not be included in a text and almost always follow the Arabic system, rather than either of the two Syriac systems in use. Similarly, two dots over the letter assist us in determining whether a final *hē* is intended to be a *tāʾ marbūṭa* or a final *h*. Lastly, the *shadda* occasionally appears in its Arabic form. On other occasions, it shows up as a tilde over the doubled consonant or a neighbouring one. Gemination was rare enough in Classical Syriac that it did not merit its own special diacritic.

The full listing of the most common orthography is found in the table below:

Arabic	Garshūnī	Arabic	Garshūnī	Arabic	Garshūnī
ا	ܐ	ش	ܫ	م	ܡ
ب	ܒ	ص	ܨ	ن	ܢ
ت	ܬ݂/ܬ	ض	ܛ݂/ܨ݂	و	ܘ
ث	ܬ݂	ط	ܛ	ي	ܝ
ج	ܓ̰/ܓ	ظ	ܛ݂/ܛ	ه	ܗ
ح	ܚ	ع	ܥ	ء	–
خ	ܟ	غ	ܓ݂	آ	ܐ
د	ܕ	ف	ܦ	ؤ	ܘ
ذ	ܕ݂	ق	ܩ	ة	ܗ̈
ر	ܪ	ك	ܟ݂/ܟ	ى	ܝ
ز	ܙ	ل	ܠ	ئ	ܝ
س	ܣ				

In traditional Syriac texts, similar to those in Hebrew and Arabic, the letters are also assigned numerical values. These numbers are often denoted by a line over the individual graphemes. This tradition was carried over into many of the Garshūnī texts used in this section.

The traditional Syriac system of numeration is as follows (Healey 2005, 93):

Syriac Grapheme	Numeral	Syriac Grapheme	Numeral
ܐ	1	ܠ	30
ܒ	2	ܡ	40
ܓ	3	ܢ	50
ܕ	4	ܣ	60
ܗ	5	ܥ	70
ܘ	6	ܦ	80

ܙ	7	ܨ	90
ܚ	8	ܩ	100
ܛ	9	ܪ	200
ܝ	10	ܫ	300
ܟ	20	ܬ	400

British Library Or MS 4435; 12r

Transcription

1. ܐܠܦܨܠ ܐܠܬܐܡܢ ܥܫܪ ܦܝ ܐܢܗ ܠܡܐܕܐ ܐܪܣܠ ܓܒܪܐܝܠ ܘ ܠܡ ܝܪܣܠ ܡܠܐܟ ܐܚܪ.
2. ܦܢܩܘܠ ܐܢܗ ܟܡܐ ܩܕ ܓܐ ܠܥܢܕ ܕܐܢܝܐܠ ܗܘ ܓܒܪܐܝܠ ܐܠܝ ܙܟܪܝܐ.
3. ܩܕ ܒܫܪ ܥܢ ܐܠܚܒܠ ܒܝܘܚܢܐ ܗܟܕܐ ܘ ܐܠܒܬܘܠ ܗܘ ܒܫܪܗܐ
4. ܦܠܘ ܟܐܢ ܓ̰ܝܪܗ ܩܕ ܒܫܪ ܙܟܪܝܐ ܦܓ̰ܝܪܗ ܩܕ ܒܫܪ ܐܠܒܬܘܠ ܟܠ ܘ ܓ̰ܝܪ ܡܨܕܩ ܥܢܕ ܐܠܣܐܡܥܝܢ ܡܢ ܟܠ ܒܕ
5. ܠܟܢ ܐܘܠܐ ܩܕ ܐܪܣܠ ܐܠܝ ܕܐܢܝܐܠ ܘ ܬܐܢܝܐ ܐܠܝ ܙܟܪܝܐ ܘ ܬܐܠܬܐ ܐܠܝ ܡܪܝܡ
6. ܦܗܕܐ ܬܚܩܩ ܟܠܐܡ ܐܠܡܠܐܟ ܠܐܢܗ ܩܕ ܣܒܩ ܒܫܪ ܕܐܢܝܐܠ ܘ ܙܟܪܝܐ ܘ
7. ܩܐܠ ܩܘܡ ܐܢ ܓܒܪܐܝܝܠ ܗܘ ܪܝܣ ܪܬܒܗ̈ ܐܠܡܓ̰ܕܗ̈ ܐܠܬܐܠܬܝܗ̈ ܡܢ ܐܠܡܠܐܝܟܗ
8. ܘ ܩܕ ܐܪܣܠ ܗܕܐ ܠܟܝ ܝܘܨܚ ܟܝ ܚܒ ܕܐܢܝܐܠ ܦܝ ܐܠܬܒܥܝܗ.
9. ܠܝܩܕ ܦܡ ܐܠܢܒܘܗ̈ ܐܠܡܐܠܝܡ ܠܟܠ ܟܠܡܬܐ ܗܘ ܐܫܥܝܗ ܘ ܟܩܡܬܗ
10. ܘ ܬܐܢܝܐ ܠܟܝ ܝܒܫܪ ܐܠܬܠܡܝܕ̈ ܘ ܝܟܠ ܐܠܓ̰ܕܝܕܗ̈
11. ܘ ܠܐܓ̰ܠ ܕܠܟ ܩܕ ܐܪܣܠ ܐܠܝ ܙܟܪܝܐ ܘ ܡܪܝܡ

Arabic Transcription

1. الفصل التامن عشر في انه لمادا ارسل جبرايل و لم يرسل ملاك اخر.
2. فنقول انه كما قد جا لعند دانيال هو جبرايل الي زكريا.
3. قد بشّر عن الحبل بيوحنا هكدا و البتول هو بشرها
4. فلو كان غيره قد بشر زكريا فغيره قد بشر البتو كل و غير مصدّق عند السامعين من كل بد
5. لكن اولا قد ارسل الي دانيال و تانيا الي زكريا و تالتا الي مريم
6. فهدا تحقّق كلام الملاك لانه قد سبق بشر دانيال وزكريا و

7. قال قوم ان جبرايل هو ريس رتبة السجمة التحتانيه من الملايكه
8. و قد ارسل هدا لان اسمه كان عند دانيال في العتيقه.
9. ليسّد فم اليهود القايلين لعل عبتا هو اسمه و خدمته
10. و تانيا لكي يخرج العتيقة و يدخل الجديدة
11. و لاجل دلك قد ارسل الي زكريا و مريم

Translation

(1) Section 18, regarding why Gabriel was sent and not another angel. (2) We say that it was the same as in the case of Daniel, (and) when Gabriel came to Zachariah. (3) He similarly presaged the pregnancy (of Elizabeth) with John and he also brought good tidings to the Virgin. (4) So, if it had been someone else who brought good tidings to Zachariah, it would also have been someone else who brought good tidings to the Virgin. And someone else would have been believable to the listeners in any case. (5) But first He sent [him] to Daniel, and second to Zachariah, and third to Mary. (6) This proves the words of the angel, because previously he brought good tidings to Daniel and Zachariah. (7) Some people said that Gabriel is the head of the lower stream of His angels. (8) And He sent this one because his name was already associated with Daniel in the Old [Testament] (9) in order to shut the mouths of Jews who were saying that perhaps his name and task were not to be taken seriously; (10) and secondly so that he [Gabriel] would leave the Old [Testament] and enter the New [Testament]. (11) And for that reason, He sent him to Zachariah and Mary.

British Library Or MS 7205, 1v

A book of Christian theology in questions and answers

Transcription

1. ܒܣܡ ܐܠܐܒ ܘܐܠܐܒܢ ܘܐܠܪܘܚ ܐܠܩܕܣ ܐܠܐܠܗ ܐܠܘܐܚܕ ܐܡܝܢ
2. ܟܬܐܒ ܐܠܬܥܠܝܡ ܐܠܡܣܝܚܝ ܒܛܪܝܩ ܐܠܣܘܐܠ ܘܐܠܓ̰ܘܐܒ ܒܝܢ ܐܠܡܥܠܡ ܘܐܠܬܠܡܝܕ܀
3. ܣܘܐܠ ܝܐ ܐܟ̰ܝ ܡܢ ܙܡܐܢ ܐܢܐ ܡܫܬܐܩ ܐܠܝ ܡܥܪܦܗ̈ ܐܠܬܥܠܝܡ ܐܠܡܣܝܚܝ
4. ܦܐܢ ܟܐܢ ܥܢܕܟ ܥܠܡܐ ܒܗ ܦܥܠܡܢܝ ܫܝܐ ܡܢ ܗܕܐ ܐܠܥܠܡ ܐܠܫܪܝܦ ܐܠܡܒܐܪܟ
5. ܓ̰ܘܐܒ ܢܥܡ ܥܠܝ ܐܠܪܐܣ ܘܐܠܥܝܢ ܐܢܐ ܐܥܠܡܟ ܡܡܐ ܥܛܐܢܝ ܐܠܠܗ
6. ܘܐܢܥܡ ܥܠܝ ܡܢ ܟܪܡ ܦܝܛ̤ܗ.
7. ܦܐܥܠܡ ܐܢ ܐܠܥܠܡ ܐܠܡܣܝܚܝ ܗܘ ܬܥܠܝܡ ܡܪܟܒ ܡܢ ܟܠܐܡ ܐܠܐܢܓ̰ܝܠ ܐܠܡܩܕܣ
8. ܘ ܡܢ ܪܣܐܝܠ ܐܠܚܘܐܪܝܘܢ.
9. ܘ ܒܘܣܐܛܗ̈ ܗܕ̤ܐ ܐܠܟܠܐܡ ܐܠܡܣܝܚܝ ܬܥܠܡ ܡܐ ܝܢܒܓ̇ܝ ܠܗ
10. ܘ ܡܐ ܗܘ ܛܪܘܪܝ ܠܐܡܪ ܟ̰ܠܐܨܗ ܐܠܐܒܕܝ.
11. ܣܘܐܠ ܐܬܕܪܝ ܡܢ ܗܡ ܐܠܡܠܙܘܡܝܢ ܐܢ ܬܥܠܡܘܐ ܗܕܐ ܐܠܬܥܠܝܡ ܐܠܡܦܝܕ.
12. ܓ̰ܘܐܒ ܓ̰ܡܝܥ ܐܠܡܣܝܚܝܝܢ ܗܡ ܐܠܡܠܙܘܡܝܢ ܒܬܥܠܝܡܗ.
13. ܐܠܟܒܐܪ ܡܢܗܡ ܘ ܐܠܨܓ̇ܐܪ ܐܠܪܓ̰ܐܠ ܘܐܠܢܣܐ ܡܢ ܟܠ ܒܕ ܘ ܣܒܒ.

Arabic Transcription

1. بسم الاب والابن والروح القدس الاله الواحد امين
2. كتاب التعليم المسيحي بطريق السوال والجواب بين المعلم والتلميذ
3. سوال يا اخي من زمان انا مشتاق الي معرفة التعليم المسيحي
4. فان كان عندك علما به فعلمني شيا من هدا العلم الشريف المبارك
5. جواب نعم علي الراس والعين انا اعلمك مما عطاني الله
6. وانعم علي من كرم فيظه.
7. فاعلم ان العلم المسيحي هو تعليم مركب من كلام الانجيل المقدّس
8. و من رسايل الحواريون
9. و كوساطة هذا الكلام المسيحي تعلم ما ينبغي له
10. و ما هو طروري لامر خلاصه الأبدي.
11. سوال اتدري من هم الملزومين ان تعلموا هدا التعليم المفيد
12. جواب جميع المسيحيين هم ملزومين بتعليمه.
13. الكبار منهم والصغار الرجال و النسا من كل بد و سبب.

Translation

(1) In the name of the Father, the Son and the Holy Ghost, the Sole God, amen. (2) The Book of Teaching for a Christian, by means of Questions and Answers between the teacher and the student. (3) Question: Oh, my brother, for some time now, I have been doubtful about the Teachings for Christians. (4) If you are in possession of any knowledge about it, impart upon me something from this honourable, blessed knowledge. (5) Answer: Yes, on [my] head and [my] eye, I will teach you what God has given me (6) and has bestowed upon me from the garden of his abundance. (7) I shall teach [you] that Christian knowledge is teaching composed of the Word of the Holy Gospels (8) and from the epistles of the Apostles. (9) And as a medium of this, the Word of the Lord [Messiah] taught what was necessary for this, (10) and what was essential, for the issue of eternal salvation. (11) Question: Tell [me], who are they who should learn this useful teaching? (12) Answer: All Christians are required to learn it. (13) Adults among them and children; men and women; for all desires and reasons.

Commentary

The above extracts come from two Garshūnī Arabic manuscripts housed at the British Library. I have sought to mirror the texts as closely as possible, and have therefore left in as many idiosyncrasies as can be reflected in a word-processed document.

Information about the provenance of these manuscripts is scant at best. For the most part, British Library records provide only the title of the work, its pagination, and the date of its acquisition. Garshūnī manuscripts were sourced from across the northern Middle East, including modern day Syria, Turkey, and Iraq. As such, they represent the copying traditions of these communities.

The first extract, Or. 4435 is a collection of stories to be told at Christian festivals. I have chosen a short extract explaining angelic visitation. The manuscript itself was likely copied in the 19th century in the vicinity of Malatya, Turkey (Margoliouth 1899, 42). More information can be gleaned from the catalogue of Forshall and Rosen (1838) for the second extract, Or. 7205. This Catechism in the form of questions and answers, we learn from the catalogue, is likely to have been penned in the 15th or 16th century. An addition at the back of the manuscript tells us that it was purchased by Father Elyas from Father Suleiman of Mosul in 1799. From this we know that the work was likely still in use until the end of the 18th century (Forshall and Rosen 1838, 101).

Most of the unique attributes of Garshūnī mapping can be seen in both manuscripts. Consider, to start with, the repurposing of the *ṭēt*, equivalent of the Arabic *ṭā*ʾ, as a *ḍād*, which is seen only in the extract from Or. 7205:

Or. 7205

Line 6

ܦܝܛܗ *fayṭihi* [fayḍihi] 'his abundance'

Line 10

ܛܪܘܪܝ *ṭarūrī* [ḍarūrī] 'necessary'

Next, we find in the two texts the use of the *gāmal* to reflect both the Arabic *jīm* and *ghayn*:

Or. 4435

Line 2

ܓܒܪܐܝܠ *Gibrāʾīl* [Jibrāʾil] 'Gabriel'

Line 4

ܦܠܘ ܟܐܢ ܓܝܪܗ *fa-law kān gayroh* [fa-law kāna ghayrihi] 'if it were not him'

Or. 7205

Line 5

ܓܘܐܒ *gawāb* [jawāb] 'answer'

Line 13

ܐܠܨܓܐܪ *al-ṣigār* [al-ṣighār] 'the small ones'

Finally, the following examples demonstrate the lack of transference of complete Arabic orthography into Arabic Garshūnī, with an example of a lack of *hamza*:

Or. 4435

Line 11

ܠܐܓܠ *li-agal* [li-ajli] 'because'

Or. 7205

Line 8

ܪܣܐܝܠ *rasāil* [rasāʾil] 'letters'

As a final remark, the texts under examination, along with many of the other Arabic Garshūnī texts in the British Library collections, do not demonstrate usage of Syriac lexical items in any notable proportion. Nonetheless, it is interesting to point out the carry-over of some of the biblical names in their Syriac orthography, such as

Or. 4435

Line 2

ܕܐܢܝܐܠ *Dāniyāl*, which we can compare to the Arabic دانييل (ܕܐܢܝܝܠ in Arabic Garshūnī orthography) and the Syriac ܕܐܢܝܐܝܠ.

8. EXCERPT FROM YŪSUF AL-MAĠRIBĪ'S DAFᶜ AL-IṢR ᶜAN KALĀM AHL MIṢR (1606)

Liesbeth Zack

The following is an excerpt from *Dafᶜ al-iṣr ʿan kalām ahl Miṣr*, 'Removing the burden from the speech of the Egyptians' (henceforth *Dafᶜ al-iṣr*), written in the year 1014–1015/1606 by the Egyptian Yūsuf ʾAbū al-Maḥāsin Jamāl al-Dīn b. Zakariyyā b. Ḥarb al-Maġribī al-Miṣrī al-ʾAzharī (ca. 1562–1611).

Al-Maġribī was born and raised in Cairo as the descendent of North African immigrants. He grew up in the Ibn Ṭūlūn quarter, which was the meeting point for North African pilgrims, and the living quarter of a large number of North African immigrants. After first being set up in the fabric trade by his uncles following the death of his father, al-Maġribī went to study at al-Azhar University and subsequently worked in a government position. Al-Maġribī knew Persian and Turkish and translated some literary works from these languages into Arabic, but these translations have not survived.[1] He does, however, comment on Turkish and

---

[1] For more information on al-Maġribī's life and works, see Zack (2009, 9–19).

 https://doi.org/10.11647/OBP.0208.14

Persian words and phrases and cites some poetry in these languages in *Dafʿ al-iṣr*.

Dafʿ al-iṣr is a dictionary of Egyptian Arabic words that al-Maġribī checked for consistency with Classical Arabic, mainly using al-Fīrūzābādī's (1329–1415) *al-Qāmūs al-Muḥīṭ* as his reference, but also citing from the Qurʾān and ḥadīth and from Classical Arabic poetry. Al-Maġribī introduces the Egyptian words and phrases by the word *yaqūlūna* 'they say', which was usual in the so-called *laḥn al-ʿāmma* literature. Al-Maġribī was acquainted with this genre, having written an arrangement of, and appendix to, al-Ḥarīrī's *Durrat al-ġawwāṣ fī awhām al-xawāṣṣ*. However, al-Maġribī's objective was the opposite of that of the *laḥn al-ʿāmma*-literature, because whereas the authors of *laḥn al-ʿāmma* works set out to correct 'mistakes' that people made in the Arabic language, al-Maġribī's purpose for writing *Dafʿ al-iṣr* was to prove that many words and expressions that were generally thought to be 'incorrect' actually had equivalents in the Classical Arabic language (Zack 2009, 31–32; see Pellat (2012b) on *laḥn al-ʿāmma* literature). If a word used in the Egyptian dialect was found with the same meaning either in one of the Classical Arabic dictionaries, in the Qurʾān or ḥadīth, or in Classical Arabic poetry, al-Maġribī would classify it as *ṣaḥīḥ* 'correct'; if not, he would comment in terms of *lam yuʿlam* 'it is unknown', *wa-laysa ka-ḏālik* 'it is not like this', *ġayr ṣaḥīḥ* 'incorrect', and similar phrases (Zack 2009, 50–51).

Besides being an important source for Egyptian Arabic in the 17th century,[2] *Dafᶜ al-iṣr* also contains numerous interesting observations on Egyptian culture, such as games, food and drink, clothing, and household utensils. Al-Maġribī also makes comments about his own friends and acquaintances as well as about noteworthy events, as the selected text fragment will show. Al-Maġribī often digresses from the original word under discussion. Most of his comments were triggered by reading something in *al-Qāmūs al-muḥīṭ* that interested him or that reminded him of something that he had experienced. This is demonstrated in his entry for *ṭabṭab* 'to pat', where a note in *al-Qāmūs al-muḥīṭ* about the nickname *ṭabāṭabā* for someone who pronounced the *qāf* as *ṭāʾ* reminded him of one of his own acquaintances with the same speech impediment.

Only one manuscript of *Dafᶜ al-iṣr* has survived—the autograph, which is kept in the St. Petersburg University library (catalogued under no. MS OA 778). In its present form, it consists of 134 folios, but originally it contained 25 *kurrāsas* 'quires', of which quires 3–13 have been lost. The manuscript appears to be a first draft of *Dafᶜ al-iṣr*, as there are a large number of corrections, additions, and comments (such as *unẓur* 'look up') added in the margins in the author's handwriting.[3] An abbreviated version, based on the complete manuscript, was written by Ibn Abī

---

[2] Another important source is Yūsuf al-Širbīnī's *Hazz al-quḥūf fī šarḥ qaṣīd Abī Šādūf*, description by Davies (1981), text edition and translation by Davies (2016).

[3] For more information on the manuscript and the contents of *Dafᶜ al-iṣr*, see Zack (2009, 21–35).

al-Surūr (1589–1590). This book, titled *al-Qawl al-muqtaḍab fīmā wāfaqa luġat ahl Miṣr min luġat al-ʿarab* 'The abbreviated speech concerning what corresponds in the language of the people of Egypt to the language of the Arabs', contains only one-third of the original lemmata of *Dafʿ al-iṣr*, namely those that had the same meaning in Egyptian Arabic and Classical Arabic. Furthermore, it is stripped of all cultural information, poetry, and anecdotes, which is precisely what makes *Dafʿ al-iṣr* an important source of information on Egyptian language and culture in the 17th century.[4]

The excerpt from *Dafʿ al-iṣr* presented here is from the chapter *bāʾ*, section *ṭāʾ* and the first part of section *ʿayn*. Note that words are arranged according to the last letter of the root, like in other dictionaries, such as *Lisān al-ʿarab* and *al-Qāmūs al-muḥīṭ*, so that, for instance, the word *ʿazab* is found in chapter *bāʾ*, section *ʿayn*. The excerpt starts on fol. 16r line 10 of the manuscript, and ends at fol. 17r line 13. The orthography is kept exactly as it was written in the manuscript. The text fragment is followed by a translation and commentary.

Transcription

fol. 16r

10. فصل الطا يقولون طبطب على الشي
11. وله مناسب قال فى القاموس الطبطبة صوت الما وصوت تلاطم السيل
12. والطبطبية الدرّة وطبطب صوت فانده طباطبا لقب
13. اسماعيل بن الحسن بن الحسين بن علي رضى الله عنهم لقب به لانه كان
14. يبدل القاف طآ او لانه اعطي قبا فقال طباطبا يريد قباقبا انتهى

[4] For more information on *al-Qawl al-muqtaḍab* see Zack (2009, 35–36).

15. قال الفقير وقد سمعت المرحوم ابن الشيخ الغيطي وكان يبدل حروفا
16. بالطا يقول ناطس بعض وريطاط اي ناقص بعض وريقات
17. رحمه الله ونفعنا باسلافه الكرام والطبطاب طآير له اذنان كبيرتان
18. ويقولون حصل لفلان الطرب يخصّونه بحركة الفرح وهو يطلق
19. علي حركة الفرح والحزن من الاضداد ورجل مطراب وطروب وقد
20. ظهر الان ان قولهم لو اتفق حماران لاطربا اي حركا حركة حزن لا
21. حركة فرح اذ صوت الحمار بمفرده يحرك حركة الحزن ويستعاذ منه
22. فكيف مع الازدواج فانده طرب ككتف اسم فرس النبي صلي الله عليه وسلم

fol. 16v

1. ويقولون طاب للّذي يلعبون به وطابة للكرة ايضا
2. ولم اعلم لهما مناسبا[5] والطابة في اللغة الخمرة وطيبة المدينة
3. وعذق بن طاب نخل بها او ابن طاب ضرب من الرطب كذا في القاموس
4. فقد يمكن علي بعد ان يكون الطاب من احدهما فانه من النخل وهي
5. طاب علي الاول او من نخل بها ابن طاب علي الثاني والطياب
6. ككتاب نخل بالبصرة[6] [7] ويقولون على الاجر الطوب وهو صحيح
7. وعلي المزح المطايبة وهو صحيح ايضا ومن الحوادث
8. الحوادث[8] التى وقعت في هذا العام وهو عام اربعة عشر والف
9. ببلاد مصر العشبة التى اشتهرت باسم طابغه يشربون دخانها
10. وقد زاد استعمالها الان حتى صار يباع منها في كل يوم بدنيا
11. لها جرم وعمت البلوي بها سآير الجنوس في دكاكين خاصة
12. بها ويخطر فى الفكر ان تفتح بيوت لخصوصها كالقهاوي[9]
13. ولم اعرف فيها خبرا صادقا قالوا جات من بلاد الغرب ومدحت
14. بقصيدة مطولة سمعت بها وقد مصصت من دخانها قليلا فحصل
15. عندي شبه الدوخه ولا بدع فان الدخان ويقال له الدخ قريب منها
16. فصل العين يقولون العبّ علي ما يلي الصدر و

---

[5] Margin: انظر الطاب والطابه

[6] Margin: واما الطابة فلم تعلم صح

[7] Margin: ويقولون طاوب لفلان اي انه طاطا في السلام عليه انظرها

[8] *Sic.*

[9] Margin: بيع منها كل رطل بثلاثة ذهب

17. الصحيح انه الكم[10] قال في القاموس العب بالضم الرّدن وقال في
18. الردن اصل الكم جمعه اردان ويقولون عتبة الباب يريدون
19. ما يلي سفل الباب والذي في القاموس انه اسكفة الباب والعليا
20. منها انتهي وانظر الفرق بين المعطوف والمعطوف عليه[11] فظاهره ان اسكفة
21. هي السفلى ثم قال وما عتبت بابه اي لم اطا عتبته وهذا دليل على انها سفلي
22. فائده قوله تعالي وان يستعتبوا فما هم من المعتبين اي ان
23. يستقيلوا ربهم لم يقلهم اي لم يردهم الي الدنيا البتة ويقولون

fol. 17r

1. عرقب الدابة اذا قطع عرقوبها وهو صحيح واما المثل المشهور
2. مواعيد عرقوب فهو معبد بن اسد من العمالقة اكذب اهل زمانه
3. اتاه سآيل فقال اذا اطلع نخلي فلما اطلع قال اذا ابلح فلما ابلح قال
4. اذا ازهي فلما ازهي قال اذا ارطب فلما ارطب قال اذا اتمر فلما اتمر
5. جذه ليلا ولم يعطه شيا فقال الاشجعي، وعدت فكان الخلف منك سجية،
6. مواعيد عرقوب اخاه بيثرب، ومن قصيدة بانت سعاد، كانت
7. مواعيد عرقوب لها مثلا، وما مواعيدها الا الاباطيل، ويقولون
8. علي بعض الحرس ليلا العزب وله مناسبة لان العزب لغةً من لا
9. اهل له ولا يحرس هذه الحراسة من له اهل غالبا وكذلك من لا زوجة
10. له عزب ولا تقل اعزب او قليل جمعه اعزاب وهي عزبة وعزب
11. والفعل كنصر وتعزّب ترك النكاح نادره كما ان تعزّب بالزاي ترك
12. كذلك بالرآءِ فانه ترك وطنه وكذلك يعزب بمعني يغيب فالقرب في
13. اللفظ والمعني وقد علم ان الرجل عزب وهي عزبه لا عازبة كما يقولون

---

[10] Margin: العب الكم

[11] Margin: انظر الفرق

Translation

fol. 16r

(10) Section *ṭā*ʾ. They[12] say: *ṭabṭab ʿalā al-šay*, (11) and this has an equivalent.[13] [Al-Fīrūzabādī] said in *al-Qāmūs*: "*al-ṭabṭaba* is the sound of water and the sound of the dashing of the torrent (12) and *al-ṭabṭabiyya* is a whip and *ṭabṭab* is a sound." Interesting fact: "*ṭabāṭabā* is the nickname (13) of Ismāʿīl b. al-Ḥasan b. al-Ḥusayn b. ʿAlī—may God be pleased with them—which was given to him because he used to (14) replace *qāf* with *ṭā*ʾ, or because he was given a *qabā*ʾ,[14] so he said: *ṭabāṭabā*, but he meant *qabāqabā*", end [of the quotation]. (15) The *faqīr*[15] said: I heard the late son of sheikh al-Ġayṭī, who replaced letters (16) with *ṭā*ʾ, say *nāṭis baʿḍ wurayṭāṭ*, that is, *nāqiṣ baʿḍ wurayqāt*,[16]—(17) may God rest his soul, and we have profited much from his noble ancestors—"*Al-ṭabṭāb* is a bird with big ears". (18) They say: so-and-so experienced *al-ṭarab*, which they apply to the agitation[17] of joy,

[12] I.e., the Egyptians.

[13] I.e., it can be found in *al-Qāmūs al-Muḥīṭ*.

[14] An outer garment with sleeves.

[15] Al-Maġribī always refers to himself in the third person with the epithet *al-faqīr* 'the poor', or 'living for the Lord alone' (see Nizami 2012 for the use of this term in the context of Sufism). Al-Maġribī had connections with some of the Sufi orders in Cairo (see Zack 2009, 15–16).

[16] "some little papers are missing"

[17] Lane (1863–1893): "طَرَبٌ Emotion, or a lively emotion, or excitement, or agitation, or unsteadiness [...] by reason of joy or grief [...]" (1888a); "حَرَكَةٌ motion; commotion; agitation" (556b).

and it is used [in Classical Arabic] (19) for the agitation of both joy and grief, [so this is] one of the words with two opposite meanings, and "a man who is *muṭrāb* and *ṭarūb*."[18] (20) It seems now that the saying "if two donkeys happen to meet, [their voices] agitate," means that they evoke the agitation of grief, not (21) joy, because the voice of a single donkey evokes grief, from which one should seek protection, (22) so what would it be like if it were doubled? Interesting fact: *ṭarib* "like *katif*[19] is the name of the horse of the Prophet—God bless him and grant him salvation."

fol. 16v

(1) They say *ṭāb* to [the game] they play, and also *ṭāba* to the counter.[20] (2) I do not know a corresponding [word in Classical Arabic] for these two words.[21] *Al-ṭāba* in the [Classical Arabic] language is "wine, and *Ṭayba* is al-Madīna, (3) and *ʿaḏq ibn ṭāb* is a type of date palm in [al-Madīna], or *ibn ṭāb* is a type of date." It is written thus in *al-Qāmūs*, (4) so it could just be that *ṭāb* is [derived] from one of these two, because it is [made] from the palm tree, so it is (5) *ṭāb* from the first one, or it is from the palm trees in [al-Madīna] [called] *ibn ṭāb*, from the second one. And

---

[18] This means that these are the two adjectives derived from the word *ṭarab*, i.e., 'a man who is filled with joy or grief'.

[19] That is, with the same vocalisation as *katif*.

[20] Literally: 'ball'. See the Commentary below for a discussion of the Egyptian Arabic terms in the text.

[21] Margin: Look up *ṭāb* and *ṭāba*.

ṭiyāb (6) like *kitāb* is a type of palm tree in Baṣra.[22, 23] They call baked bricks *ṭūb*, and this is correct, (7) and [they call] joking *muṭāyaba*, which is also correct. One of the events (8) events [*sic*] that happened this year, which is the year 1014,[24] (9) in the land of Egypt, is the herb that has become known under the name of *ṭābġa* 'tobacco'. They inhale[25] its smoke, (10) and its use has now increased to the point that it is being sold every day in a world (11) full of vice and it has become a general necessity, all types in designated shops, (12) and now the idea has come up to open special houses for it like cafés.[26] (13) I don't have reliable information about it. They say that it came from the West, and it is praised (14) in a long poem that I have heard. I have sucked up a little bit of its smoke and got (15) a kind of *dawxa*, dizziness, and no wonder, because *duxxān* 'smoke', which is also called *duxx*, is close to it.[27] (16) Section *ʿayn*. They say *al-ʿbb* to that which is next to the chest, but (17) the correct [meaning] is that it is the sleeve. [Al-Fīrūzābādī] said in *al-Qāmūs*: "*al-ʿubb* with the vowel *u* is *al-rudn*, the sleeve," and [al-Fīrūzabādī] said about

---

[22] Margin: As to *ṭāba*, it is not known; correct.

[23] Margin: They say: he *ṭāwb* to someone, which means that he bowed his head in greeting to him, look this up.

[24] 1605–1606 CE.

[25] Literally: 'drink'.

[26] Margin: A *raṭl* of it is sold for three gold pieces. [Note: the *raṭl* is a unit of weight.]

[27] Here, al-Maġribī makes a connection between *dawxa* 'dizziness' and *duxx* 'smoke', because they sound similar.

(18) *rudn*: "the base of the sleeve, its plural is *ardān*."[28] They say: *ʿatabat al-bāb*, with which they mean (19) that which is at the bottom of the door, and what is written in the *Qāmūs* is that it is "*uskuffat al-bāb*, the threshold of the door, and the upper part (20) of it," end of quotation.[29] It appears that *uskuffa* (21) is the lower part; then [al-Fīrūzābādī] said "*mā ʿatabtu bābahu* means: I did not step upon his threshold," and this is a sign that it is the lower part. (22) Interesting fact: the words of the Sublime *and if they ask amends yet no amends shall be made to them*[30] mean that if (23) they ask their Lord to forgive their fault, he will definitely not do so, which means that he will not return them to the world. They say

fol. 17r

(1) he *ʿarqab* the riding animal, if he hamstrung it, which is correct, and as for the famous expression (2) "the promises of ʿUrqūb, this is "Maʿbad b. Asad, one of the Giants, who was the most untruthful person of his time. (3) Once a beggar came to him, so he told him: when my palm trees put forth the spadix [I will give you alms],[31] so when that happened, he said: when it brings forth

---

[28] Margin: *al-ʿbb* is the sleeve.

[29] Margin: Look up what the difference is between the two conjuncts. [Note: *Al-maʿṭūf* and *al-maʿṭūf ʿalayhi*: a word to which another word is conjoined, for instance by the particle of conjunction *wa-*, in this case: *uskuffat al-bāb wa-l-ʿulyā minhā*.]

[30] Qurʾān 41:24, translation by Arberry (1963, II:187).

[31] See Lane (1863–1893, 1919c) for the meaning of أطلع النخل. The طَلْع, translated by Lane as the spadix (1921b) is a fleshy stem with small flowers that turn into dates if the palm tree is female.

dates, so when that happened, he said: (4) when the redness appears in the dates, and when that happened, he said: when the dates become ripe, so when that happened, he said: when the dates become dry, and when that happened, (5) he cut them off at night, and did not give [the beggar] anything." Al-Ašjaʿī[32] said: "You made a promise, but not fulfilling it was in your character (6) Like the promises of ʿUrqūb to his brother in Yaṯrib." And from the poem *Suʿād is gone*:[33] (7) "The promises of ʿUrqūb were for her a model tall-tale promises, empty talk." They call (8) someone of the night guards *ʿazab* 'bachelor', which has an equivalent, because in the [Classical Arabic] language *ʿazab* is "someone who does not (9) have a family", and someone who has a family as a rule does not do this [night] watch, and someone who does not have a wife (10) is also a *ʿazab*, "and do not say *aʿzab*, or it is rare; the plural is *aʿzāb* and the feminine *ʿazaba* and *ʿazab*, (11) and the verb is like *naṣara*;[34] and *taʿazzaba* means he abstained from marriage." A curiosity: just like *taʿazzaba* with a *zāy* means 'to abstain', (12) so also with a *rāʾ*,[35] because it means that he left his land, and likewise *yaʿzibu* with the meaning 'to be absent', so the proximity is in both (13) the pronunciation and the

---

[32] Abū ʿĀmir Ibn Šuhayd al-Ašǧaʿī (992–1035) was an Andalusian poet, man of letters, and vizier. See Pellat (2012a).

[33] This is from the *lāmiyya* known as the *Burda*, by Kaʿb b. Zuhayr, a contemporary of the Prophet. See Basset (2012). Translation of this verse by Sells (1990, 149).

[34] I.e., it has the vowels *a-a*, so *ʿazaba*.

[35] I.e., *taʿazzaba* and *taʿarraba* have the same meaning.

meaning. It is known that the man is *ʿazab* and the woman *ʿazaba*, not *ʿāziba* as they say.

Commentary

This section is divided into two parts: the first will discuss the orthography of the Classical Arabic component of the text, and the second part will focus on the Egyptian Arabic entries.

Classical Arabic: Orthography

The main body of the text, which consists of al-Maġribī's comments on the Egyptian Arabic words under discussion, and contains quotations from *al-Qāmūs al-muḥīṭ* and other dictionaries, the Qurʾān, ḥadīth, and poetry, are all in Classical Arabic in terms of morphology, syntax, and vocabulary. However, the orthography is not according to the standards of Classical Arabic, but follows patterns that are well-known from Middle Arabic texts. Al-Maġribī's biography shows that he was an educated man, who studied at the Azhar University, was interested in the Arabic language, and had good knowledge of dictionaries and other works on linguistics. He also composed poetry in Classical Arabic. This is indicative of his excellent knowledge of the Arabic language. The fact that the orthography he used does not adhere to the standards of Classical Arabic can therefore not be attributed to insufficient knowledge of the language. As Lentin (2011) points out, "many writers have left us works written both in faultless or even sophisticated Classical Arabic and works written in Middle Arabic. For those writers at least, one has to abandon the idea of their inadequacies in Classical Arabic." We have to bear in mind that in many text editions, the orthography has been standardised by the editors, and that many Classical Arabic texts originally contained Middle Arabic features (Lentin 2011). In fact, the history of Arabic orthography has not been sufficiently studied yet; in order to do so, more text editions that are faithful to the original orthography need to be published (Den Heijer 2012). As for *Dafᶜ al-iṣr*, the most important orthographic features are highlighted in the sections that follow (see also Zack 2009, 77–83).

The *hamza*

The *hamza* has been omitted in many cases. As the text is in Classical Arabic, this omission of the *hamza* is unlikely to be indicative of its loss in the pronunciation. Rather, as Blau (2002, 32) suggests, it could reflect "an ancient orthographic habit preserved also through N[eo-]A[rabic] influence."

Some examples of omission of the *hamza* (see also Blau 2002, 32–33):

initial *hamza*: اي 16r, ln. 16 (أي); الاضداد 16r, ln. 19 (الأضداد).
medial *hamza*: جات 16v, ln. 13 (جأت); طاطا 16v, margin (طأطأ); شيا 17r, ln. 5 (شيئا).
final *hamza*: الشي 16r, ln. 10 (الشيء); الما 16r, ln. 11 (الماء); بالطا 16r, ln. 16 (بالطاء).

When the *yāʾ* is the seat of the *hamza*, it is written below the *yāʾ*, e.g., طآير 16r, ln. 17 (طائر); سآيل 17r, ln. 3 (سائل). It can also be omitted, as in فايده 16r, ln. 12[36] (فائدة); سآر 16v, ln. 11 (سائر).

[36] And other instances; in such cases, only one line number is given here.

The *madda*

The *madda* is sometimes omitted, e.g., in الان 16r, ln. 20 (الآن). However, more interesting is that the *madda* is added on the *ʾalif* to write the combination *āʾ*: سآر 16v, ln. 11 (سائر); طآ 16r, ln. 14 (طاء). Often for good measure an extra *hamza* is added as well: طآءِر 16r, ln. 17 (طائر); بالرآءِ 17r, ln. 12 (بالراءِ).

The *yāʾ* and *ʾalif maqṣūra*

The *yāʾ* and *alif maqṣūra* are often used interchangeably.

> *alif maqṣūra* instead of *yāʾ*: فى 16r, ln. 11; رضى 16r, ln. 13; التى 16v, ln. 8.
> *yāʾ* instead of *alif maqṣūra*: صلي 16r, ln. 22; البلوي 16v, ln. 11; ازهي 17r, ln. 4; بمعني 17r, ln. 12.

The *tāʾ marbūṭa*

The *tāʾ marbūṭa* is often written without dots, even if it is the first part of a genitive construction. Examples: الطابه 16v, margin; الدوخه 16v, ln. 15; نادره 17r, ln. 11; عزبه 17r, ln. 13.

Egyptian Arabic Lemmata

ṭabṭab 'to pat': this entry provides a good example for how al-Maġribī comments on Egyptian Arabic vocabulary. In most cases he does not give a definition of the word under discussion, assuming that his readers know what it means. In Egyptian Arabic, *ṭabṭab* is used nowadays with the meaning of 'to pat' (Badawi and Hinds 1986, 530b; see also Dozy 1881, 2:21b); the combination with *ʿalā* given by al-Maġribī makes it likely that it meant just that in the 17th century, but the quotation from *al-Qāmūs al-muḥīṭ* does not give the exact same meaning. The entry also shows how al-Maġribī integrates anecdotes about his own acquaintances and events from his own life into the dictionary.

al-ṭarab 'agitation': as in al-Maġribī's time, in modern Egyptian Arabic it is used to mean only pleasure, not sadness, but more specifically the pleasure derived from listening to singing (Badawi and Hinds 1986, 534a).

ṭāb 'the *ṭāb*-game': the game of *ṭāb* is still played today in Egypt. It is a "game for two players with stone counters and four strips of palm branch, each strip having one green side and one white side; the strips are thrown against a vertical surface and the various combinations of green and white govern the movement of the stones on a grid drawn in the dust" (Badawi and Hinds 1986, 528a). Lane (1863–1893, 55–58) gives a detailed description of the game and how it is played (Zack 2009, 74, 243; see also Dozy 1881, 2:65a–b).

ṭāwb 'to bow one's head in greeting': no references found in Classical Arabic or Egyptian Arabic dictionaries.

ṭūb 'bricks': from Coptic τωωβε 'brick' (Crum 1939, 398a; Badawi and Hinds 1986, 548b). The reason that al-Maġribī does not refer to its non-Arabic origin is that al-Fīrūzābādī (1999, 103a), al-Maġribī's main source, does not mention that it is a loanword.

muṭāyaba 'joking': as in Classical Arabic (Lane 1863–1893, 1952c).

ṭābġa 'tobacco'. Tobacco was introduced in Egypt in 1603–1604 (Matthee 2012), two years before al-Maġribī wrote *Dafᶜ al-iṣr* (Zack 2009, 70–71). His comments show how tobacco very rapidly became popular, with special shops and coffee houses where customers could smoke being established within the two years of its introduction. Al-Maġribī did not view the smoking of tobacco favourably, as he comments on how he tried it and became dizzy and considered it a vice. He returns to the subject of tobacco on fol. 75v, where he mentions that there were discussions about whether it was permissible to smoke tobacco while fasting during Ramadan, with one sheikh ruling that it was indeed allowed. Al-Maġribī found this reprehensible (he mentions this anecdote in the lemma *raḏil* 'depraved'). Badawi and Hinds (1986) do not mention the word *ṭābġa* for tobacco, and neither does Spiro (1895).[37] It is mentioned by Steingass (1884, 162b) as *tabġ* and by Dozy (1881, 2:141a) as *tibġ*.

ʿbb 'bosom of a garment'. It still has the same meaning in modern Egyptian Arabic, vocalisation *ʿibb* (Badawi and Hinds 1986, 558b; *ʿubb* in Classical Arabic, where it means 'base of the sleeve', as demonstrated in the quotation from al-Fīrūzābādī mentioned by al-Maġribī).

ʿataba 'threshold'. According to al-Maġribī, this applied only to the lower part of the door frame, but in modern Egyptian Arabic it is both the lower and upper part (Badawi and Hinds 1986, 558b).

ʿarqab 'to hamstring', i.e., incapacitate by cutting the hamstring tendon. The word is still in use in modern Egyptian Arabic (Badawi and Hinds 1986, 574a).

[37] Badawi and Hinds (1986) mention *tumbāk* / *ṭumbāk* (136a, 546b) and *duxxān* (282a). Spiro (1895) mentions the Turkish *tutun* (68a) as well as *duxxān* (194b).

ʿazab 'member of the night guard': this meaning was derived from the original meaning 'bachelor', because only men who did not have a family would work in the night guard.[38] Dozy (1881, 2:124a) mentions 'milice bourgeoise'. The 17th-century meaning of 'member of the night guard' disappeared in the 19th century, as it is not mentioned by Spiro (1895, 396b). Badawi and Hinds (1986, 574b–575a) mention only the forms *ʾaʿzab* and *ʿāzib* 'bachelor', not *ʿazab,* although they do mention the feminine form *ʿazaba* (alongside *ʿazba* < *ʿāziba*).

[38] See Cezzâr (1962, 32) for more information on the night guard in Ottoman Egypt.

9. LEBANON: CHRONICLE OF AL-ṢAFADĪ (EARLY 17TH CENTURY [?])

Jérôme Lentin

In the first annex to their edition of al-Ṣafadī's chronicle (about the period 1612–1624) Bustānī and Rustum (1969, 208–41) published a section dealing specifically with the years (1613–1618) Faḫr al-Dīn spent in Italy. For them, al-Ṣafadī (a scholar born in Ṣafad, who studied in Al-ʾAzhar in Cairo, and the author of learned works as well as of travelogues) is not the author of this text, an opinion which seems reasonable, but is not shared by all scholars.

A recent edition is the 2007 volume *Riḥlat al-ʾAmīr Faḫr al-Dīn ʾilā ʾĪṭāliyā, 1613–1618.* Faḫr al-Dīn al-Maʿnī al-ṯānī, ḥaqqaqahā wa-qaddama lahā Qāsim Wahb. Beirut: Al-Muʾassasa al-ʿarabiyya li-l-dirāsāt wa-l-našr and Abu Dhabi: Dār al-Suwaydī li-l-našr wa-l-tawzīʿ (*Irtiyād al-ʾāfāq*).

Transcription

وفي مدينة فرنسيا وغيرها بيمارستانات لاجل الضعفاء واي من[1] ضعف[2] وكان له خاطر[3] يروح[4] الى البيمارستانات يلاقي الحكما موجوده وجميع[5] ما يحتاج الضعيف[6] ولو كان اقل الناس واراد له ادويه بالف غرش يداووه[7] بها من غير منية[8] واكله وشربه وفرش ولحف وناس معدة لخدمة المرضى بجميع ما يحتاجوا اليه ولما يعرف الحكيم انه طاب يطالعوه[9] من غير كلفه وما يحط[10] الضعيف درهم الفرد[11] وجميع المصروف من اوقاف البيمارستانات وكذلك لهم

 https://doi.org/10.11647/OBP.0208.15

ديوره[12] فيها خدامين[13] ومراضع كلما خلق ولد للنسوان[14] من الذي[15] تحت القسط او من النسوان الذي يخلق لهم ولد وما مرادهم[16] يشهروه حتى اذا احد من الفقراء ولد له ولد وكان له اولاد كثيره يرميه في هذا الموضع كرامة ترباته[17] وهذا الدير له طاقة من رخام على قدر ما يسع الولد حين يخلق تجيبه[18] الحرمه[19] ملفوفا وترميه في الليل من هذه الطاقة ولها ناس ينتظروها من جوا[20] واذا نزل الولد يستلقوه ويعطوه الى[21] المراضع يدبروه واذا كبروا[22] الاولاد يحطوهم في القراءة والصناعة ويحطوا الذكور وحدهم واذا بلغوا الاولاد الاناث يدوروهم في المدينه وكل من قبل على جواز يجوزوه[23] بنت منهم ان كان من اولاد المتربيين[24] في الدير او من الناس الذي برا[25] يجوزوه البنت الذي علمها وكلفة تربيتهم وجوازهم من اوقاف الدير ومن كيس السلطان لان السيره عندهم المراة تعطي الرجال[26] النقد كل من هو على قدر حاله على قدر مراتبهم وكذلك لهم ديوره للبنات الاكابر وديوره الى بنات العامة الذي يرهبوا فيهم البنات وعلى هذا المنوال ديوره الى الاولاد والرجال وجميع من يدخل الى هذه الديورة كلفته من اوقاف الدير واولاد الاكابر ياتيهم من اهلهم

Translation

In the town of Florence, as in others, there are hospitals for ill people. Whoever falls ill and wants to go to the hospital will find there doctors and everything needed by an ill person. Even those with the most limited means, if medicines costing one thousand piasters are necessary, they treat them without any return obligation. They also get food, drink, bed, and blankets. People are there ready to provide all the care patients need. When the doctor sees that the ill person has recovered, they let him out without paying anything: he doesn't pay a single dirham. All these expenses are funded from the endowment income [*waqf*-s] of the hospitals. They also have monasteries with attendants and wet nurses. Every time a woman of disrepute gives birth to a child, or a woman wants to keep the birth of her child a secret, or even when a poor man with many children has a [new] child, [in all these cases] they can leave the child at this place, to have it brought up. This monastery has a marble window *the size of a new-born child. The woman brings the baby in swaddling clothes and drops it at night through this window. People are there inside waiting for her and when the baby comes down, they catch it and give it to the wet nurses who take charge of it. When the children grow up, they pay for them to learn to read [and write] and to learn a handicraft—but only the boys. As for the girls, when they reach puberty, they go around the city with them and marry any one of these girls to whoever agrees to do so. Whether it is to one of the children raised in the monastery or to one of the people outside, they give to him as a wife the girl he has singled out. The costs of their upbringing and marriage are covered by the endowment* income of the monastery and at the expense of the sultan, because this is their way of doing things: the woman gives to the man the dowry—each according to his situation and to their [respective] rank. They also have monasteries for the daughters of the notables and monasteries for the daughters of the common people, where they turn them into nuns. And the same goes for the monasteries for boys and men. All those who enter the monasteries [in the case of the children of the common people] have their costs paid from the endowment income [*waqf*-s] of the monastery. As for the children of the notables, they are funded by their families.

Commentary

1 اي من *ʾaymən* 'whoever' (colloquial).

2 ضعف 'to get sick, to fall ill' (colloquial); compare no. 6.

[3] له خاطر + (subjunctive) imperfect 'to want, wish, desire to, to feel like doing sth' (colloquial).

[4] يروح *rāḥ* (and less frequently *rawwaḥ*) is the usual verb in MA for 'to go' and 'to go to'. For this last meaning, the more stylistically elevated توجّه is also widely.

[5] جميع + noun / pron. is the most common quantifier in (Levantine) MA for 'all'; 'whole, entire', even before a singular (pro)noun.

[6] الضعيف 'ill, sick' (compare no. 2).

[7] يداووه. The (colloquial) -*ū* form (and not -*ūn*) is used most of the time in MA for the second and third person plural of the imperfect; the -*ūn* form is used either in classicising passages or as a marked form, for instance after final conjunctions (contrary to Classical usage). Compare the many other examples of -*ū* forms in this text: يحطوهم, يدبروه, يستلقوه ويعطوه, ينتظروها, يطالعوه, يحتاجوا, يحطوا, يدوروهم, يجوزوه (2x), يرهبوا.

[8] منية. Colloquial, see Barthélemy (1935–1969, 804); see also Dozy (1881, vol. II, p. 616).

[9] طالع is used with its colloquial meaning 'to throw out, pull out, remove, dismiss, expel', etc.

[10] حط 'to put, place', here figuratively 'to pay (an amount of money)' (colloquial).

[11] درهم الفرد *fard* = 'one and only, one and the same'; this construction, Ø + N sing. + art. + فرد, is mainly used after a negation, as is the case here; it can be as a whole modified by the article (الدرهم الفرد, i.e., [الـ[درهم الفرد]). See Lentin (1997, 312).

12 ديوره (also ديورا) is the most frequently used (colloquial) plural of دير 'convent, monastery' in Ottoman MA texts (see Lentin 1997 184–186, §4.3.7.5).

13 خدامين. The formerly mpl oblique case sound form *-īn* is predominantly used in MA regardless of the syntactic function of the noun (the *n* being generally retained in construct state). The Classical nominative *-ūn* form is reserved for stylistically marked use.

14 خلق ولد ل lit. 'a child is created (born) to…' (colloquial *ḫiliq*); compare the following ولد له ولد (speaking of a man).

15 للنسوان من الذي. Invariable الذي is extremely common in MA. Compare الناس الذي برا.

16 ما مرادهم يشهروه. Most probably a transposition of colloquial *ma bidd-hon yišəhrū*.

17 ترباته. Colloquial verbal noun of *rabbā* (*tərbāy*, *tərbāye*, etc.).

18 تجيبه *žāb*, *yžīb* 'to bring' is probably the most frequently used colloquial verb in MA, and can be considered a typical 'plain MA' verb.

19 الحرمه 'the woman' (colloquial).

20 من جوا lit. 'from inside'. Colloquial *žuwwā* (adverb and preposition, construct state *žuwwāt*) 'inside' and *barrā* (*barrāt*) 'outside' are widely used in MA.

21 ديوره الى بنات العامة (and ديوره الى الاولاد والرجال). The use of الى, where either Classical or colloquial Arabic would have ل, is typical of a frequent MA procedure whereby a partial correspond-

ence between a colloquial and a Standard preposition is generalised into total interchangeability (often bringing about a pair of stylistically contrasting variants).

[22] كبر 'to get old' (colloquial *kibir*).

[23] جواز and يجوزوه. Colloquial forms (compare Classical Arabic *zawāj* and *zawwaja*).

[24] اولاد المتربيين. Ø + N + art. + active participle qualifying N (= الاولاد المتربيين). متربيين is morphologically colloquial (*mitrabbyīn*).

[25] برا. See no. 20.

[26] الرجال is the colloquial singular form (*rəžžāl*), whereas in الاولاد والرجال it is the plural (Classical *rijāl*, colloquial *ržāl*).

10. A JEW'S TESTIMONY REGARDING A STATEMENT MADE IN HIS PRESENCE BY A MUSLIM, TESTIFIED ON MONDAY 20TH KISLEV 5418 (1657)[1]

Werner Diem

Transcription

אייש חאל (2) כ̇אטרך עלה יעקב וחק וחק סועוב[2] עלייה קדר מא (3) סועוב עלה אוכ̇תו ואמראתו ואכתר ופי יום אין ג̇א אל (4) כ̇בר אין מא עוודשי רוחת נפתש פי נחיית אל בסאתין (5) ואנא ראייח קבלני וואחד מסלם רפיקי בייאע לבן וכונת (6) אנא ויעקב נדכ̇ול ונכ̇רוג̇ פי בייתו למא כונא נרום לסוכר (7) פי קאלי אל מסלם אל לבאן יא חג̇ מ״ח אייש דאייר (8) תעמל הנא פי קולתלו מא תערף יעקב רפיקי טלע (9) ליילית אמס ידפן ולליידאת ווארח[3] ומא עאווד פי קאלי אל (10) לבאן תעאלה מעי נרוחו נפתשו עליה פרוחנא פתשנא (11) ומא לקיינשי פי[4] תאני יום ג̇א אל לבאן מחמל באל לבן (12) יביעו הנה פקאלי אנה נצ̇רת אתניין מרמיין מכסרין (13) איידיהום ורג̇לייהום ואל דם נאזיז מן

[1] Published in Diem (2014, 9–10). Reproduced from the journal *Mediterranean Language Review* with kind permission of the editor, Prof. Matthias Kappler.

[2] סועוב for צועוב *ṣuʿub*.

[3] ווארח for וראח.

[4] פי here *fi-* (< *fa-*).

 https://doi.org/10.11647/OBP.0208.16

רוסהום פי טל פיהום (14) אל לבאן פי ערף יעקב פי קאללי אל לבאן תעאלה מעי (15) נווריהום לך פרוחנא אנא ואל לבאן פתשנא מא ווג׳ידנאשי

Arabic Transcription

اييش حال (2) خاطرك عله يعقب وحق وحق سوعوب علييه قدر ما (3) سوعوب عله اوختو وامراتو واكتر وفى يوم اين جا ال (4) خبر اين ما عوودشى روحت نفتش فى نحييت البساتين (5) وانا راييح قبلنى وواحد مسلم رفيقى بيياع لبن وكونت (6) انا ويعقب ندخول ونخروج فى بييتو لما كونا نروم لسوكر (7) فى قالى المسلم اللبان يا حج محـ(ـمد) اييش داير (8) تعمل هنا فى قولتلو ما تعرف يعقب رفيقى طلع (9) ليبليت امس يدفن ولييدات ووارح وما عاوود فى قالى ال (10) لبان تعاله معى نروحو نفتشو عليه فروحنا فتشنا (11) وما لقيينشى فى تانى يوم جا اللبان محمل باللبن (12) يبيعو هنه فقالى انه نضرت اتنيين مرمبين مكسرين (13) اييديهوم ورجلييهوم والدم نازيز من روسهوم فى طل فيهوم (14) اللبان فى عرف يعقب فى قاللى اللبان تعاله معى (15) نووريهوم لك فروحنا انا واللبان فتشنا ما ووجيدناشى

Translation

What do (2) you think about Jacob? Seriously, I was very sad about him, as (3) were his sister and wife, and even more. On the day when the (4) news reached (us) that he had not returned (home), I went to look (for him) near al-Basātīn. (5) While I was walking, one of the Muslims, a friend of mine, a seller of milk, met me. (6) Jacob and I had frequented his house when we wanted sweets. (7) The Muslim milkman said: "O Ḥajj Muḥ(ammad), what are you doing (8) here?" I said to him: "Don't you know that Jacob, my friend, went out (9) yesterday night to bury little girls, he went and did not come back." Then the milkman (10) said to me "Come with me! We'll go and look for him!" So we went to look, (11) but did not find him. On the next day, the milkman came carrying milk (12) in order to sell it here. He said to me: "I saw two who had been struck down, with broken (13) hands and feet, and blood oozing from their heads." When the milkman looked down on them, (14) he recognised Jacob. So, he said to me: "Come with me! (15) I will show them to you." Then the milkman and I went to look for them, but we did not find them.

11. A JEW'S TESTIMONY REGARDING A STATEMENT MADE IN HIS PRESENCE BY A MUSLIM (1681)[1]

Werner Diem

מה הום כל אל יהוד סוא פלאן (2) ופלאן יאכולו מן אכלנא ומן לחמתנה ויישתרו מן אל
(3) סוק ויג̇יבו לנא נטבוכ̇ו להום ויאכלו מענא אמה אצלן (4) אל טוויל אלי מן ענדכם
אללה ירחמו דאך מאסיך עלה (5) דינו לא יכול מן אכלנא ולא ידוק לנא טועאם ומעמלתו[2]
(6) טייבה על אל צודק כונת אנא והוא ושריכו מעה פי סוק (7) ברכאתה חביינא נעדו
אנה והום למחלת אבו עלי פי (8) נהאר אלי כאן עג̇אג̇ ואל ריח וכאן ענדי אנה מה נעמיל
(9) פי אל סוק סבקוני וטלעו פי אל מעדייא ג̇יית אנה (10) ללבאחר לאג̇ל מה נעדי למחלת
א׳ עלי קאלולי אנה (11) אצלן אל טאוויל ורפיקו טלעו פי אל מעדיא אצגירה[3] (12)
ואנקלבת ביהום ולא טלע מן אל מעדייא חד גייר וואחד׳[4] (13) מרה מסכת פי קורון אל
בקרה היא אלי טלעת

Arabic Transcription

مه هوم كل اليهود سوا فلان (2) وفلان ياكولو من اكلنا ومن لحمتنه وييشترو من الـ (3) سوق
ويجيبو لنا نطبوخو لهوم وياكلو معنا امه اصلن (4) الطوويل الى من عندكم الله يرحمو داك

---

[1] Published in Diem (2014, 22–23). Reproduced from the journal *Mediterranean Language Review* with kind permission of the editor, Prof. Matthias Kappler.

[2] Based on *muʿāmala*.

[3] Phonetic spelling instead of אל צגירה.

[4] Feminine form, abbreviated at the end of the line.

https://doi.org/10.11647/OBP.0208.17

ماسيك عله (5) دينو لا يكول من اكلنا ولا يدوق لنا طوعام ومعملتو (6) طييبه عل الصودق
كونت انا وهوا وشريكو معه فى سوق (7) بركاته حبيينا نعدو انه وهوم لمحلت ابو على فى (8)
نهار الى كان عجاج والريح وكان عندى انه مه نعميل (9) فى السوق سبقونى وطلعو فى
المعدييا جييت انه (10) للباحر لاجل مه نعدى لمحلت ا(بو) على قالولى انه (11) اصلن
الطاوويل ورفيقو طلعو فى المعديا اصغيره (12) وانقلبت بيهوم ولا طلع من المعدييا حد غيير
وواحد(ه) (13) مره مسكت فى قورون البقره هيا الى طلعت

Translation

Not all Jews are alike. So-and-so (2) and so-and-so eat from our food and from our meat, and buy from the (3) market and bring (it) to us so that we cook (it) for them, and they eat together with us. Concerning Aṣlān (4) the Tall, who belongs to you (Jews)—may God have mercy on him—he adheres to his (5) religion. He does not eat from our food. He does not taste our dishes. His behaviour is (6) excellent in terms of piety. He and I, and his business partner with him, were at the (7) Sūq Barakātih (market). We, they and I, wanted to cross to Maḥallat Abū ʿAlī on that (8) day, when there was dust and wind. I had something to do in (9) the market, so they went ahead of me and went on the ferry. (When) I came to (10) the river in order to cross to Maḥallat ʿAlī, they told me that (11) Aṣlān the Tall and his companion went on the small ferry. (12) It capsized with them on board and no one escaped from the ferry except for a woman, who grabbed on to the horns of the cow,[5] and she (alone) came out of it.

[5] The speaker presupposes the listener's knowledge of a cow that had been in the ferry.

12. A BASRA PASSOVER HAGGADAH WITH JUDAEO-ARABIC TRANSLATION (CA. 1700)

Omer Shafran

Location of the manuscript: Jerusalem, The National Library of Israel Ms. Heb. 8°713 [B 296 (8°713)].

Transcription

Aramaic/Hebrew

הא לחמא עניא די אכלו אבהתנה בארעא
דמצרים כל דכפין יתי וייכול כל דצריך
ייתי ויפסח השתא הכא לשנה הבאה בארעא
דישרﭏ השתא הכא עבדי לשנה הבאה
בארעא דישרﭏ בני חורין.

Judaeo-Arabic

האדׄא כבז ﭏ מסכין ﭏדׄי אכלו אבאיינא
פי בלד מצר כל גׄועאן ייגׄי ויאכל
כל מעתאז ייגׄי וייפסח הסנא נחנא הון
לי סנת ﭏ גׄאייא פי בלד יסראיל הסנא
נחנא עביד ליסנת ﭏ גׄאייא פי בלד יסראיל
בנין ﭏ מטלוקין.

 https://doi.org/10.11647/OBP.0208.18

Arabic Transcription

هاذا خبز ال مسكين الذي اكلو ابايينا
في بلد مصر. كل جوعان ييجي وياكل,
كل معتاز ييجي ويفسح. هسنه نحن هن,
لي سنه ال جاييا في بلد يسرايل. هسنا
نحنا عبيد, ليسنت ال جاييا في بلد يسرايل
بنين ال مطلوقين.

Translation

'Lo! This is the bread of the afflicted, which our ancestors ate in the land of Egypt; let all those who are hungry enter and eat thereof; and all who are needy, come and celebrate the Passover! This year we are here, but next year we hope to celebrate it in the land of Israel. This year we are slaves here, but next year we hope to be freemen in the land of Israel.' (English translation with slight alterations drawn from Russotto 1912).

Commentary

The Hebrew/Aramaic influence is obvious in this Judaeo-Arabic passage: the element ה, in הסנא *has-sana* 'this year', is an apocopation of the demonstrative *hāḏi*, as is common on Southern Iraqī.[1] Its use in this context may additionally have been facilitated by the homophonous Hebrew definite article. The verbal form ייפסח *yifsaḥ*, here 'he will celebrate the Passover', is peculiar to the language of the Jews, and is derived from the festival name *Pesaḥ* 'Passover'; this verb appears also in the original Aramaic/Hebrew text (see above, יפסח). The structure לי סנת אׄ גאייא

[1] I am grateful to Prof. Clive Holes for this suggestion.

reflects the spoken Arabic of Iraq, where constructions such as *sana l-jāya* 'next year', *bab iš-šārgi* 'the eastern gate', and *ṣōb al-janūbi* 'the southern direction' are common.[2] It is an old construction that has disappeared from Modern Standard Arabic, but is still very common in the dialects, and its usage in this place may have been reinforced by its being a calque of the analogous Hebrew construction לשנה הבאה, *le-šana* (indefinite, thus in this passage) *hab-baʾa* (definite) 'next year'.

[2] Again, I am indebted to Prof. Clive Holes for his comments on the phenomenon.

13. QAHWA ‘COFFEE’ (16TH–17TH CENTURIES)

Ghayde Ghraowi

Transcription

"قهوة" من دفع الإصر عن كلام أهل مصر للمغربي:[1]

يقولون قهوة للمستخرج من البن وليس في اللغة قال (القهوة الخمرة والشبعة المحمكة واللبن المخض كالقهة كعدة والرائحة والقهوان التيس الضخم القرنين المسنّ واقهي دام على شرب القهوة واطاع السلطان) انتهى ولم ينص على القهوة المستعملة الان حتى ان البن الذي هو اصلها ليس له ذكر في كتب الطبّ وانظر عدم ذكر صاحب القاموس لها هل حدثت بعده ذكر لي شيخنا الشيخ الحاكمي ان صاحبه المرحوم ابو السعود الذي كان يكتب تقرير شيخه الشيخ القدسي الواعظ وهو على الكرسي وعظ يوما في بعض الماجد وكان الشيخ الحاكمي هناك فسمعه يقول وهذه القهوة التي ابتلت الخلائق بها وورد في الحديث النهي عنها لانه ورد النهي عن القهوة وهي هذه فقام الشيخ الحاكمي وكانه لا يعرفه أصلا فقال يا شيخ افهم ما تقول فقال له كانك ممّن ابتلى بها فقال تامل ما تقول فانه كذب على النبي صلى الله عليه وسلم ما تعريف الخمر اليس انه عصير العنب فقال نعم فقال فاين القهوة منه فسكت وخشي انني اعلم الأستاذ البكري بذلك فارسل بعض الاصحاب للصلح وانه من الان لا يذكر القهوة بشي فرضيت ولم اخبر الأستاذ وللاستاذ مدح كثير فيها وللشيخ ابي الفتح المالكي وقلت

في قهوة القشر ارى فضيلة * اذا ناى من ليس فيه مرحمهْ
حكمتها من اجل صلح بيننا * فيا لها من قهوة محكّمهْ

[1] Zack (2009, 202–3). My transcription here follows that of Zack’s edition, leaving orthographical particularities from the manuscript source uncorrected.

https://doi.org/10.11647/OBP.0208.19

شعر قهوة البن لابراهيم ابن المبلط من الكواكب السائرة بأعيان المئة العاشرة للغزي:[2]

إبراهيم الشيخ الفاضل الأديب الشاعر برهان الدين ابن المبلط القاهري شاعر القاهرة من شعره في قهوة البن:

يقول عذولي قهوة البن مرّة * وشربة حلو الماء ليس لها مثل
فقلت على ما عبتها بمرارة * قد اخترتها فاختر لنفسك ما يحلو

وقال:
أرى قهوة البن في عصرنا * على شربها الناس قد اجمعوا
وصارت لشرّابها عادة * فليست تضرّ ولا تنفع

وقال وهو مشهور عنه:
يا عائباً لشراب قهوتنا التي * تشفي شفاء النفس من أمراضها
أو ما تراها وهي في فنجانها * تحكي سواد العين وسط بياضها

ولبعضهم في هذا المعنى:
اشرب هنيئاً قهوة البن التي * تحلو مع الأخوان والخلان
سوداء في المبيض من فنجانها * تحكي سواد العين للإنسان

قلت أحسن منه قولي:
إشرب من القهوة صاعين * ولو ببذل الورق العين
سوداء في بيض فناجينها * كأنها الإنسان من عين

موشح قهوة البن من ديوان محمد البكري:[3]

أدر القهوة في كأس البها
قهوة البن وناهيك بها

[2] Al-Ghazzī (1979, 3:92–93).

[3] Muḥammad al-Bakrī, *Dīwān* (MS 59 Bibliothèque Nationale du Royaume du Maroc, 1586, fols 99b–100a). It is important to note the coincidence of the manuscript's copy date and the death of its author. Also, the first three stanzas appear in Kīlānī (1965, 194–95). My thanks to Adam Sabra for providing me with the manuscript source.

هي حل ما نهى عنها نُهى
فاسقني يا صاح

شنف الكاسات واسمع ما أقول
إنها شرب الأجلاء الفحول
أولياء الله أرباب الوصول
لحمي الفتاح

ما علينا من عذول جاهل
مفترى زور كلام باطل
خامل الذكر وميت زائل
راح مع من راح

ان يقل تنشي اقل سكر القلوب
مثل ما يشمل ابطال الغيوب
قد يودي الأمر فيها الموجوب
فاجل لي الاقداح

إنما ينكر ما يقترب
بأمور مثلها لا يحسن
فأبهج سنة قوم احسنوا
في احتسا الراح

Translation

'Coffee' from *Dafʿ al-iṣr ʿan kalām ahl Miṣr* by al-Maghribī:

[The Egyptians] say: coffee (*qahwa*) for the extract of the bean, but this usage is not in the standardised language [according to al-Fayrūzabādī], who says, "*qahwa* is wine, a thoroughly[4] satiating drink, and a froth-less, clear[5] yogurt. It is like *qiha/qaha* (one of the names of the narcissus) [?] and it is an aroma. The word *qahwān* means a large aged goat with two horns. The verb *aqhī*[6] means to persist in drinking *qahwa* and to obey the sovereign." These definitions don't indicate coffee used today, and even the bean, which is its source, has no mention in the medical textbooks, so bear in mind their lack of mention by the author of *al-Qāmūs*—did it occur after him? Shaykh al-Ḥākimī[7] gave me an account of his deceased companion, Abū al-Ṣaʿūd,[8] who was writing down the statements of his master, the preacher Shaykh al-Qudsī one day when he was preaching in one of the mosques.[9] Shaykh al-Ḥākimī was there, and heard him say, "Coffee (*qahwa*) is that with which the people are afflicted, and its prohibition appears in the Ḥadīth. This is so because of the prohibition against *qahwa* (i.e., *khamr*)." Then Shaykh al-Ḥākimī stood as if he did not know this already, and said, "O Shaykh, take note of what you're saying." So, Shaykh al-Qudsī said to him, "It is as though you are of those who are afflicted by *qahwa*." So, al-Ḥākimī replied, "Contemplate what you are saying." And because

---

4 While the original reads *muḥmaka*, this is likely an error on al-Maghribī's part, as the edition of *al-Qāmūs al-muḥīṭ* shows *muḥkama*. See al-Shami and Ahmad (2008, 1378).

5 *Makhḍ* (*sic* – read *maḥḍ*).

6 *Sic* – read *aqhā*.

7 As in Zack's study, this figure remains unidentified.

8 As in Zack's study, this figure remains unidentified.

9 Mājid (sic – read masājid).

it seemed that he was lying about the Prophet [he added,] "What is the definition of wine (*khamr*)? Is it not the juice of grapes?" Shaykh al-Qudsī said, "Yes." So, al-Ḥākimī said, "So, where does coffee fit in this?" He was then speechless and feared that I would inform al-Ustādh al-Bakrī[10] of this. So, he sent some companions to make peace over the matter, and to this day he doesn't mention coffee in anything. So, I was pleased, and didn't inform al-Ustādh [al-Bakrī], who has many poems in praise of coffee—as does Shaykh Abū al-Fath al-Mālikī.[11] I wrote the following:

> I witnessed a virtue in the coffee husk
> when he who is without compassion is far
> I judged it fairly to make peace between us
> as this virtue from coffee is a just arbiter

Entry for Ibrāhīm ibn al-Muballaṭ from *al-Kawākib al-sā'ira bi-aʿyān al-mi'a al-ʿāshira* by Najm al-Dīn al-Ghazzī:

The Eminent Shaykh, litterateur, poet Ibrāhīm Burhān al-Dīn ibn al-Muballaṭ al-Qāhirī, poet of Cairo. The following comes from his poetry on the coffee bean:

> My critic says, "coffee is a bitter drink
> water is the sweet beverage without equal"
> So, I replied, "what you disparage with bitterness
> I've chosen—So, chose for yourself that which is sweet"

---

[10] Given the prominence of the Bakrī family during this period it is difficult to ascertain to which member this reference is made. Al-Maghribī died nearly a quarter century after Muḥammad al-Bakrī, author of the below mentioned *muwashshaḥ*. It is possible but improbable that al-Maghribī's reference is being made to the same al-Bakrī.

[11] Muftī and poet who lived in Damascus, died 1567/8.

He has also said:

These days, I see the coffee bean
is what people have agreed upon drinking
Drinking it became a custom
it neither hurts nor helps

He is also noted for these lines:

O critic of the imbibing of our coffee which
cures the soul of what ails it
Or you do not see it, when in its cup
it speaks the eye amidst its white

Another poet has a verse with the same motif:

Drink, savoring the coffee bean
that is sweet with brothers and friends
A blackness within the whiteness of the cup
speaks of the man's eyeball

I [al-Ghazzī] have said even better than this, here:

Drink two cups of coffee
even if it costs an extra coin, silver or gold
A blackness in the white of its cups
as though they were of the man's eyes

Coffee *Muwashshaḥ* from the *Dīwān* of Muḥammad al-Bakrī:[12]

Pass the coffee in the glass at hand
of the coffee bean, how excellent, how grand
What sound reason considers contraband

---

[12] For commentary on the first three stanzas of this *muwashshaḥ* see Larkin (2006, 231). Note my translation here departs selectively from the literal text in order to retain the rhyme scheme of the poem.

So, friend, for me have a drink poured

Adorn the cups, hear what I disperse
it's the drink of the masters of verse
Allah's privileged, endowed with his forthcoming force
for the protection of the lord

Upon us is an ignorant censor
who with invalid speech is a lie dispenser
a fleeting death, a memory obscure
he has gone with wine, poured

It's said at the slightest drink hearts grow intoxicated
just as the brave of the unseen get inebriated
the matter now finished, the hearts morally obligated
But surely, the glasses I've scored.

Though he denies what he nears
there's nothing better than these frontiers
people's most joyous practice, they're the best, it appears,
at drawing out the wine, poured.

Commentary

The role of coffee in early modern Ottoman society has been addressed from many historiographical perspectives, from its importance as a traded commodity to the religious-legal debates surrounding its illicit status in Islamic law. What is less understood, perhaps, is the intellectual and literary impact of coffee. Presented here are three samples from the linguistic and literary corpus of 16th- and 17th-century Ottoman Arabic. First, an abridged version of Yūsuf al-Maghribī's (d. 1019/1610), entry on coffee (*qahwa*) in his dictionary of colloquial Egyptian Arabic, followed by a few verses of coffee poetry from Najm al-Dīn al-Ghazzī's (d. 1060/1650) centenary biographical dictionary. Lastly, a *muwashshaḥ* (strophic poem) by Muḥammad al-Bakrī (d. 994/1586), in which the subject of coffee merges into that of wine, demonstrating the generic link in between the two substances in Arabic literature. While these samples have primarily been translated here for readers' enjoyment, they also invite us to think of coffee as a linguistic and literary problematic during the Ottoman period.

14. EGYPT: DAMURDĀŠĪ'S CHRONICLE OF EGYPT (FIRST HALF OF 18TH CENTURY)

Jérôme Lentin

Chronicle of al-ʾamīr ʾAḥmad al-Damurdāšī (middle of the 18th century), *Al-durra al-muṣāna fī ʾaḫbār al-kināna* (manuscript: British Museum OPB MSS OR 173, copied by Miḫāʾīl Ṣabbāġ, Ms pp. 218–19; ed. Crecelius and ʿAbd al-Wahhāb 1991, 198; ed. ʿAbd al-Raḥīm 1989, 121–22)[1]

Transcription

وبنرجع[1] الى عبدين باشا اخر سنتهُ[2] سعوا له فى عبد الله افندي الروزنامجي فاراد قتله فاتاه الخبر فوزع ما يعز عليه وقص دقنهَ ولبس لبس قرندلي يولداش وخرج[3] ملبس اخذه معه وما يحتاج اليه الامر و نزل / بولاق[4] بكسمه[5] فراش فنزل فى معاش[6] وسافر دمياط ومنها نزل فى غليون وسافر الى الشام له معنا [كلام][7] يوم الثلاثا دور عليه الباشا لم وجده[8] ارسل ضبط[9] كامل الذي[10] وجده فى بيتهِ وكان له بيتين[11] بيت للحريم وبيت للعيله والمطبخ ثم ان الاغا المعين اراد يدخل[12] بيت الحريم منعته اولاد الحاره وقالوا له لم له شى[13] فى هذا البيت اخذ ما وجد وطلع[14] وجعلوا ان[15] عليه مال للميري وكان موجر حصصهُ الى اختيارية[16] فى الاوجاق الجاويشيه لانهُ قد كان يولداش عندهم

---

[1] For images see https://ia801308.us.archive.org/zipview.php?zip=/21/items/M-0004/09794-.zip: 114/الدرة المصانة.tif (pp. 217–18); 115/الدرة المصانة.tif (pp. 219–20).

 https://doi.org/10.11647/OBP.0208.20

فبذلك حمو لحصصه من الباشا وجعلوا انهم اشتروهم منه وان لهم سنتين[17]
والمقاطعات اخبر بمن يدفع المال اقام بالشام ثمان سنوات

Translation

(Crecelius and ʿAbd al-Wahhab Bakr 1991, 199)

Let us come back to ʿAbdīn Bāšā. At the end of his year [as governor], some people worked to set him against ʿAbdallah ʾAfandī the *rūznāmjī* (executive director of the Treasury) and he planned to kill him. But this latter got informed. He distributed the possessions dear to him, cut his beard, dressed up as a Kalandar dervish [*qarandalī yūldāš*], took a saddlebag where he put clothes and things he could need, and went to Būlāq disguised as a servant. He embarked on a *germe* boat and sailed to Damietta, from where he embarked on a galleon to Syria. We will come back to him later. On Tuesday, he [= ʿAbdīn Bāšā] searched for him but he could not find him. He ordered that everything that could be found in his house be seized. He [= ʿAbdallah ʾAfandī] had two houses, one for his women, and one for his servants and the kitchen. When the appointed *ʾāġā* wanted to enter the house of the women, the people of the quarter prevented him, saying: "He has nothing in this house." The *ʾāġā* [just] confiscated what he had found and left. They [= ʿAbdallah ʾAfandī's friends] claimed that he owed money to the land administration and that he had rented his shares to the elders [commanding officers] of the Jawīšiyya unit since he was their fellow. By doing that, they protected his shares from the Pasha. They pretended that they had bought them from him two years earlier, and that the renting-contracts are the best source of information on who pays. ʿAbdallah ʾAfandī lived in Damascus for eight years.

Commentary

[1] *b*- has inexplicably been omitted in the two editions.

[2] سنتهُ. For *ḍamma* in ـهُ representing the vowel [u] or [o] of the 3ms suffixed pronoun, see Lentin (2012, §3.9, 225–26).

[3] خرج 'saddleback' (classical *ḫurj*, colloquial *ḫərəž*).

[4] نزل بولاق. In Egyptian MA texts, verbs of movement often take a direct object (as they do in colloquial); cf. سافر دمياط (but note سافر الى الشام).

[5] كسم 'clothes, dress' (colloquial).

[6] معاش a kind of (small) boat.

[7] له معنا [كلام]. The form كلام is rightly restored by the editors. This expression is frequently used in the text, as is also common in 'popular' literature, especially in the *sīras*.

[8] لم وجده. On *lam* used with the suffix conjugation, see Lentin (1997, 764–67).

[9] ارسل ضبط. Similar to *baʿaṯa/baʿat*, the verb *ʾarsal(a)* often functions as a factitive auxiliary (see Lentin 1997, §14.5.1, 633–36); the auxiliary verb is generally in the perfect.

[10] كامل الذي وجده. In Egyptian MA texts, كامل is the most common quantifier for 'all, whole, entire', even before a singular (pro)noun, as is the case here. It is the exact equivalent of Levantine MA جميع (see text II.9, no. 5).

[11] كان له بيتين. The former oblique case of the dual form *-ayn/ -ēn* is the dominant form used in MA, regardless of the syntactic function of the noun (exactly like *-īn* in the sound mpl form, see text II.9, no. 13).

[12] اراد يدخل. Modal auxiliaries are very often asyndetically constructed in MA texts.

[13] لم له شى. For *lam* negating some types of nominal clauses see Lentin (1997, 782).

[14] The colloquial verb طلع is the normal (Near Eastern) MA verb for 'to walk out, go away, leave'.

[15] جعلوا ان. For the meaning 'to claim, pretend to', see Dozy (1881, I 198).

[16] اختيارية. Plural of اختيار 'old man, senior'.

[17] لهم سنتين. Colloquial turn of phrase indicating duration: prep. *l(a)*- + pers. pron. + noun indicating a period of time + predicative clause 'he… for a (two, three…) year(s)/month(s)'.

15. MATENADARAN COLLECTION MS NO.1751: A MEDICAL WORK (1726)

Ani Avetisyan

Transcription

(1) באסם אללה אל רחמאן אל רחים ומא תופֿיקי אלא איאה יקול אל עבד אל פֿקיר אלי אלאה אל ואחד אל בארי. (2) מחמד אבן אבראהים אבן סאעד אל אנצארי עאמלה אללה בלטפֿה "אל חמד ללאה. (3) מנור אל אלבאב ומלהם אל צואב" ובעד פֿהדא מכ̇תצר ישתמל עלי עלם אל פֿצד ועמלה. (4) ומא יתצל בה סמיתה נהאית אל קצד פֿי צנאעת אל פֿצד ורתבתה עלי באבין. (5) "אל באב אל אול פֿי מא יג̇רי מן הדי אל צנאעה מג̇רי אל ג̇זאיאת[1] ואל כליאת והו עשרון פֿצלא פֿי חד אל פֿצד. (6) וכיפֿיתה ושרוטה ומנאפֿעה ומא יתעלק בדאלךּ יתצל בה" אל באב אל תאני פֿי מא יג̇רי מן הדי אל צנאעה. (7) מג̇רי אל ג̇זייאת והו דכר כל ואחד מן אל ערוק אל מקצודה עלי אנפֿראדה וכיפֿית פֿצדה ומנאפֿעה. (8) ומא יחדר מן כ̇טאה יתופֿק פֿיה ואללה אסאלךּ אן ינפֿע בה. (9) "אל באב אל אול פֿי מא יג̇רי מג̇רי אל ג̇וייאת ואל כליאת והו עשרון פֿצלא". (10) אל פֿצל אל אול פֿי חד אל פֿצד הו תפֿרק אתצאל אראדי יתבעה אסתפֿראג̇ עלי מן אל ערוק. (11) אל פֿצל אל תאני פֿי כיפֿיתה ודאלךּ הו אן יחס אל ערק קבל אל שד. (12) לינצ̇ר חאל אל שראיין פֿיבתעד ענהא לאנהא לא תצ̇הר בעד אל שד. (13) תם ירבט אעלא מוצ̇ע אל עצ̇ד רבטא מעתדלא וימלא אל ערוק באל אבהאם ליצ̇הר ויחס באל סבאבה. (14) ליחקק מוצ̇עה ויקיד באבהאם אל יד אל יסרי ליואמן חרכתה תחת אל מבצ̇ע. (15) תם יחדת עלי מקדאר ג̇ור אל ערק וירסל אל מבצ̇ע בחסבה ג̇מזא. (16) ויקףּ וקפֿה וינצ̇ר הל אצאב אל ערק פֿינתר

[1] Two different spellings of the word جزئيات appear in the passage; ג̇זייאת/ג̇זאיאת which could be a consequence of a copying mistake.

 https://doi.org/10.11647/OBP.0208.21

אל מבצ̇ע ליוסע אל פ̇תחה בקדר אל ג̇רץ̇. (17) ואן לם יכון אצאב אל ערק סל אל מבצ̇ע מן ג̇יר נתרא וסעה אל פ̇תחה אבלג̇ פ̇י אל תנקיה. (18) ואמכן לל דם אל ג̇ליץ̇ לכנהא לא שד סל סריעא ויכ̇שי מנהא אל ג̇שי ואל טול ובטי אל אלתחאם. (19) ולא יצלח לל ערוק אל דקיקה ואל ערצ̇י סריע אל אלתחאם ויכרה לל דקיקה כ̇וף בתרהא ואל מורב. (20) אופ̇ק ואעדל ואדא שד ערק ערק פ̇י אל יד ולם יצ̇הר חל רבאטה ואעיד מרארא ויעלק באל יד שי תקיל ליצ̇הר אל ערק.

Arabic Transcription

(1) بسم الله الرحمن الرحيم وما توفيقي الا اياه يقول العبد الفقير الى الله الواحد البارئ. (2) محمد ابن ابراهيم ابن ساعد الانصاري عامله الله بلطفه "الحمد لله. (3) منور الالباب وملهم الصواب" وبعد فهدا مختصر يشتمل على علم الفصد وعمل. (4) وما يتصل به سميته نهاية القصد في صناعة الفصد ورتبته على بابين. (5) "الباب الاول فيما يجري من هدي الصناعة مجري الجزئيات والكليات وهو عشرون فصلا في حد الفصد. (6) وكيفيته وشروطه ومنافعه وما يتعلق بدالك يتصل به" الباب الثاني فيما يجري من هدي الصناعة. (7) مجري الجزئيات وهو دكر كل واحد من العروق المقصوده على انفراده وكيفية فصده ومنافعه. (8) وما يحدر من خطأه يتوفق فيه والله أسألك أن ينفع به. (9) "الباب الأول فيما يجري مجري الجزئيات والكليات وهو عشرون فصلا". (10) الفصل الأول في حد الفصد هو تفرق اتصال ارادي ويتبعه استفراغ على من العروق. (11) الفصل التاني في كيفيته ودالك هو ان يحس العرق قبل الشد. (12) لينظر حال الشرايين فيبتعد عنها لانها لا تظهر بعد الشد. (13) ثم يربط أعلا موضع العضد ربطا معتدلا ويملأ العروق بالابهام ليظهر ويحس بالسبابة. (14) ليحقق موضعه ويقيد بابهام اليد اليسري ليوأمن حركته تحت المبضع. (15) ثم يحدث على مقدار غور العرق ويرسل المبضع بحسبه غمزا. (16) ويقف وقفة وينظر هل أصاب العرق فينتر المبضع ليوسع الفتحة بقدرالغرض. (17) وان لم يكون أصاب العرق سل المبضع من غير نترا وسعة الفتحة أبلغ في التنقية. (18) وأمكن للدم الغليظ لكنها لا شد سل سريعا ويخشي منها الغشى والطول وبطء الالتحام. (19) ولا يصلح للعروق الدقيقه والعرضي سريع الالتحام ويكره للدقيقه خوف بترها والمورب. (20) اوفق واعدل وادا شد عرق عرق في اليد ولم يظهر حل رباطه واعيد مرارا ويعلق باليد شي ثقيل ليظهر العرق.

Translation

(1) “In the name of God, the Merciful, the Compassionate” and my good fortune is only Him, recites the poor self to the One God.

(2) Muḥammad ibn Ibrahim ibn Saʿid al-Anṣari, May God, treat him with kindness. (3) Praise be to God, the one who enlightens the hearts and inspires the righteous ones. This compendium contains the science of phlebotomy and its uses. (4) As for the practice of phlebotomy, I called it "The end of search in the art of phlebotomy" and divided it into two volumes. (5) The first volume concerns procedure with regard to the details and generalities of this art. It consists of twenty chapters concerning the manner, (6) conditions, rules and benefit of phlebotomy, and what is related to its practice. The second chapter concerns the details of this art (7) and mentions each individual vein separately, with characteristics of its phlebotomy and benefits. (8) It warns against mistakes that may occur. God, I ask you that there may be benefit in it. (9) The first chapter is concerned what transpires with regard to the details and generalities, and it consists of twenty chapters. (10) The first chapter concerns the manner of phlebotomy, focussing on the separation of voluntary joining, followed by draining of the veins. (11) The second chapter is on its characteristics, and that is to feel the vein before the binding, (12) in order to see the condition of the arteries; and to stay away from them, as they are not discernible after the binding. (13) Then the upper part of the humerus is bound with a moderate tie, veins are filled up (using) the thumbs to become visible and be felt with the forefinger (14) in order to establish its place, and it should be bound with the thumb of the left hand in order to avoid it moving under the scalpel. (15) Then it should be extended, corresponding to the depth of the vein and the scalpel is pointed according to the touch. (16) It should remain in place

and it should become apparent whether it hits the vein. The scalpel should be inserted to widen the opening as much as intended. (17) And if it does not hit the vein, remove the scalpel without pulling apart the wideness of the opening to facilitate cleanliness (18) and allow the blood to clot, because it does not heal quickly, and from it can occur unconsciousness, prolongation, and slowness of closing.[2] (19) Fast closing is not suitable for the thin and horizontal veins. It should be detested for thin ones for fear that they might be cut off and tightened. (20) Make it suitable and balance it, and if the vein becomes thick in the hand and the loosening of the binding has not made it become apparent, repeat it several times; and suspend something heavy from the hand in order for the vein to appear.

Commentary

The late Judaeo-Arabic medical treatise *Nihāyat al-qaṣd fī ṣināʿat al-faṣd* (henceforth NQSF) of MS No.1751 is written in a register close to Classical Arabic, despite the lateness of the text.

It exhibits regular occurrences of the Classical Arabic demonstratives *hāḏā* and *ḏālika*. The vernacular pronoun *hāḏi* is rare, but also employed in the text (line 5).[3]

[2] Or 'Allow the blood to clot, however, it does not heal quickly; there is a fear that there would be unconsciousness, prolongation, and slowness of closing' according to the earlier Arabic version of the text وأمكن للدم الغليظ لكنها لا تندمل سريعا ويخشي منها الغشى والطول وبطء الالتحام.

[3] As Wagner (2010, 75) has argued, this may reflect Modern Egyptian Arabic di + the presentative prefix hā. It is worth mentioning, that two different spellings of *hādi*; האדי, הדי are found in the text.

In NQSF the numerals composed of single digits and tens adhere to the rules of the Classical Arabic; (i) they are followed by the accusative singular and (ii) have a single-digit numeral in gender polarity to the counted noun (lines 5, 9). Numerals almost exclusively appear fully written.

16. A CLERICAL LETTER BY RAFAEL AL-ṬŪḴĪ FROM THE PRIZE PAPERS COLLECTIONS (1758)[1]

Esther-Miriam Wagner and Mohamed Ahmed

Transcription

Envelope

1. بعونه تعالي
2. يصل الى ناحية دجرجة بصعيد مصرويسلم
3. بلتم القس روكس قدسي امانه مرسله
4. بالخير

Recto

5. الي جناب حضرة اخينا وحبيبنا بالرب القس المكرم روكس قدسي دام الله بقاه
6. بعد تقبيل الايادي نعرض على **حضرتكم** بان وصلت لعندنا مشرفتكم
7. العزيزه في اليوم 20 من شهر اوطبُره اعني به شهر **بابه** سنه 1758
8. وفيها اعلمتمونا عن وصول الكتب التي ارسلتها لعندكم وعن
9. سلامتكم وصار عندنا **فرح جزيل** من اجل ذلك لكن من جهة اخري

[1] The letter is part of the box HCA 32/212 in the National Archives. Analyses of this letter were previously included in the linguistic description in Wagner and Ahmed (2017). At the time, the authors gave this letter the siglum NAL 46.5, as the letters had not yet been catalogued by the National Archives.

 https://doi.org/10.11647/OBP.0208.22

10. صعب علينا موت اخينا المرحوم القس عوض رحمة الله وعزاكم فيه
11. ويكون فيكم العوض لاننا ما نقدر نفعل شياً الا **الدعا** اليه بالخير
12. من **الباري وتنيح نفسه** تم نرجوكم بان تعرفونا عن الصور
13. الكبار امتعتنا التي **كانتن**[2] عنده وعن بعض كتب اعطيتهم
14. له في روميه ليبيعهم لنا فاذا تعرفونا عن الجميع وبالخصوص
15. عن الصور لانها **وقف للكنيسة** ولا احد يقدر يتصرف فيها
16. اخيراً نرجوكم بان تواصلونا باخباركم ولا يكون عندكم تقصير
17. في دلك كمثل سابقاً لان من مدة طويلة لم وصلنا من عندكم
18. خبر الا هدا المكتوب الذي وصلنا هذه السنه بعد ما تعوق
19. في الطريق ثلاثة عشر اشهر فاذاً فيما بعد لا تنسونا هكذا
20. مده طويله كسابقاً واخيرا اهدوا منا السلام على كل الاخوه الذين
21. عندكم المحبوبين بالرب المعلم مشرقي الباسكي واهل
22. منزله وعلى اهالينا وكل من **يلود بحضرتكم**_اهدوه السلام

Signature

23. المحب المخلص
24. رافاييل الطوخي
25. قس بنعمة الله

Date

26. سط في 22 **هتور** (نوفمبر)
27. سنه 1758
28. مسيحية

Translation

[Written in the hand of Yūḥannā Marqūryūs al-Farārjī]

Envelope

1. With the help of God.

---

[2] Why the *nūn* was added to this form is not quite clear.

2. (The letter) should arrive to Girga in Upper Egypt, and be delivered
3. into the fingertips of the priest Rūks (?) Qudsī by care of the messenger.
4. In wellness.

Recto

(5) To the Excellency, our brother and beloved in God, the honourable priest Rūks Qudsī—may God prolong his life. (6) After kissing hands, we acknowledge to your respected self that your precious letter reached us (7) on the 20th of the month *Ottobre*, i.e., the month Baba, in the year 1758, (8) in which you inform us about the arrival of the books that I sent to you, and about (9) your safety, and we were greatly content to hear that. But on the other hand, (10) we were sorry about the death of our brother, the deceased priest ʿAwaḍ—My God's mercy be upon him, and may God give you consolation (11) and may there be recompense for you, because we cannot offer anything but prayers for him and his welfare (12) from the Creator and peace for his soul. Then we would like to ask you to inform us about the large (13) paintings that belong to us that were in his keeping and about some other books we gave to him (14) in Rome to sell on our behalf. So, please inform us about everything, especially (15) about the paintings, because they belong to the Church's charitable organisation (*waqf*) and no one has the right to dispose of them. (16) Finally, we wish you to keep in touch and not delay in (17) doing as you did previously, because for a long time we have received nothing (18) from you but this letter, which reached us this year

after a thirteen-month (19) delay. From now on, please do not forget us for such a long period again. (20) Finally, send our greetings to all the brothers who (21) are with you, the beloved in God; the Master Mushraqī al-Bāskī and his family; (22) and to our relatives and to all who are under your protection send our greetings,

Signature

23. Your sincere friend
24. Rafael al-Ṭūḵī
25. a priest by God's grace

Date

26. written on 22nd Hathor
27. of the year 1758
28. of the Lord

Commentary

There is a marked difference in register within the corpus of Arabic Prize Papers between letters written by merchants and those written by clerics. The clerical letters overall show more literary forms, such as the future particle *sa-* and much-increased use of the negation particle *lam*. These forms are used as stylistic markers of the clerical register and were probably introduced through exposure of the clerics to literary Arabic texts, which led to the development of a particular clerical register.

At the same time, vernacular, non-literary forms occur in particular sociolinguistic circumstances and we also find phonological and morphological Middle Arabic forms similar to those found in the traders' correspondence.

Line 7

الدعا 'prayer'. As in most Middle Arabic texts, *hamza* is not spelled.

Line 13

من مدة طويلة لم وصلنا من عندكم خبر 'for a long time, no news reached us from you'. The negation particle *lam* is a register marker in various Middle Arabic varieties.[3] In the clerical Prize Paper letters, as in many other Middle Arabic texts, *lam* has considerably enlarged its functions, and occurs with the perfect, in contradiction to Classical Arabic grammar.

With the imperfect, *lam* negates the present and with the perfect, past tense forms. The use of *lam* appears to be related to register in the Prize papers, with clerical writers much more likely to use it than mercantile authors.

Line 15

ثلاثة عشر اشهر '13 months'. In most of the Arabic Prize papers under HCA 32/212, there is little marking of the Standard Arabic interdental fricatives /ḏ/and /ṯ/, and they are usually spelled as *dāl* and *tāʾ*. The writer of the letter, Rafael al-Ṭūḵī, is an exception in his use of marking /ṯ/ with three dots.

[3] For an extensive discussion of *lam* in spoken and written varieties of Arabic, see Wagner (2010, 141–50).

17. A CHRISTIAN MERCANTILE LETTER FROM THE PRIZE PAPERS COLLECTIONS (1759)[1]

Esther-Miriam Wagner and Mohamed Ahmed

Transcription

Envelope

1. بعونه تعالي
2. يصل الي محروسة مصر يسلم ليد الأخ العزيز الخواجه ديمتري خير
3. بالخير
4. ب م

Recto

5. الي جناب الاخ العزيز الخواجه ديمتري المكرم دام الله بقاه
6. بعد مزيد كترة الاشواق اليكم لا يخفاكم قبل تاريخه ارسلنا لكم مكتوب صحبة مركب القبطان بانوفيسك
7. راكوزي جواب مكاتيبكم انشالله تكونوا اتطلعتوا عليه بخير واخبرناكم بوصول اربعة بالاة

[1] The letter is part of the box HCA 32/212 in the National Archives. In the analyses for the Prize Papers project, this letter was given the provisional NAL 45.6, as the letters had not yet been catalogued by the National Archives.

https://doi.org/10.11647/OBP.0208.23

8. عصفر وبالتين شمع وستة فروق بن الذين ارسلتوهم من حسابنا علي طريق دمياط فمتي
9. عرفتونا التمن بالمصروف قيدناهم لكم واخبرناكم ايضاً ان انطون عمل لكم قايمة
10. الحساب بجميع الداخل والخارج كما هو مسطر في الدفاتر وارسلها لكم صحبة بانوفيك ثم
11. اخبرناكم من جهة بالة العصفر الذي ناقصه وبالتين القماش كتبنا الي يوسف
12. فرنجي انه يفحص دفاترنا الذين في سكندريه وينظر ان كان فقدوا في مراكب الذين ضاعوا
13. ام حاصل غلط فهلبت تعرفونا عن ذلك حتي لا يسهي عليه وعند اتطلاعكم
14. علي القايمه المذكوره تخلصوا الحساب وتعرفونا صحته وترسلوا لنا قايمه نقيضه
15. حتي ننظر الغايه ونخلص من هذا الحساب لان حالته طالت وما في غير مراجعه
16. من طرفكم لطرفنا ومن طرفنا لطرفكم فالمراد هذه نهايت الحساب الذي ارسله لكم
17. انطون وخلافه ما في واخبرناكم ان من عبود شلبي لم حضر لنا مكاتيب ولا
18. عندنا خبر كيف مراده في هذه الحجاره الذين ارسلتوهم فالمرجوا

Signature Bottom Left

19. محب مخلص لكم
20. يوسف
21. بكتي
22. م

End Right Margin (Date)

23. سنه 1759 في
24. 16 شهر كانون
25. اخر غ

Right Margin

26. يا اخي في حال وصول هذا المكتوب لكم ترسلوا
27. له مكتوب وتعرفوه يرسل لنا جواب ويعرفنا
28. مراده لاننا اصرفنا نصين طيبه علي شغل
29. هذه الحجاره وتركيبهم وهي معطله علينا

30. واخبرناكم ايضاً ان ترسلوا لنا غلاق حساب
31. اخينا المرحوم الذي كان قبل اخيكم الخواجه
32. يوسف حتي ننظر قدره ونقطع حسابكم مع اخينا
33. المرحوم ثم بعده حضر لطرفنا مركب القبطان اندربولي
34. كورنيز من سكندريه وصحبته حضر لنا عزيز مكتوبكم
35. الكريم محرر في 15 شهر تشرين اول فقريناه وفهمنا
36. كامل ما شرحتم وحمدناه الله علي صحتكم صار معلومنا
37. وصول مكتوبنا لكم صحبة مركب السويد مقاولة انطون
38. والمذكور [...] يتوجه لدمياط يشحن ارز والحال لم
39. هو محقق لان مركب الارز الذي حضر من دمياط تخزن
40. جميعه في الحواصل وبيع جمله ما في اما قفتين وتلاته

Top Margin

41. سعر 14 وسعر 14,25 صار معلومنا احوال واسعار طرفكم وحضور الحج فربنا يلطف
42. بالحال عرفتونا ان باقي عندكم برميل قزدير والحال اتصرفوا فيه بزايد ام
43. بناقص كذلك باقي عندكم جانب حب هال عرفنا ابن خالتنا يتصرف فيه
44. ثم ان سالتم عن احوال هذا الطرف علي ما هي واسعار البن سعر 23 والعصفر
45. تبهدل ونزل الي سعر 10,25 وموجود منه كتير وطلب من برا ما في والصمغ
46. سعر 8 وسعر 8,25 واصناف القمايش جميعها مايته وبعد تاريخه نعمل لكم
47. قايمه بصافي جميع البضاعه الذي وصلتنا من يدكم والحرير بعنا منه
48. خمسماية ليبره والباقي قاعد مرادنا نعمل له حال ونخلص منه.
49. واسعار الحرير البيروتي سعر 16 والطرابلسي سعر 16 وسعر 17 والباياسي
50. سعر 14 والقبرصي سعر 12 وباقي الاسعار علي ماهي يكون ذلك معلومكم
51. هذا ما عندنا اخبرناكم فالمرجوا لا تمنعوا عنا اخبار صحتكم وما
52. لكم من الخدمه والمصالح عرفونا علي الراس والعين بلغوا مزيد اشواقنا
53. الي اخوتكم واولادهم العزاز والي اخوتنا وكامل المحبين حضر
54. من عندنا يسلموا عليكم واولاد اخينا يقبلوا يديكم وطال الله
55. بقاكم والسلام

Translation

Envelope

1. With the help of God
2. To be sent to Cairo, to the hands of the dear brother Ḵawāja Dimitri Ḵayr
3. in well-being
4. b m

Recto

(5) To the Excellency, my dear brother Ḵawāja Dimitri the honourable, may God prolong his life. (6) After (expressing) our intense longing for you, it will not have escaped your notice that previously we sent you a letter with the ship of captain Panofisk (7) Raguzī in answer to your letters. God willing, (the letter) found you well. We informed you about the arrival of the four bales (8) of safflower and two bales of yellow wax and six packets of coffee that you sent on our account via Damietta. When (9) you inform us about the price including expenses, we will register it for you. Also, we told you that Antwān made (10) a list of the income and expenditures as set down in the records, and he sent it to you with Panofisk. Then (11) we informed you about the missing bale of safflower and two bales of cloth. We wrote to Yūsuf (12) Faranjī to check our records in Alexandria and to see if they were lost in the ships which were lost (13) or whether there was a mistake. You should urgently inform us about this so that he does not forget about it. When you have inspected the (14) aforementioned list, you should close the account. You should inform us of its correctness and send us an annulled list

(15) so that we can see the extent of it, and close the account, because it has taken so much time. There is nothing left but a revision (16) from your side to our side and vice versa. Now, we hope that this will be the end of the account that Antwān sent to (17) you and there is no disparity. We informed you that we did not receive letters from ʿAbūd Šalabī, we do not (18) know what his desire for these stones that you sent is. So please

Signature Bottom Left

19. Your sincere friend
20. Yūsuf
21. Baktī
22. m

End Right Margin (Date)

23. Year 1759 (written) on
24. 16th of the Second
25. Kānūn

Right Margin

(26) My brother, when this letter reaches you, you should send (27) a letter to him and inform him to send us a reply and to tell us (28) what he wants, because we spent two good half-dinars on the preparation (29) of these stones and on setting them, which has been delaying us. (30) Also we informed you to send us the final account calculation (31) of our deceased brother, which was (for the period) before your brother Ḵawāja (32) Yūsuf's (account) so that we would know how much is it, and to cut off your account from the one of our deceased (33) brother. Then, the ship

of captain Andropoly Korniz arrived in our area (34) from Alexandria, with it came to us your dear honourable (35) letter dated to 15th Tishreen Awwal. We have read it and understood (36) all of what you had explained. We thanked God for your well-being. We knew about (37) the arrival of our letter at yours with the Swedish ship hired by Antwān (38) and the mentioned [...] who had the intention of heading to Damietta to load rice. Well, this is not (39) confirmed, because the rice ship that came from Damietta was stored entirely (40) at the (government) corn stores, and there is no outright sale option, only two or three baskets are available

Top Margin

(41) at a price 14 and 14,25. We learned about the prices and the conditions (of merchandises) in your area during the time of *Hajj*, may God (42) give his mercy. You informed us that there is one barrel of tin plating left with you. Now, you should get rid of it (literally: sell it out with profit or loss). (43) Also, there is some cardamom left with you. We informed our cousin to sell it. (44) If you are asking about the news in our area, it is as usual. The coffee price is 23 and the safflower (45) is depreciated, and its price went down to 10,25. There is enough available, and there is no demand for it from abroad. The gum arabic is (46) priced at 8 and 8.25. All types of clothes sales are dead. Afterwards, we will prepare for you (47) a list of the net of all merchandises that arrived from your side. Concerning the silk, we sold (48) five hundred libra from it; the rest is sitting (on the shelves). We wish that we could manage to sell it. (49) The prices of the Beiruti silk

is 16, and the Tripolitan is 16 and 17, and the Bāyāsī (50) is at 14, and the Cypriot is at 12. The rest of the prices are unchanged; you should know this (51) for now, this is all the news we have. We wish that you do not cut us off from news about your health. Whatever (52) you need and desire, please let us know (we will do it) with pleasure. Send our many greetings (53) to your brothers and their dear children, and to our brothers and all the beloved. People (54) from here are sending you greetings. The children of our brother are kissing your hands. May God prolong your (55) life. Peace.

Commentary

Line 7

اربعة بالاة 'four bales'. Final *tā'* is frequently spelled as *tā' marbūṭa.*

Line 8

الذين ارسلتوهم 'which you sent' (see also twice in line 12 and in line 18). The use of the plural relative pronoun for inanimate objects is slightly unusual here. The writer, Yūsuf Baktī, appears to favour this hypercorrect form, perhaps seen as more elevated style, as it also appears in another letter of his to a different addressee, interestingly, a Muslim correspondent.

Line 13

اتطلاعكم 'your inspection'. The colloquial *itfaʿʿala* stem appears frequently in the mercantile letters of the Prize Papers.

Line 16

نهايت الحساب 'the end of your account'. Just as final *tā'* may be spelled with *tā' marbūṭa*, so *tā' marbūṭa* is spelled with *tā'*.

Line 17

لم حضر لنا مكاتيب ‘the end of your account’. In the mercantile letters, *lam* is not as frequent as in clerical letters, but it does occur, here with the perfect to negate the past.

18. ḤANNĀ AL-ṬABĪB, RIḤLAT AL-SHAMMĀS ḤANNĀ AL-ṬABĪB ILĀ BALDAT ISTANBŪL (1764/65)

Feras Krimsti

Gotha Research Library, Gotha, Ms. orient. A 1550. The text excerpt is selected from folios 14a–14b.

Transcription

Folio 14a

13. بلاودون وصلنا اليها بعد ستة ساعات وطريقها سهل جميل جداً
14. وقبل الدخول الى بلاودون مبني جسر على نهر وطول هذا الجسر نحو من ثلاثة
15. ساعات ونهايته النهر ومنه الى بلاودون واعلم ان طريق استنبول من
16. خروجك من انطاكيه حتى تدخل الى استنبول جميعه قلدريم مبني بنا مثل الجسر
17. وهذا الاعتنا اعتناه راغب باشا من مال اسعد باشا لانه رم طريق
18. استنبول جميعه وصيره سهل جداً لان اولاً ما كان هذا الطريق ينسلك
19. الا بعد العجز وبعد انكسار هلقدر دواب وضيعان احمال ومشقا وعنا
20. عظيم والان صيره راغب باشا طريق تنسلك به الاخشاب والتخوت بكل سهوله
21. وقريب الى البلد جسر اخر يشتمل على خمسين قنطره منهم كبار ومنهم صغار
22. جسر مكلف جداً هو والرصيف المذكور اما بلاودون فهي قصبه متوسطه
23. مابين قريه وبلد وهي عامره وبها خمسة جوامع بموادن وجامع الواحد له

Folio 14b

1. قبه رصاص وهو جامع مكلف وماء هذه البلده جيد وهي بلاد مرخصه لاننا اخذنا في

 https://doi.org/10.11647/OBP.0208.24

2. بالاودون ثلاثة دجاجات بتسعة مصاري وسبعة اواق تفاح احمر يشهي النظر من
3. حسنه ورايحته بمصريه واحده والعنب كثير والبطيخ والجبس وكل شي كثير وخبزها
4. طيب وجبنها طيب وبها كستنه اي ابو فريوه كل سبعة اواق بمصريه وكل واحده قدر
5. جوزه كبيره وجديد شي ما يجي منه الى هذه البلاد ولهذه المدينه سوق عامر
6. وموجود به كل شي ولها خانين برسم الحجاج وهم خانين مكلفين وبها بعض احجار
7. مكلفه مصوره واحجار عليهم صلبان ولها قساطل ماء مكلفات بنا ملوك قدما
8. وعليها دلايل القدميه وانها من مدن ملوك الروم الكبار بساتينها قليله
9. ويباع بها سمك كثير وكبار ولذيذ لانه قريب اليها نهر كبير الذي ذكرناه
10. وقريب اليها بحرة ماء صغيره يوجد بها اسماك كثير والحطب بهذه القريه وفي
11. كل هذه النواحي بغاية الرخص لان الحمل الذي وزنه ثلاثون واربعون رطل يباع
12. في هذه النواحي بخمسة مصريات واقل والفحم ايضاً كثير ورخيص اما العنب والجبس
13. والتفاح وبقية الفواكه فلا تسال عنهم شي مثل الكذب اسال لمن سافر في طريق
14. استنبول ايام الفواكه وما الكستنا اي ابو فريوه موجود في كل مكان بالاحمال
15. ويوجد بها تتن ينكجا مال استنبول وبها كرخانة فاخوري يعمل بها اواني
16. الفخار الجيد وبها خان مكلف ظهره رصاص واما اهل هذه البلده بهم اناسه
17. قليل الا انهم اتراك قبا نزلنا في خانها تلك الليله وفي الصباح يوم السبت
18. في 27 تشرين اول رحلنا قاصدين بياض

Translation

Bolvadin

[14a] (13) We reached it after six hours and the road is easy and very beautiful. (14) Before Bolvadin, a bridge was built over the river, and the bridge is about three (15) hours long and leads to the river [= Akar Çayı] and from there to Bolvadin. You should know that the road to Istanbul, from (16) when you leave Antakya until you enter Istanbul, is all *kaldırım*, built like a bridge. (17) Ragıp Paşa provided this, using Asʿad Paşa's money, by repairing the road (18) to Istanbul and making it very easy. Because

initially one could only pass along the road (19) if one put up with weariness, many an injured beast, the loss of burdens, troubles, and great problems, (20) but now Ragıp Paşa made the road so easy that wood and litters can be transported easily. (21) Close to the town, there is another bridge consisting of fifty arches, big ones and small ones, (22) a very pretty bridge this is with the aforementioned pavement. As for Bolvadin, it is a medium-size keep, (23) between a village and a town, and it is prosperous. In it are five mosques with minarets one of which [14b] (1) has a leaden dome and it is a pretty mosque. The water of this town is also good. It is a cheap town because we bought in (2) Bolvadin three chickens for nine *misriya*, seven ounces of red apples, which whet the appetite with their (3) beauty and their scent, for a single *misriya*, many grapes, honey melons, and water melons, a lot of everything. [Bolvadin's] bread (4) is delicious and its cheese is delicious. There are also chestnuts, i.e., Abū Furaywa; seven ounces of them cost a *misriya* and each single one of them has the size (5) of a big walnut. There is nothing new that would not come to this town. This city has a prosperous market (6) and everything is available there. It has two *khāns* for pilgrims and they are two pretty *khāns*. There are some (7) pretty carved stones and stones with crosses on them. [The city] has pretty water fountains, built by ancient kings (8) and displaying evidence of their antiquity, and they come from the big cities of the Greek kings. There are few gardens (9) and a lot of tasty big fish is sold in them, because a big river, which we mentioned before, (10) is close and a small lake with a lot of fish is also close. The wood in this village, (11) and in the entire area, is very cheap because a load that weighs thirty and forty *raṭl* is sold (12) in this area for fifty *misriya* or less, and charcoal is also plentiful and cheap. As for the grapes, the honey melons (13), the apples, and the rest of the fruit, don't ask about them—it is as if they were illusions. Ask someone who travels on the road (14) to Istanbul during the fruit season. As for the chestnuts, i.e., Abū Furaywa, loads of them are available everywhere. (15) There is *tütün yananca* belonging to Istanbul in [the town], a pottery workshop where good earthenware is produced, (16) and a pretty *khān* the roof of which is leaden. As for the people of this town, they are hardly civil, (17) just vulgar Turks. During that night, we stayed in the [town's] *khān* and on Saturday morning, (18) 27 October [1764], we departed, heading to Bayat.

Commentary

Ḥannā al-Ṭabīb (c. 1702–1775) was a Maronite physician from Aleppo with contacts among bureaucratic circles in Istanbul. While his travelogue in general contains numerous dialectal elements, the text is not colloquial in the strict sense; rather, a striving for the use of classical Arabic can be detected, e.g., in the excerpt *sahl jiddan*, and not *ktīr*, for 'very easy'; *yūjad bihī asmāk*, and not *fī asmāk*, for 'there is fish'; *ayḍan* 'also', instead of *kamān*; etc. It is not clear if the travelogue was intended to be read aloud or silently in a private setting, but the style is generally unofficial, as evinced in the excerpt by the frequent recurrence of casual phrases, e.g., the water of the town is said to be 'good' (*jayyid*), bread and cheese are 'delicious' (*ṭayyib*)—without further specification. The narrator addresses the reader directly with imperatives, here, notably, *iʿlam* 'you should know' and *lā tasʾal ʿanhum* 'don't ask about them'. Also quite notable is the tendency to use emphatic language, e.g., phrases like *shī mithl al-kadhib* 'it is as if they were illusions.'

Folio 14a, line 16

قلدريم. Ottoman Turkish *kaldırım* 'pavement.'

Folio 14a, lines 17, 19; 14b, line 7

اعتنا, عنا, قدما, and further instances. The absence of final *hamza* can be regularly observed in so called 'Middle Arabic' texts. See Lentin (2011, 220).

Folio 14a, line 18

صيره سهل جداً 'he made it very easy' (to traverse).

Folio 14a, line 19

هلقدر 'to such a degree', here 'so many'. *Ha* + *l* + *qadar* is equivalent to the demonstrative construction *hādha l-qadar* and the result of the assimilation of the demonstrative pronoun. See Kallas (2012, 236–37) and Barthélemy (1935–1969, 870–71).

Folio 14a, line 22; 14b, lines 1, 6, 7, 16

مكلف / fem. مكلفه / dual مكلفين here 'pretty'. The extremely frequent use of this word is a peculiarity of Ḥannā al-Ṭabīb's writing style (in the excerpt six times, in the entire travelogue more around three hundred occurrences). In Arabic, the use of the word *mukallif* with this meaning is rather unusual. Ḥannā may have used Ottoman Turkish *mükellef*, which means 'great, grandiose, magnificent'.

Folio 14a, line 23

بموادن. *Hamza* in the plural *maʾādhin* is replaced by *wāw*. The *dhāl* is replaced by a *dāl*. Interdentals shifting into postdental plosives are a regular feature in the Aleppo dialect and can be detected elsewhere in 17th- and 18th-century travel accounts. See Kallas (2012, 224–26, especially 225–26).

Folio 14b, lines 2, 3, 4, 12

مصريه / plural مصاري or مصريات. Currency, a para.

Folio 14b, lines 2, 4

اواق (plural of اوقية) weight measurement. The Aleppo *ūqiyya* corresponded to 100 dirhams or 320 gr. See Barthélemy (1935–1969, 905).

Folio 14b, line 2

يشهي النظر literally 'which impassionate the eye'.

Folio 14b, lines 4, 14

ابو فريوه literally 'the father of the little fur'. The *kunya* refers to the furry shell of chestnuts.

Folio 14b, line 4

قدر 'of the size, of the dimensions'.

Folio 14b, line 5

وجديد شي ما يجي منه الى هذه البلاد. The phrase is syntactically awkward; it supposedly means 'there is nothing new that would not come to this town'; however, the negation 'there is nothing' is missing.

Folio 14b, line 6

كل شي *kull shī* < *kull shayʾ* 'everything'. On the absence of final *hamza*, see above. On the different uses of *shī*, see also Barthélemy (1935–1969, 421–22).

Folio 14b, line 11

حمل 'the load of a beast of burden'. See Barthélemy (1935–1969, 178).

Folio 14b, line 11

رطل a weight measurement. The Aleppo *raṭl* corresponded to the weight of 800 dirhams (2.566 kg). See Barthélemy (1935–1969, 284).

Folio 14b, line 13

شي مثل الكذب 'it is as if they were illusions', i.e., they are so fantastic that they can only be made up.

Folio 14b, line 15

تتن ينكجا. Probably Ottoman Turkish *tütün yananca* 'tobacco that burns'. The reference may be to tobacco that is smoked (as opposed to smokeless tobacco).

Folio 14b, line 15

كرخانة Ottoman Turkish *kerhane* 'workshop', here a 'pottery workshop'. On the dialectal word in Arabic, *karkhāna*, see also Barthélemy (1935–1969, 709).

Folio 14b, line 17

قبا Ottoman Turkish *kaba* 'rough, vulgar'.

19. SYRIA 1: CHRONICLE OF IBN AL-ṢIDDĪQ (1768)

Jérôme Lentin

The chronicle of Ibn al-Ṣiddīq (Ḥasan, al-šahīr bi--), *Ġarāyib al-badāyiʿ wa-ʿajāyib al-waqāyiʿ*, covers the events between 1182/1768 and 1185/1771 and is a contemporary account. We have no information about the author. The manuscript (a unicum) is part of the Wetzstein Collection, in the Staatsbibliothek zu Berlin – Preußischer Kulturbesitz (We II 417, Ahlwardt's catalogue vol. 9 n° 9832). The edition by Yūsuf Nuʿaysa (1988) is very faulty, full of mistakes and inaccurate readings. Long passages are omitted or mixed up. The text below is taken from the manuscript (p. 70; Ms f° 80b–81a).

Transcription

فعلوا اهل حران ما امرهم فراحوا[1] كبسوا اطراش[2] ابن احسين ارشيد وجابوه[3] الى الشام فدري ابن حبي قبل ما[4] يصل فراح يركض الى الصرايه[5] ودخل الى الكخية وعيط عليه وصرخ وقلوا[6] دين ايمان مالكم[7] وقول مالكم كيف باشتك[8] يعطيني بيورلدي الامان وتبعثوا[9] انتوا[10] فى قفاي من بعد جبتوا انا واعطيتوا[11] قول كمان[12] تبعثوا الى حران وتنهبوا طرشوا وماله او رزقوا الى الشام وحيات راس السلطان ما بقيم[13] قدمي من هون[14] الى ما تكتبوا بيورلدي آخر برجوع الطرش فكتبهم قوة واقتدار ولبّس ابن احسين ارشيد[15] قوة واقتدار يوم ثمانيه في شهر رجب عمل عصمان[16] باشا قلّت عقل بالشام وجميع[17] الخلق سبوه وقالوا هذا الرجل صار مجنون وجاب محمد اغا ابن الرّومي وعزلوا من قلعة المزيريب وعمل بدلوا صبي صفير مسكون الريح لانه هو

 https://doi.org/10.11647/OBP.0208.25

فسق بتاع[18] اولاد ابن احسين اغا الذي قتل فى سوق الاروام سلموا كل امور الحج ووكالة الدروز وحوران وجميع الناس سبوه ولعنوه وقالوا اهل الشام ان تم هذا الرجل على هذا العقل الفاسخ يروح الشام دخان ويوم تسعه فى رجب اجا[19] جوقدار من عند متسلم حمص ومعه مكتوب الى الباشا ومضمون المكتوب يا افندينا انّا نخبرك انّ اهالى حمص بدّها[20] ترحل من اخبار الذي[21] شاعت علينا ما فعل نعمان باشا في مجي الى حما فطلب منّا ذخيرة ثمن تيام[22] جميع اهل حمص لما دريوا[23] اعتمدوا انهم يرحلوا ويهربوا في البراري والقفار[24] فارسلنا واخبرناكم ونستنا[25] منك الجواب فحالا ارسل جواب الى متسلم حمص كلما طلب نعمان تعطيه

Translation

The people of Ḥarrān [= Ḥarrān al-ʿawāmīd, in the vicinity of Damascus] did what he had ordered them to do and they went and looted the cattle of Ḥusayn Rušayd and brought it to Damascus. Ibn Ḥibbī got aware of this before its arrival and he rushed inside the Palace to find the *kaẖiya* [intendant] and shouted and screamed at him and said: you, man of no faith! You traitor to your word! How is it that your Pasha gives me a written order (*buyuruldī*) granting me safe-conduct and quarter and that you send [people / messages] behind my back [to harm / discredit me], after I have brought it to you and after you have given your word. Moreover, you send [people] to Ḥarrān to loot his cattle and his goods and livelihoods and bring them to Damascus. By the life of the Sultan, I will not remove my foot from here until you write a new written order ordering that the cattle must go back. He compelled them to write [it] by force. He bestowed marks of honour upon Ibn Ḥusayn Rušayd by force. On the 8 Rajab, ʿUṯmān Bāšā behaved improperly in Damascus. All the people insulted him, saying: this man has turned crazy! He let

Muḥammad ʾĀġā Ibn al-Rūmī come, dismissed him from the fortress of al-Muzayrīb and replaced him by a mentally ill young boy – because of his depravity with young boys. He entrusted the son of Ibn Ḥusayn ʾĀġā, who had been killed in the *Sūq al-ʾArwām*, with the leadership of the pilgrimage, and made him his representative [*wakīl*] for [the region of] the Druzes and Ḥawrān. All the people insulted and cursed him and the Damascenes said: should that man continue with his depraved mind, Damascus will go up in smoke. On the 9 Rağab a *jūqadār* (*čūẖadār*) [here: a high rank messenger] sent by the *mutasallim* of Homs arrived bearing a letter to the Pasha saying: Sir (*ʾAfandīnā*) we are informing you that the people of Homs are about to move away, because of the news that spread out and reached us about what ʿUṯmān Bāšā did when he arrived to Hama: he required of us [that we supply] the provisions for eight days. When the people of Homs heard about that, they decided they would move and run away to the steppe and the desert. We have already sent you a message to inform you and we are waiting for your response. Right away, he sent his answer to the *mutasallim* of Homs [saying]: Grant ʿUṯmān whatever he might ask.

Commentary

[1] راحوا. See text II.9, no. 4.

[2] اطراش. The usual plural of this (colloquial) word is *ṭrūš*; *(ʾa)ṭrāš* is probably a classicising form.

[3] جابوه. See text II.9, no. 18.

[4] قبل ما, although attested in the Classical language, is most probably the colloquial form of this conjunction.

[5] الصرايه. Shift of s > ṣ; cf. *sarāy(a)*.

[6] قلوا *qal-lo* (< *qāl l-o*). Notice also the *ʾalif wiqāya* after the final *-o/-u* (a common feature of MA orthography); cf. طرشوا *ṭarš-o*, جبتوا *žibt-o*, رزقوا *rizq-o*, عزلوا *ʿazal-o*, بدلوا *badal-o*.

[7] مالكم < **mā l-kum* 'not to you' = 'you don't have'.

[8] باشتك. Borrowings like *bāšā* often have a *-t* in the construct state (and are often written with a *tāʾ*, e.g., باشة, also in the absolute state).

[9] تبعثوا. For the *-ū* form (and not *-ūn*) of the 2pl of the imperfect see text II.9, no. 7. The verb *baʿaṯa/baʿat* often functions as a factitive auxiliary (see Lentin 1997, §4.5.1, 633–36); the auxiliary verb can follow immediately or be preceded by the conjunction *wa*, as in the just following تبعثوا الى حران وتنهبوا 'you send [people] to Ḥarrān to loot his cattle', which could very well be translated 'you let loot his cattle in Ḥarrān'. Cf. also text II.14, no. 9.

[10] انتوا colloquial pron. (*ʾintu*). Notice also the *ʾalif wiqāya* after the final *-u* (cf. n. 6).

[11] اعطيتوا. The (colloquial) *-ū* form (and not *-um*) is used most of the time in MA for the 2mpl and 2fpl of the perfect.

[12] كمان *kamān*, colloquial adverb.

[13] بقيم: *b(a)qīm*, i.e., *b-* + 1cs of *qām*, with *i* theme vowel (cf. Classical *ʾaqāma*) 'to remove'. The *b(i)-* imperfect, significantly used here in the first person and in reported (direct) speech, indicates modality (here modal future in a strong assertion) as well as the commitment of the speaker.

[14] هون *hawn/hōn*, colloquial adverb.

[15] احسين and ارشيد. The initial prosthetic *ʾalif* indicates (in this case) that the noun begins with CC-. Thus, we have to read something like *Ḥsēn* and *Ršēd* (*Rašīd* is never abbreviated as **Ršīd*).

[16] عصمان **ʿUṯmān* > *ʿUsmān* > *ʿUṣmān*.

[17] جميع. See text II.9, no. 5.

[18] بتاع is one of the numerous 'genitive particles' used in MA texts (see Lentin 1997, §17.8.2, 745–47). Its particular (qualificative) value here is not frequent.

[19] اجا *ʾiža* (/*žā*) 'to come' (Classical *jāʾa*) occurs regularly in MA texts.

[20] بدّها *bidd-hā*. Colloquial *bidd-* + pronominal suffix 'to want, wish' or 'to be intending/going to' is common in (the most colloquialising) MA texts.

[21] اخبار الذي invariable الذي (see text II.9, no. 15). Also notice the construction Ø + N + relative clause (= Classical الاخبار التي).

[22] ثمن تيام colloquial *ṯmən-t-iyyām*.

[23] دريوا *diryū*. Morphologically colloquial (*diri* 'to become aware, hear').

[24] في البراري والقفار. This literary cliché is very common in 'popular' literature, especially in the *sīras*.

[25] نستنا *nistanna* (colloquial).

20. A LETTER TRANSMITTED BY AMBASSADOR HAJJ MAHDĪ BARGASH FROM SULTAN MUḤAMMAD BIN ʿABDALLAH TO SULTAN ABDUL ḤAMĪD (1789 CE)

Ahmed Ech-Charfi

CBH. 226/10511

A letter transmitted by Ambassador Hajj Mahdī Bargash from Sultan Muḥammad Bin ʿAbdallah to Sultan Abdul Ḥamīd informing him that he is sending a present of four ships and 536 liberated Ottoman prisoners.

Transcription

المقام المتوج بتاج العز والسيادة والمحلى بحلية الفضل والمجادة البالغ في أفعال الخير حد النهاية والكوكب الطالع في برج اليمن والسعادة معدن السادات الأجلاء الأخيار سلسلة المجاهدين لأعداء الله الكفار من جعلهم الله من حماة الإسلام وممن أنام سبحانه في ظلهم جميع الأنام سلطان البرين وخاقان البحرين وخديم الحرمين الشريفين السلطان بن السلطان السلطان عبد الحميد خان بن السلطان أحمد خان جعل الله أيامهم السعيدة كلها محمودة ومآثرهم الكريمة شهيرة مشهودة سلام عليك ورحمة الله تعالى وبركاته وتحياته ورضوانه أما بعد فيصل حضرة أخينا السلطان عبد الحميد نصره الله صحبة خديمنا الحاج المكي برقاش ولد قبطان باشى أربعة مراكب من مراكبنا الجهادية هدية منا إليك ونطلب الله النصر والتمكين والفتح المبين لنا ولكم ولسائر المسلمين وأن تكون عساكر المسلمين أعزة منصورة وأعداء الله الكفرة أذلة مقهورة وها خديمنا القايد محمد بن عبد الله وارد عليكم بخمسمائة أسير وستة

 https://doi.org/10.11647/OBP.0208.26

وثلاثين أسيرا مَنَ الله تبارك وتعالى عليهم وأنقذهم من الأسر والحمد لله على ذلك الذي مَنَّ الله علينا بإنقاذ إخواننا المسلمين من يد أعداء الله الكفرة. والخديم المذكور من يصلكم فيه كفاية الخبر والذي يقول لكم فخرا أمرناه به والسلام في أوائل شعبان المبارك عام 1203.

Translation

Your Majesty, with a crown of splendour and sovereignty and adorned with favours and glory; you, perpetrator of deeds of ultimate generosity; you, a planet in the horoscope of good omen and happiness; you, who come from a lineage of the best noble sovereigns forming a chain of *mujāhidīn* against unbelievers and enemies of Allah, the *mujāhidīn* whom Allah has given the responsibility to protect Islam and provide peace for all people; you, sultan of the two lands, Khagan of the two oceans, and custodian of the two holy mosques; a sultan and son of a sultan; Sultan Abdul Ḥamīd, son of Sultan Aḥmed Khan, may Allah grant them everlasting happiness and make their good achievements famous and celebrated; peace, mercy, and blessings of Allah be upon you!

There will be delivered to our brother—Sultan Abdul Ḥamīd; May Allah make him glorious—by our servant Hajj Al-Makkī Bargash, son of Captain Pasha, four of our navy vessels, as a gift from us to you. We ask Allah for glory, empowerment, and further conquests to us and to you and all Muslims so that Muslim armies always prevail and their enemies be vanquished and humiliated. Also, our servant Caid Mohammed bin Abdellah will deliver to you five hundred and thirty-six (Ottoman) prisoners freed by the help of Allah—we thank Him for that and for helping us to liberate our Muslim brothers from the hands of unbelievers, Allah's enemies. The aforementioned servant will provide you with more information on the operation he carried out under our order.

Peace be upon you,

Early Shaʿbān of the year 1203

21. ARAB MERCHANT LETTERS FROM THE GOTHA COLLECTION OF ARABIC MANUSCRIPTS

Boris Liebrenz

Arabic letters concerning personal and business matters abound in the pre-Ottoman period, but become extremely scarce afterwards. Since the early 19th century, the Forschungsbibliothek Schloss Friedenstein, Gotha (Germany) has held seven volumes of merchant letters dating from the middle of the 18th century until 1806. Numbering more than 1,600 letters, this repository seems to be the largest one preserved from the period.

The writers and addressees are both Christian and Muslim and examples of both will be given here. There are some overlaps, but in general the Christian letters cover a network of merchants of Syrian origin that operated between Cairo, Alexandria, Damietta, Jaffa, Jerusalem, and Damascus, with mentions of further extensions to Istanbul, Cyprus, and Rhodes. The letters by Muslims (with few Christian examples) belong to several networks of Muslim merchants centred in Cairo. In the case presented here, the network revolves around two brothers Abū Qaṣīṣa and letters are exchanged primarily between Jedda, Suez, and Cairo.

 https://doi.org/10.11647/OBP.0208.27

The language of the Christian network is marked by unequivocal embracing of the colloquial. Its features include: loss of gender distinction, plural, or dual; replacement of emphatic consonants with their unemphatic counterparts (ص > س; ض > د; ط > ت; ظ > ز), but also occasionally the reverse (e.g., دراهم regularly becomes ضراهم); case endings lost or wrong (بكل خيراً); negation of all tempi with *lam* followed by a verb in perfect tense (*lam kān*) or even negation with *lam* with no verb at all (*lam huwa bāqī*); imperfect verb forms are often prefixed with a ب. The lexicon includes not only several words of Italian and French origin (بوليصه), but also several particles of colloquial usage (*šū*, *layš*, *minšān*). The orthography changes with the individual scribes, but some features are prevalent: *tāʾ marbūṭa* becomes *tāʾ* and vice versa; *plene* writing of long vowels that are regularly omitted (ذاالك); the *ʾalif* of the article is dropped when the initial *hamza* is silent (بلسلامة); individual words can be joined into one when contracted in speech (قلله = *qul lahū* > *qillu*). The letters of Abū Qaṣīṣa's network are generally more in line with the grammatical and orthographic rules of written Arabic although any of the aforementioned phenomena may occur.

The address differs between the two networks in layout and sometimes wording. Those from the Red Sea and Egypt are written in one line at the top of the verso side. The Syrians write several lines at the centre of what was the outer side of the folded letter. The same can be observed from other contemporary letters from the Ottoman Empire north of Egypt. This formal feature appears to mark a general division between letters written in

Greater Syria and north of it (of which the Syrian merchant diaspora is an Egyptian extension to the south) on the one side, and those coming from Egypt, the Arabian Peninsula, and further south, on the other.

Transcription

MS Gotha orient. A 2837, doc. 1

Fransīs Bernard Dumyān to his cousin Giovanni Rūk / Rocco and his maternal uncle Yūsuf Anṭūn Tarjumān Talāmās / Giuseppe Talamas in Damietta. The writer's unnamed sister[1] is also mentioned in the internal address.

The details of the matter reported in this latter are not always clear to me.[2] Yet the contours of dramatic events revolving around two fierce legal cases taking place in Rosetta are evolving. They first pitted Fransīs against a powerful consul, while he believes he has the whole community of consuls on his side, securing documents from as far as Istanbul. The second case is that of a murder that had taken place in the Frankish quarter and sees the consuls united against the city's governor, who is unable to present the murderer.

1. بمنه تعالى
2. يصل الى ثغر دمياط ويسلم ليد جناب حضرة ابن عمنا الخواجه
3. جواني روك وخالنا الخواجه يوسف انطون ترجمان تلاماس

[1] Theresia, according to other letters.

[2] The matter is taken up again in Forschungsbibliothek Gotha, Ms. orient. A 2837, no. 27 (dated Ṣafar 30, 1219), which this one must precede, since the murder is mentioned as an immediate case here unlike in no. 27.

4. المحترمين امانه مرسله بالخير

MSig. Guiseppe Talamas Incaricato dell'Agenzia d Spagna opera altiss. Giovanni Rocco in Damietta

Recto

1. حفظهم الباري تعالى
2. امين
3. جناب حضرة شقيقتنا المصيونة وابن عمنا سنيور جواني وخالنا سنيور يوسف المحترمين

4. غب عروض الشوق اليكم مع تزايد الاشتياق لجنابكم المعروض لبين اياديكم
5. هو انه قبله تقدم لكم مكتوب عن سكت راشيد تحت يد الخواجه بطروشي وهي عرفناكم
6. بوصولنا لاجل الاطمان انشا الله تعالى يكون وصلكم وانتم بخير الان
7. نخبر جنابكم بخصوص القنصل حين لقا كافت القناصل شادين على يدنا بلحق
8. والطريقا لسبب لم يمشو مثله على طمع الفلوس فلمذكور رد جواب للجميع
9. انني صحيح رسلت وراه انه يحضر ولاكن الان لم لي عنده ولا له عندي
10. فطلبناه للشرع عند ا[..]لا قنصل الذي هو يريدو بحضور كافت القناصل
11. لم كان يقبل ورجل الباين انه عارف حاله لم هو باقي لسبب ذالك
12. معلط وقصده ياكل العرابون ..ـه ٣ (نصف) ٥٥٣ خلاف المصاريف ولاكن انشا الله تعالى
13. ووجود المحبين منبظر عينه بوصط كرفوه لان كافت القناصل ختمو لنا الاوراق
14. ايضا الرويسة افرنج وروم ووجهناهم بسلامت الله تعالى الى كرفوه للسناتو اول (...)
15. ولجل البخت توجه ايضا والد الاب المحترم ابونا ديونيسيوس وكيل الروم فجنابه
16. سلمهم لوالده وايضاً بمكتوب منه للبرينشبه حكم ما ردنا نحن فنساله تعالى

17. دعاكم فرنسيس
18. مـــــد
19. برنا دميان

20. ١٢١٩

21. سنة

Righthand Margin

22. ان يطول بعمر المحبين فلرجا دايماً تكونو مطمنين
23. علينا ولم يكون لكم علينا فكرة بوجه من الوجوه
24. وعمالين كل يوم بعزومه ايام عند القناصل ايام عند
25. التجار والمحبين نساله تعالى ان يقضدرنا [كذا] علي مكافت
26. الجميع ورد شملنا وياكم بجبران خاطر عن قريب
27. بجاه والدت السياده وابنها الحبيب وكافت
28. القديسيين امين
29. الان رسلنا الكنباري الى راشيد لاجل
30. يحصل محضر المركب من بيترو اتر امارني
31. عن يد الخواجه روشيتي انما ارجوكم
32. ترسلو لنا الورقة الذي حضرت من
33. اسلانبول بختم كنشليريت [السبع]
34. جوزر[3] ومكتوب فيها حساب
35. محضر المركب وبتجادوها بين
36. الاوراق الفرنجية لان الكنباري
37. ينساها الرجا ارسالها حالاً
38. مع قوطم الجوخ الزروق بتوع
39. الابيتو الذي عليه السبابيطا
40. ووجه دوشك من الصوفر ع ١ واربع
41. وجوه امخدات بلونو ام خمسة

[3] This short-lived Republic of the Seven Islands or Septinsular Republic comprised several islands off the coast of modern Greece in the Ionian Sea, among them Corfu, mentioned in the letter. It was established by a joint Ottoman-Russian military intervention that took the territories from the French and it existed between 1800 and 1807, after which they were first annexed by Napoleon and then transformed into a British protectorate from 1815 to 1864.

42. ذالك ما ارجوه منكم مع الدعا

Top Margin

43. دايماً وسلامنا للجميع كل حي
44. باسما وايضاً الاخ يعقوب غطاس
45. ومنا بتقبل (...) كافة الامهات جميعاً جناب
46. ابونا باصلي وجناب ابونا يوسف والبيتريو واكل
47. الكبير ووكيل القدس والسنايتي والاب عيسا جارنا
48. ودايماً نسالهم الدعا خط عجله وعمركم يطول
49. ومزيد سلامنا لجناب الخواجه باصيلي فخر والخواجه
50. عيروت المحترمين

Verso

1. يستولي
2. قبله واحد اجر دلي قوس ترجمان اسويسيا
3. ونابولي بلقرابينا وبساعة قتل اخدوه دفنوه
4. ورسلو كافت القناصل للحاكم وطلبو منه الرجل حتا
5. شنقو بحارت الافرنج فلحاكم فتش عليه لم وجد فقال
6. لهم بسلمكم واحد اجردلي غيرو وقتلوه يبقا واحد
7. قدام واحد فلم قبلو ولحد تاريخه يفتشو علي الذي
8. قتل وبادين يعمرو بوابات ويعملو حارت الافرنج
9. لوحدها فقامت اهل البلد لم رادو فلزم انهم يحررو
10. لسعادت الباشه ومستنزرين الجواب وعملين يبنو
11. بلسد وكل يوم سو خره على اولاد البلد فربنا
12. يجعل النهاية خير لان الحال واقف على الجميع وكل
13. شي غالي يكون معلومكم الرجا من ابن عمنا سنيور جواني
14. ايذا راد ولقا مناسب يسرف بضاعتو بطرفكم انسب
15. من هنا ومن راشيد وانما مصر لم بنعرف الاسعار
16. وانما الحرب دايماً حد ذالك كفاية دمتم

Translation

With His blessing
May it arrive at the harbour Damietta and be expedited to the hand of his excellency our cousin the master
Juwānī Rūk and our maternal uncle the master Yūsuf Anṭūn Tarjumān Talāmās,
the esteemed, safe and sound.

Recto

(1) May the Exalted protect them!
(2) Amen.
(3) [To] his Excellency our sister, our cousin Signor Juwānī, and our maternal uncle Signor Yūsuf, the esteemed.
(4) After expressing the longing for you with exceeding yearning for your Excellency, what we have to put before you (5) is this: you previously received a letter regarding the mint of Rāšīd by hand of the master Baṭrūshī, in which we informed you (6) about our arrival to put you at ease. God willing, it reached you and you are fine. Now (7) we want to report to your Excellency on the issue of the consul when he found all the consuls in support of us (8) because, unlike him, they were not driven by greed for money. Said consul answered to the crowd: (9) "It is true that I sent after him so that he would appear. But right now I have no claim against him, as he has none against me. (10) We had cited him to court at [...] a consul who wanted him in the presence of all the consuls, (11) which he refused." It is clear that this is a man who knows his ways and won't stay blemished because of that. (12) His intention is to pocket the down payment—533 ½

[piasters and] 3 [*miṣriyya*] plus expenses—but—God willing—(13) with the presence of loving friends, he will be thwarted, with the mediation of Corfu. Because all the consuls have sealed papers for us, (14) also the heads of the monasteries of the Europeans (Ifranj) and the Orthodox (Rūm). We delivered them to Corfu for the Senate first [...]. (15) And for good luck, the father of the esteemed Father Diyūnīsiyūs, guardian of the Orthodox, His Excellency (16) directed them to his father, too. And also a letter from him to the Principe according to our answer. We ask God

(17) Praying for you Fransīs

(18) ...

(19) Barnā Dumyān

(20)–(21) in the year 1219.

Righthand Margin

(22) to prolong the lives of our friends. Please, always be at ease (23) about us, and don't spare a thought on us. (24) We spend our days being invited, sometimes with the consuls, sometimes with (25) the traders. About the friends we ask God to enable us to satisfy (26) them all and that he would unite us in good spirit soon, (27) through the power of the Mother of the Lord, her beloved son, and all (28) the saints. Amen.

(29) Now: we sent al-Kunbārī to Rāšīd so that (30) he would get the ship's manifest from Pītrū Atrāmārnī (31) by way of the master Rūšītī. I ask you only (32) to send the paper that arrived from (33) Islāmbūl with the seal of the consul's office of the Seven (34) Islands, as well as a letter with the account (35) of the ship's manifest. You will find it between (36) the *franjī*

(Italian or in Latin characters?) papers. (This is) because al-Kunbārī (37) (might?) forget it. Please send it immediately (38) together with: a (قوطم?) of blue broadcloth belonging to (39) the dress on which are the shoes; (40) and 1 kind of (دوشك?) from (الصوفر?); and four (41) or five coloured pillows.

(42) This is what I ask from you, with my constant prayers,

Top Margin

(43) and greetings to everyone, each (44) by their names! Also to the brother Yaʿqūb Ġaṭṭās. (45) And from us (…) all the mothers kiss (the hands of) His Excellency (46) Our Father Bāṣilī and His Excellency Our Father Yūsuf and al-Bītrīyū, the great (47) guardian, and the guardian of Jerusalem, and al-Sanāyitū, and Father ʿĪsā, our neighbour. (48) We always ask for their intercession. This is written hastily! May your life be prolonged! (49) Extensive greetings to His Excellency the master Bāṣīlī Faḫr and the master (50) ʿAyrūt, the esteemed.

Verso

(1)–(2) Previously, one (اجر دلي) overpowered the dragoman of Switzerland (3) and Napoli with a carabine and (the dragoman) was immediately killed. They took him and buried him (4) and all the consuls sent for the governor to demand the perpetrator. They wanted to (5) strangle him in the Frankish quarter. The governor searched for him but did not find him. So he said (6) to them: “I will hand over another (اجر دلي) for you to kill. Thus it’s still one (7) for one.” But they did not accept. And up to date they are still looking for the (8) killer. They want to fortify the gates and make the Frankish quarter (9) isolated. The local people rose up and will certainly write (10) to His Excellency the pasha. And they are waiting for his answer. They set out to build (11) on the wall. The worst curse on the local people every day! May our Lord (12) give a good outcome because all business stops at this state of affairs and (13) everything is expensive. This is to let you know.

We ask of our cousin, Senior Giovanni, (14) if he so pleases, to find a better opportunity to turn his merchandise into cash (15) than here or in Rāšīd—for Cairo we don't know the prices. (16) The war is always an obstacle for this. Enough now! May you live long!

Commentary

The address is in Italian and the lexicon of the writer, too, seems to show familiarity with Italian terms (*l'abito, principe*).

Recto

Line 12

العرابون. I interpret this to be a form of *ʿarabūn*, which, according to de Biberstein-Kazimirski (1860, 209) means *arrhes*, i.e., 'deposit, down payment'.

Line 38

بتوع. Like the more prevalent form بتاع, this term signifies a connection or belonging between two nouns, equivalent to the terms ذو/ذات and تابع.

Line 39

الابيتو. This word appears to be of a non-Arabic form and I interpret it as a rendering of the Italian *l'abito* 'the dress'.

Line 48

خط عجله. A standard excuse for a letter written in haste.

Verso

Line 2

اسويسيا. This seems to reflect the Italian version of Switzerland, *Svizzera*.

Line 8

بادين. This is the dialectal expression of intention and desire which is usually formed today and in the letters with بد (*badd*) as an invariable noun to which a personal pronoun is attached to express gender and number, e.g., بدهم. But in this rare case, as in a few other places throughout the letters, it is formed like a verb, e.g., بدني.

MS Gotha orient. A 2837, doc. 148

Makkī Rawāy to Ṣāliḥ Abū Qaṣīṣa at the Wikālat al-Naššārīn in Cairo. The letter was presumably sent from Suez, where Makkī was posted.

Transcription

Recto

1. يصل ان شا الله تعالى الى محروسة مصر يسلم ليد المحترم المكرم الاخ العزيز الحاج صالح ابو قصيصة بوكالت النشارين ٨٦٤٢

Verso

1. الجناب المحترم المكرم الاخ العزيز الحاج صالح ابو اقصيصة اعزه الله تعالى
2. بعد مزيد السلام عليه وكثرة الاشواق اليه لا يخفاكم نعرفكم سابق تاريخه
3. ارسلنا لكم مكتوب وفيه قايمة بعلم المشحون ان شا الله تعالى يكون
4. وصلكم واتطلعتوا عليه وانتم بخير ويوم تاريخه قدمنا لكم
5. في داو العيدروس خرز ١٥ وداو السعيدي خرز ١٥ على با هارون خرز ٢٢ هذا غلاق
6. الخرز ونعرفكم من قبل اصحاب الثلاثة داوات المزكورة فهم عندكم
7. في مصر اياك تنولوا في كل داو خمسة احمال لاجل شحنت الشامية
8. الذي لكم لان بلغنا انهم بينولوا في مصر وخايفين يحضروا
9. ويكونوا غلفوا الشحنة في مصر يكون في علمكم واستلموا لنا
10. على الاخ الحاج محمد ابن قيموا وكل من يسال عنا والسلام
11. السيد مكي
12. رواي
13. (علامة)
14. ١٢١٠
15. سنة
16. في ٥ رجب

Translation

Recto

(1) May it arrive, God willing, to the well-protected Cairo and be delivered to the hand of the esteemed and noble one, the beloved brother al-ḥājj Ṣāliḥ Abū Qaṣīṣa at the Wikālat al-Naššārīn 8642

Verso

(1) His Excellency, the esteemed and noble one, the beloved brother al-ḥājj Ṣāliḥ Abū Qaṣīṣa, may God strengthen him!

(2) After copious greetings for him and much longing for him, it shall not be concealed from you that we inform you that

previously (3) we sent you a letter which included a cargo manifest, God willing it has (4) reached you and you looked at it and are in good health. As of today, we have forwarded to you, (5) on the dhow of al-ʿAydarūs, 15 beads, and on the dhow of al-Saʿīdī 15, and on (that of) Bā Hārūn 22. And that is the rightful passage of possession (*ġilāq*) (6) of the beads. We also inform you on behalf of the three captains of the aforementioned dhows, that when they are with you (7) in Cairo you can load five loads (*aḥmāl*) on each dhow because of the Syrian cargo (*šaḥnat al-Šāmiyya*) (8) that is with you. Because it has reached us that they load in Cairo and are afraid to come, (9) they will wrap the cargo in Cairo. So that you know.

Greet on my behalf (10) the brother al-ḥājj Muḥammad Ibn Qīmū and everyone who asks after us. Peace!

(11) al-sayyid Makkī

(12) Rawāy

(13) [signature]

(14)–(16) on 5 Rajab in the year 1210 (=15.1.1796)

Commentary

Recto

Line 1

٨٦٤٢ '8642'. This number has an apotropaic function. The letters of the southern network of mostly Muslim writers who corresponded between Cairo, the Red Sea, and the Hejaz, rarely exclude it. But it is sometimes also found in correspondence of the northern, mostly Christian network.

Verso

Line 5

غلاق. I am not certain about the meaning of this word. My translation is based on Lane's (1863–1893, VI: 2284) translation of the verb غلق and its infinitive nouns غَلَقٌ and غُلُوق as "The pledge was, or became, a rightful possession [i.e. a forfeit] to the receiver of it," although this remains an unsatisfactory explanation.

22. A JUDAEO-ARABIC LETTER FROM THE PRIZE PAPERS COLLECTION, HCA 32/1208/126.2 (1796)

Matthew Dudley

Transcription

1. בע"ה
2. תונס יום כ"א לח' חשון ש' התקנז
3. אהובינו וחמודינו ה"ר שלמה בושערה יצ"ו
4. אחדש"ו מן בעד כטרט אסלאם עליך ב"ש והאד אלחרפין בקצור באש נעלמך אלי קבלט מעה
5. אלמסעי פ׳י וסט ברייט ה"ר דאענוס עז בראטך תאריך ט"ו לח' הנצ"ל וערפט מה פיהא
6. ומנהא פרחט נסמע ביך טייב ת״ל ורייטך תחרסני באש נכברך סום אלקאהווא אש
7. תסווא ענדה פי סבט ענדך מנהא תעלם יא סידי אלי אלקאהווא פאטו תסווה מייא
8. וסטין למייה וכמסה וסטין לקונטאר וכו"פ גאט מרכב מן מאלטא וגאבת אלקאהווא
9. ואלבארח גאט מרכב דוברה מן דזאייר מוחוק בזביב וגא פ׳יהא אלקאהווא אלי
10. גא ואחד אלמסלם סמייט אראמוש גאב פ׳יידו מייא ועשרין קונטאר כולק אלגור
11. אלי גאלהום אלי סיגורו יסטחק אטיח סומהא פי סבט כולחד יחאב יביע ואלי
12. יסיר לקודאם נכברך ואנה ידהורלו וידא לקוט סום טייב פי קצמטינה אלא ביע
13. אחסן מן תונס פי סבט אליום זמאן שטה ולקאהווא וידא לחקט למא עדמט
14. ואנטי ומה ידהורלך ומן אלפלוס לאכרין אלי רסלטלו ראהום באקיין מטבועין
15. פ׳י קפ׳אפ׳הום בטאבעך באש תבקה עלה באל אלי אנטי ומא תאמרני כיפאש
16. תעמל פ׳יהום וכו"פ׳ אסאעה קצירא ומא ענדי חדוש באש טנוול עליך כאן
17. בלכ׳יר ועאפ׳ייה וכאן תסטחקשי חאגה אמרני טקציהא עלה ראצי ועינייה ושו"ש
18. ע"ה שלמה צמח
19. ס"ט

 https://doi.org/10.11647/OBP.0208.28

Arabic Transcription

1. בע"ה
2. תונס יום כ"א לח' חשון ש' התקנז
3. אהובינו וחמודינו ה"ר שלמה בושערה יצ"ו
4. אחדש"ו من بعد كطرط اسلام عليك ב"ש وهاد الحرفين بقصور باش نعلمك إلي قبلط معه
5. المسعي في وصط برييط ה"ר داعنوس عز براطك تاريخ ט"ו לח' הנצ"ל وعرفط ما فيها
6. ومنها فرحط نسمع بيك طييب ת"ל ورايطك تحرسني باش نخبرك سوم القاهووا اش
7. تسووا عنده في سبط عندك منها تعلم يا سيدي إلي القاهووا فاطو تسووه مييا
8. وسطين لمييه وخمسه وسطين لقنطار וכו"פ جاط مركب من مالطا وجابت القاهووا
9. والبارح جاط مركب دوبره من دزايير موحوق بزبيب وجا فيها القاهووا الي
10. جا واحد المسلم سمييط اراموش جاب فييدو مييا وعشرين قونطار خولق الغور
11. الي جالهم الي سيغورو يسطحق اطيح سومها في سبط كولحد يحاب يبيع والي
12. يسير لقدام نخبرك وانه يدهورلو ويدا لقوت سوم طييب في قصمطينة الا بيع
13. احسن من تونس في سبط اليوم زمان شطه والقاهووا ويدا لحقط لما عدمط
14. وانطي ومه يدهورلك ومن الفلوس الاخرين الي رسلطلو راهوم باقيين مطبوعين
15. في قفافهوم بطابعك باش تبقه عله بال الي انطي وما تامرني كيفاش
16. تعمل فيهوم و וכו"פ اساعه قصيرا وما عندي حدوش باش طنوول عليك كان
17. بالخير وعافييه وكان تسطحقشي حاجة امرني طقضيها عله راضي وعينييه וש"ו"ש
18. ע"ה שלמה צמח
19. ס"ט

Translation

(1) With the help of God. (2) Tunis on the 21st of Cheshvan 5557, (3) Our beloved and dear Rav Shlomo Bushʾara[1]—may his Rock

[1] Although I have provided the direct transliteration 'Bushʾara' in line with that of Richard Ayoun (2010), there is a great deal of variation in transliterations of this surname in primary sources related to HCA 32/1208. For example, in HCA 32/901/276 spellings range from 'Bouchara' (n.48r), 'Bochara' (n.41r), 'Busciara' (n.37r), and 'Bocharra' (n.35r). Most of the papers and letters in HCA/32/1208 appear to have

keep him and grant him life. (4) Much peace upon you in the name of God. I am sending these two letters in order to briefly inform you that I have received from (5) the messenger in between the letter of the respected Rav Daʾnos dated the fifteenth of the aforementioned month and having taken note what's in it (6) and from it, I was happy to learn that you are well (thanks be to God) and your perspective in supervising me so that I should inform you of the sale of what the coffee (7) totals to on Saturday, informing you, sir, that you have ground coffee totalling one-hundred (8) sixty and one-hundred sixty-five [*reales*] per *qantar* and also the vessel arrived from Malta carrying the coffee, (9) yesterday a Dobra [Ragusan] vessel arrived from Algiers loaded with raisins and had with it the coffee (10) that the Muslim named Aramouche came bringing [with] one-hundred twenty *qantar* in hand, of inexperienced character (11) he told them surely it is worth granting its sale, on Saturday everyone likes selling and [through] that (12) which was sent we had previously informed you that it appears also for foodstuffs [there is] an agreeable sale in Constantine, (13) it is better selling there than in Tunis on Saturday, it is now wintertime and the coffee also was afflicted when it became unavailable, (14) and letting you know from the money for the others I sent [what] are the remaining balances (15) in their baskets, following your supervision in order to [meet that which] is on your mind and [awaiting] what you direct me to do with how (16) to handle them and also the

belonged to Shlomo Bushʾara and were captured aboard the cargo ship *Venus* in late-October 1800, after the vessel ran aground in the port of Mahon.

time is short and I have nothing new in order to prolong [this letter], may (17) you be well and healthy, if there is anything else required command me and I will gladly carry it out, with great care, peace and happiness
(18) Shlomo Ṣemaḥ,[2] servant of God
(19) a good Sefardi

Commentary

The letter features a variety of linguistic elements characteristic of Maghrebi Arabic. These components include the interrogatives *āsh* (אש/اش) and *kīfāsh* (כיפאש/كيفاش), as well as the conjunction *bāsh* (באש/باش) and the demonstrative pronoun *hād* (האד/هاد). Additionally, the author makes use of the common Maghrebi verbal construction 'to be', through the conjugation of رأي in the third-person plural (ראהום/راهوم). Ṣemaḥ's writing also demonstrates instances of code-switching to vocabulary from Judaeo-Spanish (line 11), and Hebrew (lines 4 and 16).

Another overarching feature within the letter is the author's reference to the potential sale of the coffee 'on Saturday' (lines 7, 11, 13). This arrangement should give readers pause due to the fact that it stands in violation of both biblical and rabbinic injunctions against conducting business on the Sabbath. The two

[2] As with the recipient's surname, the transliteration 'Ṣemaḥ' directly portrays the sender's Hebrew orthography. That said, alternate Latinised versions of the surname surely existed in the late-18th century. One example is the spelling 'Semah', which is attested in the 1784 communal census records of the Livornese Massari (*Tribunale dei Massari*, vol. 10, f. 388r, Archivio Storico della Comunità Ebraica di Livorno).

Jewish merchants in question therefore likely relied on the assistance of Muslim or Christian trading partners to carry out this transaction. Besides the obvious temporal dimensions of the phrase פי סבט/في سبت, it may also imply the location for the coffee's sale. More specifically, the inclusive tone of Ṣemaḥ's affirmation in line 12 to the effect that 'on Saturday everyone likes selling', may suggest the existence of a Saturday market (*Sūq es Sebt*).

Line 1

בע"ה–בעזרת השם 'with the help of God' (lit. 'with the help of the Name') (Hebrew).

Line 2

לח' = לחודש 'in the month' (Hebrew).

ש' = שנה 'year' (Hebrew).

Line 3

ה"ר = הרב 'the master' (Hebrew).

יצ"ו = ישמרהו צורו ויחיהו 'may his Rock keep him and grant him life' (Hebrew; Hacker 2015, 75).

Line 4

ב"ש = בשמו lit. 'in His name' (Hebrew).

אחדש"ו = אחר דרישות שלומו 'after inquiring about your (lit. his) health' (Hebrew).

בקצור 'briefly' (Hebrew).

Line 5

ברייט 'letters' (Maghrebi Arabic بريات).

Line 6
ת"ל = תודה לאל 'thanks be to God'.

Line 7
The term فاتو/פאטו/*fatto* is possibly a borrowing from Italian via Judaeo-Spanish, more specifically, the past participle of the Italian verb *fare* 'to make, to do'. Accordingly, the 'made' or 'finished' coffee may indicate that it had already been ground or processed in some manner.

Line 8
כו"פ = כלל ופרט lit. 'generally and particularly', but used colloquially as 'also' (Hebrew).

Line 10
This prepositional construction 'in hand' is perhaps a hybridisation of the Hebrew 3ms possessive suffix (ו-) and the Arabic preposition (في) with the cognate 'hand' (يد-יד). Furthermore, the mention of خولق الغور/כולק אלגור 'inexperienced character' in this line stems from the likelihood that the merchant Aramouche did not offer the proper valuation for the coffee he brought from Algiers. From another letter we learn that the latter cargo sold for only one hundred forty *reales* per *qantar*, while the cargo of coffee from Malta sold for one hundred sixty-five *reales* per *qantar*.[3]

Line 11
سيغورو/סיגורו = *seguro* 'certainly' (Castilian).

Line 16
חדוש 'news' (Hebrew).

---

3 Shlomo Ṣemaḥ to Shlomo Bushʾara, 4 Kislev 5557, HCA/32/1208/126.1, British National Archives.

Line 17

ש"וש = שלום ושמחה 'peace and happiness' (Hebrew).

עיניה/عينييه lit. 'my eyes' is used here colloquially as a parting word of affection that translates to 'with great care'.

Line 18

ע"ה = עבד השם 'servant of God' (lit. 'servant of the Name') (Hebrew).

Line 19

ס"ט = ספרדי טוב 'a good Sefardi' (Hebrew).

23. THE CAIRO-RAMLA MANUSCRIPTS, OR THE RAMLE KAR, 13 (1800S)

Olav Ørum

Transcription

(1:א2) ﭏבאב ﭏד̇י פי מכאיד (2) ﭏנסא (3) יוחכא ען אמראה פאגרה כאן (4) להא בעץ̇ אצחאב והי (5) מתזוגה ברגול סמיע מוטיע פלמא (6) כאן בֵעץ̇ ﭏאיאם אראד יסאפר פעבא (7) זאד וקומאנייה וודע אמראתו וראח (8) פמא צדקת אנו ראח למא אנהא ארמלת (9) כ̇לף אצחאבהא תנדר עליהום פאתא (10) ﭏאוול ומעהו כ̇מסת ארטﭏ לחם ומא (11) קעד קליל ﭏא וﭏתאני אקבֵל פנפדת ﭏ (12) אוול טלעתו ﭏ מקעד ודכ̇ל ﭏתאני (13) גלס ﭏא וﭏ תﭏת טרק ﭏבאב פכ̇בת

(1:ב2) ﭏ תאני פי זיר עארג ודכ̇ל ﭏ תﭏת פמא (2) לחק יגלס ﭏא וﭏ ראבע טרק ﭏבאב (3) פלפתו פי חציר ודכ̇ל ﭏראבע הו פי (4) ﭏכלאם ﭏא וגוזהא טרק ﭏבאב פאכ̇דת (5) ﭏראבע וצ̇עתו פי צנדוק ופתחת לגוזהא (6) דכ̇ל קﭏת לו מא לך רגעת קﭏ נסית (7) ﭏ שרוﭏ פנאולתהו ﭏ שרוﭏ וגא ירוח (8) פודעתהו וצארת תבכי ותקול יא אבן (9) עמי תרוח ותכ̇ליני למין קאם אוצבאעו (10) נחית ﭏ סמא וקﭏ כ̇ליתך לדא קﭏת (11) לו ומין יכ̇בז לי ﭏעגין ומן ישתרי (12) לי ﭏ לחם ויטול עלייא קﭏ להא אהו (13) יא בנתי פוקנא חאצ̇ר נאצ̇ר קﭏת לו (14) ומן יקצ̇יני חאגה ומן יונסני ומן ירוד (15) עלייא ﭏ כלמה קﭏ להא מא קולת לך

(1:א3) יא בנתי אהו פוק ראסנא סאמע כִלאמנא (2) מא יעוזך לחד קﭏ וכאן ﭏ רגול (3) ﭏדי פי ﭏ מקעד מצטנת עליה (4) טַן אן ﭏ כלאם לו קﭏ לו אחכי לי ליש אנא (5) כונת כ̇דאמך תגיב ﭏחאגה כולהא עלייא (6) מא לקית ﭏאנא האת חאגה עלא ﭏי פי ﭏ (7) חציר האת חאגה עלא ﭏי פי ﭏזיר חאגה (8) עלא ﭏי פי ﭏ צנדוק פאנבהת ﭏ רגול (9) ואשתלק עלא לעבתהום וטלק ﭏ (10) מרא ·

https://doi.org/10.11647/OBP.0208.29

(3א:11) וחוכי אן אמראה כאן להא צאחב (12) תחבהו מחבה ופקה (13) פאתדלל עלייהא וחלף אדא לם יואצלהא (14) גנב זוגהא מא עאד יאתיהא ולם כאנת (15) תטיק פוראקו פקﭏת לו ﭏ לילה תעﭏא

(3ב:1) אקף ורא ﭏ באב פאדא סמעת ﭏ סוקאט (2) אנקאם אפתח ﭏ באב בלטאפה ואדכׄול (3) תלתקי מרבוט פי ﭏ סוקאט כׄיט אמסכו (4) ואמשי עליה יגיבֵך לי פתכון אשיאהך (5) מצלחה תלתקיני פי אסתנטׄארך תקצׄי (6) ארבך ותרוח קﭏ להא וגב וצבר לל (7) עשא וגא וקף ורא ﭏ באב · (8) וכאנת ﭏ כׄאינה רבטת כׄיט פי ﭏ (9) סוקאט בעד אן עשת זוגהא ונײמתהו (10) וקללת זית ﭏ קנדיל ואוצלת ﭏ כׄיט (11) ללפרש ורבטתו עלא טרף אוצבאעהא (12) ונאמת גנב זוגהא ובאמרן קדרהו ﭏלה (13) תעﭏא פאק זוגהא פי תלך ﭏ לילה (14) פצאר יתחדת מע ﭏ מרא ויחסס עליהא (15) פוקע בﭏ כׄיט קﭏ להא ודא איש יא בהגה

(4א:1) קﭏת די חכמה אתעלמתהא מן סתי (2) ﭏ מרחומה קﭏ להא ואיש תכון דל חכמה (3) קﭏת לו אדא חסית בברגׄות קרצני (4) נהרוש לחמי בﭏ כׄיט לאן ﭏצׄפר (5) יאסי עלא ﭏ לחם קﭏ להא צדקת ﭏלה (6) ירחמהא די כאנת אומﭏ חכימה ואנא דאים (7) אסמע דל כלאם תאריה ען צחיח ולם (8) יזﭏ יהרס למא צׄרבהא דם נאמת ﭏ מרא (9) והו לם יאתיה נום פקעד יתפכר ויתחס בן (10) דרעו[1] בֵרגׄות גא יחוך ﭏמוצׄע בצׄפרו (11) אפתכר כלאם ﭏ מרא קﭏ פי נפסו אדי (12) וקתך ופך ﭏ כׄיט מן אוצבאע ﭏ מרא (13) ורבטו עלא אוצבאעו[2] והרש לחמו (14) אנקאם ﭏ סוקאת טׄן אל רגול אנהא ﭏ (15) אשארה ﭏ מעהודה פפתח ﭏ באב

(4ב:1) בחסן עבארה מטאפה ודכׄל מסך (2) ﭏ חבל בﭏ שמﭏ וצאר ילעב פי דכרו (3) בﭏ ימין וכׄטר ברפק וצנעה[3] למא (4) ללפרש וכאן ﭏ קנדיל אנטפא (5) פטׄן[4] ﭏ רגול אנהו ואקף עלא ﭏ מרא (6) פתקדם סחב רגלין ﭏ ראגל אתחזם (7) בהום וכבס עליה חס בנפסו אנהו ראיח (8) יתסיךׄ בסיךׄ פז קאים ודק פי דכר ﭏ (9) ראגל דקה שדידה בקבצׄתוּ ונבֵה ﭏ (10) מרא בﭏ עגל קאמת מסרועה וקﭏת (11) מﭏך מﭏך קﭏ להא יא כׄי קומי אנצׄורי

---

[1] דרעו; MS: לרעו.

[2] ורבטו עלא אוצבאעו; MS: ורבטו עלא ~~ﭏ~~ אוצׄבאעו.

[3] וצנעה; MS: וצׄנעה.

[4] אנטפא פטׄן; MS: אנטפא ~~וﭏרגׄול~~ פטׄן.

(12) דל דאהיה באין חראמי כבס עלייא כאן (13) ראיח ידכ̇ול פייא באין ﭏ ערץ ﭏמערץ (14) יחסבני מרקד וﭏ כ̇ורוסתאן פלחקת (15) ﭏ כ̇אינה בﭏ וקעה ארתעדת ואט̇הרת

(1:א5) כ̇וף וקﭏת יא כ̇יבתי יא דהותי וזעקת (2) עלא זוגהא וקﭏת רוח קיד לי פתילה (3) ואכ̇שא ﭏלה פייא אנא ולייתך טול (4) עומרי טאהרת ﭏ דיל אנבהת ﭏ ראגל (5) פי נפסו וכ̇אף לא תבתלי ותקעוד (6) פי עוצמתו קﭏ להא אמסכי אמסכי למא (7) אקיד לך פתילה מן בית גארתנא אצחי (8) יפלת מן אידך קﭏת האת האת יא סידי (9) פנאולהא דכר ﭏ רגול פי ידהא ואמנהא (10) עליה וראח יקיד פתילה מא כאנת כסלאנה (11) נפדת עשיקהא ראח ﭏ סטח וענדהא (12) עגל שנבארי ואקף פי ﭏ חוש דכ̇לת (13) בו ﭏא חד ﭏפרש ואכ̇רגת לסאנהו קבצ̇ת (14) עליה ולם תזﭏ קאבצ̇ה ﭏא אן אתא זוגהא (15) בﭏ פתילה אנאר ﭏ מחל פטל ראה ﭏ

(1:ב5) עגל נהצ̇ת עליה ﭏ מרא וקﭏת יוה יוה (2) וצ̇חכת לחתא מﭏת וקﭏת תאריה (3) ﭏעגל ﭏי ענדנא יא דהותי רב כ̇יי̈בֶך (4) וזקזקת חט ﭏ ראגל אידו עלא שפתיה (5) וקﭏ ﭏלה[5] יכ̇ייבד מן דון ﭏבהאים (6) ולכִן די עמאילך אקף[6] עלייא יא (7) אבן ﭏ זנא וראח יגרי עמר ﭏ קנדיל (8) ווקדו וצאר יקול והו מאשי אן כִאן (9) מורִאדך תעאמלנא בדול וחיאתך (10) אפרגך תום אנו גא אתסלם לסאן (11) ﭏ עגל מן יד ﭏ מרא ﭏתקאה טרי (12) קﭏ להא יא כ̇י איש מענה מן סאעה (13) כאן לסאנו מתל ﭏ חטבה ודל וקת (14) בקא טרי קﭏת לו יו איוה בִן כאן עטשאן (15) ודל וקת ערק לסאנו פי אידי קﭏ להא

(1:א6) צדקתי יא בנת ﭏנאס רוחי האתי סכין (2) חצליני בהא וגר ﭏעגל למא גאבו (3) לל דורקאעה ומﭏ עליה ענקלו (4) רמאה וקיידו פנאולתו ﭏ מרא ﭏ (5) סכין וקﭏת לו ראיח תעמל איה קﭏ (6) ראיח אדבח תעריס ואכ̇יר מא יסרח (7) עלינא תאני מרה ﭏ לילה די סרח עלייא (8) לילה אוכ̇רא יסרח עליך דא מלעון (9) באין עליה יאכ̇וד שהותו בלסאנו וﭏלהי (10) יא מרא כבס עלייא כבסה · לו לא זהקת (11) מן תחתו לכאן אבצר איש גרא ומסך (12) ﭏסכין וגרהא מתלמה קﭏ לל מרא (13) האתי ﭏמסן כ̇נא נחדקהא פנאולתו (14) ﭏ מסן וקף יסן ﭏ סכין וקדמו עלא (15) עונק ﭏ עגל דאיס עליה

(1:ב6) קﭏ ﭏ ראוי הדא מא כאן מן (2) אמרו ואמא מא (3) כאן מן אמר ﭏ רגול ﭏדי נפדתו פוק (4) ﭏסטח פאנו סמע ﭏ הרג ואקע (5) גא לל דואר טל בדמאגו פוגד ﭏ (6) רגול ואקף יסן ﭏסכין פקעד יתפרג (7) עליה · קﭏ וכאן באמרן קדרהו ﭏלה (8) תעﭏא

---

[5] וקﭏ ﭏלה; MS: וקﭏ ~~יהב~~ ﭏלה.

[6] עמאילך אקף; MS: עמאילך ~~ﭏלר~~ אקף.

ענדהום כבש פחל פי ﭏ סטח (9) אתכ̇ייל בﭏ רגול אתזאול מנו (10) פאתוכ̇ר וחכם צ̇הרו וקדחו בקרונו (11) וקע עלא ﭏ עגל ונט וקף קﭏ לו (12) ﭏ ראגל דא איש דא איש קﭏ לו פיק (13) ואצחא לבﭏך אמין ﭏ מדבח סאכ̇ן (14) גנבֵבּום סמע אנך נאוי תדבח ﭏ (15) עגל בעתני לך יטלוב מנך ארבע

(7א:1) קרוש גאת עליך אן כאן לך גרץ̇ קﭏ (2) ﭏ ראגל ואנא יגיני מן אין ארבע קרוש (3) יא סידי דל וקת רוח רוח יא סידי (4) רוד עליה וקול לו דאך נדם עלא (5) דבחו קﭏ לו בכ̇אטרך אפתח לי ﭏ (6) באב וכ̇נא נרוח נרוד עליה פפתח (7) לו ﭏ באב ואכ̇דו מן אידו סלכו טלע (8) ראח והדא בעץ̇ פעאילהום (9) תם

Arabic Transcription

(2و 1) الباب الذى فى مكايد (2) النسا (3) يوحكا عن امراه فاجره كان (4) لها بعض اصحاب وهى (5) متروجه برجول سميع موطيع فلما (6) كان بعض الايام اراد يسافر فعبا (7) زاد وقومانييه وودع امراتو وراح (8) فما صدقت انو راح لما انها ارملت (9) خلف اصحابها تندر عليهوم فاتا (10) الاوول ومعهو خمست ارطال لحم وما (11) قعد قليل الا والتانى اقبل فنفدت ال (12) اوول طلعتو ال مقعد ودخل التانى (13) جلس الا وال تالت طرق الباب فخبت

(2ظ 1) ال تانى فى زير عارج ودخل ال تالت فما (2) لحق يجلس الا وال رابع طرق الباب (3) فلفتو فى حصير ودخل الرابع هو فى (4) الكلام الا وجوزها طرق الباب فاخدت (5) الرابع وضعتو فى صندوق وفتحت لجوزها (6) دخل قالت لو ما لك رجعت قال نسيت (7) ال شروال فناولتهو ال شروال وجا يروح (8) فودعتهو وصارت تبكى وتقول يا ابن (9) عمى تروح وتخلينى لمين قام اوصباعو (10) نحيت ال سما وقال خليتك لدا قالت (11) لو ومين يخبز لى العجين ومن يشترى (12) لى ال لحم ويطول علييا قال لها اهو (13) يا بنتى فوقنا حاضر ناضر قالت لو (14) ومن يقضينى حاجه ومن يونسنى ومن يرود (15) علييا ال كلمه قال لها ما قولت لك

(3و 1) يا بنتى اهو فوق راسنا سامع كِلامنا (2) ما يعوزك لحد قال وكان ال رجول (3) الدى فى ال مقعد مصطنت عليه (4) ظن ان ال كلام لو قال لو احكى لى ليش انا (5) كونت خدامك تجيب الحاجه كولها علييا (6) ما لقيت الانا هات حاجه علا الى فى ال (7) حصير هات حاجه علا الى فى الزير حاجه (8) علا الى فى ال صندوق فانبهت ال رجول (9) واشتلق علا لعبتهوم وطلق ال (10) مرا ٠

(3و 11) وحوكى ان امراه كان لها صاحب (12) تحبهو محبه وفقه (13) فاتدلل علييها وحلف ادا لم يواصلها (14) جنب زوجها ما عاد ياتيها ولم كانت (15) تطيق فوراقو فقالت لو ال ليله تعالا

(3ظ 1) اقف ورا ال باب فادا سمعت ال سوقاط (2) انقام افتح ال باب بلطافه وادخول (3) تلتقى مربوط فى ال سوقاط خيط امسكو (4) وامشى عليه يجيبك لى فتكون اشياهك (5) مصلحه تلتقينى فى استنظارك تقضى (6) اربك وتروح قال لها وجب وصبر لل (7) عشا وجا وقف ورا ال باب . (8) وكانت ال خاينه ربطت كيط فى ال (9) سوقاط بعد ان عشت زوجها ونييمتهو (10) وقللت زيت ال قنديل واوصلت ال خيط (11) للفرش وربطتو علا طرف اوصباعها (12) ونامت جنب زوجها وبامرن قدرهو الله (13) تعالا فاق زوجها فى تلك ال ليله (14) فصار يتحدث مع ال مرا ويحسس عليها (15) فوقع بال خيط قال لها ودا ايش يا بهجه

(4و 1) قالت دى حكمه اتعلمتها من ستى (2) ال مرحومه قال لها وايش تكون دل حكمه (3) قالت لو ادا حسيت ببرغوت قرصنى (4) نهروش لحمى بال خيط لان الضفر (5) ياسى علا ال لحم قال لها صدقت الله (6) يرحمها دى كانت اومال حكيمه وانا دايم (7) اسمع دل كلام تاريه عن صحيح ولم (8) يزال يهدس لما ضربها دم نامت ال مرا (9) وهو لم ياتيه نوم فقعد يتفكر ويتحس بن (10) لرعو برغوت جا يحوك الموضع بضفرو (11) افتكر كلام ال مرا قال فى نفسو ادى (12) وقتك وفك ال خيط من اوصباع ال مرا (13) وربطو علا اوصباعو[7] وهرش لحمو (14) انقام ال سوقات ظن ال رجول انها ال (15) اشاره ال معهوده ففتح ال باب

(4ظ 1) بحسن عباره مطافه ودخل مسك (2) ال حبل بال شمال وصار يلعب فى دكرو (3) بال يمين وخطر برفق وصنعه[8] لما (4) للفرش وكان ال قنديل انطفا (5) فظن[9] ال رجول انهو واقف علا ال مرا (6) فتقدم سحب رجلين ال راجل اتحزم (7) بهوم وكبس عليه حس بنفسو انهو رايح (8) يتسيخ بسيخ فز قايم ودق فى دكر ال (9) راجل دقه شديده بقبضتو ونبه ال (10) مرا بال عجل قامت مسروعه وقالت (11) مالك مالك قال لها يا خى قومى انضورى (12) دل داهيه باين حرامى كبس علييا كان (13) رايح يدخول فيا باين ال عرض المعرص (14) يحسبنى مرقد وال خوروستان فلحقت (15) ال خاينه بال وقعه ارتعدت واظهرت

---

[7] وربطو علا اوصباعو; MS: وربطو علا ~~ال~~ اوصباعو.

[8] وصنعه; MS: وضنعه.

[9] انطفا فظن; MS: انطفا ~~والرجول~~ فظن.

(5و 1) خوف وقالت يا خيبتي يا دهوتي وزعقت (2) علا زوجها وقالت روح قيد لي فتيله (3) واخشا الله فيبيا انا وليبيتك طول (4) عومري طاهرت ال ديل انبهت ال راجل (5) في نفسو وخاف لا تبتلي وتقعود (6) في عوصمتو قال لها امسكي امسكي لما (7) اقيد لك فتيله من بيت جارتنا اصحي (8) يفلت من ايدك قالت هات هات يا سيدي (9) فناولها دكر ال رجول في يدها وامنها (10) عليه وراح يقيد فتيله ما كانت كسلانه (11) نفدت عشيقها راح ال سطح وعندها (12) عجل شنباري واقف في ال حوش دخلت (13) بو الا حد الفرش واخرجت لسانهو قبضت (14) عليه ولم تزال قابضه الا ان اتا زوجها (15) بال فتيله انار ال محل فطل راه ال

(5ظ 1) عجل نهضت عليه ال مرا وقالت يوه يوه (2) وضحكت لحتا مالت وقالت تاريه (3) العجل الى عندنا يا دهوتي رب خيّيبك (4) وزقزقت حط ال راجل ايدو علا شفتيه (5) وقال الله[10] يخيبيك من دون البهايم (6) ولكِن دي عمايلك اقف[11] علييا يا (7) ابن ال زنا وراح يجري عمر ال قنديل (8) ووقدو وصار يقول وهو ماشي ان كِان (9) مورادك تعاملنا بدول وحياتك (10) افرجك توم انو جا اتسلم لسان (11) ال عجل من يد ال مرا التقاه طري (12) قال لها يا خي ايش معنه من ساعه (13) كان لسانو متل ال حطبه ودل وقت (14) بقا طري قالت لو يو ايوه بِن كان عطشان (15) ودل وقت عرق لسانو في ايدي قال لها

(6و 1) صدقتي يا بنت الناس روحي هاتي سكين (2) حصليني بها وجر العجل لما جابو (3) لل دورقاعه ومال عليه عنقلو (4) رماه وقييدو فناولتو ال مرا ال (5) سكين وقالت لو رايح تعمل ايه قال (6) رايح ادبح تعريس واخير ما يسرح (7) علينا تاني مره ال ليله دي سرح علييا (8) ليله اوخرا يسرح عليك دا ملعون (9) باين عليه ياخود شهوتو بلسانو واللهي (10) يا مرا كبس علييا كبسه ، لو لا زهقت (11) من تحتو لكان ابصر ايش جرا ومسك (12) السكين وجرها متلمه قال لل مرا (13) هاتي المسن خنا نحدقها فناولتو (14) ال مسن وقف يسن ال سكين وقدمو علا (15) عونق ال عجل دايس عليه

(6ظ 1) قال ال راوي هدا ما كان من (2) امرو واما ما (3) كان من امر ال رجول الدي نفدتو فوق (4) السطح فانو سمع ال هرج واقع (5) جا لل دوار طل بدماغو فوجد ال (6) رجول واقف يسن السكين فقعد يتفرج (7) عليه ، قال وكان بامرن قدرهو الله (8) تعالا عندهوم كبش فحل في ال سطح (9) اتخييل بال رجول اتزاول منو (10) فاتوخر وحكم ضهرو وقدحو بقرونز (11) وقع علا ال عجل ونط وقف قال لو (12) ال راجل دا ايش دا ايش قال لو فيق

---

[10] وقال الله; MS: وقال ~~يهى~~ الله.

[11] عمايلك اقف; MS: عمايلك ~~الل~~ اقف.

(13) واصحا لبالك امين ال مدبح ساكِن (14) جنبكِوم سمع انك ناوى تدبح ال (15) عجل بعتنى لك يطلوب منك اربع

(7و 1) قروش جات عليك ان كان لك غرض قال (2) ال راجل وانا يجينى من اين اربع قروش (3) يا سيدى دل وقت روح روح يا سيدى (4) رود عليه وقول لو داك ندم علا (5) دبحو قال لو بخاطرك افتح لى ال (6) باب وخنا نروح نرود عليه ففتح (7) لو ال باب واخدو من ايدو سلكو طلع (8) راح وهدا بعض فعايلهوم (9) تم

Translation

(2a:1) The Chapter of the (2) Wives' Schemes.
(3) It has been told about this brazen wife, that she (4) had some male friends while being (5) married to a man of the listening and abiding kind. (6) One day, he wanted to travel, so he packed (7) provisions and supplies, said farewell to his wife and left.

(8) She couldn't believe it [and could hardly wait for him to leave. As soon as he had left], she pretended (9) she had become a widow, and her [male] friends came after her. (10) The first one came, bringing with him five *raṭls* of meat. He hadn't (11) sat for long before the second one approached. So she rushed the (12) first one into the loft room, just as the second one entered. (13) He had barely sat down, when the third knocked on the door. So she hid (2b:1) the second one in a clay pot, and the third one entered inside. He didn't (2) even get time to sit down before the fourth knocked on the door. (3) She wrapped the third in a woven rush mat, and in came the fourth. He had just (4) opened his mouth when her husband knocked on the door. So she took (5) the fourth one, put him in a box and opened up for her husband. (6) "What's the matter with you? You came back," she said when he came inside. "I forgot (7) my trousers," he answered. So she handed him the trousers, and he made a move to

leave. (8) She said farewell and started crying, saying, (9) "My dear cousin, you are abandoning me! With whom will you leave me?" He pointed his finger (10) in the direction of the sky and said, "I leave you with Him." She answered, (11) "If not you, then who'll bake me dough and who'll buy (12) me meat and accompany me?" (13) "There He is, my girl," he said, "above us, present and witnessing." She said, (14) "Who will do stuff for me? Who will provide (15) me human contact and amuse me? Who will give me answers?" "I told you, (3a:1) my girl," he said, "there He is, above us, listening to what we are saying. (2) You won't need anyone else!" The man (3) from the loft room upstairs said, (4) thinking the errands were meant for him, "That's unheard of! (5) Am I your servant or something? One who'll bring you whatever you ask for? (6) Haven't you found anyone else but me for doing all this? Give something to the guy inside the (7) mat! And what about giving something to the guy inside the clay pot! And something (8) to the guy inside the box!" So the man finally got it, (9) understood their little game and divorced the wife. (3a:11) And it has been told that there was a woman who had a friend (12) that she loved wholly and dearly. (13) He flirted with her, and swore that if he couldn't have an affair with her (14) when next to her husband, he would not commit to her any more. She couldn't (15) bear being apart from him, so that evening she told him, "Come (3b:1) and stand behind the door. If you hear the door latch (2) move, gently open the door and enter the room. (3) There you'll find a thread tied to the door latch. Grab it (4) and go with it, and it will take you to me and you can 'have yourself (5) a good time.' (?) You will find me waiting for you.

So do (6) your thing and leave." He told her, "You got it!" He waited for the (7) evening and came to stand behind the door. (8) So the unfaithful one tied a thread to the (9) door latch after she had prepared dinner for her husband and put him to bed. (10) She turned down the oil-lamp and brought the thread with her (11) to bed. She tied it to the tip of her finger (12) and lay down next to her husband. And by the will and power of Allāh—(13) may He be exalted—her husband woke up that night (14) and started talking to the wife, touching her a bit. (15) He got caught up in the thread, and asked, "What's that, my dear?" (4a:1) "This is a piece of wisdom, a trick that I learned from (2) my deceased grandmother," she said. "And what be so that piece of wisdom?" (3) he asked. "If I feel a flea biting me, (4) I scratch my skin with the thread. That's because my fingernail (5) will damage the skin." "She was right," he said, "may Allāh (6) protect her. That was a piece of wisdom, indeed! I always (7) listen to those words, and they seem so right!" And (8) he continued to scratch until he started to bleed. While the wife fell asleep, (9) he could not, so he sat up pondering. He felt (10) a flea on his arm. He was about to scratch with his nail, (11) when he remembered what his wife had told him. He said to himself, "Now (12) is your chance!" and untied the thread from the wife's finger (13), tied it onto his own, and scratched his skin. (14) The door latch then moved, and the man outside thought that it was the (15) 'promised' sign. He opened the door, (4b:1) and gently passed inside. He entered, grabbed (2) the thread with his left hand and started playing with his penis (3) with his right hand. Then he proceeded in a proud and elegant manner. When (4) he was next to the bed where the oil-lamp had gone out, (5) the man thought that he was standing over the wife. (6) So he pulled the husband's legs around his hips, held (7) them firmly and lay on top of him. The husband got the feeling that he was going to (8) get penetrated, so he jumped up and punched the (9) man in the crouch with a hard fist punch, and (10) quickly alerted the wife. She got up in a hurry and said, (11) "What's the matter with you?" "Get up, my dear! Look!" (12) he replied, "Look at that sly bastard! That criminal lay on top of me and was (13) about to enter inside me! The unscrupulous pig (14) thought I was sleeping, and then the fairy..." (15) The unfaithful one overcame the shock (?), trembled, and appeared to be (5a:1) afraid. "Good Lord," she said and shouted (2) to her husband, saying, "Go and light an oil-lamp wick for me. (3) By the fear of Allāh, I have been your woman all (4) my life and my tale is but pure!" The husband (5) was shocked, and became afraid that this would affect (6) his reputation. He said to her, "Grab this! Grab this! When (7) I light the wick from my neighbour's house for you, be on the alert, (8) let it go from your hand." "Give it to me, give it to me, my dear," she said. (9) So he handed the man's penis in her hand, trusted her (10) with it, made sure she held it strong, and went to light the wick. She reacted quickly (11) and released her lover, who rushed to the roof of the house. (12) She had a beef calf standing in the courtyard which she (13) took inside, next to the bed. She pulled out its tongue and held (14) onto it until her husband came back (15) with the wick. He lit up the place and came to see the (5b:1) calf. The wife came on to him and said, "Well, well!" (2) and laughed until she was tired of laughing, and said, "Actually, it was (3) the calf who was here. Good Lord, God damn you!" (4) and chirped. The man put his hand on his lips (5) and said, "May Allāh curse you, that thing was not the cattle! (6) So this what you are doing to me? He was standing over me, you (7) son of a bitch." He rushed over to fix the oil-lamp, (8) lit it, and started moving while saying, "If (9) your intention is to treat [our marriage] like this, I swear by your life, (10) I'll show you!" After that he came and took the tongue (11) of the calf from the wife's hand and found it moist. (12) He said, "My dear, that doesn't make sense! (13) A moment ago, his tongue was like a piece of wood, and suddenly (14) it became moist?" She said, "Boy, o boy, he was thirsty (15) and now his tongue started sweating in my hands." He said, (6a:1) "That's right, oh good girl. Go get me a knife. (2) Give it to me, and drag the calf along with you." When he had taken it (3) to the courtyard, he wrestled it down (4) and threw it to the ground and tied it. The wife gave him (5) the knife, and said to him, "What are you going to do?" He replied, (6) "I am going to slaughter a wedding feast, of the last thing that grazes (7) on us ever again. This night it grazed on me, (8) another night it grazes on you. He is cursed, (9) he who has to take on his cravings with his tongue. (10) Wallah, I swear, o woman, it really squeezed onto me. If I hadn't pulled myself (11) from beneath him, I sure know what would have happened." So he took (12) the knife along with him and told the wife, (13) "Give me the sharpening iron, let's sharpen it." So she handed him (14) the sharpening iron. He stood up, sharpened the knife and brought it to (15) the neck of the calf and pushed down.

(6b:1) The storyteller has said that this is what happened with (2) the husband. About what (3) happened with the man that she hid on (4) the roof, [it has been said that] he had heard the ongoing chaos, (5) and came back to the house and peaked over the edge with the top of his head. He saw the (6) husband standing there, sharpening his knife, so he sat down and watched (7) him. It has also been said that, by the will and power of Allāh—(8) exalted be He—they had a stud bull goat on the roof. (9) The husband thought he saw something moving on the roof, (10) so the lover, who was on the roof, quickly leaned back. The lover grabbed the goat by its neck and tried to pull it towards the edge of the roof (?), when the goat suddenly pushed him with his horns, (11) and he fell down on top of the calf. He made a jump, standing up, and the husband said to him, (12) "What's this? What's this?" The lover replied, "Wake up! (13) Wake up, the supervisor butcher lives (14) right next to you. He heard that you had decided to slaughter the (15) calf and sent me to you to ask for four (7a:1) *qirsh*. You have to pay up if you want to slaughter the calf." (2) "And from where will I get four *qirsh*, (3) my friend?" the man said, "Go, go away now, my friend, (4) go to him and tell him that it is a remorse on (5) his slaughter." He said to him, "Be so kind, open (6) the door for me and let us go and give him an answer." So he opened (7) the door for him, took him by his hand and led him out. (8) So the lover got out and left. And that's some of the things they did.

(9) The End.

Commentary

Preliminary note:

The present text seems to have been strongly influenced by the Egyptian or Cairene vernacular, and is most likely representative of the period between the 17th and the 19th centuries.[12] As a general observation, it is relevant to note that the present text exhibits many linguistic characteristics which have already received extensive treatment in the field of Judaeo-Arabic. For example, the Classical Arabic (CA) short vowels *i*, *a*, and *u* are frequently rendered in *plene* script by means of the orthography of the text. Some examples illustrating this practice are כ׳יבתי 'my impostor, swindler' (5a:1); אכ׳יר 'last' (6a:6); ראגל 'man' (*passim*; but also רגול 2a:5); ואקף 'he stopped' (*passim*; but also וקף *passim*); עומרו 'his life' (1b:5); ירוד 'he answers' (2b:14); אוצבאע 'fingers' (*passim*); יטלוב 'he requests' (6b:15); etc. Not surprisingly, the findings in the present text indicate a stronger presence of *plene* written the CA short vowel *u* than of *i* and *a*. From a morphological and morphosyntactic point of view, one could draw attention to the apparent lack of vowel harmony between word boundaries, viz. *ʿalayhum* < *ʿalayhim*; *h*-less pronominal suffixes, viz. *-u* / *-ū* (< *-ū(h)* < *-uhu*); the seemingly random separation of words, especially concerning the definite article; and invariable

[12] This assumption is based on the fact that the MS displays a fragmented short story about Goḥa/Nasreddin (not included in this sample), whose earliest MS is dated to 1571. The MS treated here is dated by the National Library of Israel to the 19th century, but it is not clear whether it is a copy of an earlier *Vorlage* or if it was written down directly from an oral source.

reflections of different pronouns and particles, all of which characteristic of a language variety which some scholars would regard as analytic, or simply as reflecting the style and register employed by the popular or 'lower' strata of the society. Most of these characteristics deviate from CA conventions, and many seem to reflect the actual speech of the social environment in which the text acquired its present shape. Those interested in a more general description of the Judaeo-Arabic language, including the characteristics noted above, may gain further insight by consulting Blau (1999).

2a:1–2

ﭏבאב ﭏדֿי פי מכאיד ﭏנסא 'The Chapter of the Wives' Schemes; lit. the chapter in which [are found] the schemes of the wives'. An example of *h*-less alternant to CA *fīhī* 'in it' (> *fīh* > *fī*).

2a:6

בֵעץׄ 'some'. *Imāla* in "inhibiting content" (Cantineau 1960, 23)," reflected in vocalisation. See also אקבֵל 'he approached' (2a:11); בֵרגֿות 'flea' (4a:10).

אראד יסאפר 'he wanted to travel'. The expression displays either the hypocorrect absence of the conjunction *an*, an earlier chronological stage, or a stylistic or social stratum in which the verb 'to want' was represented by the verb *arād* in speech.

2a:12

ﭏ מקעד 'the loft room'. Reflecting the *alif-lām* ligature and a separate definite article. This occurs *passim* throughout the MS.

2b:7

שרוﭏ 'sirwal trousers'. Shift from CA *s* to *š*.

2b:10

בּליתך לדא 'I left you with that'. Demonstrative pronoun *da*.

2b:11

לו ומין יכבז לי איעגין 'if not you, then who'll bake me dough?'. Conjunction *law* + *wa-*.

2b:12

אהו 'that (demonstrative)'. Displaying the intensifying interjection *a-* (as in أَلَا and أَمَا 'verily, truly, indeed; isn't it'). See also 3a:1.

2b:13

חאצׄר נאצׄר 'present and witnessing'. Displaying Islamic content; see, e.g., Mullā ʿAlī al-Qāriʾ's *Miškāt al-Maṣābīḥ* 10:210.

נאצׄר 'witnessing'. De-spirantisation reflected in a shift from CA *ẓ* (*ḏ̣*) to *ḍ*. See also 4b:11; 6b:10.

2b:15

מא קולת לך 'I told you (indeed)'. Intensifying particle *mā*.

3a:1

כּלאמנא 'our words, what we speak of'. A non-standard Modern Egyptian Arabic (MEA) vowel pattern reflected in the vocalisation of short *i*.

3a:3

אלדי 'who (demonstrative)'. See also 6b:3; דכרו 'his penis' (4b:2, 8). An apparent de-spirantisation reflected in a shift from CA *ḏ* to *d*. There is also one occurrence of fricative *ḏ* being employed in the demonstrative; however, this is found only in the heading of the chapter (2a:1).

3a:4

ליש 'why'. Displaying an earlier chronological stage of the more common MEA interrogative variant *lē(h)*.

3a:6

אלי 'who (demonstrative)'. See also 3a:7; 3a:8; 5b:3. Note that the two invariant demonstrative particles אלי and אדי are used interchangeably throughout the manuscript.

3a:12

מחבה ופקה 'wholly and dearly'. See also (possibly) דקה שדידה 'a hard punch' (4b:9). Final *-h* reflecting the adverbial ending *-a* or *-ā*, thus alternating from CA *-an*. Similar use of final *-h*, when reflecting CA final *-ā* (by means of ى or ا), is also attested in מענה 'meaning' (5b:12) and מתלמה 'just as' (6a:12), respectively.

ובאמרן קדרהו אלה 'by the will and power of Allāh'. Use of genitive *-in*, an ending which here may be considered hypercorrect according to CA conventions. See also 6b:7.

3a:14–15

ולם כאנת תטיק פוראקו 'and she couldn't bear being apart from him'. *lam* + verb in the perfect tense negating a past or completed action.

3b:15

ודא איש 'what is that?'. Demonstrative pronoun *da* preceding the noun. See also 6b:12.

איש 'what'. An earlier chronological stage of the more common, MEA interrogative variant *ē(h)*.

4a:1

די חכמה 'that is [a piece of] wisdom'. Demonstrative pronoun *di*. See also 4a:6; 5b:6.

4a:2

דל חכמה 'that [piece] of wisdom'. A merger of the demonstrative with the following definite article, viz. *d-il-* / *di-l-*. It can be added that it is written separately from the noun which it precedes.

4a:4

נהרוש 'I scratch'. Use of the so-called *nekteb*-paradigm in the singular. See also 6a:13.

4a:14

סוקאת 'door latch' (but סוקאט *passim*). De-emphatisation reflected in a shift from CA *ṭ* to *t*.

4a:16

דאים 'always'. Omitting of adverbial ending (*-ā* and) *-an*.

4b:7–9

ראיח 'going to'. An earlier chronological stage of the MEA future particle *ha* / *ḥa* by means of the variant *rāyiḥ*. See also 4b:13; 6a:5; 6a:6.

5a:12

שנבארי '[*shanbar*] beef cattle'. Used here in the meaning of MEA *kandūz* 'meat from a mature buffalo or cow' (Hinds and Badawi 1986, 480, 766).

5b:8–10

אן כְאן מורְאדך תעאמלנא בדול 'if your intention is to treat [our marriage] like this (?) [...]'. Demonstrative pronoun *dōl*.

אן כְאן מורְאדך 'if your intention is'. A double occurrence of the heavy *ie-imāla*, a feature which has fallen out of use in all modern dialects. It thus represents an earlier chronological stage of the *e-imāla*, which is common in MEA.

5b:12

איש מענה מן סאעה 'that doesn't make sense!' Displaying *iš* (or a variant of it) as a negating particle.[13]

5b:13

דל וקת 'this time, i.e., now'. The apparent separation of the two items (*dil* + *waqt*) reflects an early variant and use of the modern variant *dilwaʾt(i)* 'now'. See also 5b:15; 7a:3.

6a:7

ﭏ לילה די 'that evening'. Displaying the demonstrative adjective *di* following the noun.

6a:13

כֿנא נחדקהא 'let's sharpen it'. Displaying a shortened variant of the modal auxiliary expression *xallina* (> *xina*) 'let's...'. See also 6b:14.

6b:14

גנבֵכֿום 'next to you'. Evidence of a slightly palatalised or fronted consonant *k*, viz. **ganb*^{e}*k*^{i}*um*.

7a:9

וכֿנא נרוח נרוד עליה 'so, let's go and answer him'. Displaying lack of *nektebū* in the plural (see the use of *nekteb* in the singular, in 4a:4).

---

[13] See, e.g., the use of *iš* (or a variant of it) as a negating particle in Spanish Arabic *apud* Corriente (1977, 145).

24. A 19TH-CENTURY JUDAEO-ARABIC FOLK NARRATIVE[1]

Magdalen M. Connolly

The manuscript BnF Hébreu 583[2] (dated 1839 CE) contains, amongst other material, three Egyptian Judaeo-Arabic (JA) tales,[3] depicting fictional events in the life of Abraham ibn ʿEzra (c. 1089–1167), the renowned Jewish biblical scholar and polymath. This edition focuses on the third of these tales, in which Abraham ibn ʿEzra, brought from Cairo by two students at the urgent behest of a rabbi, saves the life of the rabbi's son and secures the freedom of the town's Jewish community. While the

[1] This short piece is a condensed and updated version of Connolly (2018, 392–420). I am grateful to the University of Uppsala Press for allowing me to reproduce the article, here.

[2] This manuscript was kindly made available to me by the Département de la reproduction at the Bibliothèque nationale de France, Paris. As of 2016, the manuscript is available to view online at http://gallica.bnf.fr/html/und/manuscrits/manuscrits.

[3] These three tales are found in fols 134v–140v. The first tale is in fols 134v–137r, line 18; the second tale is in fols 137r, line 19–139r, line 18; and the third tale—reproduced here— is contained within fols 139r, line 19–140v, line 20. Another version of this tale is found in CUL T-S Ar.46.10.

 https://doi.org/10.11647/OBP.0208.30

literary content of this tale and its socio-historical context[4] are doubtless worthy of exploration, this short contribution is restricted to a transliteration of the original text, with transcoding into Arabic script,[5] and an English translation.[6]

---

[4] Of particular note in this tale is the blood-libel accusation—directed throughout the middle ages at Jewish communities by Christians within Europe and, later in the 1800s, by Syrian Christian communities at their Jewish counterparts. Here, the blood-libel accusation is inverted and levelled against a Christian community. Tensions between Christian and Jewish communities in Egypt and Syria began in the late 17th century, driven by shifts in the political landscape, which—in the case of Egypt—had profound economic and social consequences for Cairo's Jewish inhabitants (Masters 2001, 117). The colophon on f. 174v dates the copying of these tales to Monday, 16th Ṭevet 1839. It, therefore, predates the infamous 'Damascus Affair' of 1840 by a few months (see Frankel 1997; Masters 2001; and Florence 2004 for details of the 'Damascus Affair'). As such, this text adds another dimension to Master's assertion that blood-libel accusations were circulating among (Syrian) Christian Arabs before the Damascus Affair (Masters 2001, 123). This tale indicates that some Jews were engaging with the accusation and turning it back on their Christian neighbours.

[5] In transcoding the text into Arabic script, I hope to make this JA text, with its many interesting linguistic features, available to a wider audience interested in varieties of Middle Arabic. In so doing, I follow the practice pioneered by Diem (2014) and suggested to me by Dr. Esther-Miriam Wagner (in conversation).

[6] A Hebrew edition of three tales from the manuscript BnF Hébreu 583 was first produced by Yitzhak Avishur (1992). Avishur's interest in the folk narrative appears to have been predominantly literary and

As is evident in the spelling of consonantal *wāw* and *yā*ʾ with double *vav* and *yod*, respectively, frequent Hebrew lexical items, the occurrence of *niktib-niktibū* forms, and the consistent separation of the definite article,[7] this folk narrative contains several features often referred to as characteristic of late JA. These features are found alongside classical JA features, limited CA influence, Middle Arabic practices, and contemporaneous Arabic dialectal features.

From the *plene* spelling of short vowels and the denotation of the 3ms pronominal suffix with *vav* to the presence of the colloquial verb *gāb* 'to bring', the fifth form's prosthetic *ʾalef*, and the use of the construct-state particle *bitāʿ*, this text reveals numerous colloquial features that are characteristic of Modern Cairene Arabic. In the presence of the JA relative pronoun, CA-influenced demonstrative pronouns, and complex adverbial subordinators, the text also displays a preoccupation with raising the register above the quotidian, an aspiration which is partially achieved through these aforementioned features.

Furthermore, the use of the diacritical dot and consonantal representation indicate both a continuation of classical JA

---

historical and his transliteration does not reflect the true state of the text's orthographic features. A new transliteration is, therefore, required for the manuscript to be of use to broader audiences; linguistic as well as literary and historical. This paper serves as a supplement to the existing edition by Avishur, presenting a new transliteration and translation of one of three Egyptian Judaeo-Arabic tales found in the manuscript BnF Hébreu 583.

[7] For a discussion of the separation of the definite article in JA, see Connolly (2021).

spelling practices—for example, in the representation of *ḍād* with *ṣade* and a supralinear diacritical dot, and the enduring, albeit limited, influence of contemporaneous Arabic orthographic practices evident in the application of the diacritic to graphemes such as *pe* for *fāʾ*, *dalet* for *ḏāl*, and *kaf* for *ḫāʾ*, in imitation of the physical form of their Arabic graphemic equivalents.[8]

Notes on the Edition

The text has been as faithfully rendered as possible, including all diacritics and orthographic idiosyncrasies found in the original manuscript. The JA text has then been transcoded into Arabic script, grapheme-for-grapheme. No adjustments or amendments have been made to the text in its transcoded form. As for the English translation, any additions intended to aid comprehension and readability are enclosed in parenthesis ().

Transliteration

139r.

19. איצׄה אכׄברו אן כאן פׄי בלד מן בלאד אל ערלים[9] כאנו כל
20. סנה פׄי עידהום יאכׄדו ואחד יאודי יעמלוה קורבן לל ע''ז[10]
21. וכאנו אל יאוד יעמלו גורל עלא אוולאד אל יאוד לאגׄל מא
22. יערפׄו מין אלדׄי ינעמל קורבן אל סנה אל אתייה לאגׄל אן יטלע
23. מצרופׄו מן ענד אל ערלים טול אל סנה · וחין יגׄי אל מיעאד

---

[8] On the use of diacritical dots in late JA, see Connolly *forthcoming*.

[9] The term ערלים ‘uncircumcised’ (sg. עָרֵל) is used to refer to Christians (Jastrow 2005, 1119).

[10] ע"ז: ‘idolatry’ (עבודה זרה).

139v.

1. יאכ̇דוה במוכב עט̇ים וכל אלד̇י יטלוב ינול · פ̇י סנה מן אל סנין
2. עמלו אל ג̇ורל טלע עלא אבן אל רב בתאע ד̇אלך̇ אל בלד וכאן
3. עומרו עשרין סנה ולם כאן אל ראב ענדו כ̇לאפ̇ו וכאן ד̇אלך̇ אל ולד
4. ליס להו נט̇יר פ̇אל דונייא מן אל פ̇צאחא ואל קראייה וכ̇לאפ̇ו פ̇י חין אלד̇י
5. טלע אל ג̇ורל עלא אל ולד קאמו באל בוכא ואל צייאח ואל נוואח ואל חוזן
6. וכאן מיעאד אלד̇י יאכ̇דו אל ולד יקרבוה יחכום אוול לילת פסח פ̇י
7. אלתפ̇ת אל ראב לאתנין מן אל תלמידים וקאל להום תערפו תרוחו מצר
8. לענד אל רב אברהם ן̇ עזרא עא"ס תסלמו להו האד̇א אל ג̇וואב ותערפו
9. פי האד̇י אל דעווה ומן ג̇יהת אהל מנזלכום נחן נצרופ̇ עליהום
10. לחין מא תחצ̇רו ובשרט לם תתעווקו פ̇אל טריק · לאן מן האד̇י אל
11. בלד למצר תלת אושהור רוואח ותלת אושהור מג̇יי · והלבת
12. תקעודו פ̇י מצר שהר יציר סבעת אושהור לחין מא תחצ̇רו פ̇י
13. קאלו להו סמיע מוטיע יא סיידנא פ̇י כתב להום ג̇וואב ואתווג̇הו
14. למצר מן בעד תלת אושהור חוצ̇רו פ̇י מצר · וג̇דו ואחד עני
15. מאשי פ̇אל סכה סאלוה פ̇ין בית אל רב אברהם ן̇ עזרא פ̇י קאל להום
16. הנא[11] אנא · אעטו להו אל ג̇וואב · פ̇י קאל להום לם פ̇יה באס
17. בע"ה[12] נתווג̇ה מעאכום נקצ̇י האד̇י אל דעווה ולם יכון אלא כ̇יר · פ̇י
18. אכ̇דהום אלא מנזלו וקעדו ענדו · ובעד שהר קאלו להו יא סיידנא
19. נרידו נתווג̇הו לאג̇ל אל דעווה תתמהא פי קאל להום אל ראב לם
20. עודתו תכ̇אטבוני פ̇י שאן ד̇אלך̇ אנה וקת מא נריד נתווג̇ה פ̇קעדו
21. ללילת ערב פסח מן בעד מא עמל אל רב בדיקת חמץ ואראחו
22. פ̇י קראייה קעדו לארבע סעאת מן אל ליל לחין מא פ̇רג̇ית אל קראייה
23. פ̇י פרקו כעך̇[13] בסירג פ̇י אעטו לל ראב כעכתין ואל תלמידים כל

---

[11] This may read הוא 'he' rather than הנא 'here'.

[12] בע"ה: 'With the help of God' (בעזרת השם).

[13] כעך̇: In Arabic كعك\كحك *kaʿk/kaḥk* "cookies of flour, butter, and sometimes a sweet filling or a dusting of sugar, baked for special occasions" (Hinds and Badawi 1986, 737). In light of the context in which these 'cookies' are consumed in this tale, however, it is possible that *kaʿk* here refers not to celebratory cookies but to *matzōt*, the unleavened bread consumed during Passover (see preceding footnote).

24. ואחד כעכתין ואתווג̇הו לחאלהום פ̇י אכ̇ד טריקו אל רב אב̇ ן̇ עזרא ואל
25. תלמידים

140r.

1. תלמידים מעו ואתווג̇הו פ̇י עוואץ̇ מא יתווג̇הו לל בית חוכם אל
2. ג̇ארי טלעו נאחיית אל כ̇ליה פ̇י קאלו אל תלמידים יא סיידנא לאין
3. מתווג̇הין נחן דא אחנא בקינא פ̇אל כֵ̇ליה פ̇י קאל להום אל ראב אמסכו
4. פ̇י טרפ̇י פ̇י מסכו טרפ̇ו וקרי שם לם טלע עליהום אל פ̇ג̇ר אלא
5. והום פ̇אל בלד בתאע אל דעווה · פ̇י נט̇רו אל תלמידים אל בלד
6. ואתעג̇בו · ואחד יקול האד̇י אל בלדנא וואחד יקול לם היא בלדנא
7. נחן פ̇י מצר ואל רב אברהם מאשי קודאמהום לחין מא וצלו לבית
8. אל חכ̇ם פ̇י טרקו עלא אל באב · פ̇י טלע אל חכ̇ם פ̇תח אל באב
9. וג̇ד אל רב אברהם ואקפ̇ עלא אל באב פ̇י כ̇מנו אנו סַאֵל · פ̇י קאל
10. להו אל חכ̇ם מא תריד לם תעלם בחאלנא פ̇י קאל להו אל רב אברהם
11. נעם עלם בדעוותך̇ ולאכן אתכל עלא אללה ס"ו[14] והוא יעמל לך̇ נסים
12. אלתפ̇ת אל חכ̇ם וג̇ד אל אתנין אל תלמידים אלד̇י כאן ארסלהום למצר
13. לל רב אברהם ן̇ עזרא · פ̇י סלם עליהום וקאל להום אחכו לי מא ג̇רא
14. פ̇י קאלו להו יא סיידנא אל רב אב' ן̇ עזרא הוא אלד̇י ואקפ̇ קוצאדך̇ פ̇י
15. קדם עליה ואכ̇דו ודכ̇ל בו אל בית · פ̇י מא בעד מא צלו פ̇אל כניס
16. חכו אל תלמידים לל סי' חכ̇ם באלד̇י ג̇רא ופ̇רג̇ו להו אל כעך̇ בסירג̇
17. אלד̇י מעאהום · ואתעג̇ב אל ח' עלא ד̇אלך̇ · ואל רב̇ אב̇ ן̇ עזרא ע"ה[15]
18. קאל לל ולד אלד̇י נאוויין יאכ̇דוה יעמלוה קורבן לל ע"ז · חין מא יג̇ו
19. באל מוכב יאכ̇דוך̇ קול להום אן נכון אנא מעאך̇ · וחין מא יקולו
20. לך̇ אתמנא תועטא קול להום אלד̇י יתמנא רפ̇יקי · פ̇י קאל להו אל ולד
21. סמיע מוטיע · פ̇י בעד סאעתין אלא וג̇ו אל ערלים במוכב עט̇ים
22. לאג̇ל אנהום יאכ̇דו אל ולד יווכבו בו פ̇אל בלד · פ̇י קאל להום אל
23. ולד כ̇דוני אנא ורפ̇יקי מעי ואלד̇י יתאתא עלייה יתאתא עלא
24. רפ̇יקי · פ̇י קאלו אל ערלים אחנא לנא ואחד ואד̇א כאן תעטונא אתנין

---

[14] ס"ו 'Praise the Lord!' (سبحان الله).

[15] ע"ה: 'Peace be upon him' (עליו השלום).

140v.

1. אחסן ואחסן · פׄי רכב אל רב אב' ןׄ עזרא עא"ס הוא ואל ולד פׄי קלב
2. אל תכׄתרואן וקאלו להום אל ערלים אתמנו תעטו · פׄי קאל להום אל רב
3. אב' ןׄ עזרא אתמנא אן תגׄעלו אל קסיס אל כביר פׄי זכיבה ותרבטו
4. פׄום אל זכיבה פׄאל תכׄתרואן לחין ינתם אל מוכב · פׄי קאלו אל ערלים
5. סמיע מוטיע פׄי אכׄדו אל קסיס אל כביר וחטוה פׄי זכיבה ורבטו
6. פׄום אל זכיבה פׄאל תכׄת רואן[16] [sic.] ואנגׄר אל מוכב ולפׄו אל בלד וראחו
7. אל כניסה · פׄי סאלוהום איש תרידו תאכלו פׄי טלב מנהום אל ראב
8. אברהם פׄרכׄתין פׄי גאבו להום פׄרכׄתין · פׄי טלע אל ראב אברהם לל
9. כניסה ונדה על ע"ז אל כבירה אלדׄי ביעמלו להא אל קורבאן וקאל יא
10. ממזר אנזל מן מכאנךׄ וסן אל סכינה · פׄי נזל אל ע"ז וקעד יסן
11. אל סכינה פׄי אנבהתו גׄמיע אל ערלים ונזל עליהום אל פׄזע אל
12. עטׄים · פׄי מא בעד נדה אל רב אב' על ממזרתה וקאל להא אנזלי
13. מן מכאניךׄ ולעי אל נאר לאגׄל מא נטבוך אל פׄראךׄ פׄי נזלית אל
14. ממזרתה וקעדית תנפׄוך אל נאר · פׄי חין מא שאפׄו אל ערלים
15. כדׄאלךׄ וקעית קלובהום וגׄשיית עיניהום וקאלו יא סייד אל יאוד ארפׄע
16. גׄצׄבךׄ עננא ורגע לנא אל אצנאם אלא מכאנהום וכׄוד אל יאודי מעךׄ
17. ואתווגׄה ונחן נכתב לכום פׄרמאן אן מן אל יום לם עודנא נטלבו
18. ואחד כל סנה אבדן פׄי אל חין כתבו להום פׄרמאן וכׄתמו ואעטו
19. להום ואכׄדו טריקהום ואתווגׄהו למנזלהום ועמלו עיד פסח לם להו
20. נטׄיר אבדן ואתווגׄה אל ראב לבלדו זכׄותו יגׄן עלינו אמן כי"ר:·[17]

Arabic Transliteration

139r.

1. ايضه اخبرو ان كان في بلد من بلاد ال ערלים كانو كل
2. سنة في عيدهوم ياخدو واحد ياودي يعملوه קורבן لل ע"ז
3. وكانو ال ياود يعملو גורל علا اوولاد ال ياود لاجل ما
4. يعرفو مين الذي ينعمل קורבן ال سنة ال اتيية لاجل ان يطلع

[16] תכׄת רואן: ‘sedan chair’ is written here in two parts, whereas elsewhere it reads as a single word (תכׄתרואן).

[17] כי"ר: ‘His will be done!’ (כן יהי רצון).

5. مصروفو من عند ال ערלים طول ال سنة · وحين يجي ال ميعاد

139v.

1. ياخدوه بموكب عظيم وكل الذي يطلوب ينول · في سنة من ال سنين
2. عملو ال גורל طلع علا ابن ال רב بتاع ذالك ال بلد وكان
3. عومرو عشرين سنة ولم كان ال ראב عندو خلافو · وكان ذالك ال ولد
4. ليس لهو نظير فال دونييا من ال فصاحا وال قراييية وخلافو في حين الذي
5. طلع ال גורל علا ال ولد قامو بال بوكا وال صيياح وال نوواح وال حوزن
6. وكان ميعاد الذي ياخدو ال ولد يقربوه يحكوم اوول ليلت פסח في
7. التفت ال ראב لاتنين من ال תלמידים وقال لهوم تعرفو تروحو مصر
8. لعند ال רב אברהם ן עזרא עא"ס تسلمو لهو هاذا ال جوواب وتعرفو
9. في هاذى ال دعووة ومن جيهت اهل منزلكوم نحن نصروف عليهوم
10. لحين ما تحضرو وبشرط لم تتعووقو فال طريق · لان من هاذى ال
11. بلد لمصر تلت اوشهور رروواح وتلت اوشهور مجيي · وهلبت
12. تقعودو في مصر شهر يصير سبعت اوشهور لحين ما تحضرو في
13. قالو لهو سميع موطيع يا سييدنا في كتب لهوم جوواب واتووجهو
14. لمصر من بعد تلت اوشهورحوضرو في مصر . وجدو واحد عني
15. ماشي فال سكة سالوه فين بيت ال רב אברהם ן עזרא في قال لهوم
16. هنا انا · اعطو لهو ال جوواب · في قال لهوم لم فيه باس
17. בע"ה نتووجه معاكوم نقضي هاذى ال دعووة ولم يكون الا خير· في
18. اخدهوم الا منزلو وقعدو عندو · وبعد شهر قالو لهو يا سييدنا
19. نريدو نتووجهو لاجل ال دعووة تتمها في قال لهوم ال ראב لم
20. عودتو تخاطبوني في شان ذالك · انه وقت ما نريد نتووجه فقعدو
21. لليلت ערב פסח من بعد ما عمل ال רב בדיקת חמץ واراحو
22. في قراييية قعدو لاربع سعات من ال ليل لحين ما فرغيت ال قراييية
23. في فرقو كعك بسيرج في اعطو لل ראב كعكتين وال תלמידים كل
24. واحد كعكتين واتووجهو لحالكوم في اخد طريقو ال רב אב ן עזרא وال
25. תלמידים

140r.

1. תלמידים معو واتووجهو في عوواض ما يتووجهو لل بيت حوكم ال
2. جاري طلعو ناحييت ال خلية في قالو ال תלמידים يا سييدنا لاين
3. متووجهين نحن دا احنا بقينا فال خلية في قال لهوم ال ראב امسكو

4. في طرفي في مسكو طرفو وقرى שם لم طلع عليهوم ال فجر الا
5. وهوم فال بلد بتا ع ال دعووة · في نظرو ال תלמידים ال بلد
6. واتعجبو· واحد يقول هاذا ال بلدنا وواحد يقول لم ה"א بلدنا
7. نحن في مصر وال רב אברהם ماشي قودامهوم لحين ما وصلو لبيت
8. ال חכם في طرقو علا ال باب · في طلع ال חכם فتح ال باب
9. وجد ال רב אברהם واقف علا ال باب في خمنو انو سال · في قال
10. لهو ال חכם ما تريد لم تعلم بحالنا في قال لهو ال רב אברהם
11. نعم علم بدعووتك ولاكن اتكل علا الله ס"ו והוא يعمل لك נסים
12. التفت ال חכם وجد ال انتين ال תלמידים الذي كان ارسلهوم لمصر
13. لل רב אברהם ןֿ עזרא · في سلم عليهوم وقال لهوم احكو لي ما جرا
14. في قالو لهو يا سييدنا ال רב אב' ןֿ עזרא הוא الذي واقف قوصادك في
15. قدم عليه واخدو ودخل بو ال بيت · في ما بعد ما صلو فال كنيس
16. حكو ال תלמידים لل سي' חכם بالذي جرا وفرجو لهو ال كعك بسيرج
17. الذي معاهوم · واتعجب ال חֿ علا ذالك · وال רבֿ אבֿ ןֿ עזרא ע"ה
18. قال لل ولد الذي ناوويين ياخدوه يعملوه קורבן لل ע"ז · حين ما يجو
19. بال موكب ياخدوك قول لهوم ان نكون انا معاك · وحين ما يقولو
20. لك اتمنا توعطا قول لهوم الذي يتمنا رفيقي · في قال لهو ال ولد
21. سميع موطيع · في بعد ساعتين الا وجو ال ערלים بموكب عظيم
22. لاجل انهوم ياخدو ال ولد يووكبو بو فال بلد · في قال لهوم ال
23. ولد خدوني انا ورفيقي معي والذي يتاتا عليبه يتاتا علا
24. رفيقي · في قالو ال ערלים احنا لنا واحد واذا كان تعطونا اتنين

140v.

1. احسن واحسن · في ركب ال רב אבֿ ןֿ עזרא עא"ס הוא وال ولد في قلب
2. ال تختروان وقالو لهوم ال ערלים اتمنو تعطو· في قال لهوم ال רב
3. אב' ןֿ עזרא اتمنا ان تجعلو ال قسيس ال كبير في زكيبة وتربطو
4. فوم ال زكيبة فال تختروان لحين ينتم ال موكب · في قالو ال ערלים
5. سميع وموطيع في اخدو ال قسيس ال كبير وحطوه في زكيبة وربطو
6. فوم ال زكيبة فال تختروان وانجر ال موكب ولفو ال بلد واراحو
7. ال كنيسة · في سالوهوم ايش تريدو تاكلو في طلب منهوم ال ראב
8. אברהם فرختين في جابو لهوم فرختين · في طلع ال ראב אברהם لل
9. كنيسة ونده על ע"ז ال كبيرة الذي بيعملو لها ال קורבאן وقال يا
10. ממזר انزل من مكانك وسن ال سكينة · في نزل ال ע"ז وقعد يسن
11. ال سكينة في انبهتو جميع ال ערלים ونزل عليهوم ال فزع ال

12. عظيم · في ما بعد نده ال רב אב' על ממזרתה وقال لها انزلي
13. من مكانيك ولعي ال نار لاجل ما نطبوخ ال فراخ في نزليت ال
14. ממזרתה وقعديت تنفوخ ال نار· في حين ما شافو ال ערלים
15. كذالك وقعيت قلوبهوم وغشييت עינ'هوم وقالو يا سييد ال ياود ارفع
16. غضبك عننا ورجع لنا ال اصنام الا مكانهوم وخود ال ياودي معك
17. واتووجه ونحن نكتب لكوم فرمان ان من ال يوم لم عودنا نطلبو
18. واحد كل سنه ابدن في ال حين كتبو لهوم فرمان وختمو واعطو
19. لهوم واخدو طريقهوم واتووجهو لمنزلهوم وعملو عيد פסח لم لهو
20. نظير ابدن واتووجه ال ראב لبلدو זכותו יגן עלינו אמן כי"ר:

Translation

139r.

(19) They also recounted that in one of the towns of the uncircumcised, every (20) year during their feast day, they would take one of the Jews, making him a sacrifice for the(ir) idols. (21) (Every year,) the Jews would cast lots for the children of the Jews in order that (22) they might know who would be made a sacrifice the following year, so that he might take (23) his expenses from the uncircumcised during the (remaining) year. When the appointed time came,

139v.

(1) they would take him in a great procession, and all that he asked for would be granted. One year, (2) they cast the lot, (and) it fell on the son of the rabbi of that town. He was (3) twenty years old and the rabbi had no other (children) besides him. This boy had (4) no equal in the world in terms of eloquence and the recitation (of the Torah), and so on. When (5) the lot fell on the boy, they began weeping, wailing, mourning, and grieving. (6)

(The) date on which they would take the boy and present him as a sacrifice was decided as the first night of Passover. (7) So, the rabbi turned to two of (his) students, saying to them, "You know you will go to Cairo, (8) to the place of Rabbi Abraham ibn ʿEzra, peace be upon him! You will deliver this letter to him and you will inform (him) (9) of this appeal. As for the people of your home(s), we will support them (10) until you return[18] and on the condition that you do not tarry on the road. From this (11) town to Cairo it is three months going and three months coming back. No doubt (12) you will stay in Cairo for a month. It will, thus, be seven months until you return." (13) They replied, "We hear you and are obedient, O, our master." So he wrote a letter for them and they set off (14) for Cairo. After three months, they arrived in Cairo and they happened upon a poor man (15) walking along the sidestreet. They asked him, "Where is the house of Abraham ibn ʿEzra?" He replied, (16) "Here I am!" They gave him the letter. Then he said to them, "There's nothing for it! (17) With God's help, I will come with you and I will answer this appeal and all will be well." He then (18) took them to his home, (where) they stayed with him. After a month, they said to him, "O our master, (19) we wish to go so that you can see to the appeal." The Rabbi replied, "You should (20) no longer address me with regard to this matter. I will go when I see fit." So, they stayed (21) until

[18] I am grateful to Dr. Nadia Vidro for her suggested translation of this sentence.

the night of the eve of Passover. After the Rabbi did the *chametz*[19] check, they went (22) for recitation. They sat for four hours during the night until the recitation was finished. (23) Then, they distributed the *kaʿk* with sesame oil. They gave two *kaʿk* to the Rabbi and two *kaʿk* to each of the (24) students. Then, they set out to (tend to) their business. Rabbi Abraham ibn ʿEzra went on his way, and the (25) (catchword)

140r.

(1) students accompanied him and they set off (together). Instead of going to the house (from which) the current (2) decree (came), they went off in the direction of the wilderness. The students exclaimed, "O, our master, where (3) are we going? This (seems to us like) we are still in the wilderness!" The Rabbi replied, "Stay (4) close to me." So they stayed where they were. He called out a Name (but) not till dawn broke over them (did they realise that) (5) that they were in the town from which the appeal came. The students saw the town (6) and were astonished! One (of them) said, "this is our town!" But the other exclaimed, "this is not our town, (7) we're (still) in Cairo!" Rabbi Abraham walked in front of them until they arrived at the house of the (8) sage. They

[19] *Chametz* refers to food that contains grains which have been mixed with water, and left to rise. In Judaism, it is forbidden to eat any products containing *chametz* from the day before Passover until the end of Passover. During this period, only *matzōt* (unleavened bread) is consumed. On the day before Passover, all *chametz* food must be removed from the house, hence, the '*chametz* check'.

knocked on the door. The sage came down, (and) opened the door (9) and found Rabbi Abraham standing on his doorstep. The sage assumed that he was a beggar, so he (10) said to him, "What do you want? Do you not know of our situation?" Rabbi Abraham replied, (11) "Yes, (I) know about your appeal, but you should trust in God, He is exalted! He will perform miracles for you!" (12) The sage turned and found the two students whom he had sent to Cairo (13) (in search of) Rabbi Abraham ibn ʿEzra. He greeted them and said to them, "Tell me what happened!" (14) They replied, "O our master, it is Rabbi Abraham ibn ʿEzra who stands in front of you!" So (15) he introduced himself and they took (him along with them) and he entered the house. After they had prayed in the synagogue, (16) the students told the master, (the) rabbi, about what had happened, and they showed him the *kaʿk* with sesame oil, (17) which (they still had) with them. The rabbi was amazed at this. (Meanwhile,) Rabbi Abraham ibn ʿEzra—may God help him—(18) spoke to the boy who was intended to be taken, and made an offering to the idols, "When they come (19) in the procession to take you, tell them that I will be with you. And when they say (20) to you, '(whatever) you wish for, you will be granted', say to them, 'what(ever) my companion desires.'" The boy replied, (21) "I hear (and) am obedient." After only two hours, the uncircumcised came in a great procession (22) in order to seize the boy (to) parade him through the town. The boy said to them, (23) "Take me and my companion with me, and what(ever) is done to me, shall be done to (24) my companion." The uncircumcised replied, "We have one (already), but if you have given us two,

140v.

(1) so much the better!" So, Rabbi Abraham ibn ʿEzra rode, along with the boy, in the middle of (2) the sedan chair. The uncircumcised said to them, "(Whatever) you wish for, you will be granted," to which Rabbi (3) Abraham ibn ʿEzra replied, "I wish you to put the high priest into a large gunny sack and bind (4) the opening of the sack to the sedan chair until the procession is over." The uncircumcised said, (5) "We hear and are obedient." So they took the high priest, lowered him into a sack, and tied (6) the opening of the sack to the sedan chair. The procession was swept along as they went around the town. Then they went (7) (to) the church. They asked them, "What do you want to eat?" Rabbi Abraham ibn ʿEzra asked them (8) for two chickens. So they brought two chickens for them. Then Rabbi Abraham went into the (9) church and he summoned (the) large idol(s) to which they made the sacrifice(s). He said, "O, (10) bastard! Get down from your place and sharpen th(is) knife!" The idol got down and sat, sharpening (11) the knife. All of the uncircumcised were speechless and great fear descended upon them. (12) Afterwards, Rabbi Abraham ibn ʿEzra summoned his (i.e., the male idol's) female bastard, saying to her, "Get down (13) from your place, and kindle the fire, so that we may cook the chickens!" The female idol (14) descended and sat, blowing (on) the fire. When the uncircumcised saw (15) this, she stilled their hearts and darkened their eyes. They exclaimed, "O, lord of the Jews, dispel (16) your anger towards us and return the idols to their places for us, take the Jew with you, (17) and go! We will write an edict for you

that from today we will never again claim (18) one (of your people), each year." Then, they wrote an edict for them, signed (it), and gave (it) (19) to them. Then they went on their way, setting off for their home, (where) they made a Passover festival, the like of which (20) had never been seen. Then, Rabbi Abraham ibn ʿEzra returned to his town. May His virtue protect us! Amen. His will be done!

25. LIBYA 1: ḤASAN AL-FAQĪH ḤASAN'S CHRONICLE AL-YAWMIYYĀT AL-LĪBIYYA (EARLY 19TH CENTURY)

Jérôme Lentin

Transcription

According to al-ʾUsṭā and Juḥaydar (eds) ([1984] 2001, 1:534)

يوم الاربعاء ١٣ ذي الحجة ١٢٤٦ هـ

توجه[1] محبنا الحاج مصطفى بن موسى الى سانية القنصل وكتب سدتو[2] انقليز وجاء القنصل الانقليز الى سيدنا واخبره بذلك والسلام

يوم السبت ١٦ ذي الحجة ١٢٤٦ هـ

وبحساب الروم فى ٢٨ من مايو سنة ١٨٣١ وقعت فيه فيشطة[3] متا ع[4] الراي[5] الانقليز عند القنصل الانقليز وعمل بدكان جانبوبه الرومى المالطى ثلاثة بتاتى شراب وتينده[6] قدام الدكان والبنديرة[7] الانقليزة فوق الدكان ونبه القنصل المذكور على جميع النصارى السدتو متاعه كل واحد ياخذ بوتيلية[8] شراب والذي عنده فاميليه[9] ياخذ على عددهم وتوجهوا إلى القنصل جميع القناصل الذين بطرابلس غرب وكذلك فيه[10] ناس مسلمين[11] توجهوا إليه وباركوا له وفرح بهم غاية الافراح والسرور هو وإبنه فادريك وأرسل الى سيدنا دام عزه وطلب منه أربع مدافع من متا ع المحلات[12] لأجل يضربوهم فعطاه سيدنا أربع مدافع بكراريصهم[13] جابوهم[14] إلى البحر قدام الكشك جابوهم طبجية القاجيجي وطلقوهم وروحوا[15] بهم والسلام

 https://doi.org/10.11647/OBP.0208.31

Translation

Wednesday 13 ḏū al-ḥijja 1246 h.

My dear friend the *ḥājj* Muṣṭafā b. Mūsā went to the garden (?) of the consul and registered as an English subject. The English consul went to inform our Lord of that. And that's all.

Saturday 16 ḏū al-ḥijja 1246 h [corresponding to] 28 May 1831 in the European calendar.

On that day there took place a *party for the King of England at the consul's residence.* He had three barrels of wine put in the shop of the Maltese Christian Gian Buba (?), an awning in front of the shop and the English flag over the shop. The consul warned all the Christians [lit. 'his subjects'] that every single person should take [only]one bottle, every man with a family should take according to their number [i.e., the number of the members of the family]. All the consuls who were in Tripoli of the West went to the consul's. There were also Muslims who went to him and presented their compliments to him, which delighted him and his son Frederic very much. He sent a message to our Sovereign—may his glory endure—asking him to send four ceremonial cannons [lit. 'of the embellished type'] to fire them. Our Sovereign gave him four cannons with their carriages. They were taken to the sea-side in front of the pavilion [which towers over the Pasha's palace] by the gunners of Al-Qājījī. They fired the cannons and brought them back. And that's all.

Commentary

[1] The verb (الى) توجّه 'to go (to)', used three times in this short passage, is common in MA texts; it can be considered the 'stylistically elevated' correspondent of *rāḥ* (cf. text II.9, no. 4).

[2] السدتو cf. Ital. *suddito*, Sp. *súbdito*. The chronicle of Ḥasan al-Faqīh Ḥasan is rich in borrowings from Romance languages (cf. the notes to lns 3, 5–9, and 13 below). No attempt is made here to determine their precise origin, and the references to Spanish (Sp.) or Italian (Ital.) are purely indicative, since these words may have been borrowed from various Italian or Spanish dialects or, more likely, in certain cases at least, from the *Lingua Franca.*

[3] فيشطة cf. Ital. *festa*, Sp. *Fiesta.*

[4] متاع colloquial genitive particle. It is attested from the 12th c. in Maghrebi MA texts.

[5] الراي cf. Ital. *rè*, Sp. *rey.*

[6] تينده cf. Ital. *tenda*, Sp. *tienda.*

[7] بنديرة cf. Ital. *bandiera*, Sp. *bandera.*

[8] بوتيلية cf. Ital. *bottiglia*, Sp. *botella.*

[9] فاميليه cf. Ital. *famiglia*, Sp. *familia.*

[10] فيه *fi* / *fih* 'there is'. Well known in Levantine dialects, but is also used in some (Eastern) Maghrebi dialects.

[11] مسلمين. For *-īn*, see text II.9, no. 13.

[12] محلات *m(u)ḥallāt* (root ḤLW/Y). The editors understand محلات 'places' and gloss *mutanaqqila* 'movable, transportable'.

[13] كراريص plur. of كروصة, cf. Ital. *carrozza*, Sp. *carroza.*

[14] جابوهم. See text II.9, no. 18.

[15] روحوا *rawwaḥū*. See text II.9, no. 4.

26. LIBYA 2: LETTER FROM ĠŪMA AL-MAḤMŪDĪ (1795–1858) TO ʿAZMĪ BĒK, DAFTARDĀR OF THE ʾIYĀLA (PROVINCE) OF TRIPOLI (UNDATED)

Jérôme Lentin

Transcription

According to Ibrāhīm (1983, 222–23)

الحمد لله وحده وصلى الله على سيدنا محمد واله وسلم

حضرة الاسعد الارشد الامجد المرعى المويد افاندينا احمد عزمي دفترلي دار[1] اكرمه الله امين السلام الاتم الاطيب الاعم عليكم ورحمة الله وبركاته ولا زيادة سوى الخير ويليه[2] اعلامكم انه اتانا الارفع جوابكم[3] قريناه[4] وفهمنا لفظه ومعناه وما ذكرت انك اتيت مع المرعي بالله سيدنا دامت معاليه في راحة الضعفاء والمساكين واعتدال الحق وخسف الباطل الحمد لله على ذالك وهذا ما كنا نريدوا[5] ومتحقق عندنا انك انت واسطة خير وصاين عرض السلطان ولاك[6] رغاب في اموال الناس تحققناه منك تحقيق[7] با انفسنا[8] وما وقع بيننا من زمان امحمد[9] رايف باشا الى ساعته التاريخ ولو ما كنت انت واسطة في انحرجت وانهزبت[10] قدام الاعمال من غير سبب وال[11] تولو غيره فعلوا معي اكبر من ذالك هاذ[12] السبب ال اجنيت انا بيه[13] وانا راجل[14] صاحب خدمه وطريق ما نستحقش[15] ايقودوني[16] لمصلحتي قود والحاصل هاه[17] سيدنا قدم ان شاء الله بالهنا على العماله وانت هاه ناظر وانا قيسوني وجربوني بشرط الخدمه ال نقدرهم كلهم[18] اليا[19] بان تقصيري على المعد وامر القدوم اولا سيدنا محل الفضل وايلاغيني على قدر عرفي وثانيا اودعوني لختيار نفسي ليا بانلي صفاوه ونرد بلا اندا[20] واما قولك اننا لم نكتب لكم جواب غير هاذا المراسله[21] خلقه الله مفاتيح الصدور ونسئل الله سبحانه ان يجعل على قدومكم راحة المسلمين وتلقوا[22] على اقوال اهل الحسد والمفسدين والله يجعل واصطتك[23]

 https://doi.org/10.11647/OBP.0208.32

خير وحسنى وهوين[24] عرفنا سيدنا بما بان لنا وما عندنا يخبركم به حامل الجواب مشافاه[25]
ميلاد بن الحاج سعيد والسلام

خديم الدوله غومه بن خليفه

Translation

God be praised, only Him, and let Him bless our *sayyid* Muḥammad and his family and grant them salvation.

Excellency, felicitous, well-guided, glorious, protected and supported, our *ʾafandī* ʾAḥmad ʿAzmī, *daftardār* (director of the financial administration of the province)—may God confer honours upon him. Amen—My fullest, best and most complete greetings to you, may the mercy of God and His blessings be upon you. Nothing is to be added, except [wishes for] the very best. Now, let me inform you that I received your precious letter, that I read it and understood its form and content, as well as what you said about what you did, with our Lord the protected by God—may his noble actions endure—for the comfort of the weak and the poor, and to raise truth and make falsehood vanish. God be praised for that, this is what I wanted. I am assured that your mediation is for the best, that you are the guardian of the Sultan's honor, and that you are not coveting the properties of the people. Of this I have become truly convinced myself from what has happened between us since the time of Muḥammad Rāyif Bāšā until this very day, even if you were not mediating for me [at that time, when] I was put on the spot and put to shame in front of the Administration of Finance without any reason. And those who took charge after him did even worse to me. *That is why I was blamed* [for a crime I had not committed], whereas I am a devoted and upright servant, and I don't need to be guided in the performance of my duties. In short, here is our Sovereign who came—let's hope—for the good of the *ʿamāla* (governorate) and here you are, [his] *nāḏir* (superintendent). As for me, evaluate me and test me, on one condition: if it appears that, among all the tasks I can accomplish, I have failed to achieve the assigned one, and if I am summoned, first, it will be by our eminent Sovereign and he will treat me according to my abilities; second, let me choose by myself and, *if it appears evident to me that he is sincere [in blaming me]*, I will start again without being asked to. And when you say that I did not write any letter to you except this correspondence… God's human creatures have the key of hearts. We ask God—be He praised—to bring ease to the Muslims with your arrival, to allow you to ignore what the enviers and those who spread disturbance say, and may He make your mediation good and successful. Here we are, we informed our Sovereign *about how things appear to us*. The bearer of this letter, Mīlād son of the ḥājj Saʿīd, will inform you [in more detail] verbally about what I think. Farewell.

The servant of the Porte Ġūma b. Ḫalīfa

N.B. The translation of the passage from 'As for…' until '…the key of hearts' is purely tentative.

Commentary

1 دفترلي دار. In this Turkish term, the suffix لي (*-lü*) must initially have been written by mistake, and then left uncrossed out.

2 يليه is an equivalent of أما بعد.

الارفع جوابكم. Notice the very unusual word order. The elegant turn of phrase ارفع جوابكم was likely meant here.

4 قريناه. MA *qara* / colloquial *qre* (cf. Classical *qaraʾa*), a C_3 = Y verb.

5 نريدوا. Colloquial form of the 1pl imperfect. Notice also the *ʾalif al-wiqāya*.

6 لاك. Colloquial negative turn (*lā* + bound 2ms pronoun) 'you are not…'. The negation is probably stronger than *mā-k*; for Takrūna in Tunisia, see Marçais and Guîga (1958–1961, 3571).

7 تحقيق. *Mafʿūl muṭlaq* of تحققنا. This turn of phrase is not frequently used in MA. Another example is ايقودوني قود.

8 با انفسنا. Two *ʾalifs* (ا ا) denoting *ʾa* (as well as *aʾ* and *āʾ*) is common in late MA orthography; see examples in Lentin (1997, 111–12), e.g., لاانهم *liʾannahum*.

9 امحمد. The initial prosthetic *ʾalif* indicates here that the initial syllable begins CC- (*Mḥammad*). Cf. text II.19, no. 15.

10 انهزبت. For the meaning, compare form II *hazzaba* in Dozy (1881, II: 756). Corriente (1997, 549) offers another meaning: 'to dumbfound' for form V *tahazzaba*.

11 ال تولو. The form ال is a form of the relative (cf. the two other examples ال اجنيت انا بيه and ال نقدرهم كلهم).

12 هاذ. Colloquial short form of the demonstrative.

13 بيه. Colloquial (prep. *bi-* + bound 3ms pronoun).

14 راجل. Colloquial *rāžəl* 'man'.

15 ما نستحقش. Colloquial 1s imperfect and colloquial 'discontinuous' (dimorphematic) negation *ma…š*.

16 ايقودوني. Colloquial *yqūdūni* (cf. note to ln. 6 above); cf. also وايلاغيني.

17 هاه. Colloquial deictic particle *hā-* + bound 3ms pronoun *-hu*.

18 الخدمه ال نقدرهم كلهم. The plural agreement of the pronouns (ـهم) with the feminine singular noun خدمه is rather uncommon.

19 اليا *elya* (and ليا *leya* below). Colloquial conditional conjunction 'if'.

20 اندا *nda* (cf. note to ln. 6 above). Cf. Classical *nidāʾ* (Boris 1958, 606 *ᵊnde*).

21 هاذا المراسله. The mascudemonstrative هاذا with the feminine noun مراسله is quite unexpected. But one should note that هاذا is written here with *ʾalif* after the *hāʾ*, whereas its other occurrences in the text read هذا. Hence one could think here of another example of ا ا noting *ʾa* (see note to ln. 8 above) and read هاذ االمراسله (with the short form of the demonstrative, cf. note to ln. 12). This hypothesis cannot be verified since there is no facsimile reproduction of the manuscript in the edition.

22 تلقوا. Probably تلغوا, with *ġ* > *q*, as is common in several Maghrebi Bedouin dialects. For the meaning, cf. Boris (1958, 557): *lġe ʿala* 'to abandon, not take care of anymore, to give up, to stop talking to'.

23 واصطتك = واسطتك. With *s* > *ṣ* (in the vicinity of *ṭ*); but see above واسطة.

24 Colloquial هوين *ha/āwēn* is a kind of presentative particle. The variant هوينه occurs in another letter of Ġūma al-Maḥmūdī (*Waṯāʾiq ʿan tārīḫ Lībiyā*... p. 244): هوينه قادم اليك 'Here he is coming to you'. Nowadays in Tripoli, *hāwēn-* is used only with a suffixed 3rd-person pronoun (*-a, -ha, -hum*) or with the frozen 3ms pronoun *-a*: *hāwēna.*[1]

25 مشافاه = مشافهة.

---

[1] I am indebted to Christophe Pereira for this information.

27. T-S NS 99.38 (1809)

Geoffrey Khan and Esther-Miriam Wagner

Transcription

1. בעהש היום יום ב׳ ١٣ רחמים קסט׳
2. אחינו אל סי׳ קארו פרנסיס נרו׳

3. אחדש״ו נערפכם יא מחבנה באן אמס תאריכו כתבנא
4. לכם מכתוב צו׳ אל סאעי וערפנאכם פי בגואב
5. מכתיבכם אלדׄי ורדת ענכם ואיצׄה יום תאריכׄו וצלנא
6. מכתוב צו׳ ברבר אל כביר ווצלנה
7. צו׳ אל רייס אל מדכור נו׳ ١٥ יכון מעלומכם
8. ויצלכם צאפינא טאי דׄאלך תטלעו עליה
9. ואנתום בכׄיר וצורת סי׳ אברהם אבו וצלתו
10. לשלום יכון מעלומכם כדה נרגוכם אן מן פצלכם
11. חאלן תאמנונא בוצול אל מורסל לכם מן נו עג٥
12. אלא נו׳ עג١١ אלדׄי ערפנאכם ענהום מן סאבק
13. ואיצׄה תערפונא בוצול מורסלנא מן חסאב
14. אל בון נו עג۴ ונערפכם באן יום תאריכׄו
15. ארסלנה לכם מאע סלמת תעאלא צו׳ רמצאן
16. שרבי תסלים אבנו אברהם אמונה נו עג١١
17. וצמנהא דכלהא תטלעו עליה ואנתום בכׄיר
18. בעה (?) לידכם לשלום באל וצול תערפונא
19. ונערפכם באן יום תאריכו חררנא עאלה אלסי׳
20. אברהם יעבץ בולצה קבץ סי׳ מחמוד חסן בפצה
21. ١٠٢٨٣ חוכם תעריפכם יכון מעלומכם ואן
22. סאלתום עאן אצעאר אל בון בטרפנה אתחסן יום
23. תאריכו בסבב אל כׄבר אלדׄי טלע בקולת אן וקע
24. צולח שאפי מן אסטמבול יכון מעלומכם

 https://doi.org/10.11647/OBP.0208.33

25. וסער אל בון בתאריכו ע׳ ٨١ ואל פרקין באקין
26. ולם נתצרף פיהום לומא יגיבה תעריף מכת[תובכם]
27. ולאן חצל ע׳ ٨٥ אוו אכתר בענאהום עא[לה]
28. קדר מא יבאן לנה וחוכם אל תגאר ואן שא אללה
29. תכונו ארסלתו לנה בית אל מיזאן ואל מיזאן
30. אחסן לאזים לנה כתיר ובלגו סלמנא עאלה
31. מחבנה יצחק פרנסיס וד״ש למחבנה אל הר אליאן
32. וצהל ובלגו סלמנא עאלה אל סי׳ נסים משיש
33. ריו וד״ש למחבנה אברהם הלוי ולכאמל אל
34. כומפנניה ד״ש ולם נטיל עליכם אלא באל
35. כיר כדמה מצלחא ערפונא נפוז בקצהא
36. עאלה אל ראס ואל עין ושלום
37. הצעיר
38. אברהם גבריאל
39. כמאן חפז
40. סט סט

Arabic Transcription

1. בעהש היום יום ב׳ ١٣ רחמים קסט׳
2. אחינו אל סי׳ קארו פרנסיס נרו׳

3. אחדש״ו نعرفكم يا محبنه بان امس تاريكو كتبنا
4. لكم مكتوب صو" ال ساعي وعرفناكم في بجواب
5. مكتيبكم الذي وردت عنكم وايضه يوم تاريخو وصلنا
6. مكتوب صو" بربر ال كبير ووصلنه
7. צו׳ ال رييس المدكور نو" ١٥ يكون معلومكم
8. ويصلكم صافينا طاي ذالك تطلعو عليه
9. وانتوم بخير وصورت سي" אברהם אבו وصلتو
10. לשלום يكون معلومكم كده نرجوكم ان من فصلكم
11. حالن تامنونا بوصول ال مورسل لكم من نو عج٥
12. الا نو" عج ١٠ الذي عرفناكم عنهوم من سابق
13. وايضه تعرفونا بوصول مورسلنا من حساب
14. ال بون نو عج ٤ ونعرفكم بان يوم تاريخو
15. ارسلنه لكم ماع سلمت تعالا صو" رمصان

16. شربي تسليم אבנו אברהם אמונה نو عج ١١
17. وصمنها دكلها تطلعو عليه وانتوم بخير
18. بعه (?) ليدكم לשלום באל وصول تعرفونا
19. ونعرفكم بان يوم تاريكو حررنا عاله السي"
20. אברהם יעבץ בולצה קבץ سي" מחמוד חסן بفضه
21. ١٠٢٨٣ حوكم تعريفكم يكون معلومكم وان
22. سالتوم عان اصعار ال بون بطرفنه اتحسن يوم
23. تاريكو بسبب ال خبر الذي طلع بقولت ان وقع
24. صولح شافي من اسطمبول يكون معلومكم
25. وسعر ال بون بتاريكو عي" ٨١ وال فرقين باقين
26. ولم نتصرف فيهوم لوما يجيبه تعريف مكت [توبكم]
27. ولان حصل عي" ٨٥ اوو اكتر بعناهوم عا [له]
28. قدر ما يبان لنه وحوكم ال تجار وان شا الله
29. تكونو ارسلتو لنه بيت ال ميزان وال ميزان
30. احسن لازيم لنه كتير وبلجو سلمنا عاله
31. محبنه יצחק פרנסיס וד"ש لمحبنه ال هر اليان
32. وصهل وبلجو سلمنا عاله ال سي"נסים משיש
33. ريو וד"ש لمحبنه אברהם הלוי ولكامل ال
34. كومفننيه ד"ש ولم نطيل عليكم الا بال
35. كير كدمه مصلحا عرفونا نفوز بقصها
36. عاله ال راس وال عين ושלום
37. הצעיר
38. אברהם   גבריאל
39. כמאן   חפז
40. סט סט

Translation

(1) With the help of God. Monday 13th of Elul (5400 +) 169 (= 5569 Era of Creation = 1809 CE). (2) (To) our brother the master Karo Francis—may God preserve him. (3) After inquiring about your (lit. his) health, we inform you, our beloved, that yesterday we wrote (4) to you a letter via the messenger. We informed you in it about the answer (5) to your letters, which arrived from you.

Also, today a letter (6) reached us with (the ship) *Barbar the Great*, it reached us (7) with the mentioned captain, (consignment) no. 15. (This) you should know. (8) Our net (profit) should reach you inside this (letter). You should understand it, (9) (and we hope) be fine with it. The purse of the lord Abraham, his father, reached him (10) safely. You should know. So we hope that you please (11) for the moment trust us with the arrival of the goods sent to you from no. 5 (12) to no. 10, which we informed you about in advance. (13) Also, inform us of the arrival of our consignment regarding (14) the coffee, no. 4. We inform you that today (15) we sent to you under God's protection with Ramaḍān (16) Šarabī by delivery of his son Abraham, the consignment no. 11. (17) Its content is inside of it. You should understand it, (and we hope) be fine with it. (18) I sent (it) to your hand safely. When it arrives, let us know. (19) We inform you that today we made out to the master (20) Abraham Yaʿbeṣ a bill of exchange belonging to the master Maḥmūd Ḥasan for (21) 10283 silver-dinars according to your instruction. You should know (this). If (22) you ask about the prices of coffee in our region, it is going well (23) today because of the news that arrived reporting that (24) a conciliatory settlement has been made from Istanbul. You should know (this). (25) The price of coffee is today at a value of 81, and two portions remain. (26) We do not have authority over them until the notification of your letter brings it. (27) Because at the value of 85 or more we sold what (28) seemed suitable to us. Concerning the traders, God willing, (29) you would have sent to us the casing of the scales. We need (30) the scales very much. Convey our greetings to (31) our beloved Isaac Francis. Greetings to our beloved *ha-rav* Ilyān (32) and (to) Ṣahl. Convey our greetings to the master Nissim Mašīš (33) Rio. Greetings to our beloved Abraham ha-Levi and to all the (34) company greetings. We will not prolong (this letter) to you except with (35) (wishing you) the best. (If there is any) service or benefit (we could assist you with), let us know and we shall be sure to carry it out (36) with pleasure. Shalom.

(37) *Ha-ṣaʿir*

(38) Abraham Gabriel

(39) Kamān Ḥefez

(39) *Simen ṭov/Sefardi ṭov Simen ṭov/Sefardi ṭov*

Commentary

Line 1

Raḥamīm is the name for Elul, the month of prayers for forgiveness and mercy.

Line 2

נרו is the abbreviation for נַטְרֵיהּ רַחֲמָנָא וּפַרְקִיהּ.

Line 3

The abbreviation אחדש״ו is used for אחרי דרישת שלומו

Line 4

In our corpus of letters, *maktūb* has replaced the word *kitāb* for 'letter' used in earlier correspondence. The abbreviation צו' stands for *ṣuḥba* 'with'. The form פי for *fīhi* 'in it' shows an unusual orthography as the suffix *-h* is not spelled.

Line 25

ע' is short for *ʿereḵ* 'value'.

28. RYLANDS GENIZAH COLLECTION A 803 (1825)

Esther-Miriam Wagner and Mohamed Ahmed

Transcription

1. בע"ה
2. ביום ٢٨ לח' סיון שנת ٨٥ ליצירה
3. אה אל סי' יעקב יעביץ נר"ו יאיר אבירא
4. אחדש"ו מן בעד מזיד אל סלאם עליכום נערפכום באין אתמול גה לטרפנה אלס' יוסף אאילייון וכׄברנה
5. עלה אל גזרה ביתאע אכׄוך בעונות אל נפׄטר פי יעלם אל שית' באין צועוב עלינה קאווי לאין
6. כאן ראגׄיל חסידא קדישא עלה מה חאכו כל אל נאס ולאכין מה ביל יד חילה אל שית' יצברכום ואל ברכה
7. פיד ופׄי ולאדו ובעד נערפכום באין סאביק תא' כתבנה ליכום וכׄברנאכום באין אלכׄוואגה בוגׄוז סאל
8. עליכום וקולנה לו סאפיר ישופ וולאדו ואתמול סאל עליכום אין כאן גית ולה לה וקולנה לו אל גומעה אל
9. גאייה ייגי פי כירה וכׄברנאכום כלפי יכׄברכום גׄירנה לנה מה תגיבוש אל חאק עלינה יכון פי שאריפ
10. עילמיכום בע"ה גוואב אל מכתוב תכונו אינתו תיחצׄרו לטרפנה חוכם מא קולתו ליל וכיל
11. וליל מבאשיר ולם ענדי מה נטול עליכום אלא ביל כיר ושלום הצעיר
12. נסים סבאח
13. ס"ט

 https://doi.org/10.11647/OBP.0208.34

Arabic Transcription

1. בע"ה
2. ביום ٢٨ לח' סיון שנת ٨٥ ליצירהא
3. אה السيـ" יעקב יעביץ נר"ו יאיר אבירא
4. אחדש"ו من بعد مزيد ال سلام عليكوم نعرفكوم بإين[1] אתמול جه لطرفنه السيـ" יוסף אאיליון وخبرنه
5. عله ال גזרה بيتاع اخوك בעונות ال נפטר في يعلم אל שית' بإين صوعوب علينه قاووى لإين
6. كان راجيل חסידא קדישא عله مه حكوا ال ناس ولاكين مه بيل يد حيله אל שית' يصبركوم وال بركه
7. فيك وفي ولادو وبعد نعرفكوم بإين سابيق تا' كتبنه ليكوم وخبرناكوم بإين الخواجه بوجوز سأل
8. عليكوم وقولنه لو سافير يشوف وولادو وאתמול سأل عليكوم إين كان جيت وله له وقولنه لو الجمعه ال
9. جاييه ييجي في خيره وخبرناكوم כלפי يخبركوم غيرنه لنه مه تجيبوش الحق علينه يكون في شاريف
10. عيلميكوم בע"ה جوواب ال مكتوب تكونو اينتو تيحضرو لطرفنه حكم ما قولتو ليل ووكيل
11. وليل مباشير ولم عندي مه نطول عليكوم الا بال خير ושלום הצעיר
12. נסים סבאח
13. ס"ט

Translation

(1) With the help of God. (2) On the 28th of Sivan of the Year 5585 of Creation (= 1825 CE). (3) (To) our beloved, the master Jacob Yabets—may God protect and preserve him—enlightened by God. (4) After inquiring about his health, and after (extending) many greetings to you, we let you know that yesterday, Mr

[1] In order to reflect the Hebrew spelling באין, we decided to use the إ sign here.

Joseph Aylloni[2] came to our area, and he informed us (5) about the punishment of your brother, dead because of (our) sins. God—may his name be blessed—knows that (this) was difficult to bear for us, because (6) he was a pious and saintly man, as all people depicted him. Yet, there is nothing we can do. May God—his name be blessed—give you patience. It is for you[3] (7) and his children to fill his place. Then we also inform you that previously we wrote to you and informed you that Mr Bogush asked (8) about you and we told him that you are travelling to see your children. Yesterday he asked about you, whether you came (back) or not. We said to him: Next (9) Friday he will come in good health. We tell you just as anyone other than us would tell you on our behalf. Do not blame it on us. You should know (10) this.[4] With the help of God, (there will be an) answer to (this) letter. You should come to our area in accordance with what you told the agent (11) and the supervisor. I have nothing to add except the best of greetings. The young man (12) Nissim Sabbāḥ, (13) a good Sefardi.

Commentary

The code-switching between Hebrew and Arabic in this letter differs markedly from what can be observed in medieval letters. In fact, code-switching involving temporal adverbs, such as *ʾetmol*

[2] For the Ladino spelling of the name, see https://he.wikipedia.org/wiki/%D7%A9%D7%9C%D7%9E%D7%94_%D7%90%D7%90%D7%99%D7%9C%D7%99%D7%95%D7%9F.

[3] A common Egyptian condolence, see Badawi and Hinds (1986, 68).

[4] Literally 'This should be to your honourable knowledge'.

'yesterday', is not normally found in medieval Judaeo-Arabic letters, but is a much more common occurrence in Yiddish and Ladino letters.[5] Medieval mercantile letters in particular avoid code-switching,[6] whereas early modern traders frequently switch into Hebrew. Similarly, words such as *nifṭar* 'deceased' are not normally used in Classical Judaeo-Arabic code-switches, whereas they are commonly used loanwords in Yiddish. It could be argued that the change in style as well as frequency of mercantile code-switching observed between medieval Judaeo-Arabic and Early Modern Judaeo Arabic, in particular in the letter at hand, was influenced by language patterns from Yiddish and Ladino through traders from Europe and Asia Minor.

Line 1

בע"ה = בעזרת השם 'With the help of God'.

Line 2

לח' = לחודש 'in the month'.

Line 3

אה = אהובנו 'our beloved'.

נר"ו = נטרה רחמנא פרקה 'may God protect and preserve him'.

Line 4

אחדש"ו = אחרי דרישת שלומו 'After inquiring about your (lit. his) health'.

---

[5] For differences in codeswitching between Judaeo-Arabic and Yiddish, see Wagner and Kühnert (2016). A cursory analysis of all Judaeo-Arabic letters written by Daniel b. ʿAzarya published in Gil (1997, 625–715) shows no temporal adverbs at all.

[6] See Wagner and Connolly (2017).

גַה. Classical Judaeo-Arabic גא, Classical Arabic جاء 'he came'.

Line 5

צוּעוּב 'difficult to bear'. The vocalisation here may reflect what Rosenbaum (2002, 37) describes as preference for *u* over Standard dialect *i* in Modern Jewish Egyptian Arabic, which would indicate the speaker's Jewish heritage and minority status for any listener.

Line 6

ראגִ֗יל. The pointing of this letter and the other letters below is somewhat random. Some of those going back to Classical Arabic ج have dots beneath, as here; others do not, for example ייגי 'he will come' in line 9. Yet, also Classical Arabic غ may receive the dot, as in גִ֗ירנה 'other than us', also in line 9. The same irregularity can be found in various letters, e.g., the pointing of כ to distinguish between [k] and [b], on the one hand, and [k] and [k̲], on the other.

חסידא קדישא. The use of this Aramaic form again is somewhat unusual for Judaeo-Arabic letters. Yet it is commonly used in Yiddish, as mentioned by Khan (2006, 358).

Line 7

ت" = تاريخه 'its (the letter's) time, i.e., today'.

Line 8

ולה לה. The dialectal term *walla* + *lāʾ* 'or not'.

וולאדו. The double spelling of ו here, as well as the double spelling of י in ייגי 'he will come' in line 9, are not consistent throughout the letter and may show a preference of double spelling if ו is followed by short [u] if and י is followed by [i].

29. SYRIA 2: CHRONICLE OF MUḤAMMAD SAʿĪD AL-ʾUSṬUWĀNĪ (1840–1861)

Jérôme Lentin

The *šayḫ* Muḥammad Saʿīd al-ʾUsṭuwānī (1822–1888) was a Damascene *ʿālim*. He was *ḫaṭīb* of the Umayyad Mosque in Damascus, and eventually held important functions in the administration of justice. In 1867, he was appointed *qāḍī* of Tripoli, and was first *qāḍī šarʿī* in Damascus between 1869 and 1873. His chronicle covers the years between 1840 and 1861. Edition that of ʾUsṭuwānī (1993).

Transcription

p. 194

وظهره رايت في الجامع الحاج عبد الرحمن الحموي اراني مكتوب[1] من ولده محمد المرسل
الى جهة بيروت مع الذين تقدموا ثاني دفعة في ١٣ ص وبه يعرف اياه انهم بداوا بتخشيبهم
من الساعة ٤ والساعة ٦ مشوهم اصبحوا في الديماس وقاموا[2] من الديماس الى خان الحسين
ماشين مخشبين عطاشى الاحد دخلوا بيروت الى القشلة وفي دخولهم صاروا النصارى الذين
سافروا الى بيروت يسمعوهم[3] الكلام الفاحش مثل وين[4] البلطات وين سيوفكم اخذينكم[5] على
الخازوق على المرسه غدا رايحين[6] على الشام طالعناكم[7] واخذنا بيوتكم ومن هذا القبيل وان
العسكر الفرنساوي حاطط[8] عن بيروت ساعة ١ وموجود[9] اوردي من ٩ الى ١٠ الف ولهم في
القشلة فكوا لهم الخشب واخذوهم على البحر انزلوهم في مركب عثملي وانهم الى الان
كذلك واقفين[10] تاريخ المكتوب في ٢٠ ص من البحر للشام

 https://doi.org/10.11647/OBP.0208.35

Translation

At noon of that day [Saturday, 22 Ṣafar 1277 = 7 September 1860], I saw in the mosque the *ḥājj* ʿAbd al-Raḥmān al-ḥamawī. He showed me a letter from his son Muḥammad, who had been sent to Beirut with those who had preceded a second wave of people driven away on 13 Ṣafar. In this letter, he was informing his father that they had first been put into wooden handcuffs at 4 o'clock. At 6 o'clock they had been forced to start walking. In the morning they were in Dīmās, from where they left for Ḫān al-Ḥusayn, walking with their hands cuffed and thirsty. On Sunday they had entered Beirut until the barracks. When they entered, the Christians who had travelled to Beirut started addressing them with impudent words like: "Where are your axes, where are your swords? They're taking you to the stake [to impale you], to the rope [of the gibbet]! Tomorrow we are going [back] to Damascus. We have dislodged you from your houses and we have taken them!" and words of the same kind. [He was adding in his letter that] the French army had settled in Beirut at 1 o'clock, and that they had an army corps, of 9 to 10,000 [soldiers] in the barracks. And that they had unfastened their cuffs and taken them to the sea, where they had embarked them on an Ottoman boat, and that, on the date he wrote his letter, sent from the sea to Damascus on 20 Ṣafar, they were still liying at a standstill.

Commentary

[1] اراني مكتوب. As a rule, 'cases' disappear in MA. Classical or classicising forms with case endings (مكتوبا) appear only in specific contexts.

[2] قاموا. Colloquial use of *qām*.

[3] يسمعوهم. For the regular *-ū* (and not *-ūn*) form in MA for the 2pl and 3pl imperfect, see text II.9, n. 7.

[4] وين. Colloquial interrogative adverb (*wayn* / *wēn*).

[5] اخذينكم على الخازوق. Notice the temporal value of the active participle (present / immediate future).

[6] غدا رايحين على الشام. Notice the temporal value of the active participle (near future, cf. *ġadan*).

[7] طالعناكم. Colloquial طالع 'to remove, expel' (see text II.9, n. 9).

[8] حاطط عن بيروت. The proposed translation follows the editor's gloss (*daḫala ʾilā*).

[9] وموجود اوردي. *Mawžūd* is frequently used in MA and can be analysed as a transposition of colloquial *fī* 'there is'.

[10] واقفين. The sound masculine plural form *-īn* is predominant (whatever the syntactic function of the noun) in MA texts, see text II.9, n. 13.

30. ARABIA: A LETTER FROM ABDALLAH ḤIṢĀNĪ TO ʿABDALLAH BĀŠĀ (1855)

Jérôme Lentin

A letter from the *šayḫ* ʿAbdallah Ḥiṣānī to ʿAbdallah Bāšā, dated 18 Rabīʿ al-ʾawwal 1272 h (28 November 1855); from the facsimile in ʾAġlū (2002, 170), since the edition (81–82) is faulty.

Transcription

تعالى

الحمد الله وحده

1. الى حضرت[1] قدوة الاكابر وعين الاعيان المحروس بعين الملك الديان افندينا عبد الله باشه حضه الله امين
2. السلام عليكم ورحمت الله وبركاته وبعد جانا[2] جوابك العزيز وفهمنا مضمونه ويو[3] جانا جوابك واردنا[4] جواب
3. سابق من امير مكه الشريف عبد المطلب ومن عند اهل مكه العما[5] والمفاتي ويذكرون ان النصار طبو[6]
4. مكه بيت الله الحرام وهذ العلم لا يرضاه لا الله ولا رسوله ولا الصلطان[7] ولا من يقول لا اله الا الله محمد رسو
5. ل الله وبعد بلغنا الامر هذا صابة[8] المسلمين غيره دون دين محمد صلى الله عليه وعلى اله وسلم ودون دينهم
6. وبغة[9] تقوم القبايل وطلبنا منهم لين[10] نبلغكم ونبلغ الباشه ونشوف[11] تحقيق الامور فان كان وكد[11] عند
7. نا على ما ذكر الشريف وهل[12] مكه على ان النصارا هتكو حرمة بيت الله فحنا[13] ما عندنا طاعه[14] لنصار ولا لمن

 https://doi.org/10.11647/OBP.0208.36

8. يعينها وقايمين[15] عليها غيرت فدين[16] ومستعينين بلا لله وبرسوله وبكلمه التوحيد كما قال الله تعالى سبحانه وتعالى
9. يا ايها الذين امنو اناما المشركون نجس فلا يقربو المسجد الحرام[17] وانا سار[18] بيني وبينك عهده على ما يرظي[19] الله ورسوله
10. وعلى ما يصلح في ارض الحرمين ومن وقت العهده اليا[20] تاريخه ما حصل تقصير في خدمتكم وخدمت الدوله العليه
11. وحنا خدامه بلا مصلحه معك ومع الدوله العليه كله في شان[21] محبة افندينا ومحبتك السبب انك
12. راع صدق[22] معي وحنا عرفنا سعادت افندينا بجواب ونرقب[23] جوابه ونرقب جواب منك وحنا مجتهدين
13. في كف القبايل قبايلنا لين يجينا جواب افندينا وجوابك هذ[24] ما لزم عرفناك[25] به والسلام صح[26] حرر وجرا يوم الوفا[27]
14. من ربيع اول سنة ١٢٧٢ من خادمك الشيخ عبد الله حصاني [ختم]

Translation

Praise be to God alone, exalted be He

(1) To his Lordship, model of the grandees and prominent among the leaders, protected by the eye of the Retributing Sovereign, our Sir (*ʾAfandīnā*) ʿAbdallah Bāšā—may God prompt him [to godly works]. Amen. (2) Greetings to you and the mercy of God and His blessings be upon you. — I have received your esteemed letter and I have perfectly understood *the contents.* The [very] day it arrived, we had [just] received a letter (3) from the *ʾamīr* of Mecca the *Sharif* ʿAbd al-Muṭṭalib and from the people of Mecca, *ʿulamāʾ*, and muftis. They were reporting that the Christians entered (4) Mecca, the Sacred House of God. Such news satisfies neither God, nor His Prophet, nor the Sultan, nor those who say that there is no deity *except God* and that Muhammad is His (5) messenger. When we heard that, the Muslims felt full of ardour [to fight] for the religion of Muḥammad (God bless him and

grant him salvation) and for their religion. (6) The tribes wanted to rise up. We asked them [to wait] until we inform you and the Pasha and until things are confirmed. If it proves true (7) that the Christians disgraced the sanctity of the House of God, as the *Sharif* and the people of Mecca said, we will yield neither to the Christians nor to those who (8) support them and we will rise against them in zeal for the religion and we will seek the help of God, of His Prophet, and of the proclamation of His unicity. As God— praised and exalted be He—said: (9) "O you who believe! The Associationists are nothing but impure, so let them not approach the Inviolable Mosque." You and I have concluded a pact [making a commitment] to do what satisfies God and His Prophet (10) and what is right in the land of the two sanctuaries. From the day we made this pact until today, I have never failed to serve you and the Sublime Porte. (11) We serve without taking any advantage from you or from the Sublime Porte, doing all this [only] for the sake of my love for our Sire and for you. This is because you are (12) truthful with me. I have informed His Grace, our Sir, in a letter and I am waiting for his answer. I am waiting as well for an answer from you. I am doing my best (13) to hold back the tribes until I receive the answer of our Sir and yours. This is what I needed to tell you. Greetings. This was written the day of *al-wafā(ʾ)* (14) of Rabīʿ al-ʾawwal 1272 by your servant the *šayḫ* ʿAbdallah Ḥiṣanı [seal]

Commentary

1 حضرت. *Tāʾ ṭawīla* for *tāʾ marbūṭa* (and vice versa, see note to ln. 7) is common in MA texts. Cf. ln. 2 رحمت, ln. 8 غيرت, ln. 10 خدمت, ln. 12 سعادت.

2 جا *žā* 'to come' is common in MA (see text 'Syria 1', note to ln. 19). Cf. the imperfect يجينا in ln. 13.

3 يو is most probably an apocopated form of يوم 'when'.

4 واردنا. Notice the perfective aspectual value of the active participle.

5 العما is probably to be read العلما. المفاتي is either an unusual plural of *muft*^{in} (Classical *muftūn*), or—less likely—the plural of مفتى 'counsel' (see Piamenta 1990–1991, II:366).

6 طبو *ṭabb* 'to enter' (colloquial). The spelling without *ʾalif al-wiqāya* is consistent in this text (as in others) for the perfect هتكو (ln. 7) and امنو (ln. 9) and the imperfect يقربو (ln. 9).

7 الصلطان *al-ṣulṭān* (< *al-sulṭān*).

8 صابة = صابت (cf. Classical أصابت). On the writing ة for ت, see note to ln. 1.

9 بغة تقوم القبايل. The (colloquial) modal auxiliary (3fs) *baġat* (on the writing ة for ت, see note to ln. 1) is constructed asyndetically, as is generally the case in MA texts.

10 لين. Colloquial *lēn* 'until' (for a further example see note to ln. 13).

11 نشوف. This colloquial verb (*šāf* 'to see') appears frequently in MA texts, even in the less colloquialising ones.

12 هل مكه = أهل مكه.

13 حنا *ḥinna*. Colloquial personal pronoun (for further examples see notes to lns 11 and 12 [2x]).

[14] ما عندنا طاعه. Colloquial negative construction (= Classical لا طاعة لنا).

[15] قايمين. For the frozen sound masculine plural form in *-īn* see text II.9, n. 13 and text 'Syria 2', n. 10. Further examples of the same in thisln. 8 مستعينين and ln. 12 مجتهدين.

[16] فدين = في الدين.

[17] Qurʾān 9 (*Al-Tawba*), 28. The canonical text reads: يا ايها الذين امنوا إنما المشركون نجس فلا يقربوا المسجد الحرام [بعد عامهم هذا] 'O you who believe! The Associationists are nothing but impure, so let them not approach the Inviolable Mosque [after this year of theirs]'.

[18] سار = صار.

[19] يرظي = يرضي.

[20] اليا. Colloquial *ilya*, cf. Classical الى.

[21] في شان. Colloquial prepositional phrase *fi šān* 'for, for the sake of'.

[22] راع 'owner', hence 'provided with' (colloquial = Classical ذو, صاحب); cf. de Landberg (1920–1942, II:1321).

[23] نرقب *ragab* 'to wait for' (colloquial).

[24] هذ. Short form of the colloquial demonstrative *hāḏa*.

[25] ما لزم عرفناك. Notice the asyndetic construction of لزم, and the perfect form of the auxiliary verb.

[26] من is crossed out in the manuscript.

[27] يوم الوفا. 77th (or 78th) day of the lunar year, 18 Rabīʿ al-ʾawwal.

31. EXCERPTS FROM YAʿQŪB ṢANŪʿ'S ABŪ NAḌḌĀRA ZARʾA AND ʿABD ALLĀH AL-NADĪM'S AL-USTĀḎ

Liesbeth Zack

This chapter presents excerpts from two of the most famous 19th-century Egyptian newspapers: *Abu naḍḍāra zarʾa* 'The man with the blue eyeglasses', founded by Yaʿqūb Ṣanūʿ in 1878, and *al-Ustāḏ* 'The professor', founded in 1892 by ʿAbd Allāh al-Nadīm. Both were satirical newspapers, critical of Egyptian society and of the regime, and both were (partially) written in Egyptian Arabic, which could be read aloud in order to make them accessible to the uneducated masses. This makes them interesting subjects for a comparative linguistic study.

Yaʿqūb Ṣanūʿ[1]

The Jewish Egyptian journalist and playwright Yaʿqūb Ṣanūʿ, also known as James Sanua, was born in Cairo in 1839. His father Rafāʾīl was a Jewish merchant who moved from Livorno in Italy to Cairo at some point in the 19th century, while his mother,

---

[1] This is an abridged version of section 2 in Zack (2014). See also http://kjc-sv036.kjc.uni-heidelberg.de:8080/exist/apps/naddara/biography.html for a short introduction to Ṣanūʿ's life and works.

 https://doi.org/10.11647/OBP.0208.37

Sara, was a Cairene by birth. Rafāʾīl Ṣanūʿ worked as an adviser to Aḥmad Pasha Yagan, the nephew of Muḥammad ʿAlī Pasha.[2] Aḥmad Pasha Yagan sponsored Yaʿqūb during the course of a three-year period of academic formation in Livorno, where he studied political economy, international law, the natural sciences, and the fine arts. Upon his return to Cairo, Ṣanūʿ began work as a teacher.[3] He became a follower of the great thinker Jamāl al-Dīn al-Afġānī, who encouraged him to apply his literary skills to the cause of reform and suggested using the theatre as an instrument of public education. The Khedive Ismāʿīl had opened two theatres in Cairo and Alexandria in 1869, on the occasion of celebrations in honour of the completion of the Suez Canal. Ṣanūʿ translated some European plays into Arabic, but also wrote others in both colloquial and Classical Arabic, setting them in Egyptian society. He was an important figure in the birth of Egyptian drama, and became known as the 'Molière of Egypt'. However, since his plays contained satirical portrayals of Egyptian society and criticism of government officials, Ismāʿīl withdrew his support and banned his plays in 1872, ending his career as a dramatist.[4]

---

[2] See Gendzier (1966, 17).

[3] Gendzier (1966, 6–17, 19).

[4] Gendzier (1966, 29–38).

In 1878, Ṣanūʿ published the first issue of his satirical newspaper *Abu naḍḍāra zarʾa* 'The man with the blue eyeglasses',[5] which was his own nickname. The publication was written in large part in colloquial Egyptian Arabic and contained imaginary dialogues and letters, sketches, fictitious minutes from meetings and dreams. In 1878, Ṣanūʿ was banned from Egypt because of his criticism of the regime. He consequently settled in Paris, but continued to publish the newspaper.[6] The final issue appeared in December 1910. Ṣanūʿ remained in France for the rest of his life, even when changed political circumstances would have allowed him to return to Egypt. He died in Paris in 1912.[7]

The excerpt presented here is from the fifth issue of *Abu Naḍḍāra* and discusses how Yaʿqūb Ṣanūʿ collected the materials for his newspaper. It is a fictional dialogue between Abu Naḍḍāra and Abu Khalīl. The dialogue is a stylistic device often used by Ṣanūʿ, as well as by the journalist ʿAbd Allāh al-Nadīm (1843–

---

5 The first issue can be found here: http://kjc-sv036.kjc.uni-heidelberg.de:8080/exist/apps/naddara/journals.html?collection=/db/data/commons/Abou_Naddara/Journals/1878/1_Garidat-Abi-Naddara-Zarka_issues-001-015. It was published on 21 Rabīʿ al-awwal [12]95 AH, which corresponds to 25 March 1878.

6 Due to censorship, he had to change the name of the newspaper regularly. There are issues entitled *Al-naḍḍārāt al-miṣriyya* 'the Egyptian spectacles', *Abu ṣuffāra* 'the man with the whistle', and *Abu zummāra* 'the man with the oboe', among others.

7 See also this webpage published by Heidelberg University for more information on *Abu naḍḍāra* and the other journals that Ṣanūʿ published in Paris: http://kjc-sv036.kjc.uni-heidelberg.de:8080/exist/apps/naddara/intro_journals.html. Scans of all the journals are available on this website as well.

1896) fifteen years later in his magazine *al-Ustāḏ*, as the next section demonstrates.

ʿAbd Allāh al-Nadīm

The Egyptian reformist ʿAbd Allāh b. Miṣbāḥ al-Ḥasanī, known as al-Nadīm 'the boon companion', was born in 1843 in Alexandria, where he studied at the mosque of Ibrāhīm Pasha. After completing his education, he worked for some time as a telegraph officer in the Delta and as an *udabātī*, an itinerant versifier.[8] Later he owned a lingerie shop, in order to earn a living beside his work as a journalist. The shop doubled as a literary salon, where poets and writers met.[9] In 1879, al-Nadīm joined the secret society *Jamʿiyyat Miṣr al-Fatāt/Union de la Jeunesse Egyptienne*, but soon left it to establish *al-Jamʿiyya al-Khayriyya al-Islāmiyya* 'the Islamic Charitable Society'. In 1881, he first founded the satirical magazine *al-Tankīt wa-l-Tabkīt* 'Joking and reproaching' and then *al-Ṭāʾif* 'The wanderer'. The latter became the organ of the followers of ʿUrābī Pasha, an Egyptian army colonel who aimed at ending the British occupation of Egypt. After the failure of the ʿUrābī revolt in 1882, al-Nadīm spent years in hiding and was finally arrested in 1891, exiled, and subsequently pardoned in 1892. Upon his return to Egypt, he founded the satirical newspaper *al-Ustāḏ* 'The professor', which ran from August 1892 until

---

[8] See Sadgrove (2012).

[9] It was not uncommon in that era for shops to double as literary salons; see Doss (1998, 144).

June 1893. He was then once again exiled and spent the rest of his life in Istanbul, where he died in 1896.[10]

Al-Ustād̲ is a weekly satirical newspaper in which criticism of the Egyptian regime, the British occupation of Egypt, and various social issues are addressed, often in the form of dialogues. The first excerpt from *al-Ustād̲* that is presented here is part of a series of dialogues entitled *Madrasat al-banāt* 'the girls' school'. The dialogue is between Zakiyya and Nafīsa. Nafīsa attends the girl's school and Zakiyya asks her about the subjects she is learning, questioning the usefulness of subjects such as French and English. The second excerpt is also a dialogue between two women, Laṭīfa and Dimyāna. The text shows the problems caused by drinking alcohol. This fragment is interesting from a linguistic point of view, because *q is consistently written with a *hamza*, imitating the way it is pronounced in Cairene Arabic.

Transcription: *Abu naḍḍāra zarʾa*

Excerpt from *Abu naḍḍāra zarʾa*, issue 5, year 1, 21 Rabīʿ T̲ānī 1295,[11] 1

(أبو خليل) أنت عبارتك ايه يابو نظاره – بقى ما عندكش لا شغله ولا مشغله الا كتابة بسلامتها الجريده – الظاهر كدا لانّ من اول نمره لتانى نمره مضت تقريبا جمعتين ومن تانى نمره للتالته جمعه وحده فقط ومن التالته للرابعه نصف جمعه ومن الرابعه للخامسه يا دوب يومين – دا احنا ما لحقناش نهضمها والله – لا بد ان مسكتك صخونة كتابة الجرانيل – طيب بس وبتجيب الكلام ده كله من أين – دول أولاد البلد بيقولوا انك فى الليل بتقلع برنيطتك دى ام طرحه وسترتك ونظارتك الزرقا وبتلبس لك عمه تخليها عشرة أرطال فى الميزان

[10] See Sadgrove (2012).

[11] = 24 April 1878.

وجبه فروزى وافطان شاهى وحزام طرابلسى وصرمه حمرا وخزرانة أولاد الفن فى يدك وبتلزق دقنك دى العريضه بحبتين صمغ حتى انها تبقى سكسوكه وتدخل فى قهوة اللياتى مش على شان تشرب حشيش الله لا يقدر انما على شان ما تسمع كلام بنى شدّاد اللطيف وتلتذ بنكاة ونوادر ظريفه تدرجها فى صحيفتك الشهيره التى صبحت فى افمام العالم كالشهد والسكر وبوظت عن قراءة الجرانيل العظيمه المفيده الكلام ده صحيح ولا كذب

(ابو نظاره) اهو من ده على ده

(أبو خليل) قال وبتروح فى دكاكين اخواننا التجار وتجتمع هناك على الشبان الفصحاء وتستنشأ منهم الاخبار الظريفه ثم انك تسبكها فى محاورات ولعب تياترو كلعبة القريداتى[12] التى حصلت فى أيام الغز وما أشبه

(أبو نظاره) أى نعم

(أبو خليل) والقصد من جريدتك الهذلية دى ايه

(أبو نظاره) تفكيه العالم واتطلاعهم على الجد بصورة الهذل

(أبو خليل) عفارم عليك يابو نظاره – واحنا يا أولاد البلد فاهمين الامر ده محبتك بتزيد يومى فى قلوبنا وبتطلب لك التوفيق – انما يا اسفاه رايح ينوبك ايه من التعب ده كله اديك ألفت لك كتب بالافرنجى مدح فى مصر وترجمت أفخر قصايد العرب لاشهار علم الاداب الشرقى فى الغرب وحسن اخلاقهم وحرية ديانتهم وما أشبه وأسست لنا تياترو عربى وصنفت لك مقدار تلاتين كوميديه من قريحتك نثر واشعار وصرفت فيها دم قلبك وعلمت ابناء الوطن التشخيص بكل مهاره فى التياترو وشرعت فى كتابة جرانيل بجميع اللغات الاوروباويه واخترعت ادوار غنا عربيه وطبقتها على موسيقه فرنساويه – يا ترى كسبت ايه من كل ده – بس ربيت لك أعداء وضديات [...]

Translation

(Abu Khalīl) What's the matter with you, Abu Naḍḍāra? You haven't got anything to do now other than writing this fine[13] news-

[12] This is a typo. It was actually called القرداتي *al-quradāti*. It was published in *Abu Naḍḍāra* issue 4, 14 Rabīʿ Ṯānī 1295 = 17 April 1878, 2–4.

[13] Literally 'with her well-being'. See Spiro (1895, 288): "بسلامته الخواجه دا this fine gentleman, this good fellow."

paper, or so it seems, because between the first issue and the second approximately two weeks passed, and only one week between the second and the third, and half a week between the third and the fourth, and hardly two days between the fourth and the fifth. By God, we haven't had time to digest it, surely newspaper writing fever has taken hold of you. All right, so where do you get all this talk from? The guys in town say that in the evening you take off this hat of yours with its veil and your coat and your blue eyeglasses, and put on a turban that weighs ten pounds on the scale, and a turquoise robe, a striped caftan, a belt from Tripoli,[14] and red shoes, with an artist's bamboo cane in your hand, and you glue that wide beard of yours with two bits of gum so it becomes a goatee. Then you go into the *Layyāti*[15] coffee shop, not to smoke hash, may God forbid, but to listen to the amusing words of the hashish-smokers[16] and to enjoy the jokes and the funny anecdotes that you put in your famous newspaper, which has become like honey and sugar in everyone's mouths and has detracted people from reading the great, useful newspapers. Is that right or is it a lie?
(Abu Naḍḍāra) A bit of this and a bit of that.

---

[14] "طرابلس *ṭarablus* silk sash of Syrian make" (Spiro 1895, 362).

[15] This is probably the name of the coffee shop or its owner. The *layy*, pl. *layyāt*, is the flexible tube of the water pipe (*šīša*), and *layyāti* is the *nisba*-adjective referring to this: 'the one with the water pipe tubes'.

[16] See Badawi and Hinds (1986, 456b). The *faʿʿāl*-form is an intensive noun, so بنى شدّاد means 'those who take pulls [from the water pipe] often'.

(Abu Khalīl) It is said that you go to the shops of our colleagues the traders and meet up there with the eloquent young men looking for funny news stories, which you then transform into dialogues and theatre plays like the play about the monkey keeper, which took place in the days of the Mameluks,[17] and the like.
(Abu Naḍḍāra) That's correct.
(Abu Khalīl) And what is the purpose of this humorous newspaper of yours?
(Abu Naḍḍāra) Amusing people, and presenting serious information in the form of humour.
(Abu Khalīl) Well done, Abu Naḍḍāra! We, the people of this country, understand this matter. Our love for you is growing daily in our hearts, and we wish you all the best of luck. But oh grief, what is all this trouble going to get you? You've[18] written books in European languages praising Egypt, you have translated the most wonderful poems of the Arabs in order to spread the word in the West about Oriental literature, their good manners, their freedom of religion, and the like, and you've founded an Arab theatre for us and have written around thirty comedies using your great talent, prose and poems, and have paid a very high price for it,[19] and you have taught the people of our country to perform skilfully in the theatre, and you have started writing

[17] The full title: القرداتى—لعبه تياتريه تاريخية حصلت فى أيام الغز سنة 1204 'The monkey keeper—A historical theatre play taking place in the days of the Mameluks in the year 1204'. The year corresponds to 1789–1790 CE.

[18] Lit. 'there you are'.

[19] Lit. 'you have spent the blood of your heart'.

newspapers in all European languages and have created Arabic songs and set them to French music—so I wonder what you have gained from all of this? You have only made[20] enemies and hostilities. […]

Transcription: *Al-Ustāḏ*

Excerpt 1: *al-Ustāḏ* year 1, no. 11, 1 November 1892, 246

مدرسة البنات

زاكيه ونفيسه

.ز. انت رحت للمعلمه النهار ده .ن. انا في المدرسة .ز. تتعلمي ايه في المدرسة يا اختي .ن. اتعلم الكتابة والقراءة والفرنساوي والخياطة والبيانو وعندنا ناس يتعلمو الانكليزي وناس يتعلمو الرقص الافرنجى .ز. طيب الكتابه والقراءة قلنا آهي تنفع تقعدي يوم تقرى في المصحف الشريف والا في كتاب تعرفي منه امور دينِك والفرنساوي والانكليزي تعملي به ايه هوانت رايحه تجوزي فرنساوي والا انكليزي .ن. لأ دلوقت كل اولاد الناس الكبار يتعلمو الفرنساوي والا الانكليزي بلكي الواحده تتجوز واحد من اللي يعرفو اللغة تبقى تتكلم وياه .ز. هوا يختي اللي رايحه تتجوزيه موش ابن عرب والا ابن ترك .ن. ايوه .ز. طيب اتعلمي انت العربي والا التركي اللي يكلمونا به اهل بلادنا واما الراجل اللي رايح يفوت لغته ويكلم حريمه بالفرنساوي والا بالانكليزي وهوا ابن عرب والا ابن ترك دا يبقي قليل الذوق هوا عارف ان احنا يا بنات الشرق فرنساويه والا انكليز لما يكلمنا بلغتهم .ن. بقى على كدا انت ما تعرفيش جرى ايه في الدنيا دلوقت بعض بنات الشام بيتعلموا في المدارس اللغات البرانية وازواجهم رخرين[21] .ز. طيب دول لبسوا آلا افرنكه وطلعوا في السكه بهدوم البيت زي ستات الافرنج واحنا يللي ما نطلع من بيوتنا الا متغطيين ولا نجتمع بالرجاله الغُرب ولا نروح تياترو ولا باللو احنا واخواتنا المحجوبين في الشام نتعلم اللغات دي ليه [...].

Translation

The Girls' School

Zakiyya and Nafīsa

---

[20] Lit. 'raised'.

[21] From الآخرين, with $l > r$.

Z: Did you go to the teacher today? N: I attend school. Z: What are you learning in school, dear?[22] N: I'm learning writing, reading, French, sewing and piano, and we have people who are learning English, and people who are learning European dancing. Z: Well, writing and reading, we'd say that, yes, they are useful so one day you can sit and read the Holy Quʾrān, or a book from which you learn things about your religion, but French and English, what are you going to do with those, are you going to marry a Frenchman or an Englishman? N: No, all the upper-class children learn French or English now. A woman may marry one of those men who know the language, so she can talk with him. Z: My dear, isn't the man whom you're going to marry a descendant of an Arab or a Turk? N: Yes. Z: Well, then learn the Arabic or Turkish language used by the people of our country when they talk to us. As for the descendant of an Arab or a Turk who puts his language aside and addresses his wife in French or English, he has no manners. He knows that we, girls from the East, are neither Frenchmen nor Englishmen, when he talks to us in their language. N: That means you're not aware of what's going in the world these days. Some girls from the Levant learn foreign languages at school and so do their husbands. Z: All right, those girls are dressed 'à la European' and have taken to the streets in house clothes like European ladies, but we, who only leave the house covered up, don't get together with strange men and don't go to the theatre or the ball, why should we and our veiled sisters in the Levant learn these languages […].

[22] Lit. 'my sister'.

Transcription: *Al-Ustāḏ*

Excerpt 2: *al-Ustāḏ* year 1, no. 7, 4 October 1892, 149–50

لطيفه ودميانه

د. نهارك سعيد. ل. نهارك سعيد مبارك دا إيه آل على رأْي اللي آل غيبوا عام وطلّوا يوم. د. انا كنت عُئْبال عندك في فرح ام جرجس وانت تعرفي انها حبيبتي ووحدانيه والواحده لمَّا يبأَى عندها زحمه زي دي متعرفشي اللي يجي مِ اللي يروح. ل. فيكِ البركه والنبي انك تعرفي الواجب يا اَم حنين. إِحنا افتكرناكِ ديك الليله واحنا عند ستي حنيفه وأُلنا يا رِيت ام حنين هنا وتتفرج. د. هيا كان عندها حاجه يختي. ل. بالك يعني حاجه زي فرح ولَّا عزومه. د. أَيوه بئُول. ل. لا دا اَحنا كنا آعدين بنتكلم في السكارى وغلبهم وهيا بتحكي لنا على ست نجيبه وانا باحكي لها على همي وغلبي شويه وجوزها داخل واترمى في وسطنا وأَعدنا نضحك عليه وأُلنا يا ريت ام حنين هنا. د. الكلام دا كان ليلة ايه. ل. ليلة التلات اللي فات. د. كنتو تعالوا انتم شوفوا همي وغلبي ولَّا انتو عندكم لفندي بتاعكم بيسكر كل جمعه ليله ولَّا كل شهر ليلتين ادُّور علي انا اللي لفندي بتاعنا يطلع من ديوانه على الخماره يفضل يشرب من المخسوف الزبيب لمَّا يبأَى ما هو شايف يمشي ويجيني مدهول[23] وساعات يئع في السكه ويجي مِظَروط هدومه والإِرشين اللي في جيبو يأْعم. والعَدْره يختي بئيت مستلفة من حنونه حَأ الطحين مرتين وتلائيني خايفه تكتر علي الديون وتخليني ابيع الحتتين السيغه اللي فاضلين عندي [...].

Translation

Laṭīfa and Dimyāna

D: Good day. L: Good day to you. What is this? Like the famous saying, you disappear for a year and then you show up for one day. D: I was at the wedding of Umm Girgis,[24] may your children follow, and you know that she's my dear friend and that she's lonely, so when someone has a crowd like that, you don't know

[23] Read *midahwil*, not *madhūl*.

[24] Lit. 'the mother of Girgis', the *kunya*: calling a man or woman by the name of their eldest son.

who's doing what.[25] L: God bless you, by the Prophet, you are always ready to help,[26] Umm Ḥinēn. We remembered you the other night when we were at Mrs. Ḥanīfa's and we said, we wish Umm Ḥinēn were here to watch this. D: Did she have something going on, sister? L: Do you have something specific in mind like a wedding or an invitation? D: Yes, that's what I'm saying. L: No, we were sitting and talking about drunkards and the nuisance they cause, and she was telling us about Mrs. Nagība and I was telling her a bit about my worries and misery, when her husband came in and fell among us and we sat laughing at him and said, we wish Umm Ḥinēn were here. D: What night did that happen? L: Last Tuesday night. D: You should have come and seen my worries and misery, your man is getting drunk one night a week or two nights a month, now it's my turn, our man leaves his office and goes straight to the bar and he keeps on drinking that damned[27] arrack[28] until he can't see where he's walking and comes to me a wreck, and sometimes he falls in the street and comes home with his clothes soiled and the few piastres[29] that were in his pocket have fallen out. By the Virgin, my sister, I have borrowed the money for the flour from Ḥannūna[30] twice and I'm

---

[25] Lit. 'you don't know the one who's coming from the one who's going'.

[26] Lit. 'know your duty'.

[27] Lit. 'sunken into the ground', see Spiro (1895, 171a) ولد مخسوف 'a damned boy, a young rascal'.

[28] A liquor made from raisins, see Spiro (1895, 246a) "عرقي زبيب native whiskey made of raisins."

[29] Lit. 'the two piastres'.

[30] Diminutive of endearment of her son's name Ḥinēn.

afraid[31] that I will get more into debt and will have to sell the few bits[32] of jewellery I still have [...].

Commentary

Orthography[33]

(Ṣ = Ṣanūʿ, N1 = Nadīm, first excerpt, N2 = Nadīm, second excerpt)

*ʾ has mostly disappeared in medial and final position, e.g., حمرا *ḥamra* (Ṣ), خايفه (N2), الزرقا (Ṣ). See also والعَذْره *wi-lʿadra* (N2) from والعذراء, in which the *hamza* has disappeared and the *ā* has shortened to *a*. There are, however, some exceptions, such as القراءة (N1), الفصحاء (Ṣ) and رأي (N2).

*q: Pronounced as a glottal stop in Cairene Arabic, except in loans from Classical Arabic. In Ṣ and N1, mostly written with *qāf*, e.g., قليل الذوق *ʾalīl izzōʾ* (N1), بتلزق دقنك *bitilzaʾ daʾnak* (Ṣ), except for افطان *ʾufṭān* (Ṣ). In N2, *q is consistently written with *hamza*, e.g., يبأى *yibʾa*, عئْبال *ʿuʾbāl*, والإرشين *ilʾiršēn*, حأْ *ḥaʾʾ*, أعدنا *ʾaʿadna*, ألنا *ʾulna* (compare قلنا in N1), بئول *baʾūl*. The Classical Arabic rules for writing the *hamza* are not followed here. For instance, in عئْبال *ʿuʾbāl* the *hamza* should have the *wāw* as its seat rather than the *yāʾ* because of the *u*-vowel. The same applies to بئول *baʾūl*. When a word starts with a glottal stop (< *q) followed by a long *ā*, this

[31] Lit. 'you find me afraid'.

[32] Lit. 'the two pieces'. The dual is often used to indicate 'some, a few', just like English 'a couple of'. See Woidich (2006, 114).

[33] See also Avallone (2016, 81–82), who analysed the orthography in a sample of 22 pages from *Abu naḍḍāra* and 21 pages from *al-Ustāḏ*.

is written with آ, as in آل *ʾāl*, even if this long *ā* is shortened in the pronunciation, as in آعدين *ʾaʿdīn*.

yāʾ and *ʾalif maqṣūra bi-šakl al-yāʾ* are interchangeable in N1, e.g., يبقي *yibʾa*, تقعدي *tuʾʿudi*, تقرى *tiʾri*. In N2, final *i* (*ī) is dotted and final *a* (*ā) undotted, e.g., باحكي *baḥki*, يجيني *yigīni*, السكارى *is-sakāra*, اترمى *itrama*. In Ṣ, both final *yāʾ* and *ʾalif maqṣūra bi-šakl al-yāʾ* are consistently written without dots, e.g., طرابلسى *ṭarabulsi*.

The 3ms possessive suffix *-u* can be written with *wāw*, e.g., جيبو *gēbu* (N2).

Plene writing of short vowels occurs in موش *muš* and هوا *huwwa* (N1) and in هيا *hiyya* (N2). In the verb, the final 2fs vowel *-i* is written *plene*, e.g., تتعلمي *titʿallimi* (N1) and تعرفي *tiʿrafi* (N2). However, in N1 انت *inti* is written without the final vowel *-i*, which is indicated with a *kasra* in N2: وانتِ. Also, the final vowel of *-ki* is indicated with a *kasra*: افتكرناكِ *iftakarnāki* (N2), rather than with the letter *yāʾ*.

Elision of letters: *min* is abbreviated to *mi-* in N2: مِ اللي for من اللي. In N2, *ya-xti* is written as يختي, while N1 writes both يا اختي and يختي.

In N1, both *walla* 'or' and *wala* 'nor' (the second part of the negation 'neither… nor') are written as والا. *walla*: في المصحف الشريف والا في كتاب; *wala*: موش ابن عرب والا ابن ترك. In N2, *walla* is written as ولّا with a *šadda*.

tāʾ marbūṭa is randomly written with or without dots in N1 and N2: المدرسة *ilmadrasa* (N1), رايحه *rayḥa* (N1), and consistently without dots in Ṣ (except in genitive constructions), e.g., شغله

šuġla, سكسوكه *saksūka*. In genitive construction, the dots are always written in the three texts: مدرسة البنات *madrast ilbanāt* (N1), ليلة التلات *lelt ittalāt* (N2), حرية ديانتهم *ḥurriyyit diyanithum* (Ṣ). In بنكاة *bi-nikāt* (Ṣ), *tāʾ marbūṭa* is written instead of *tāʾ*.

ʾalif fāṣila is sometimes written and sometimes left out: يتعلمو and بيتعلموا (N1), كنتو تعالوا (N2).

The *l* of the article is once assimilated to the next 'sun' letter: ادُّور *iddōr* (**ildōr*) (N2). In لفندي *lafandi*, the *i* of the article *il-* is elided, as is the *ʾalif* of the word افندي (N2).

Interdentals: **ḏ̣* is written with ظ in ابو نظاره *Abu naḍḍāra* (Ṣ). However, it is written with ض in the very first issue of the newspaper. The *ḏāl* in الهذليه and الهذل (Ṣ) is a hypercorrection; the root in Classical Arabic is HZL. Ṣanūʿ tends to write **ḏ* with ذ, e.g., كذب *kizb* ~ *kidb*.

Emphasis: صخونة is written with ص instead of س in Ṣ.

Shortened long vowels are generally written with long vowels, e.g., فاهمين *fahmīn* (Ṣ), الرابعه *irrabʿa* (Ṣ), رايحه *rayḥa* (N1), فاضلين *faḍlīn* (N2). An exception is وحده *waḥda* (Ṣ).

In Ṣ, historical spelling is used more often than in N1 and N2, for instance: من أين *minēn*, نصف *niṣf* ~ *nuṣṣ*. It is unclear in the second case if the Classical or dialectal pronunciation is intended, because Ṣanūʿ tends to use some Classical Arabic vocabulary.

اتطلاعهم (Ṣ), the *maṣdar* of form eight of the root ṬLʿ (اطّلاعهم) is an odd spelling and could be a typo, perhaps influenced by اتطلّع of form five.

Morphology

The demonstrative ده is not fixed to the noun in النهار ده *innaharda* (N1).

The feminine distal demonstrative ديك 'that' is used for something that has been mentioned before: ديك الليله 'that night' (N2). Nowadays, the distal demonstratives are ms *dukha*, fs *dikha*, and pl *dukham/dukhum/dukhumma*.[34] However, until the beginning of the twentieth century, forms without the suffix *h-* were still found: *dāk*, *dīk*, *dōk*,[35] especially in adverbs of time such as *dīk innahār* 'that day',[36] *dāk innōba* 'that time'.[37]

In N2, 2pl and 3pl forms with *-u* and *-um* are interchangeable: انتو and انتم are found in the same sentence; يأعم *yiʾaʿum*.

يئع (N2) may reflect *yiʾaʿ*, which has been reported in 19th-century texts.[38] Nowadays, it is pronounced *yuʾaʿ*.[39] However, it may

[34] See Woidich (2006, 46).

[35] See for instance Hassan (1869, 88). These forms are very old; there are examples such as *dīk ilʿuyūn* from 14th-century Judaeo-Arabic texts, see Palva (1993, 181–83).

[36] Gairdner (1917, 209).

[37] El-Tantavy (1848, 126).

[38] See, e.g., Spitta (1880, 223), who, however, remarks that it was more common in the countryside than in Cairo.

[39] See Woidich (2006, 81).

also reflect *yuʾaʿ*, because al-Nadīm mostly wrote the *hamza* on the *yāʾ* when occurring in the middle of the word (see above, Orthography). The *kasra* in يِأعم *yiʾaʿum* confirms that the prefix was in fact pronounced *yi-*.

The future marker is رايح (m), رايحه (f), رايحين: رايحه تجوزي (N1), الراجل اللي رايح يفوت لغته (N1). The shortened form *ḥa-* is used in modern Cairene Arabic.

Syntax

In الحتتين السيغه (N2) the first part of the genitive construction gets the article. This construction, which can also occur with *iššuwayyit* 'the bit of…' is found in modern Cairene Arabic as well, but is 'substandard'.[40]

احنا يا بنات الشرق فرنساويه والا انكليز: In this sentence, *la*, the first part of the negation *la…wala*, is missing.

Both على شان and على شان ما 'in order to', followed by a verb in the imperfect tense, are used in Ṣ. Nowadays, the form without *ma* is more common.[41]

---

[40] Woidich (2006, 207).

[41] Woidich (2006, 386).

32. A DISGRUNTLED BISHOP: A GARSHŪNĪ LETTER FROM BISHOP DINḤĀ OF MIDYAT TO PATRIARCH PETER III

George Kiraz

Beth Mardutho K2005.72–73[1]

Document BM K2005.72–73 belongs to a larger set of documents at the archives of Deir al- Zaʿfarān near Mardin. The archive was digitised between 2005 and 2010 and the digital copies are being preserved at the Beth Mardutho Syriac Institute in New Jersey. The archive consists of ca. 10,000 documents, mostly petitions written to various Syriac Orthodox Patriarchs from Elias II (Patr. 1838–1847) to Elias III (Patr. 1917–1932). The current letter,

[1] I am grateful to Mor Philoxenus Saliba Özmen, archbishop of Mardin, for giving me permission in 2005 to digitise the archive. Thanks are due also to Ephrem Aboud Ishac, who read the penultimate version and gave many valuable suggestions. For the historical background of this period, see Dinno (2017), *The Syrian Orthodox Christians in the Late Ottoman Period and Beyond: Crises then Revival* (Piscataway, NJ: Gorgias Press).

 https://doi.org/10.11647/OBP.0208.38

dated 23 August 23 1882 (Julian), is from Bishop Dinḥā of Midyat and addressed to Patriarch Peter III (Patr. 1872–1894).[2]

We do not know much about Bishop Dinḥā. An account by the contemporary ʿAbdallah of Ṣadad (later Patriarch ʿAbdallah, 1906–1915), written in 1870, mentions three monks with this name: Dinḥā of Mashta, Dinḥā of the Monastery of Qarnā in Beth Debe (Badibe), and Dinḥā of Anḥil.[3] While Dolabani, in his history of the Patriarchs (Dolabani 1990), does not mention Peter consecrating a bishop by this name, our Dinḥā has been identified by Abraham Garis as the monk from Anḥil.[4] Dinḥā's mother tongue was Neo-Aramaic Ṭūroyo (Surayt). A native of Mosul, Peter III's mother tongue was Arabic.

It appears that the congregation in Midyat wrote to the Patriarch, complaining about Bishop Dinḥā (lns 6–7). The Patriarch in turn wrote to Dinḥā (lns 4–6) to rebuke him (verso ln. 12). Dinḥā then writes back—in this document—to defend himself. The charge seems to be that Dinḥā nominated a brother or cousin (or both) to be elected for the Midyat *majlis*. Per the Ottoman Tanzimat, towns were to have councils with a specific number of Muslims, Christians, and Jews. It appears that the congregation had obtained a *firmān* from the Porte (الباب العالي) to the effect that only Syriac Orthodox individuals might serve in the Midyat *majlis* (لا مسلم ولا نصراني غير ملت سريان القديم بس, lns 12–13) which

[2] Peter III was later renumbered by Aphram Barsoum as Peter IV, counting the Apostle Peter as Peter I.

[3] I obtained the information about the three Dinḥās from Elio Aydin, who replied to my Facebook post of 24 October 2017.

[4] Reply to my Facebook post of 24 October 2017.

would have caused problems with the local Muslim population (there were no Jews in Midyat). It also seems that some members of the congregation, who were not getting their way, were threatening to convert, most likely to Catholicism (ln. 15). The bishop then goes on to complain about the members of his congregation (lns 16, 23–24, 27–28) and the fact that the Patriarch had sacked him (وايضا عزلتمونا صرنا ممنونين بذلك, ln. 20). He also complains that he has no salary (ln. 24) and asks if he can visit the Patriarch, presumably to discuss his case (ln. 26).

Often letters discuss more than one matter and this document is no exception. After making his complaint, Dinḥā petitions the Patriarch on behalf of one David Efendi, who is apparently working very hard, but going unpaid (verse ln. 3 ff.). "Did his mother give birth to him and offer him a *waqf*?" Bishop Dinḥā asks sarcastically. The letter ends with Dinḥā asking the Patriarch to save him "from this hell" [فقط نرجو تخلصنا من هذه النار]. A subscript mentions a matter regarding Karburan, a Kurdish-speaking Syriac Orthodox village. It seems that this village was also taken away from Bishop Dinḥā.

Transcription

Recto

1. ܒܥܡ ܡܪܢܐ ܕܒܠܛܪܟ. ܘܡܪܡܪܡܝܐ: ܕܕܘܠܐ ܕܒܡܪܘܬܐ ܐܒܘܢ
ܦܛܪܘܣ
ܐܠܒܠܐ
2. ܡܪܝ ܐܝܓܢܛܝܘܣ ܦܛܪ̈ ܕܟܘܪܣܝܐ ܫܠܝܚܝܐ ܕܐܢܛܝܘܟܝܐ ܕܗܘ
3. ܒܥܕ ܡܩܒܠܬ ܐܝܐܕܝܟܡ: ܒܥܪܨ ܘܠܘܡܢ ܘܐܚܬܪܐܡ. ܘܐܠܬܡܐܣ ܐܕܥܝܬܟܡ ܐܠܪܣܘܠܝܗ. ܐܠܡܥܪܘܨ
4. ܠܐܒܘܗ ܢܥܡ ܐܠܐܒܘܝܗ.. ܐܠܡܥܪܘܨ ܥܢܕ ܓܢܐܒܟܡ ܘܟܠܐ ܥܢܕ ܐܢܦܣܟܡ ܐܠܟܒܐ ܐܠܡܥܪܘܨ

5. ܦܝ ܫܗܪ ܐܒ ٢١ ܦܠܟܘܢܬܗ ܣܐܥܬܝܢ ܒܥܕ ܐܠܟܛܐܒ ܠܟ+ ܒܪܣܐ ܣܠܐܡܬܟ ܫܐܘܐܟܡ.. ܐܐܢܐ
6. ܘܨܠܢܐ ܟܬܐܒܟܡ ܐܠܝܢܐ ܡܟܬܘܒܗ ܡܢ ܐܗܠ ܡܕܝܢܬ ܟܠܗ ܡܟܬܒܢܐ ܡܫܐܟܗ ܘܡܣܪܐܘܗ
7. ܟܬܒܢܐ ܐܡܛܐܪ ܘܟܬܒܢܐ ܒܓܪܐܝܕܗܡ. ܒܥܕ ܗܕܗ ܐܠܡܟܐܬܒܗ ܗܘ ܡܢ ܝܡ
8. ܢܥܠܡ ܐܢܢܐ ܘܨܠܢܐ ܐܠܝ ܒܝܪܘܬ ܦܝ ܗܕܐ ܐܠܐܝܐܡ ܠܐܓܠ ܐܠܡܟܐܒܪܐܬ ܘܐܠܡܒܐܝܥܐܬ
9. ܐܠܬܝ ܡܥܗܡ ܟܢܐ ܐܢܗܡ ܘܨܠܘܗ ܙܘܐܢܐ ܒܥܫܩܐܢ.. ܘܗܕܐ ܐܠܐܝܐܡ ܡܢ ܐܝܡ
10. ٨ ܐܝܡܪ ܥܠܝ ܡܟܬܒ ܘܡܕܗܘ ܢܥܡ ܡܐ ܥܠܝ ܒܝܪܘܬ ܡܟܬܘܒܐܬ ܡܢ ܫܐܡ ܗܘܠܐ
11. ܐܠܡܥܬܘܒ ܟܫܐܘܐܟܡ ܒܬܪܘܗܡ ܥܠܝ ܡܩܬܒ ܒܝܘܗܡ ܦܪܚܢܐ ܫܝܝ ܡܢ ܥܠܝ ܐܠܟܠܐܡ
12. ܐܢܗ ܠܐ ܬܟܬܒ ܐܢܝ ܦܝ ܬܟܬܒ ܡܕܝܢܬ ܠܐ ܡܫܟܟܡ ܘܠܐ ܝܪܐܢ ܒܥܝܢ ܡܟܬܒ ܫܪܝܦ
13. ܐܠܬܝܡ ܒܫܦ. ܐܠܬܢܐ ܘܐܝܬܢܐ ܒܝܬܟܡ.. ܢܥܫ ܡܐܘܪܝܢ ܫܐܘܐܟܡ ܡܥܗ ܟܬܒܟܡ ܫܐܝܟܡ
14. ܘܬܟܠ ٦ ܐܝܐܪ ܦܝ ܐܠܐܝܐܡ ܘܡܐ ܬܟܬܒ ܐܢܝ ܡܥܘܡ ܠܐܓܠ ܐܢ ܫܟܪ ܡܐ ܝܟܬܒ
15. ܘܡܐ ܒܝܬܟܐ ܐܢܬܐܝܗܡ. ܒܬܟܬܒܟܡ ܘܐܢܬ ܥܠܝ ܐܝܫ ܒܫܟܘܫ ܐܡܛܐܪ ܥܐܠܐܝܐܡ
16. ܡܐ ܢܥܡܠ. ܘܗܕܐ ܐܠܟܬܒ ܟܬܒܗܡ ܡܫܫܝܢ ܟܬܒܐܢܝ ܟܗ ܡܪܝܡ ܒܟܠ ܐܠܐܪ ܡܪܝܘܡ
17. ܒܝܡ ܒܟܬܒܗܡ ܗܕܗ ܐܗܠ ܐܡܪܐܘܗܡ. ܥܠܐ ܐܠܬܫܪܝܢ ܡܢ ܐܡܪܐܘܐ ܐܢܪܦ.. ܡܢ
18. ܢܥܡ ܣܬܘܢܐ ܟܡܕܝܢܬ ܒܡܫܐܘܗܡ ܢܝܒ ܡܥܗܡ ܐܠܐܝܐܡ ܟܢܐ ١٢ ܐܘܝܡ ܡܫܪܝܢ ܬܟܬܒ ܠܐܓܠ
19. ܐܡܗܪ ܘܐܬܠܐܠ ܐܠܬܐܠܡܗ ܒܓܐܢܐ ܡܥܘܡ ܡܐ ܪܐܙ ܒܫܘܡ ܡܫܟܗ ܟܬܒܐܢܝ ܒܬܘܗ ܟܬܪܦ
20. ܘܡܐ ܐܡܟܢ ܐܠܡܫܠ ܒܫܘܡ ܒܫܦ ܐܒܝܐ.. ܘܐܡܪܐ ܒܟܠܡܬܢܐ ܪܘܢܐ ܡܫܟܘܪܝܢ ܒܝܬܟܡ. ܟܡܐ ܥܢܐ
21. ܒܝܢ ܫܐܘܐܟܡ ܒܪܬܐܢܗ ܒܬܟܬܒܟܡ ܟܫܦ ܢܥܡܐ ܦܝ ܟܬܒܐܢܗ ܡܫܪܡܢ ܐܠܝ ܡܪܘܗܠ. ܟܡܐ ܟܬܒܬܡ
22. ܡܢ ܐܗܠ ܡܐ ܥܠܝ ܟܢܐ ܐܪܫܡܗ ܒܥܕ ܡܢ ܐܡܫܦ ܡܕܝܢܐ ܐܪܫܡܗ ܢܐܡܐ ܡܢ ܒܝܬܟ
23. ܐܠܡܫܘܫ ܟܬܒܐܢܝ ܒܫܡܐܡ ܐܠܟܬܝܪ ܗܡ ܘܐܬܒܟܐܬܪܗ ܡܕܝܢܐ ܒܟܢܝ ܡܥܘܡ ܘܐܟܡ ܘܡܟܬܪܝܢ
24. ܘܪܪܗ ܒܫܦ ܡܥܡܢ ܒܫܘܡ ܬܟܬܒ ܡܐ ܡܥܡܢ ܐܪܫܡܗ ܒܥܝܢ ܡܕܝܢܐ ܡܐ ܟܢܐ ܡܟܬܘܒ. ܒܡܐ
25. ܢܥܡ ܡܐ ܗܘ ܡܫܘܗ ܣܟܢ ܢܟܬܐܐ ܡܢ ܐܠܟܬܪܐܬ ܐܪܬܝܫܡ ܟܟܢ ܒܟܬܒܟܡ ܒܟܬܒ ܐܠܐܪܫܡܗܘܟܬܐ ܐܢܟܡ ܟܟܢ

26. ܥܐܝܡܬ ܘܐܟܢ ܠܐ ܢܬܟܠ ܐܢܟܡ ܒܟܢܝܐ ܢܬܪ ܒܝܢ ܐܢܐܡܟܬܒܟܡ ܡܐ ܦܝܪܘܗ ܟܗܘܐ
27. ܐܠܟܬܒ ܡܢ ܙܗܪ ܐܣܐܪܡܟܘܡ ܘܫܐܘܘܗܡ ܐܡܫܐܠ ܡܪܐܡܗܡ ܟܟܢ ܒܟܬܒܗܡ ܒܟܢܝ ܐܢܝ ܡܐ
28. ܫܐܠܠ ܟܟܢ ܥܠܐܪ ܐܠܬܫܫ. ܒܡܐ ܢܥܡܠ ܐܡܟܢܐ ܡܢ ܗܕܐ ܐܠܟܬܒ ܐܠܡܫܝܢ. ܘܐܡܪܐ ܢܪܝܦ ܗܕܗ
29. ܫܢ ܐܠܬܝ ܒܪܬܐܢܗ ܬܬܟܬܒܟܡ ܒܫܐܘܗ ܗܝ ܐܬܐܡܪܐ ܒܝܬܟܡ ܢܬܟܠ ܒܝܡ ܐܠܡܟܐܬܒܗ

Verso

1. ܘܐܬܟܠ ܟܟܢ ܐܠܐܝܫܪ ܡܥܐܦ ܡܢ ܐܠܟܬܗ ܘܠܐ ܡܫܟܠܝܢ ܡܢ ܐܠܟܬܒ. ܘܗܕܐ ܫܢ ܐܠܬܝ ܒܪܬܐܢܗ
2. ܟܫܐܘܐܟܡ ܙܒܕܗ ܡܐ ܡܪܘܢܐ. ܘܥܐܝܡܬܟܡ ܡܫܟܠܝܢ ܐܡܪܦ ܐܠܟܪܒܗ ܢܐ ܒܡܫܬܪ ܟܡܐܘܪܗ
3. ܟܡܝ+ ܢܐ ܐܢܝܟܡ ܒܟܢܝܐ ܐܠܐܪܫܡܗ ܡܐ ܢܥܡܦ ܒܫܦ ܡܥܗ ܐܡܪ ܫܐܘܐܟܡ. ܘܐܡܪܐ ܡܢ ܥܪܘܪ ܒܟܝܡ
4. ܝܐܘܝ ܐܫܝܡ ܗܕܐ ܪܐܙ ܟܗ ܡܕܝܢܬ ܐܠܐܠ ܐܝܡܪ ܡܥܝܡ ܟܟܠ ܘܗܘܐܪ ܘܐܢܝ ܡܐ ܐܪܬܐܢܗ ܦܟܬܒ
5. ܪܬܠܐܠ ܡܫܟܠܝܢ ܟܟܠ ܢܥܫܦ ܫܐܘܐܟܡ ܐܢܝ ܬܐܫܪܗ ܡܐ ܡܟܬܘܒ ܗܕܐ ܪܐܙ ܡܥܝܪܙ ܐܠܟܦ

6. ܓܪܝܒ ܒܥܕ ܝܘܡ ܒܥܕ ܡܢ ܣܦܪܗ ܗܕܗ ܙܐܪܢܐ ܛܪܣܗ ܘܐܚܕ ܡܥܗܡ ܒܡܟܬܘܒܐܬ ܡܢܟܡ
7. ܠܓܪܐܬܗ ܗܕܐ ܡܚܠ ܐܡܣ ܘܟܬܒܬܗ ܘܨܠ ܘܟܠܗ ܨܐܪ ܘܨܠ ܬܐܟܠ ܘܡܥܪܒ ܡܢ ܐܠܟܘܦܣܗ ܣܠܡ
8. ܡܟܬܐܒ. ܓܘܒܗ ܢܥܦ ܘܐܚܕܗ. ܠܟܢ ܗܕܐ ܨܐܪ ܒܥܕ ܘܐܠܐܠܕ ܐܕܐ ܐܚܕ ܡܢܐ ܐܠܓܬܐܗ ܐܠܓܪܐܬܗ
9. ܡܢ ܐܝ ܡܟܐܢ ܘܗܕܗ ܨܐܪ ܟܡ ܝܘܡ ܒܪܟܬܐ ܠܟܝܢܟܡ ܘܡܢܐ ܓܐܘܒܬܗܘܗ ܒܥܕ
10. ܐܟܝܐ ܘܡܢ+ ܐܘܦܥ ܐܠܟܠܬܪ. ܦܒܪܟܬܐ ܐܡܘܓ ܠܟ ܐܕܐ ܡܢܐ ܡܝܘܪܐ ܛܐܠܒܟܡ ܒܟܝܪ ܟܦ ܐܠܥܕܓ
11. ܦܐܕܐ ܡܢܐ ܢܝܘܪ ܢܡܘܓ ܠܐܚܕ ܗܢ ܒܦ ܢܝܘܪ ܢܒܪܢ ܣܐܠܟܝܢ ܠܟܡ ܡܢܐ ܢܡܘܓ ܐܠܥܕܓ ܗܟܝܐ ܡܢܐ ܡܥܕܓ
12. ܢܒܘܣ ܘܡܪܢܟ ܠܟܝܪ+ ܦܣܢܣܗ ܐܘܪܓ ܒܟܝܪ ܐܠܐܟܝܪ ܦܡܟ ܢܪܓܘ ܐܡܟܪܝܐ ܡܢ ܗܘܗ ܐܠܟܐܪ
13. ܒܪܟܬܗ ܟܠ ܡܘܟܝܐ ٨٢ ܡ+ ܟܢ ܟܟܝܪ

ܦܝ ٢٣ ܡܐܪ ܐܟ+ ܘܡܪܣܦܐܬ

ܘܡܢܐ ܘܝܣܐ

[Stamp]

طالب من رب المنى
مطران دنحا
عبده
??١٨

Subscript

1. ܘܐܡܪܐ ܐܠܟܪܒܘܐܣܗ ܦܟܬܐܢܗܡ ܠܟܡ ܐܘܐܡ
2. ܐܠܟܝܪ ܐܦܬܟܬܗܘܡ ܡܢܗ ܓܡܝܥ ܐܘܐܡܗܡ
3. ܘܦܟܗܘܡ ܐܠܟ ܡܐܘܕܝ ܗܐ ܗܢܐ ܨܦܪ
4. ܐܡܪܗܡ ܦܡܟ ܡܟܘܢ ܡܥܗܡ ܢܛܪܟܡ ܟܠܗܘ
5. ܐܠܐܡܪ ܐܡܪܟܡ

Arabic Transcription

Syro-Arabic garshunography is a transliteration scheme. As the 22 Syriac consonants are insufficient for the 28 Arabic ones, a number of extensions are used:

1. The *bgadkpat* letters provide double usage where:

   a. ܓ <g> stands for ج and غ.
   b. ܕ <d> stands for د and ذ.
   c. ܟ <k> stands for ك and خ.

d. ܬ <t> stands for ت and ث.

2. Optional dots may be placed supralinearly to denote the plosives and sublinearly to denote the fricatives. Having said that, the dots are rarely used in this document apart from the following (I use a macron, ◌̄ or ◌̱, instead of dots in the Latin transliteration in angle brackets, < >): ܓܒܛܬܟܡ <gbṭtkm> غبطتكم (ln. 4), ܒܓܨܐܢܗܡ <bgṣ̄ʾnhm> بغضانهم (ln. 7), ܝܢܓܒܢ <yngbn> ينغبن (verso ln. 12), and ܐܦܬܟܐܪܢܐ <ʾftk̠ʾrnʾ> افتخارنا (ln. 8).

3. As there are no /g/ sounds in Arabic, so ܓ is reserved for ج as denoted above and may take an optional stroke inside it, ܓ̰ transliterated as <g>. The stroke appears in ܐܠܡܣܬܓܐܒܗ <ʾlmstgʾbh> المستجابة (lns 3–4), ܘܓܗܗ <wghh> وجهه (ln. 19), ܓܣܐܪܗ <gsʾrh> جسارة (ln. 29, with three strokes inside ܓ, perhaps to add emphasis!), and ܘܐܓܒ <wʾgb> واجب (verso ln. 1, also with three strokes).

4. The plural double dot Syāme, ◌̈, may be used on ܗ̈ <ḧ> to mark *tāʾ marbūṭa*. The only words to make use of it are: قبلة (ln. 3), المستجابة (lns 3–4), عزة (ln. 5), بصحة (ln. 5), والجماعة (ln. 23), لزيارة (verso ln. 2), مدة (ln. 4), and طاسة (ln. 5). The use of the dots on ܗ̈ <ḧ> for a proper ت appears in صارة for صارت (verso ln. 6). Inversely, we have سلامت for سلامة (ln. 5).

5. An optional dot inside ܛ <ṭ>, ܛ̇, denotes ظ but this is never used in the document; e.g., we have undotted ܡܛܒܛܗ <mṭbṭh> (i.e., written as مطبطه) for مظبطة. Note that in Jazīreh Arabic, many words with ظ correspond to MSA words with ض (cf. MSA مضبطة).

6. An optional dot above ܪ̇ denotes ض and appears only in ܒܓܨ̇ܐܢܗܡ <bgṣ̄ˀnhm> بغضانهم (ln. 7). A dottless ܪ may be either ص or ض.

Garshūnī writing sometimes uses Arabic vowels. Due to typographical constraints, these are not given in the Syriac-script text above, but are given in the Arabic script below.[5]

Recto

1. ܒܫܡ ܡܪܝܐ ܡܫܒܚܢܐ ܘܡܪܘܪܒܢܐ: ܪ̈ܘܪܒܐ ܕܥܘܡܪܢܐ ܐܒܘܢ
ܦܛܪܘܣ
ܐܠܚܒܪܐ
2. ܡܢ ܐܝܦܝܣܩܘܦܐ ܦܛܪ̈ ܕܦܘܪܫܐ ܡܪܕܝܢܝܐ ܘܐܬܪܘܬܐ ܕܗܘ
3. غُب قبلة اناملكم: بفرظٍ وتوقير واحترام. واستمداد ادعيتكم الرسوليه. المست
4. ـجابة على الدوام.. المعروظ لدى غبطتكم وصلنا عزيز احرفكم الدعا المحرر
5. في شهر اب[٢١] فتلوناه حامدين عزة الباري تع[+] بصحة سلامت سيادتكم.. ثانيا
6. ذكرت لخادمكم اخذت مظبطه من اهل مدياد لكي عملنا محابه ومرايّه
7. لبعظ اشخاص وبعظ بغضناهم. چونکی هذه المقاوله هي حق نحن
8. نوظع اخينا واو ابن عمنا في هذا الانتخاب لاجل افتخارنا وفايدتنا
9. الذي يكون لنا اسم وفايده روحاني وجسماني.. وهذا الانتخاب من اقدم
10. ٨ اشهر كان مبني ومهيّ نحن ما كان عندنا معلومات من سابق هولاى
11. المحررين لسيادتكم وغيرهم كان يوجد عندهم فرمان شديد من باب العالى
12. انه لا يجلس احد في مجلس مدياد لا مسلم ولا نصراني غير ملت سريان
13. القديم بس. اخطينا واذنبنا بذلك.. نفس ماردين سيادتكم مع عظم شانكم
14. وظعت ٦ انفار في الانتخاب وما جلس احد منهم لاجل اي سبب ما زعلوا
15. وما بدّلوا ايمانهم. وغبطتكم دايم كان تنشد عمومي ايمان بالالتماس
16. ما يمكن. وهذا البلد كلهم مفسدين كلواحد له مرم على الاخر يريدون
17. عدم بعظهم هذه اول ثمرتهم. قال السجره من ثمرتها تنعرف.. من

[5] Microsoft Word 2000 up to XP allowed one to add Arabic diacritics above Syriac-script text, but it seems that later versions do not permit this! As of May 2021, one can write Arabic diacritics on Syriac using Notepad and then copy the text into Word, though this risks the text being broken during typesetting by publishers.

18. يوم حظورنا لمدياد جمعناهم نريد منكم تنتخبون لنا ١٢ اوادم يسيرون مجلس لاجل
19. امور واشغال الطايفه عجّزنا منهم ما صار بينهم محبه كلواحد وجههُ بطرف
20. وما امكن القول بينهم بشي ابدًا.. وايضًا عزلتموناصرنا ممنونين بذلك. لما كنّا
21. عند سيادتكم عرظناه لغبطتكم ليس نبياً في بلدته مكرمن الى مرذول. بقا خادمكم
22. من اول ما كان لنا ابرشية چونكى قد+ تحسب مدياد ابرشية حاشا من ذلك
23. القسوس كلواحد بمقام البطرك هم والجماعة مدياد بعظ منهم والين ومتصرفين
24. ووزره كيف يمكن بينهم جلوس ما يمكن ابرشيه غير مدياد ما لنا معاش. بقا
25. نحن ما هو حيه حتى نقتات من التراب تصطرحم على عبدكم بعطى الابرشيه
26. كلها احلم على خادمك والّي لا نرجو تنعّم علينا نحظر بين انامِلكم ما قدره لهذا
27. البلد من زود تحاريكهم وفسادهم تكميل مرامهم على بعظهم بعظ احد ما
28. يسال على خلاص النفس. بقا نومّل تخلصنا من هذا البلد الشنيع. وايضًا نعرف هذا
29. شى الذي عرظناه لغبطتكم جساره هي تجاسرنا بذلك نرجو عدم المواخذه

Verso

1. واجب على الانسان يخاف من الله ولا يستحى من العبد. وهذا شى الذي عرظناه
2. لسيادتكم ربعه ما حررنا. وخادمكم مستنظر احرف البركه يا بحظور لزيارة
3. لقد+ يا تحلم علينا الابرشيه^حتى^ما نشوف كيف يكون امر سيادتكم. وايضًا من خصوص عبدك
4. داود افندى هذا صار لهُ مدة ثلاث اشهر يخدم ليل ونهار واحد ما اعطاه فلس
5. رجال يستحي على نفوس سيادتكم احد طاسة^ماء^ما يعطيهُ هذا صرف مقدار الف
6. غرش بعظ دين بعظ من كيسه هذه صارة طمّه واحد يمسك خزمتكار يعطى
7. اجرته هذا يبان امه ولدته وقف ولو صار وقف ياكل ويشرب من الوقفيه حتى
8. يقتات. چونكى نفس واحده. لكن هذا صاحب بيت واولاد اذا احد ما اعطاه اوجرته
9. من اين ينعاش وهذه صار كم دفعه عرظها لقدسكم وما جاوبتموه بشيٍ
10. ابدًا وقد+ اوسع النظر. فلربما تقول لي اذا ما قدرة طالعت خبزك كيف اعمل
11. فاذًا ما نقدر نقول لاحد شى كيف نقدر ندبر حالنا لمن ما نقول اعمل هكذا ما يعمل
12. ينغبن ويعرظ لقد+ فحينه ترزَّل ذلك العبد فقط نرجو تخلصنا من هذه النار
13. ܒܪܟܬܝ ܥܠ ܟܘܠܟܘܢ ٢٨ م+

ܚܣܝܐ ܚܛܝܐ
ܘܡܣܟܢܐ
ܘܡܕܝܢܐ ܕܢܚܐ

في ٢٣ حرر اب+

طالب من رب المنى
مطران دنحا
عبده
؟؟١٨

Subscript

1. وايضًا الكربورانيه فلتناهم لكن اوراق
2. الذي استنطقوهم مع جميع اوراقهم
3. رسلوهم الى ماردين ها هنا صفى
4. امرهم فقط يكون حسن نظكم عليه
5. الامر امركم

Translation

Recto

(1) In the name of the Lord your protector and the exalter of the rank of your high-priesthood, our Father, (2) Mor Ignatius, Patr[iarch] of the Apostolic See of Antioch, who is (1.5) Peter III.

(3) After kissing your fingertips with duty, honour, and respect, and procuring your Apostolic blessings which are answ- (4) ered all the time. It is petitioned to Your Beatitude:

We have received your precious letter [عزيز احرفكم], the supplication [الدعا], written (5) on 21 August. We read it praising the Almighty [عزة الباري تعالى] for the well-being [بصحة سلامت] of your Lordship.

Secondly, (6) you mentioned to your servant that you received a petition [مظبطة] from the inhabitants of Midyat, (complaining) that we have loved and favoured [عملنا محابه ومرايّه] (7) some individuals and hated others. *Çünki*, is this claim just [چونكى هذه المقاوله هي حق]? (8) That we nominate [نوظع] our brother and/or paternal-cousin to this election for our own pomp and benefit? [لاجل افتخارنا وفايدتنا] (9) To gain a name [الذي يكون لنا اسم] and benefit both spiritually and materially?

And this election (10) was set and prepared [مبني ومهىّ] 8 months ago [من اقدم]. We had no information beforehand. Those (11) who wrote [هولاى المحررين] to your Lordship and others possessed [كان يوجد عندهم] a strong *firmān* from the Porte (12) stating that no one is to sit in the *majlis* of Midyat, be he a Muslim or a Christian, unless he belongs to (13) the Old Syriac *millet* only [بس]. We have transgressed and are guilty of this... Even Mardin itself, despite the great significance of your position [مع عظم شانكم], (14) nominated [وظعت] six individuals [انفار] for the election. And not even one of them succeeded [جلس], for whatever reason. They did not become upset [ما زعلوا] (15) nor did they change their faith [وما بدّلوا ايمانهم]. And Your Beatitude always implored publicly that faith by solicitation [تنشد عمومي ايمان بالالتماس] (16) is not possible [ما يمكن]. And this region [البلد, i.e., Midyat], all of (its people) are malicious [مفسدين], each one takes a shot at the other [كلواحد له مرم على الاخر]. They seek (17) to destroy each other [عدم بعظهم]. This is the first of their fruit. He said, "The tree is known by its fruit."

Since (18) the day of our arrival in Midyat, we gathered them. "We want you to elect 12 individuals [اوادم] to form a *majlis*[6] for the (19) affairs and the business of the *ṭāʾifa* [لاجل امور واشغال الطايفه]. We are tired [عجّزنا] of them. There is no love amongst them [ما صار بينهم محبه]. Each one disagrees with the other [كلواحد وجههُ بطرف, lit. 'each one looks to a (different) side']. (20) Talking to them did not achieve anything [وما امكن القول بينهم بشي ابدًا].

[6] This would be a parish *majlis*, to be distinguished from the secular town *majlis*.

Also you dismissed us (from office) [عزلتمونا] and we are much obliged [صرنا ممنونين] for this! When we were (21) with your Lordship, we presented to Your Beatitude that "No prophet is revered in his town, but is reviled." Therefore [بقا], your servant (22) had no diocese from the beginning. *Çünki*, does Your Holiness consider Midyat a diocese? God forbid [حاشا من ذلك]! (23) The priests: each one of them considers himself a patriarch. They, along with the people of Midyat: some of them are *wālīs*, *mutaṣarrifs*, (24) and *wazirs*. How can one live with them [كيف يمكن بينهم جلوس]? It is not possible (in any) diocese, except Midyat!

We don't have a salary. Well [بقا], (25) we are not a snake to eat from dirt. Have mercy [تصطرحم] upon your servant [عبدكم] by giving [us] the (26) entire diocese. Have clemency [احلم] upon your servant [خادمك]. If not [والّى لا], we beg that you confer upon us [تنعّم علينا] to be present in front of your fingertips [نحظر بين اناملكم]. It is not possible to endure this (27) region due to the amount of their incitements and wickedness [تحاريكهم وفسادهم], taking shots at each other [تكميل مرامهم على بعظهم بعظ]. No one (28) seeks the salvation of the soul. Henceforth [بقا], we hope [نومّل] that you liberate us from this repulsive country [البلد الشنيع].

Additionally, we recognise [نعرف] that the (29) matter with which we are petitioning Your Beatitude is bold [جساره هي]. We have been bold [تجاسرنا بذلك]. We beg for pardon [نرجو عدم المواخذة].

Verso

(1) It is one's duty to fear God and not to be ashamed of the servant. It is about that that we have petitioned your (2) Lordship. We have not written a quarter of it. And your servant is awaiting [مستنظر] the words of blessings [احرف البركه, i.e., a reply], either by visiting (3) your holiness, or for the diocese to have mercy [تحلمعلينا الابرشية] until we see what the order of your Lordship is.

And also regarding your servant, (4) David Efendi: he has been serving, day and night, for three months and no one gave him a single *fils*. (5) He is a man who is envious for the sake of your Lordship [رجال يستحي على نفوس سيادتكم]. No one gives him a glass [طاسة] of water. This one spent about one thousand (6) *ghirsh*, some from a loan, some from his own pocket. This became a disaster [طمة]. (Even if) one hires [يمسك] a servant [خزمتكار], he pays [يعطى] (7) his salary. It seems that his mother gave birth to him as a *waqf*. And even if he was a *waqf*, he should eat and drink from the *waqf* (income), so he can (8) live. *Çünki*, is he only one person? But he is the head of a household [صاحب بيت] and children. If no one gives him his salary, (9) how would he live? And how many times [دفعه] did he petition your holiness and you did not answer him at (10) all. And Your Holiness is more prudent [اوسع النظر] (than this). Maybe you say to me, "if you cannot win your bread, how can you help?" [اذا ما قدرة طالعت خبزك كيف اعمل] (11) If we are unable to say anything (i.e., give orders) to anyone, how can we manage [ندبر حالنا]? To whomever we say, "do this" he does not do it, (12) gets upset [ينغبن], and then petitions your holiness. Then you rebuke [ترزّل] only your servant. We beseech you to save us from this flame.

(13) *Barekhmor* for forgiveness! [18]82 AD servant of servants
22 August of your holiness
Monk Dinḥā
[Stamp: Bishop Dinḥā]

Subscript

(1) Also, regarding those of Karburan: we left (the administration to) them [فلتناهم]. But the papers of (2) their affidavits [اوراق الذي استنطقوهم] along with all their paperwork [مع جميع اوراقهم]—(3) they sent them to Mardin. Here, their business is concluded [ها هنا صفى امرهم] (i.e., as far as I am concerned). (4) Only (i.e., we wish that), may you protect them [يكون حسن نظكم عليه]. (5) The command is your command.

Commentary

Line 1
It is common to address the Patriarch in Syriac and end with *Barekhmor*[7] (verse ln 13).

Line 3
غِبّ 'after' (al-Bustānī 1930, II:1617).
المستجابة extends from ln. 3 to ln. 4.

[7] For the use of liturgical *barekhmor* as a greeting, see Borbone (2015, 479–84).

Line 4

عزيز احرفكم (and verso ln. 2, احرف البركة). Such terms designate letters written by the Patriarch. One may refer to one's own letter addressed to a Patriarch as احرف العبودية.

Line 5

تع. Abbreviation for تعالى. A supralinear line, sometimes with a vertical stroke, denotes an abbreviation or number.

سلامت. Orthographic variant for سلامة.

Line 6

محابة = MSA محبّة.

Line 7

چونكى Turkish *çünki* (also ln. 22 and verso ln. 8) = modern *çünkü*. It is consistently used here as an interrogative, with a disapproving tone, where the answer is negative.

اخينا واو ابن عمنا. There is either a scribal error involving repetition of وا (in which case, read اخينا وابن عمنا) or a conjunction has been prefixed to او.

Line 10

مهىّ = MSA مهيأ.

هولاى /hawalā/ (as pronounced today in the liturgical practices of Mardin) = MSA هؤلاء.

Lines 12–13

ملت سريان قديم. This refers to what we call today Syriac Orthodox. The designation قديم goes back to the 18th century to distinguish the older Syriac Orthodox from the then newly separated Syriac Catholics.

Line 13

بس /bas/. Colloquial for 'only'.

اخطينا = MSA أخطأنا.

Line 17

السجرة من ثمرتها تنعرف (Luke 6.44); سجرة = MSA شجرة.

Line 18

مجلس. This is a parish *majlis* 'council' rather than the town's secular *majlis*.

يسيرون. Probably /yusayyirūn/ 'to manage', but <s> could have been written for /ṣ/ to form /yaṣīrūn/ 'to become'.

Line 19

كلواحد = كل واحد. An orthographic calque from Syriac ܟܠܚܕ <klḥd> for ܟܠ ܚܕ <kl ḥd>.

Line 21

ليس نبيا في بلدته مكرمن (Luke 4:24). Notice the use of ن for *tanwīn.*

Line 25

تصطرحم = MSA تسترحم.

Line 26

والّى = MSA والّا.

Line 28

نومّل = MSA نأمل 'we hope/wish'.

Verso

Line 3

تحلم علينا الابرشية. The phrase is not clear, if we assume بالابرشية, the sense would be 'or to have mercy upon us by (giving us) the diocese'.

Line 5

طاسة colloquial 'cup'.

Line 6

طمّه = MSA طامّه ‘disaster’.

خزمتكار colloquial < Turkish خدمتكار *hizmetkâr* < Arabic خدمة ‘service’ + Persian كار ‘worker, i.e. servant’ ʿĪsā ([1911, 255] 2016, 136).

Line 8

اوجرته = MSA أجرته.

Line 9

ينعاش = MSA يعيش.

33. AḤMAD B. MUḤAMMAD AL-JARĀDĪ: SĪRAT AL-ḴAWĀJA AL-ʾAKRAM AL-MARḤŪM HARMĀN AL-ʾALMĀNĪ

Alex Bellem and G. Rex Smith

The text is a report written by the Ṣanʿānī secretary of Hermann Burchardt, a German traveller and photographer. Burchardt was murdered by bandits in December 1909 near Ibb in the Yemen (Mittwoch 1926), along with the Italian consular official Benzoni (Farah 2002, 238–39).[1] Perhaps in response to a request for details of the journey and the murder, al-Jarādī (henceforth J) produced this report for the German and Italian authorities in Ottoman Yemen in early 1910. The text below is that edited by Eugen Mittwoch in 1926 from two manuscripts which, he states, are in Berlin and the Ambrosiana in Milan and which appear to have been written at different times and without connection one with the other (Mittwoch 1926, 6–7). The MSS are so far untraced and the text below is an exact copy of Mittwoch's edition. The

[1] He had undertaken several expeditions in Ethiopia and Yemen, some authorised, others not. When the Italian authorities insisted that the Sublime Porte find and punish the murderers, the Ottomans branded Benzoni a spy.

 https://doi.org/10.11647/OBP.0208.39

language is clearly Literary Mixed Arabic (LMA) and is dealt with in some depth below.

Transcription

Mittwoch (1926, 16.3–18.5)

وبعد ما نسمنا فيها ثلاثه ايام عزمنا منها ومعانا خمسه انفار من اهالي ذمار[2] محافظين فتوكلنا
على الله ونيتنا نعرف رداع[3] فسافرنا على السلامه والعافيه وخطينا من قيعان كنا نبسر الرباح
فيها والذياب مثل التراب طول اليوم ووجهنا تبت قريت سنبان ودخلنا امسينا عند يهودي
اسمه شمعون لان المقهويين معدومين في سنبان فادخلنا اليهودي المذكور مكان فيه قدر
ميتين سفره بيدبغهن والقمل ملانهن فهجمين علينا القمل حتى اسهرنا سهر عظيم ويوم ثاني
الخميس خامس شهر القعده[4] عزمنا من سنبان وخطينا من بيت المصري ودخلنا قاع فيه
الرباح ملانه وخطينا من قريت ملح وقريت المصلا ولقينا باب القريه صانع بيشتغل فريد
رداعيات هو وثلاث بناته فاخذ الخواجه رسم الصانع وبناته واعطاهم اربعه غروش وعزمنا من
عندهم ولقينا في الطريق خمسين جمل محملات ملح فاخذ الخواجه رسم الجمال برضا
الجمالين وسلم لهم فلوس وعزمنا فاشرفنا على مدينت رداع ودخلناها بالسلامه والعافيه
ووجهنا تبت السمسره الكبيره الموجوده في وصط السوق حق مدينت رداع ولم وافقت
الخواجه وبعد ذلك شلينا جميع القراش للحكومه[5] وبقيين فيها والشيخ صالح ابن صالح
الطيري موجود في المدينه فسرح الخواجه وكاتبه سلمو عليه لانه قايمقام واضافهم براس غنم
هم والعسكر المحافظين والخواجه وكاتبه طلعو الى القلعه وهي اعلا من جميع الدور حق
رداع ويوم ثاني سرح الخواجه وكاتبه والنبهاني واخذ الخواجه رسم العامريه من الاربع

[2] Ḏamār is a town some 50 miles due south of Ṣanʿāʾ; al-Hamdānī (1884–1891, 55, 80, 104, etc.), Yāqūt (1979, III:7). Interestingly, it has the *faʿāli* pattern, along with other place names in the Arabian Peninsula, like Ẓafār, the medieval town on the southern coast of Oman, now the name of the whole southern province of Oman; Smith (2004, 264–80, 276–77).

[3] A town about 35 miles due east of Ḏamār; Hamdānī (1884–1891, 55, 93 etc.); Smith (1974–1978, II:193), with full references. It may also be in the *faʿāli* pattern.

[4] 5 Ḏū al-Qaʿda = 18 November 1909.

[5] This must refer to the government building.

الجهات وهي اعظم العجايب بحسن عمارتها لانه عمرها السلطان عبد الوهاب[6] وصور
الخواجه جميع الجوامع وخرج الخواجه والعسكر الى قريه قريبه من رداع اسمها قريت
الجراف فاخذ رسمها والساكنين فيها يهود يستعملو المدر من كل جنس وفوق القريه
المذكوره جبل فاخذ الخواجه رسمه وبعد ذلك ان الخواجه ابسر خمسه محاريق الذي
يحرقو فيهن القص وبه فيهن عشر يهوديات بيضربين القص بمضارب من الخشب فاخذ
الخواجه رسمهن واعطاهن فلوس

Translation

[**16**] After we had taken our rest there for three days, we left, accompanied by five Ḏamārīs as guards. We set off with the intention of getting to know Radāʿ. We journeyed feeling safe and sound. We made our way through plains in which all day long we could see numerous baboons and wolves. We travelled in the direction of the village of Sanbān.[7] We entered and stayed the night in the house of a Jew called Simon, since there were no innkeepers in Sanbān. This Jew showed us into a room in which there were two hundred untreated hides with the hair still on them which he tans; they were full of lice. These lice attacked us and we just could not sleep. The next day, Thursday, 5 [Ḏū] al-Qaʿda, we left Sanbān and made our way through Bayt al-Miṣrī and entered a plain full of baboons. We passed through the villages of Milḥ and al-Muṣallā, coming across at the village gate

[6] Al-Manṣūr ʿAbd al-Wahhāb, third Tahirid sultan, 883–894/1478–1489; see Smith, (1988, 129–39, 137, 139). J is wrong here! The ʿĀmiriyya mosque and *madrasa* were built in 910/1504 by the first Tahirid sultan, al-Ẓāhir ʿĀmir (reg. 858–864/1454–1460); on the mosque's architecture mosque, see Porter (1992; 2017); Al-Radi (1997).

[7] We vocalise thus, although we can find no reference to the village in the geographical sources at our disposal.

someone working on Radāʿī rugs, he and three of his daughters. The gentleman took photographs of the workman and his daughters and gave them four piastres. We left them and en route met fifty camels laden with salt. The gentleman took a photograph of the camels with the consent of the cameleers and gave them some money. We pressed on and came to the town of Radāʿ. We went in feeling safe and sound and made our way to the large caravanserai situated in the middle of the town market of Radāʿ. But it was not to the liking of the gentleman and we then took all the animals to the government building, where they remained. Now Shaykh Ṣāliḥ b. Ṣāliḥ al-Ṭayrī was in town, so the gentleman and his secretary went to greet him, since he was governor. He gave them a meal of a goat, them and the guards. The gentleman and his secretary climbed up to the citadel, the highest building in Radāʿ. The next day **[18]** the gentleman, his secretary, and al-Nabhānī[8] went and the gentleman took photographs of the ʿĀmiriyyah from all sides, it being the greatest wonder because of the beauty of its construction, having been built by Sultan ʿAbd al-Wahhāb. The gentleman photographed all the mosques and he and soldiers left for a nearby village called al-Jirāf. He took photographs of it. Its inhabitants are Jews, who make clay pots of all kinds. Above this village is a mountain which the gentleman photographed. Then he noticed five kilns where they were burning lime and where there were ten Jewish women who were beating

[8] Earlier in the text (Mittwoch 1926, 10), J identifies Ḥusayn b. Muḥammad al-Nabhānī as a gendarme of the Zaydī tribe of Arḥab, appointed from the start of the expedition as Burchardt's escort.

limestone with wooden mallets. The gentleman took their photograph and gave them money.

Commentary

Line 1

nasam 'rest, take rest' (Landberg 1920–1942, III:2767; Piamenta 1990–1991, II:484).

ʿazam min 'depart, leave' (Lane 1863–1893, 2037–38; form I = CA form VIII, with a Yemeni source; Landberg 1920–1942, III:2289; Piamenta 1990–1991, II:326).

tawakkal ʿalā Allāh 'set off, out'; often reduced to *tawakkal* in the Yemen (Piamenta 1990–1991, II:531).

Line 2

ḫaṭī 'make ones way' (Piamenta 1990–1991, I:32; Qafisheh 2000, 175; Watson 2000, 313).

ribḥī, plural *rubāḥ*, 'baboon' (Landberg 1920–1942, II:1061).

ʾabsar/ʾabṣar 'see'; SA, and indeed Yemeni Arabic (YA) in general, allow both forms (Piamenta 1990–1991, I:32).

Line 3

tabt, tibt (or *ṭabt*) 'in the direction of' (Rossi 1939, 245; Serjeant and Lewcock 1983, 562); perhaps < *tabb, tubūb* 'row, line' (Landberg 1901, 264).

maqhawī 'keeper of small inn (*maqhāya/makhāya*)'. Smaller than a *samsara* (Rossi 1939, 143; Landberg 1920–1942, III:2538; Piamenta 1990–1991, II:416).

Line 4

sufra 'hide, untreated and with the hair still on it' (Rossi 1939, 226; Piamenta 1990–1991, II:224).

Line 6

farda, plural *farīd,* 'rug, mat' (Landberg 1920–42, III:2406; Piamenta 1990–1991, II:369).

Line 8

ʾašraf ʿalā 'reach, come to' (Landberg 1920–1942, III:2042; Mittwoch 1926, 66).

Line 9

samsara, plural *samāsir,* 'caravanserai'. Larger than a *maqhāya,* (Serjeant and Lewcock 1983, 592; Piamenta 1990–1991, I:232).

Line 10

šall 'take' (Landberg 1920–1942, III:2073); Goitein 1941, Glossary, 89; Piamenta 1990–1991, I:263).

qāriša, plural *qirāš,* 'animals' in general, but often used of cattle. Here we take it to mean Burchardt's riding animals, perhaps donkeys or mules, or both (Landberg 1920–1942, III:2474; Piamenta 1990–1991, II:393).

saraḥ 'go' (Piamenta 1990–1991, I:220).

Line 11

qāyimaqām, 'governor' (Redhouse 1890, 1429).

Line 14

istaʿmal 'make'; this meaning of the verb is not CA, nor does it find a place in the Yemeni lexicographical literature at our disposal, though Dozy (1881, II:157) gives us *fabriquer.*

Line 15

miḥrāq, plural *maḥārīq*, 'kiln' (Piamenta 1990–1991, I:90).

Line 16

quṣṣ/qiṣṣ usually appears as *juṣṣ/jiṣṣ* in CA (Lane 1863–1893, 428), as well as in the vernaculars (Piamenta 1990–1991, II:67–68); from the Persian *gaj* or *kaj* (Steingass 1930, 1016, 1074).

Linguistic Notes

The text is written in LMA and contains a mixture of Classical Arabic (CA) and Ṣanʿānī Arabic (SA), also including the use of purely CA features used outside the accepted norms of CA grammatical norms.[9] Before the detailed linguistic observations below, three general features of the grammar of the text may be highlighted here.

1) the masculine plural nominal and adjectival ending in the oblique case *-īn* in all grammatical environments; e.g., *li-anna al-maqhawiyyin* ***maʿdūmīn*** *fī sanbān* 'because there were no innkeepers in Sanbān' (ln. 3);

2) the complete lack of *ʾalif al-tanwīn*; e.g., *ʾasharnā* ***sahar ʿaẓīm*** (ln. 5);

3) the complete lack of *ʾalif al-wiqāyah*; e.g., ***yastaʿmilū*** (ln. 15).

Items of lexical interest are dealt with in the Commentary above. The following linguistic observations are presented line by line, as they occur in the Arabic text.

---

[9] For a fuller discussion of LMA and its features, see Bellem and Smith (2014, 9–10).

Line 1

maʿā-nā. SA has *maʿā*-hā with the 3fs pronominal suffix and *maʿā*- with all plural pronominal suffixes (Watson 1993, 196).

Lines 1–2

wa-niyyat-nā naʿrif radāʿ literally 'our intention [was] that we get to know Radāʿ'. No verb 'to be' is expressed and the subject noun (*niyyat-nā*) is linked to the verb (*naʿrif*) asyndetically.

Line 2

kunnā nubsir al-rubāḥ fī-hā is thus a relative clause whose antecedent is *qīʿān*.

Line 3

wa-wajjahnā. Form II = CA form V, *wa-tawajjahnā*.

wa-daḫalnā ʾamsaynā 'we went in and spent the night'. The two verbs are linked asyndetically.

Line 4

miyatayn sufra '200 hides'. The first part of the *iḍāfah* construction retains the final *nūn* of the dual ending.

bi-yadbaġ-hunn/bi-dbaġ-hunn 'which he tans', i.e., habitually, as a profession. The *bi*- prefix with the prefix conjugation verb "expresses continuous and habitual aspect" (Watson 1993, 62, 78 ff.); "une valeur de concomitance" (Naïm 2009, 72). The feminine singular antecedent, *sufra*, is followed in the asyndetic relative clause by the feminine plural pronominal suffix *-hunn*.

fa-hajjamayn ʿalay-nā 'they (feminine plural) attacked us'. The feminine plural suffix conjugation is always *-ayn* in SA (Watson 1993, 56). The collective noun *qaml* serving as subject following the plural verb *hajjamayn* is construed as a feminine plural here and in the previous sentence, *wa-l-qaml malān-hunn.*

ʾasharnā. Form IV = CA form I, *sahirnā,* followed by a cognate accusative, *sahar ʿaẓīm.*

Line 5

yawm ṯānī, for *al-yawn al-ṯānī,* is used commonly in the text.

Line 6

bi-yaštaġil/bi-štaġil; see above, ln. 4.

The plural noun *farīd* is qualified by the feminine plural adjective *radāʿiyyāt.*

Line 7

ḫamsīn ǧamal muḥammalāt milḥ. The numeral is followed by the singular noun *ǧamal,* which is then qualified by the feminine plural participle *muḥammalāt.*

Line 9

fī waṣaṭ al-sūq. The *ṣād* replaces the CA *sīn* in pronunciation because of the following emphatic *ṭāʾ*.

al-sūq ḥaqq madīnat radāʿ 'the market of the town of Radāʿ'. An example of the common analytic genitive; *ḥaqq* is the only possessive linker used in YA (Naïm 2009, 115–16); it can be declined (Behnstedt 1987, 62).

wa-lam wāfaqat al-ḫawāǧa 'but it [the *samsara*] was not to the gentleman's liking'. *Lam* with the suffix conjugation negating past time—a common feature in J's text.

Line 10

šallaynā 'we took'. For the vernacular suffix conjugation of the doubled verb, see Bellem and Smith (2014, 12). Watson (2009, 114) proposes that the form is due to an '*-ay-*' infix rather than the common interpretation, that a geminate verb in the vernacular is, as it were, turned into a verb with third radical *yāʾ* and the gemination retained.

Lines 10–11

fa-saraḥ al-ḫawāğa wa-kātibu-h sallamū ʿalay-h 'the gentleman and his secretary went and greeted him'. Note that *sallamū* is plural here and linked asyndetically to the preceding clause.

Line 11

wa-l-ḫawāğa wa-kātibu-h ṭalaʿū ʾilā al-qalʿa 'the gentleman and his secretary climbed up to the citadel'. The form *ṭalaʿū* is plural.

Line 12

jamīʿ al-dūr ḥaqq radāʿ 'all the buildings of Radāʿ'. See above, ln. 9.

Line 13

*li-anna-**hu** ʿamar-hā al-sulṭān ʿabd al-wahhāb* 'because Sultan ʿAbd al-Wahhāb built it'. Note the *ḍamīr al-šaʾn*, here in bold.

Lines 15–16

ʾabsar ḫamsa maḥārīq allaḏī yaḥriqū fi-hinn al-quṣṣ 'he saw five kilns in which they were burning limestone'. In an interesting example of mixed Arabic, the indefinite antecedent *maḥārīq* (grammatically feminine singular?) is qualified by the relative clause introduced by *allaḏī* followed by the feminine plural pronominal suffix *-hinn*. The form *allī* is the usual SA relative pronoun, irrespective of the number and gender of the antecedent

(Naïm 2009, 121); *allaḏī* is the only relative pronoun used throughout the text.

Line 16

bi-yaḍribayn/bi-ḍribayn. See ln. 4 above.

34. ORA VE-SIMḤA (1917)[1]

Esther-Miriam Wagner

Transcription

בעד דאך בדאת לקהל תצללי פֿי שחרית וכדא דאך לחסיד סידור מתע אצלה פֿי ידהו ובדא יקרא פרשת העקידה,[2] וחתא ולדהו כֿדא סידור פֿי ידהו, לאכן בדא יצללי פֿי צלאת ערבית[3] וקרא באלקווי **אשר בדברו מעריב ערבים בחכמה**,[4] וחין סמע אובוה קאללו האש קאעד תצללי, דלחין וקת צלאת שחרית,[5] ואנתי תצללי פֿי ערבית גֿאובהו ולדהו, אנתי קלבת עלייא אלנהאר ורדדית אלצבאח ללמגרב וצֿללמת אלעולם בין ענייה ואנא בקית נשוף אלעולם כולהא ליל מאהושי נהאר, בהאדה ילזמני נצללי אשר בדברו מעריב ערבים בחכמה, לאין קלבת עלייא צבאחי לליל פֿי האד אלנהאר אלדי רפעתני מעאך לצלא, ורעדתני בכלאמך.

Arabic Transcription

بعد داك بدات لקהל تصللي في שחרית وكدا داك لחסיד סידור متع اصله في يدهو وبدا يقرا פרשת העקידה, وحتا ولدهو كدا סידור في يدهو لاكن بدا يصللي في صلات ערבית وقرا بالقووي אשר בדברו מעריב ערבים בחכמה, وحين سمع اوبوه قاللو هاش قاعد تصللي دلحين وقت صلات שחרית، وانتي تصللي في ערבית جاوبهو ولدهو، انتي قلبت علييا النهار ورديت الصباح للمغرب وضللمت الעולם بين عينييه وانا بقيت نشوف الעולם كولها ليل

[1] Taken from the book *Ora ve-Simha* published in Jerba in 1917. I received this book as a present from Dr Melonie Schmierer-Lee, who purchased it on Ebay.

[2] The binding of Isaac.

[3] Evening prayer.

[4] Opening of daily evening prayer.

[5] Morning prayer.

https://doi.org/10.11647/OBP.0208.40

ماهوشي نهار، بهاده يلزمني نصللي אשר בדברו מעריב ערבים בחכמה لاين قلبت علييا
صباحي لليل في هاد النهار الدي رفعتني معاك لصلا ورعدتني بكلامك.

Translation

After this, the community began to pray the morning prayer. The pious man had an original prayer book in his hand. He began to read the Parasha ha-Aqedah. His son also had the prayer book in his hand, but he began to pray the evening prayer and read with force the opening of the prayer. When his father heard (this), he said to him: "What are you praying? Whereas this is the time for the morning prayer, you are praying the evening prayer." His son replied to him: "You turned the day upside down for me, and the morning has been brought to the West, and the world has grown dark before our eyes. I began to see the whole world at night not day, and therefore I must pray the opening of the evening prayer. You turned my morning into night on this day, on which you took me with you to prayer and you made me tremble with your words."

Commentary

לקהל and לחסיד. The community and the pious man are the subjects in these clauses, so these are clear examples that here and in other places the article is spelled only with *lām* instead of a ligature of *ʾalif* and *lām*.

Geminated consonants are expressed through double spelling, as in תצללי 'prays', וצללמת 'darkened', and וררדית 'has been brought'.

The phrase מתע אצלה is somewhat unclear. מתע is the Maghrebian particle expressing belonging, *aṣl* conveys 'origin, root'. I have translated this as 'original', as this made the most sense in relation to the following story.

האש 'what'. A contraction of an emphatic particle *ha-* and Maghrebian *aš*.

The root *qʿd* is used as an auxiliary verb to express present continuous action.

The verb *baqā* is used as an auxiliary verb to express the start of an action.

The short passage, as well as the whole book from which the excerpt is taken, contains a large range of unusual connectives. For example, *bash* is used to express 'so that'.

מאהושי 'is not'.

35. A 'MANDÆO-ARABIC' LETTER FROM LADY DROWER'S CORRESPONDENCE

Charles Häberl

Transcription

1. [illegible]
2. [illegible]
3. [illegible]
4. [illegible]
5. [illegible]
6. [illegible]
7. [illegible]
8. [illegible]
9. [illegible]
10. [illegible]
11. [illegible]
12. [illegible]
13. [illegible]
14. [illegible]
15. [illegible]
16. [illegible]
17. [illegible]
18. [illegible]
19. [illegible]
20. [illegible]
21. [illegible]
22. [illegible]

 https://doi.org/10.11647/OBP.0208.41

Arabic Transcription

1. اسوثا نيهويلاخ
2. مشابا ماري بلابي داخيا
3. ماكي ياسالام عاليك يأبوس إيديك
4. كلالا شيشيان اسوثا نيهويلكون ماكتوبيچ
5. جا وانا مامنون جابات گانزا كابيرا
6. عاتاقا تاريخ مايات سانا وازرازتا واقلاستا
7. وتصطير صباغا وإناني بانيان راهمي وماجموعا
8. زيدقا بريخا من ناطراس الماندا نساوائى طريانا وأنا
9. قرا لماجموعا وانياني دارافشا ماعا الاساف
10. ماكتوبيچ جانا وأنا بال حالفايا وانا خاوئي
11. مات وطالات واحيد عازيزتي كليلا واعاد بيت هييا
12. ماعلام بيه جيت يام الاحاد عالباگداد، يام
13. رأس شاهار لماندايا، يام تامان بشاهار نگاراز،
14. شاهير تاموز
15. وانا سالامات بيت لگينزي الامفاتاش لعادليا
16. ميستار دراوار
17. ميعا ماكتوب وانا ظاليت باگداد لامان ياجيني
18. ماكتوباچ عاد نتائي تاگولين اشاوف باعاني لكاتاب
19. عازيزتي كليلا، انا موش كاداب تاگولين عات مايات رابيا
20. وانا مانا فاقير وا[انا] حاباناچ ~~تلراني~~ هايات بات هييا
21. بيت لگانزيئي صار عالايا بمايا وتامانين رابايا
22. من قير نا ولي شياخ كمات رام بر ياسمان

Translation

(1) [M]May you have health![M] (2) [M]I praise God with my pure heart.[M] (3) Makki says hello, he kisses your hand. (4) Klila Shishyan, [M]may you have good health.[M] Your letter (5) has arrived, and I am grateful. I brought a large, (6) ancient *Treasure*, a hundred years old, and an amulet, a *Liturgical Prayerbook*, (7) a ruling template, and a *Book of Refrains*. There are devotions in the *Refrains* and a collection of the Blessed (8) Oblation when we set up the

mandi. We make the *ṭaryāna*, (9) and I read the collection and the banner hymns. Unfortunately, (10) your letter came to us when I was in Ḥalfaya, my brother (11) having died, and I left afterwards. My dear Klila, I swear by the House of Life (12) that I did not know it. (13) I came on Sunday to Baghdad, (14) the first day of the Mandaean month, which we celebrate on the eighth day of (15) the month of July, and I delivered the library [to] the Justice Inspector, (16) Mr Drower. (17) He was not at his office, and I had left Baghdad when (18) your letter came. As a result, you are saying, 'I will examine the book with my eye'. (19) Dear Klila, I am not a liar, you say, 'I'll give 100 rupees', (20) and I'll be poor from it, and I truly love you, sister of the House of Life. (21) The library cost me 180 rupees. (22) From Qurna, W.Sh. Kumayt Rām bar Yasmīn.

Commentary

This is an undated letter from the personal correspondence of Stefana Drower (1879–1972) appearing here courtesy of Jorunn J. Buckley. The author of the letter is Sh. Kumayt Rām bar Yasmīn, a priest of the Mandowī family who was then resident in the city of al-ʿAmāra, roughly 340 km southeast of Baghdad. The letter details the purchase of the Drower Collection manuscripts 13, 14, and 22 (herein described as 'the *Treasure*'), which are presently in the Bodleian Library, Oxford. The letter is written in a form of colloquial Arabic similar to the Iraqi standard, but with a few unexpected features, such as the use of the personal pronoun *ʾana* instead of *ʾāni*. Its orthography shares some features with Mandaic, such as the elimination of the preposition *b-* before the word *bīt* 'house' and the spelling of final *-ī*. Additionally, the author indiscriminately represents the vowels *i*, *ō*, and *ē* with the letter ه, which possibly reflects the phenomenon of *ʾimāla* or raising, as this sound is often realized as a mid front [ɛ] in the received pronunciation of Mandaic in Iraq, corresponding to the articulation of historical /a/ (*fatḥa*) in the *gelet* Arabic dialects. In the transcription below, I have normalised the Mandaic words to conform to Arabic orthography, to reflect the traditional Iraqi pronunciation of Mandaic and to minimise potential confusion between the two systems.

Line 1

asūṯa nihwīlik̠. The first few lines consist of Classical Mandaic formulae. These particular formulae are employed to open many compositions, particularly letters. The verb is a base stem imperfective from the root *h-w-*$^{w}/_{y}$, in the 3ms form, with a 3ms enclitic indirect object, literally meaning 'may it (health) be for you'.

Line 2

mšabba mārī b-libbī dakya. The first word is a passive participle from the causative stem of the verb √*š-b-*$^{w}/_{y}$ 'to praise'.

Line 3

Makkī yusallim ʿalēk yabūs ʾīdeek. Sh. Kumayt refers here to his son, the famous Iraqi actor Makkī Al-Badrī (16/6/1925–5/8/2014), whom Drower first met when he was still a small child.

Line 4

klīla šīšyān asūṯa nihwīlḵun. The salutation returns to Mandaic, using the same standard formula found in ln. 1, albeit with the 2pl suffix ('may there be health for [all of] you'). *Klīla* 'crown' is the Mandaic equivalent of Drower's given name, *Stefana*; *Šīšyān* is the Mandaic form of her mother's name.

Lines 4–5

maktūbič jā w-ana mamnūn. It is in the second of these lines that we find the first colloquial features of this text, namely the form of the 2fs possessive suffix *-ič* instead of the more standard *-ki*. Also noteworthy in this context is the apparent lenition of the glottal stop in *jā* 'it came' (< *jāʾa*) and *w-ana* 'and I' (<*wa-ʾana*).

Lines 5–7

jābit Ginza kabīra ʿatīqa tarīḫ miyyat sinna wa-zrazta wa-Qlasta wa-taṣṭīr ṣbāġa w-ʾAnyānī. Here one encounters the colloquial verb *jāb* ~ *yjīb* 'to bring' together with the names of some well-known Mandaic compositions, the *Ginza Rabba* or *Great Treasure*, and the *Qulasta* and *Inyānī*, which were published together as the *Canonical Prayerbook of the Mandaeans* (Drower 1959). The hundred-year-old *Treasure* mentioned here was likely accessioned into the Drower Collection as DC 22, which is dated to 1831 and was purchased by Drower in 1936 (Buckley 2010, 106–7). The words *taṣṭīr* [sic] *ṣbāġa* (تسطير صباغة) refer to the template used when ruling manuscript pages to ensure that the writing follows straight lines, a photo of which appears in Buckley (2010, Plate 8).

Lines 7–8

b-Anyānī rahmī wa-majmūʿa Zidqa Briḫa min niṭras ʾil-manda, nsawwī ṭaryāna. The Blessed Oblation (*Zidqa Briḫa*) is a ritual performed on certain occasions, in this instance for the consecration of the *mandī*, the structure which is the site of many Mandaean rituals, and the making of the *ṭaryāna*, the clay table on which the ritual is performed. The use of *min* 'at the time' is another colloquial feature of this text. The verb derived from √*t-r-ṣ* (often √*ṭ-r-s*) 'to consecrate' derives from Mandaic and is particular to the Mandaean ritual vocabulary.

Lines 8–9

w-ana qrā ʾil-majmūʿa w-anyāni darafša. The word *darafša* or *darfaš* refers to the ritual banner employed during baptism, consisting of a length of white silk wrapped around a wooden crosspiece. Banner hymns (cf. Drower 1959, 330–47) are recited during the ritual of erecting, unfurling, and dismantling this banner in the Jordan.

Lines 9–11

maʿa-l-asaf maktūbič jāna w-ana b-il-Ḥalfaya w-ana ḫūyya māt wa-ṭal̤lit ʾaḫar. Ḥalfaya is a plateau 35 km southeast of al-ʿAmāra. The colloquial form *ḫūyya* 'my brother' appears here in place of the standard *ʾaḫī*. The colloquial form *ṭal̤lit* replaces standard *ṭalʿit*, in which the ʿ has assimilated to the preceding *l*.

Lines 11–12

ʿazīztī klīla w-aʿad Bīt Hayya m-aʕlam bih. The House of Life is a location within the 'lightworld', although it often stands metonymically for the latter. While one would expect the preposition *b-*, in Mandaic texts this preposition is regularly not written before the word *bīt*.

Lines 12–14

jīt yōm il-aḥad ʿal-Baġdād, yōm rās šahar il-mandāya, yōm tāmin b-šahar ngarraẓ šahar Tammūz. The form *ngarraz* is evidently *nuqarraẓ* 'we celebrate, extol'. During the 24-year period in which Drower lived in Baghdad, the 8th of Tammūz (July) fell on a Sunday (*yōm il-aḥad*) in 1923, 1928, 1934, and finally in 1945. The aforementioned *Treasure* (DC 22) was the subject of a letter from another priest, Sh. Negm, who wrote Drower on 2 February 1936 to inform her that it had arrived and that he would send it with the next mail. Therefore, it seems likely that this letter was composed in 1934. In that year, the date 8 July indeed corresponded to the first day of *Ṭābit / Gadyā*, the twelfth month of the Mandaean calendar.

Lines 15–16

w-ana sallamit bēt il-ginzī li-mfattiš il-ʿadl Mistar Drawar. The phrase *bēt il-ginzī* 'library', an Arabic calque on Mandaic *bīt ginzī*, literally means 'house of the treasures' or 'treasury'. Edwin Drower, Stefana Drower's husband, served as the Inspector-General of the Iraqi Ministry of Justice from 1922 to 1946.

Lines 17–18

mū ʿamaktab[a] w-ana ṭaḷḷit Baġdād liman yajīni maktūbič. The first two words of this sentence appear to be *miʿa maktūb*, but this would be meaningless in this context. We know from context that Drower had not yet acquired the manuscript or paid for it. So they must mean something along the lines of 'he was not at his office'. For *ṭaḷḷit*, see ln. 11 above.

Line 18

ʿād ʾintī tagūlīn ʾašawwif b-ʿēnī li-ktāb. The conjunction *ʿād* 'but; therefore, as a result' is another colloquial feature, as is the voicing of *q* in *tagūlīn* 'you (f) say'.

Line 19

ʿazīztī klīla, ʾana mūš kaddāb. The negative particle *mūš* is a colloquial feature, as is the plosivisation of the fricative *ḏ* in *kaddāb*.

Lines 19–20

tagūlīn ʿāt miyyat rūbiyya w-ana minna faqīr w-a[na]*ḥibannič* ~~*taranī*~~ *ḥayat Bīt Hayya*. Drower glosses the verb *ʿāt* as 'I will give', probably reflecting standard Arabic *ʾu*[ʿa]*ti*; in its place, one would expect *ʾanṭi*. If this is indeed the meaning, it is conjugated as if it came from a hollow root. The form *ʾaḥibannič*, standard Arabic *ʾuḥibu-ki*, is less problematic, save for the anomalous *-n-* before the object suffix. This may reflect an energic form. The colloquial form *ḫayat* 'sister' appears here in place of standard *ʾuḫt*. For *Bīt Hayya*, see ln. 11 above.

Line 21

bēt l-ginzī ṣār ʿalēya b-miyya w-tamānīn rūbiyya. For *bēt l-ginzī*, see ln. 15 above. As with the word انتيك *intī*, Sh. Kumayt sometimes indicates final *-ī* by means of the letters يك, a device borrowed from Mandaic orthography.

Line 22

min qurna, walī šīeḫ Kmēt Rām bar Yasmīn.

Sh. Kumayt closes his letter with a few words that have presented particular difficulties for its readers, including native speakers of Iraqi Arabic. The location from which (*min*) Sh. Kumayt writes is evidently Qurna, a town roughly 100 km due south of al-ʿAmāra and 74 km northwest of Basra, but he has written this word with the letter ࡉ (**qirna**) rather than the expected ࡅ (***qurna**). The spelling of his title, *šīeẖ* (for standard Arabic *šayẖ* 'old man; sheikh') reflects the monophthongization of the historical diphthong and its subsequent division into two segments, which is characteristic of colloquial Arabic in this region. Between the two words is the word *walī* 'guardian; authorized agent', which possibly refers to Sh. Kumayt's role in securing these documents on Drower's behalf.

36. AN ANECDOTE ABOUT JUḤĀ (1920S)

Tania María García-Arévalo

Unknown author. Printed by Maḵlūf Najar in Sousse, Tunisia, first half of the 20th century.

Transcription

ג̇חא וברמת אללחם
כאן יטבך פ̇י תלת לחמאת פ̇י ברמה פ̇דכ̇לו עליה תלת אצחאבהו. פ̇תקדדם ואהד מנהם וקאם לחמה וכלאהא וקאל: אללחם מססוס וילזמך תזידהו אלמלח. פ̇אם אלתאני וכ̇דא לחמה אוכ̇רא וכלאהא: תם קאל: אלטביך יכ̇צהו אלכ̇ל. ובעד אלתאלת כדא אללחמה אלתאלתה וכלאהא. תם קאל: האד אללחם יכ̇צהו אלקארץ. פ̇קאם ג̇חא וקלב אלברמה פי אלקאעה וקאל:
האד אלברמה יכ̇צצהא אללחם!

Arabic Transcription

جحا و برمة اللحم
كان تطبك فى تلت لحمات فى برمة فدخلو عليه تلت أصحابه . فتقدم واحد منهم وقام لحمة وكلاها وقال: اللحم مسسوس ويلزمك تزيده الملح. فقام التانى وخدى لحمة وأُخرى وكلاها : تم قال: الطبيك يخصه الخل. وبعد كممل التالت خدى الحمة التالتة وكلاها. تم قال: هاد اللحم يخصه القارص. فقام جحا وقلب البرمة فى القاعة وقال:
هاد البرمة يخصصها اللحم!

 https://doi.org/10.11647/OBP.0208.42

Translation

Juḥā and the meat pot

While he was cooking three pieces of meat, three of his friends came in. One of them came forward, picked up a piece of meat, ate it, and said: "The meat is bland and you have to add salt." The second got up and took another piece of meat and ate it. Then he said: "The cook was short on vinegar." Finally, the third took the third piece of meat and ate it. Then he said: "This meat lacks heat." Juḥā stood up, turned the pot over on the ground, and said: "This pot is missing the meat!"

Commentary

One of the most relevant issues in Judaeo-Arabic literature in its modern and contemporary period is its spelling. In the case of North Africa, the phonetic principle of how to transcribe Arabic divides the area into two groups. The orthography of the first group, consisting of Libya, Tunisia, and eastern Algeria, closely followed Classical Judaeo-Arabic norms, differing from the orthography characteristic of the second group, comprising Oran, Morocco, and western Algeria, which was further removed (Tobi, 2014, 142). The text presented here is, in fact, a faithful reflection of the evolved Arabised orthography produced in modern Tunisia.

General features that both groups exhibit are the reduplication of consonants to represent medial, but never final, *šadda* (gemination), as well as *ʾalef* to represent the different types of *ʾalif* (*maqṣūra*, *mamdūda*, *waṣla*) without any distinction between them. Also, *ʾalif* is used to represent the morphophonemic definite article *al-*, without any changes before 'sun' or 'moon' letters. As in most Judaeo-Arabic texts, the interdentals are lost in favour of dentals, corresponding to Jewish dialects in Tunisia, which in their oral variety have lost this feature, too.

The verbal system of modern Tunisian Judaeo-Arabic does not differ dramatically of that of Classical Arabic. The main divergences can be found in the phonetic rules applied to the conjugations and in the use of afformatives and preformatives. We find a similar situation in nominal morphology, where nominal patterns do not vary from Classical Arabic, and the changes are restricted to vocalisation due to the impossibility of short vowels in open syllables.

REFERENCES

ʿAbd al-Raḥīm, ʿAbd al-Raḥīm ʿAbd al-Raḥmān (ed.). 1989. *Kitāb al-durra al-muṣāna fī ʾaḫbār al-Kināna fī ʾaḫbār mā waqaʿa bi-Miṣr fī dawlat al-Mamālīk min al-sanāǧiq wa-al-kuššāf wa-al-sabʿat ʾūǧāqāt wa-al-dawla wa-ʿawāyidihim wa-al-bāšā ʾilā ʾāḫir sanat ṯamānin wa-sittīn wa-miʾa wa-ʾalf / Livre dʾAl-durra al-muṣāna dans* [*sic*] *Aḫbār ak-Kināna par Aḥmed Katḫoda ʿAzbān al-Demerdāšī.* (Nuṣūṣ ʿarabiyya wa-dirāsāt ʾislāmiyya / Textes arabes et études islamiques 28. Cairo: Al-maʿhad al ʿilmī al-firansī li-l-ʾāṯār al-šarqiyya bi-l-Qāhira / Institut français d'Archéologie orientale du Caire.

ʾAġlū, Sinān Maʿrūf. 2002. *Najd wa-l-Ḥijāz fī l-waṯāʾiq al-ʿuṯmāniyya: Al-ʾaḥwāl al-siyāsiyya wa-l-ijtimāʿiyya fī Najd wa-l-Ḥijāz ḫilāl al-ʿahd al-ʿuṯmānī.* Beirut: Dār al-Sāqī.

Aguadé, J. 2018. 'The Maghrebi dialects of Arabic'. In *Arabic Historical Dialectology: Linguistic and Sociolinguistic Approaches*, edited by Clive Holes, 29–64. Oxford: Oxford University Press.

Al-Sanhūrī, Muḥammad ibn Mahfūẓ. 2016. *Risible Rhymes, or The Book to Bring a Smile to the Lips of Devotees of Proper Taste and Style through the Decoding of a Sampling of the Verse of the Rural Rank and File (Kitāb Muḍḥik dhawī l-dhawq wa-l-niẓām fī ḥall shadharah min kalām ahl al-rīf al-ʿawāmm).* Library of Arabic Literature. New York: New York University Press.

Arad, Dotan. 2016. '"A Pleasant Voice and an Expert on Every Matter": On Karaite and Rabbanite Cantors in 16th-century Egypt'. *Ginzei Qedem* 12: 147–69. [Hebrew]

Arberry, Arthur J. 1963. *The Koran Interpreted.* 2nd imprint. London: George Allen & Unwin.

Avallone, Lucia. 2016. 'Spelling Variants in Written Egyptian Arabic: A Study on Literary Texts'. In *Arabic Varieties: Far and Wide—Proceedings of the 11th International Conference of AIDA, Bucharest, 2015*, edited by George Grigore and Gabriel Biţună, 79–86. Bucharest: Bucharest University Press.

Avishur, Yitshak. 1992. 'New Folk Tales about Abraham b. ʿEzra (and his Sons) from Egypt and Iraq'. In *Studies in the Works of Abraham b. ʿEzra*, edited by Israel Levin and Mashah Itzhaki, 163–92. Tel-Aviv: Tel-Aviv University Press. [Hebrew]

Ayoun, Richard. 'Bushʾara (Bouchara) Family'. In *Encyclopedia of Jews in the Islamic World*, edited by Norman Stillman (Brill: Leiden, 2010), https://referenceworks.brillonline.com/entries/encyclopedia-of-jews-in-the-islamic-world/bushara-bouchara-family-SIM_0004720.

Badawi, El-Said, and Martin Hinds. 1986. *A Dictionary of Egyptian Arabic: Arabic-English.* Beirut: Librairie du Liban.

Barthélemy, Adrien. 1935–1969. *Dictionnaire Arabe-Français, Dialectes de Syrie: Alep, Damas, Liban, Jérusalem.* Paris: P. Geuthner.

Basset, R. 2012. 'Kaʿb b. Zuhayr'. In *Encyclopaedia of Islam*, 2nd edition, edited by P. Bearman, Th. Bianquis, C. E. Bosworth, E. van Donzel, W. P. Heinrichs. http://dx.doi.org/10.1163/1573-3912_islam_SIM_3733

Behnstedt, Peter. 1987. *Die Dialekte der Gegend von Ṣaʿdah (Nord-Jemen)*. Wiesbaden: Harrassowitz.

Bellem, Alex, and G. Rex Smith. 2014. 'Middle Arabic? Morpho-Syntactic Features of Clashing Grammars in a Thirteenth-Century Arabian Text'. In *Languages of Southern Arabia*, edited by Orhan Elmasz and Janet C. E. Watson, 9–19. Supplement to the Proceedings of the Seminar for Arabian Studies 44. Oxford: Archaeopress.

de Biberstein-Kazimirski, Albert. 1860. *Dictionnaire Arabe-Français*. 2 vols. Paris: Maisonneuve.

Blanc, Haim. 1985. 'Egyptian Judeo-Arabic: More on the Subject of R. Mordekhai b. Yehuda Ha-Levi's *Sefer Darkhe Noʿam*'. *Sefunot* n.s. 3/18: 299–314. [Hebrew]

Blau, Joshua. (1965) 1999. *The Emergence and Linguistic Background of Judaeo-Arabic*. Jerusalem: Yad Izhak Ben-Zvi.

———. 2002. *A Handbook of Early Middle Arabic*. Jerusalem: The Max Schloessinger Memorial Foundation and The Hebrew University of Jerusalem.

———. 2006. *A Dictionary of Judaeo-Arabic Texts*. Jerusalem: The Academy of the Hebrew Language.

Borbone, Pier Giorgio. 2015. 'Syro-Mongolian Greetings for the King of France: A Note About the Letter of Hülegü to King Louis IX (1262)'. *Studi Classici e Orientali* 61: 479–84.

Boris, Gilbert. 1958. *Lexique du parler arabe des Marazig*. Études arabes et islamiques, Études et documents I. Paris: Imprimerie Nationale and Librairie Klincksieck.

Bosworth, Clifford Edmund. 1976. *The Mediaeval Islamic Underworld*. Leiden: Brill.

Buckley, Jorunn J. 2010. *The Great Stem of Souls: Reconstructing Mandaean History*. Piscataway, NJ: Gorgias.

al-Bustānī, ʿAbdallah. 1930. *Al-Bustān wa-huwa muʿjam lughawī*. Beirut: American Press.

al-Bustānī, Fuʾād, and ʿAsad Rustum (eds). 1969. Al-Ṣafadī, ʿAḥmad b. Muḥammad al-Ḫālidī [d. 1625], *Lubnān fī ʿahd al-ʾamīr Faḫr al-Dīn al-Maʿnī al-ṯānī [1572–1635]*. Beirut: Publications de l'Université Libanaise, Section des Études historiques XVI.

Cantineau, Jean. 1960. 'Études de linguistique arabe: Mémorial Jean Cantineau'. *Études arabes et islamiques: Études et documents* II. Paris: C. Klincksieck.

Carter, Michael G. 1998. 'Ibn Ājurrūm'. In *Encyclopedia of Arabic Literature*, edited by P. Starkey and J. Meisami, I: 308–9. London and New York: Routledge.

Cezzâr, Aḥmed. 1962. *Ottoman Egypt in the Eighteenth Century: The Niẓâmnâme-i Miṣir of Cezzâr Aḥmed Pasha*. Edited and translated from the original Turkish by Stanford J. Shaw. Cambridge, MA: Harvard University Press.

Connolly, Magdalen M. 2018. 'A Nineteenth-century CE Egyptian Judaeo-Arabic Folk Narrative: Text, Translation and Grammatical Notes'. In *Studies in Semitic Linguistics and Manu-*

scripts, edited by Nadia Vidro, Ronny Vollandt, Esther-Miriam Wagner, and Judith Olszowy-Schlanger, 392–420. Studia Semitica Upsaliensia 30. Uppsala: University of Uppsala.

———. 2019. 'Revisiting the Question of Ğīm from the Perspective of Judaeo-Arabic'. *Journal of Semitic Studies* 64/1: 155–83.

———. 2021. 'Splitting Definitives: The Separation of the Definite Article in Medieval and Pre-Modern Written Judeo-Arabic'. *Journal of Jewish Languages* 9: 32–76.

———. Forthcoming. *Judaeo-Arabic Folk Tales and Letters from the Pre-Modern Period: A Study in Linguistic Variation.* Études sur le judaïsme medieval. Leiden: Brill.

Corriente, Federico. 1977. *A Grammatical Sketch of the Spanish Dialect Bundle*. Madrid: Instituto Hispano-Árabe de Cultura, Dirección General de Relaciónes Culturales.

———. 1997. *A Dictionary of Andalusi Arabic*. Leiden: Brill.

Crecelius, Daniel, and ʿAbd al-Wahhab Bakr (eds). 1991. *Al-Damurdāšī's Chronicle of Egypt*, 1688–1751. Leiden: Brill.

Crum, Walter Ewing. 1939. *A Coptic Dictionary*. Oxford: Clarendon Press.

Davies, Humphrey Taman. 1981. 'Seventeenth-century Egyptian Arabic: A Profile of the Colloquial Material in Yūsuf al-Širbīnī's Hazz al-Quḥūf fī Šarḥ Qaṣīd ʿAbī Šādūf'. PhD dissertation, University of California, Berkeley.

———. (ed.). 2016. Yūsuf al-Shirbīnī's *Brains Confounded by the Ode of Abū Shādūf Expounded (Hazz al-quḥūf bi-sharḥ qaṣīd*

Abī Shādūf). 2 vols., translated by Humphrey Davies. Library of Arabic Literature. New York: New York University Press.

Davis, S. 1995. 'Emphasis Spread in Arabic and Grounded Phonology'. *Linguistic Inquiry* 26/3: 465–98.

———. 2011. 'Velarization'. In *Encyclopedia of Arabic Language and Linguistics*, edited by Kees Versteegh et al., IV: 636–38. Leiden: Brill.

Den Heijer, Johannes. 2012. 'Introduction'. In *Middle Arabic and Mixed Arabic: Diachrony and synchrony*, edited by Liesbeth Zack and Arie Schippers, 1–25. Leiden: Brill.

Diem, Werner. 2014. 'Ägyptisch-Arabisch im 17. Jahrhundert. Die arabischen Zeugenaussagen in Mordechai ha-Levis *Sefer Darke Noʿam* (Venedig 1697)'. *Mediterranean Language Review* 21: 1–89.

Dinno, K. 2017. *The Syrian Orthodox Christians in the Late Ottoman Period and Beyond: Crises then Revival*. Piscataway, NJ: Gorgias Press.

Dolabani, Y. 1990. ܦܛܪ̈ܝܪܟܐ ܕܐܢܛܝܘܟܝܐ/*Die Patriarchen der syrisch-orthodoxen Kirche von Antiochien*. Glane and Losser: Bar-Hebraeus Verlag. [Syriac]

Doss, Madiha. 1998. 'Dialecte égyptien et questions de langue au XIXe siècle: Le case de ʿAbd Allāh Nadīm'. *MAS-GELLAS nouvelle série* 8: 143–70.

Dozy, R. P. A. 1845. *Dictionnaire détaillé des noms des vêtements chez les Arabes: Ouvrage couronné et publié par la troisìeme classe de l'Institut Royal des Pays-Bas*. Amsterdam: J. Müller.

———. 1881. *Supplément aux dictionnaires arabes*. 2 vols. Leiden: Brill.

Drower, E. Stefana. 1959. *The Canonical Prayerbook of the Mandaeans*. Leiden: Brill.

El-Tantavy, Mouhammad Ayyad. 1848. *Traité de la langue arabe vulgaire = Aḥsan al-nuxab fī maʿrifat lisān al-ʿarab*. Leipzig: Guillaume Vogel Fils.

Farah, Caesar E. 2002. *The Sultan's Yemen: Nineteenth-Century Challenges to Ottoman Rule*. London and New York: I. B. Tauris.

al-Fīrūzābādī, Majd al-Dīn Muḥammad b. Yaʿqūb. 1999. *Al-Qāmūs al-muḥīṭ. ṭabʿa jadīda wa muwaṯṯaqa wa muṣaḥḥaḥa*. Cairo: Dār al-Fikr li-l-Ṭibāʿa wa-l-Našr wa-l-Tawzīʿ.

Florence, Ronald. 2004. *Blood Libel: The Damascus Affair of 1840*. Madison: University of Wisconsin Press.

Forshall, Josiah, and Friedrich, Rosen. 1838. *Catalogus codicum manuscriptorum orientalium qui in Museo Britannico asservantur: 1 Codices Syriacos et Carshunicos amplectens*. London: British Museum.

Frankel, Jonathan. 1997. '"Ritual Murder" in the Modern Era: The Damascus Affair of 1840'. *Jewish Social Studies* 3/2: 1.

Friedman, Mordechai Akiva. 2016. *A Dictionary of Medieval Judaeo-Arabic*. Jerusalem: Ben Zvi Institute.

Gairdner, W. H. R. 1917. *Egyptian Colloquial Arabic: A Conversation Grammar and Reader*. Cambridge: W. Heffer & Sons.

Gendzier, Irene L. 1966. *The Practical Visions of Yaʿqub Sanuʿ*. Cambridge, MA: Harvard University Press.

al-Ghazzī, Najm al-Dīn Muḥammad ibn Muḥammad. 1958. *Al-Kawākib al-sāʾira bi-aʿ yān al-miʾa al-ʿāshira*. Beirut: American University of Beirut.

Goitein, S. D. 1941. *Travels in Yemen: An Account of Joseph Halévy's Journey to Najran in the Year 1870 Written in Sanʾani Arabic by his Guide Hayym Habshush*. Jerusalem: The Hebrew University Press.

———. 1972. 'Townsman and Fellah: A Geniza Text from the Seventeenth Century'. *Asian and African Studies* 8: 257–61.

Hacker, Joseph. 2015. 'Jewish Book Owners and Their Libraries in the Iberian Peninsula, Fourteenth–Fifteenth Centuries'. In *The Late Medieval Hebrew Book in the Western Mediterranean: Hebrew Manuscripts and Incunabula in Context*, edited by Javier del Barco, 70–104. Leiden: Brill.

al-Hamdānī, Al-Ḥasan b. ʾAḥmad. 1884–1891. *Ṣifat Ǧazīrat al-ʿArab*, edited by D. H. Müller. Leiden: Brill.

Hanna, Nelly. 1998. 'Culture in Ottoman Egypt'. *The Cambridge History of Egypt*, edited by M. W. Daly, II: 87–112. Cambridge: Cambridge University Press.

Hary, Benjamin. 1987. 'Judeo-Arabic, Written and Spoken in Egypt in the Sixteenth and Seventeenth Centuries'. PhD dissertation, University of California, Berkeley.

———. 1992. *Multiglossia in Judeo-Arabic, with an Edition, Translation, and Grammatical Study of the Cairene Purim Scroll*. Leiden: Brill.

———. 1996. 'Adaptations of Hebrew Script'. In *The World's Writing Systems*, edited by W. Bright and P. Daniels, 727–34, 741–42. Oxford: Oxford University Press.

———. 2009. *Translating Religion: Linguistic Analysis of Judeo-Arabic Sacred Texts from Egypt*. Leiden and Boston: Brill.

———. 2017. 'Spoken Late Egyptian Judeo-Arabic as Reflected in Written Forms'. *Jerusalem Studies in Arabic and Islam* 44: 11–36.

Hassan, Anton. 1869. *Kurzgefasste Grammatik der vulgär-arabischen Sprache mit besonderer Berucksichtigung auf den egyptischen Dialekt*. Vienna: K.K. Hof- und Staatsdruckerei.

Hava, J. G. 1899. *Arabic-English Dictionary for the Use of Students*. Beirut: Catholic press.

Havlin, Shlomo Zalman (ed). 1995. *History of the Oral Law and of Early Rabbinic Scholarship by Rabbi Menahem ha-Meiri*. Jerusalem/Cleveland: Ofeq Institute. [Hebrew]

Healey, John F. 2005. *Leshono Suryoyo: First Studies in Syriac*. Piscataway, NJ: Gorgias Press.

Heidelberg University. n.d. *Abou Naddara Collection: Introduction: Journals*. http://kjc-sv036.kjc.uni-heidelberg.de:8080/exist/apps/naddara/index.html

Heidelberg University. n.d. *James Sanua: Biography*. http://kjc-sv036.kjc.uni-heidelberg.de:8080/exist/apps/naddara/biography.html

Hinds, Martin, and el-Said Badawi. 1986. *A Dictionary of Egyptian Arabic: Arabic-English*. Beirut: Librarie du Liban.

Hoffman, A., and P. Cole. 2011. *Sacred Trash: The Lost and Found World of the Cairo Geniza*. New York: Nextbook and Schocken Books.

Holes, Clive. 2019. 'Confessional Varieties'. In *Handbook of Arabic Sociolinguistics*, edited by Enam Al-Wer and Uri Horesh, 63–80. London: Routledge.

Ibrāhīm, ʿAbd Allāh ʿAlī (ed.). 1983. *Waṯāʾiq ʿan taʾrīḫ Lībiyā fī l-qarn al-tāsiʿʿašar. Al-juzʾ al-ʾawwal, ṯawrat Ġūmat al-Maḥmūdī 1835–1858*. Tripolis (Libya): Markaz dirāsāt jihād al-Lībiyyīn ḍidd al-ġazw al-ʾīṭālī.

ʿĪsā, Razzūq. 2016. Reprint of *Al-Manḥūṯ al-ʿāmmī wa-l-lufẓ al-dakīl fī luġat Baġdād* (originally in *Majalla luġat al-ʿarab* 1911, issue 6, p. 255) in *Baġdād fī luġat al-ʿarab*, Part III, p. 136. Karbalāʾ.

Jastrow, Marcus. (1903) 2005. *A Dictionary of the Targumim, the Talmud Babli and Yerushalmi, and the Midrashic Literature*. Peabody, MA: Hendrickson.

Kallas, Elie. 2012. 'The Aleppo Dialect According to the Travel Accounts of Ibn Raʿd (1656) Ms. Sbath 89 and Ḥanna Dyāb (1764) Ms. Sbath 254'. In *De los manuscritos medievales a internet: La presencia del árabe vernáculo en las fuentes escritas*, edited by Mohamed Meouak et al., 221–52. Zaragoza: Universidad de Zaragoza, Área de Estudios Arabes e Islámicos.

de Kazimirski, A. 1860. *Dictionnaire arabe-francais contenant toutes les racines de la langue arabe: Leurs derives, tant dans l'idiome vulgaire que dans l'idiome litteral, ainsi que les dialectes d'Alger et de Maroc*. Paris: Maisonneuve.

Khan, Geoffrey. 1991. 'A Study of the Judaeo-Arabic of Late Genizah Documents and Its Comparison with Classical Judaeo-Arabic'. *Sefunot* n.s. 5/20: 223–24.

———. 1992. 'Notes on the Grammar of a Late Judaeo-Arabic Text'. *Jerusalem Studies in Arabic and Islam* 15: 220–39.

———. 2006. 'A Judaeo-Arabic Commercial Letter from Early Nineteenth-Century Egypt'. *Ginzei Qedem* 2: 37–59.

———. 2007. 'Judaeo-Arabic'. In *Encyclopedia of Arabic Language and Linguistics*, edited by Kees Versteegh et al., II: 526–36. Leiden: Brill.

———. 2010. 'Vocalised Judaeo-Arabic Manuscripts in the Cairo Genizah'. In *'From a Sacred Source': Genizah Studies in Honour of Stefan C. Reif*, edited by B. Outhwaite and S. Bhayro, 201–18. Leiden and Boston: Brill.

———. 2018. 'Judaeo-Arabic'. In *Arabic Historical Dialectology: Linguistic and Sociolinguistic Approaches*, edited by Clive Holes, 148–70. Oxford: Oxford University Press.

Kīlānī, Muḥammad. 1965. *Al-Adab al-Miṣrī fī ẓill al-ḥukm al-ʿuthmanī*. Cairo: Dār al-Qawmiyya al-ʿArabiyya.

de Landberg, Comte. 1901. *Etudes sur les dialectes de l'Arabie méridionale, i, Ḥaḍramoût*. Leiden: Brill.

———. 1920–1942. *Glossaire daṯînois*. 3 vols. Leiden: Brill.

Lane, Edward William. 1863–1893. *An Arabic-English Lexicon, Derived from the Best and the Most Copious Eastern Sources*. Edited by Stanley Lane-Poole. London: Williams and Norgate.

Larkin, Margaret. 2006. 'Popular Poetry in the Post-Classical Period'. In *Arabic Literature in the Post-Classical Period*, edited by Roger Allen and D. S. Richards. Cambridge: Cambridge University Press.

Lentin, Jérôme. 1997. 'Recherches sur l'histoire de la langue arabe au Proche-Orient à l'époque moderne'. PhD dissertation, University of Paris III.

———. 2008. 'Middle Arabic'. In *Encyclopedia of Arabic Language and Linguistics*, edited by Kees Versteegh et al., III: 215–24. Leiden: Brill.

———. 2011. 'Middle Arabic'. In *Encyclopedia of Arabic Language and Linguistics Online Edition*, edited by Lutz Edzard, Rudolf de Jong. http://dx.doi.org/10.1163/1570-6699_eall_EALL_COM_vol3_0213

———. 2012. 'Normes orthographiques en moyen arabe: Sur la notation du vocalisme bref'. In *Middle Arabic and Mixed Arabic: Diachrony and Synchrony*, edited by Liesbeth Zack and Arie Schippers, 209–34. Studies in Semitic Languages and Linguistics 64. Leiden: Brill.

Marchand, Trevor (ed.). 2017. *Architectural Heritage of Yemen: Buildings that Fill my Eye*. Berkeley, CA: Gingko Library.

Marçais, William, and Abderrahmân Guîga. 1958–1961. *Textes arabes de Takroûna* II. *Glossaire: Contribution à l'étude du vocabulaire arabe*, tomes I–VIII, Paris: Imprimerie Nationale, CNRS, and P. Geuthner.

Margoliouth, G. 1899. *Descriptive List of Syriac and Karshuni MSS. in the British Museum Acquired since 1873*. London: British Museum.

Masters, Bruce Alan. 2001. *Christians and Jews in the Ottoman Arab World: The Roots of Sectarianism*. Cambridge Studies in Islamic Civilization. Cambridge; New York: Cambridge University Press.

Matthee, R. 2012. 'Tutun'. In *Encyclopaedia of Islam*, 2nd edition, edited by P. Bearman, Th. Bianquis, C. E. Bosworth, E. van Donzel, W. P. Heinrichs. http://dx.doi.org/10.1163/1573-3912_islam_COM_1266.

McCollum, Adam Carter. 2014. 'Garshuni as It Is: Some Observations from Reading East and West Syriac Manuscripts'. *Hugoye: Journal of Syriac Studies* 17/2: 215–35.

Mittwoch, Eugen. 1926. *Aus dem Jemen: Hermann Burchardts letze Reise durch Südarbien.* Leipzig: Deutsche Morgenländische Gesellschaft, in Kommission bei F. A. Brockhaus.

al-Nadīm, ʿAbd Allāh. (1892–1893) 1994. *Al-Aʿdād al-ḥāmila li-majallat al-Ustāḏ.* 2 vols. Cairo: Al-Hayʾa al-Miṣriyya al-ʿĀmma li-l-Kitāb.

Nahem, Ilan. 1996. *The "Metzaḥ Aharon" Commentary on the Pentateuch by Rabbi Aharon Garish.* Jerusalem: Ben Zvi Institute. [Hebrew]

Naïm, Samia. 2009. *L'Arabe yéménite de Sanaa.* Leuven and Paris: Peeters.

Nizami, K. A. 'Faḳīr'. In *Encyclopaedia of Islam*, 2nd edition, edited by P. Bearman, Th. Bianquis, C. E. Bosworth, E. van Donzel, W. P. Heinrichs. http://dx.doi.org/10.1163/1573-3912_islam_SIM_2252.

Nuʾaysa, Yūsuf. 1988. *Ibn al-Ṣiddīq, Ġarā'ib al-badā'iʿ wa-ʿajāʾib al-waqāʾiʿ: Al-ḥayāt al-ʿarabiyya fī l-qarn al-ṯāmin ʿašar al-mīlādī.* Damascus: Dār al-maʿrifa.

Palva, Heikki. 1993. 'Ḥikāya fī ḏamm al-nisāʾ, a Story in Dispraise of Women: A 14th-century (?) Egyptian Judaeo-Arabic Manuscript'. In *The Middle East: Unity and Diversity—*

Papers from the Second Nordic Conference on Middle Eastern Studies, Copenhagen 22–25 October 1992, edited by Heikki Palva and Knut S. Vikør, 176–88. Copenhagen: Nordic Institute of Asian Studies.

Pamuk, Sevket. 2000. *A Monetary History of the Ottoman Empire*. New York: Cambridge University Press.

Pellat, Ch. 2012a. 'Ibn Shuhayd'. In *Encyclopaedia of Islam*, 2nd edition, edited by P. Bearman, Th. Bianquis, C. E. Bosworth, E. van Donzel, W. P. Heinrichs. http://dx.doi.org/10.1163/1573-3912_islam_SIM_3379.

———. 2012b. 'Laḥn al-ʿĀmma'. In *Encyclopaedia of Islam*, 2nd edition, edited by P. Bearman, Th. Bianquis, C. E. Bosworth, E. van Donzel, W. P. Heinrichs. http://dx.doi.org/10.1163/1573-3912_islam_SIM_4613.

Piamenta, Moshe. 1990–1991. *Dictionary of Post-classical Yemeni Arabic*. 2 vols. Leiden: Brill.

Porter, Venetia. 1992. 'The History and Monuments of the Tahirid Dynasty of the Yemen, 858–923/1454–1517'. PhD dissertation, University of Durham.

———. 2017. 'The Bani Tahir and the ʿAmiriyya Madrasa: Architecture and Politics'. In *Architectural Heritage of Yemen: Buildings That Fill My Eye*, edited by Trevor Marchand, 51–59. Berkeley, CA: Gingko Library.

Qafisheh, Hamdi A. 2000. *Yemeni Arabic Dictionary*. Chicago: NTC.

al-Radi, S. 1997. *The Amiriya in Radaʾ: The History and Restoration of a Sixteenth-Century Madrasa in the Yemen*. Oxford Studies in Islamic Art 13. Oxford: Oxford University Press for the

Board of the Faculty of Oriental Studies, University of Oxford.

Redhouse, James W. 1890. *A Turkish and English Lexicon.* Constantinople: Printed for the American Mission by A. H. Boyajian.

Reif, Stefan C., 2000. *A Jewish Archive from Old Cairo: The History of Cambridge University's Genizah Collection.* Richmond, Surrey: Curzon.

Rosenbaum, Gabriel. 2002. 'Spoken Jewish Arabic in Modern Egypt: Hebrew and Non-Standard Components'. *Massorot* 12: 117–48. [Hebrew]

Rossi, Ettore. 1939. *L'Arabo Parlato a Ṣanʿāʾ.* Rome: Istituto per l'Oriente.

Russotto, Henry A. (ed. and trans.) 1912. *Passover Hagadah with Music.* New York: Hebrew Publishing Company.

Sadgrove, P. C. 2012. 'Al-Nadīm, al-Sayyid ʿAbd Allāh'. In *Encyclopaedia of Islam*, 2nd edition, edited by P. Bearman, Th. Bianquis, C. E. Bosworth, E. van Donzel, W. P. Heinrichs. http://dx.doi.org/10.1163/1573-3912_islam_SIM_5713.

Ṣanūʿ, Yaʿqūb. 1878. *Abū naḍḍāra zarqāʾ: Jarīdat musalliyyāt wa-muḍḥikāt.* http://kjc-sv036.kjc.uni-heidelberg.de:8080/exist/apps/naddara/index.html#.

Sells, Michael A. 1990. '*Bānat Suʿād*: Translation and Introduction'. *Journal of Arabic Literature* 21/2: 140–54.

Serjeant, R. B., and Ronald Lewcock (eds). 1983. *Ṣanʿāʾ: An Arabian Islamic City.* London: World of Islam Festival Trust.

al-Shami, Anas Muhammad, and Zakariyya Jabir Ahmad (eds). 2008. Al-Fayrūzabādī's *Al-Qāmūs al-muḥīṭ*. Cairo: Dār al-Ḥadīth.

Smith, G. Rex. 1974–1978. *The Ayyubids and Early Rasulids in the Yemen*, 2 vols. E. J. W. Gibb Memorial Series, n. s. 26. London: Luzac & Co.

———. 1988. 'The Political History of the Islamic Yemen Down to the First Turkish Invasion (1–945/622–1538)'. In *Yemen: 3000 Years of Art and Civilisation in Arabia Felix*, edited by W. Daum, 129–39. Innsbruck: Umschau-Verlag.

———. 2004. 'The Classical Arabic Pattern *faʿāli* Revisited'. In *Biblical and Near Eastern Essays: Studies in Honour of Kevin J. Cathcart*, edited by Carmel McCarthy and John F. Healey, 264–80. Journal for the Study of the Old Testament Supplement Series 375/The Library of Hebrew Bible/Old Testament Studies 375. London and New York: T&T Clark.

Spiro, Socrates. 1895. *An Arabic-English Vocabulary of the Colloquial Arabic of Egypt, Containing the Vernacular Idioms and Expressions, Slang Phrases, etc., etc., Used by the Native Egyptians*. London: Bernard Quaritch.

Spitta, Wilhelm. 1880. *Grammatik des arabischen Vulgärdialektes von Aegypten*. Leipzig: J.C. Hinrichs.

Steingass, F. 1884. *The Student's Arabic-English Dictionary*. London: Crosby Lockwood.

———. 1930. *A Comprehensive Persian-English Dictionary*. London: Kegan Paul, Trench, Trubner.

Tobi, Y. 2014. 'Judaeo-Arabic Printing in North Africa, 1850–1950', in *Historical Aspects of Printing and Publishing in Languages of the Middle East*, edited by G. Roper, 129–150. Leiden: Brill.

al-ʾUsṭā, Muḥammad, and ʿAmmār Juḥaydar (eds). (1984) 2001. *Ḥasan al-Faqīh Ḥasan's Al-yawmiyyāt al-lībiyya.* Silsilat Nuṣūṣ wa-waṯāʾiq 1–7. Benghazi: Dār al-Kutub al-Waṭanī.

ʾUsṭuwānī, ʾAsʿad (ed). 1993. Al-ʾUsṭuwānī, Muḥammad's *Mašāhid wa-ʾaḥdāṯ Dimašq fī muntaṣaf al-qarn al-tāsiʿ ʿašar (1256–1277 h. / 1840–61 m.).* Damascus (?).

Wagner, Esther-Miriam. 2010. *Linguistic Variety of Judaeo-Arabic in Letters from the Cairo Genizah.* Leiden: Brill.

———. 2014. 'Subordination in 15th- and 16th-century Judeo-Arabic'. *Journal for Jewish Languages* 2: 143–64.

———. 2018. 'Birds of a Feather: Arabic Scribal Conventions in Christian and Jewish Arabic'. In *Studies in Semitic Linguistics and Manuscripts: A Liber Discipulorum in Honour of Professor Geoffrey Khan*, edited by Nadia Vidro, Ronny Vollandt, Esther-Miriam Wagner, and Judith Olszowy Schlanger, 376–91. Studia Semitica Upsaliensia 30. Uppsala: Acta Universitatis Upsaliensis.

Wagner, Esther-Miriam, and Mohamad A. H. Ahmed. 2017. 'From Tuscany to Egypt: Eighteenth Century Arabic Letters in the Prize Paper Collections'. *Journal of Semitic Studies* 62/2: 389–412.

Watson, Janet C. E. 1993. *A Syntax of Ṣanʿānī Arabic.* Semitica viva 13. Wiesbaden: Harrassowitz.

———. 1999. 'The Directionality of Emphasis Spread in Arabic'. *Linguistic Inquiry* 30/2: 289–300.

———. 2000. *Waṣf Ṣanʿāʾ: Texts in Ṣanʿānī Arabic*. Semitica viva 23. Wiesbaden: Harrassowitz.

———. 2002. *The Phonology and Morphology of Arabic*. Oxford Linguistics; Phonology of the World's Languages. Oxford and New York: Oxford University Press.

———. 2009. 'Ṣanʿānī Arabic'. In *Encyclopedia of Arabic Language and Linguistics*, edited by Kees Versteegh, IV: 106–15. Leiden: Brill.

Wehr, Hans. 1994. *A Dictionary of Modern Written Arabic (Arabic-English)*. 4th ed. New York: Spoken Language Services.

Woidich, Manfred. 2006. *Das Kairenisch-Arabische: Eine Grammatik*. Porta linguarum orientalium, n. s. 22 Wiesbaden: Harrassowitz.

Wright, William. 1870–1872. *Catalogue of Syriac Manuscripts in the British Museum Acquired since the Year 1838*. 2 vols. London: British Museum.

Yāqūt, al-Ḥamawī. 1979. *Muʿǧam al-buldān*. 5 vols. Beirut: Dār Ṣādir.

Zack, Liesbeth. 2009. *Egyptian Arabic in the Seventeenth Century: A Study and Edition of Yūsuf al-Maġribī's 'Dafʿ al-iṣr ʿan kalām ahl Miṣr'*. Utrecht: LOT.

———. 2014. 'The Use of the Egyptian Dialect in the Satirical Newspaper *Abu Naḍḍāra Zarʾa*'. In *Alf lahja wa lahja: Proceedings of the 9th Aida Conference*, edited by O. Durand, A. D. Langone, and G. Mion, 465–78. Vienna: Lit Verlag.

———. 2016. 'Nineteenth-century Cairo Arabic as Described by Qadrī and Naḫla'. In *Arabic Varieties: Far and Wide—Proceedings of the 11th International Conference of AIDA, Bucharest, 2015*, edited by G. Grigore and G. Bițună, 557–67. Bucharest: University of Bucharest Press.

Cambridge Semitic Languages and Cultures

General Editor Geoffrey Khan

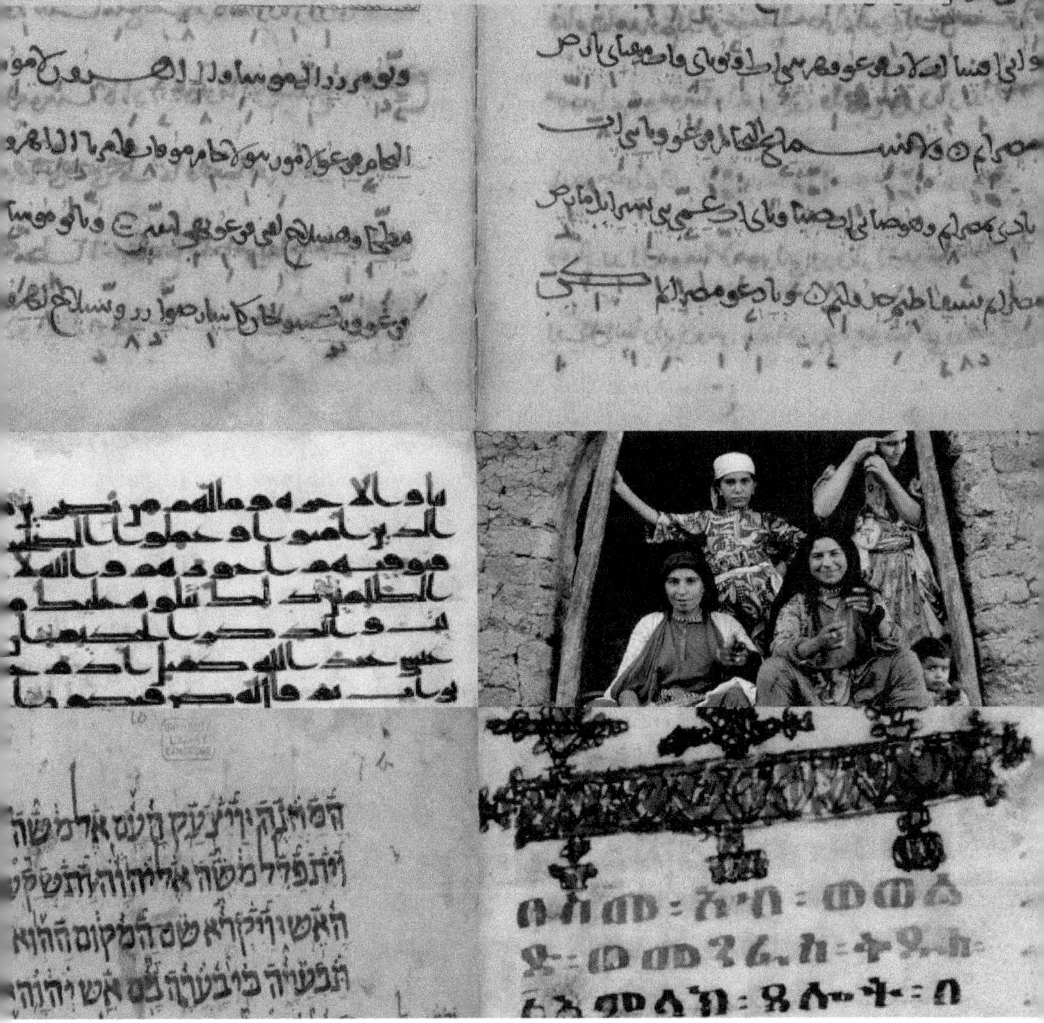

OPEN ACCESS

Cambridge Semitic Languages and Cultures

About the series

This series is published by Open Book Publishers in collaboration with the Faculty of Asian and Middle Eastern Studies of the University of Cambridge. The aim of the series is to publish in open-access form monographs in the field of Semitic languages and the cultures associated with speakers of Semitic languages. It is hoped that this will help disseminate research in this field to academic researchers around the world and also open up this research to the communities whose languages and cultures the volumes concern. This series includes philological and linguistic studies of Semitic languages, editions of Semitic texts, and studies of Semitic cultures. Titles in the series will cover all periods, traditions and methodological approaches to the field. The editorial board comprises Geoffrey Khan, Aaron Hornkohl, and Esther-Miriam Wagner.

This is the first Open Access book series in the field; it combines the high peer-review and editorial standards with the fair Open Access model offered by OBP. Open Access (that is, making texts free to read and reuse) helps spread research results and other educational materials to everyone everywhere, not just to those who can afford it or have access to well-endowed university libraries.

Copyrights stay where they belong, with the authors. Authors are encouraged to secure funding to offset the publication costs and thereby sustain the publishing model, but if no institutional funding is available, authors are not charged for publication. Any grant secured covers the actual costs of publishing and is not taken as profit. In short: we support publishing that respects the authors and serves the public interest.

Other titles in the series

Diversity and Rabbinization: Jewish Texts and Societies between 400 and 1000 CE
Gavin McDowell, Ron Naiweld, Daniel Stökl Ben Ezra (eds)
doi.org/10.11647/OBP.0219

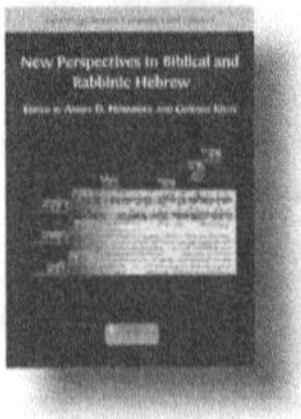

New Perspectives in Biblical and Rabbinic Hebrew
Aaron D. Hornkohl and Geoffrey Khan (eds)
doi.org/10.11647/OBP.0250

UNIVERSITY OF CAMBRIDGE
Faculty of Asian and Middle Eastern Studies

You can find more information about this serie at:
http://www.openbookpublishers.com/section/107/1